AN ACCOUNT

OF THE

WAR IN PORTUGAL

BETWEEN

DON PEDRO AND DON MIGUEL.

BY

ADMIRAL CHARLES NAPIER.

VOL. I.

The Naval & Military Press Ltd

Published by

The Naval & Military Press Ltd
Unit 5 Riverside, Brambleside
Bellbrook Industrial Estate
Uckfield, East Sussex
TN22 1QQ England

Tel: +44 (0)1825 749494

www.naval-military-press.com
www.nmarchive.com

In reprinting in facsimile from the original, any imperfections are inevitably reproduced and the quality may fall short of modern type and cartographic standards.

TO

HIS ROYAL HIGHNESS

PRINCE AUGUSTUS FREDERICK,

DUKE OF SUSSEX,

&c. &c. &c.

I dedicate this work to your Royal Highness, because you are the friend of Portugal and of freedom.

I have the honour to be,

Your Royal Highness's

Most obedient servant,

CHARLES NAPIER.

Merchistoun-Hall, Horndean,
5th July, 1836.

PREFACE.

VARIOUS accounts have been given of the war in Portugal, both by French and English officers who served in the armies of the Queen and of Don Miguel, but they relate chiefly the operations which came under their own observation, and touch little on what was going on in other parts of the country.

I have endeavoured to give an impartial account of the whole war, praising and blaming where it is due without favour or affection. I am not accustomed to write histories or prefaces, therefore the less I say the better—the reader may judge for himself.

CONTENTS.

CHAPTER I.

State of Portugal after the decease of Don John. Perfidy of Don Miguel. Troops at Oporto declare against the usurper. The constitutional party is crushed. A Regency is formed at Terceira. Folly of Don Miguel in not granting an amnesty. He is warned by the Duke of Wellington. British vessels captured. The author is sent to Lisbon, to demand satisfaction. French expedition to the Tagus. Exertions of the Regency at Terceira. The author proceeds to the Western Islands. Fayal and St. Michael's captured. The author's plan for attacking Portugal. Captain Sartorius appointed to the command of Don Pedro's squadron. Character of M. Mendizabal. Don Pedro arrives in the Western Islands. He assumes the Regency. . . Page 1

CHAPTER II.

Administration formed by Don Pedro. Character of it. First measures of the new ministry. Errors of the ministry. Irregular conduct of the British auxiliaries. Expedition projected against Madeira. Folly of it. Indefatigable activity of Don Pedro. Absurd conduct of the ministry with respect to the British auxiliaries. The foreign corps are disliked by the government. Orders given that the expedition shall be collected at St. Michael's. The troops of the expedition are reviewed by Don Pedro. The expedition embarks. Procrastinating character of the Portuguese. Don Pedro an exception. The expedition sails for Portugal. Proclamations of Don Pedro to the inhabitants and troops. . . . . Page 14

CHAPTER III.

Feelings of the troops and islanders. Force of the fleet and convoy. The expedition reaches the coast of Portugal. Sanguine hopes of Don Pedro. Futility of them practically shown. Fruitless summons sent to Villa de Conde. The army effects a landing. Inactivity of the Miguelite general Cardoza. Character of Count Villa Flor. The priests hostile to Don Pedro. Blunders of the Miguelites. Oporto evacuated by them. The army of Don Pedro enters Oporto. It is coldly received. The admiral anchors in Oporto roads. Capture of Villa Nova and the Serra convent. Incapacity of Don Pedro's war minister. Unpromising appearance of affairs in Oporto. Movements of the Miguelites. The Miguelites are defeated at Penafiel by Colonel Hodges. The troops of Don Pedro are worsted in a second attack.

Page 27

CHAPTER IV.

General attack on the Miguelite army behind the Souza. Gallant charge made by the Miguelite cavalry. No advantage gained by the battle. Cause of the failure. Terror in Oporto during the battle. Don Pedro becomes aware of his perilous situation. The priests attempt to destroy the army, by setting fire to the barracks. Resolution taken to fortify Oporto. Description of the works. Shameful misconduct of the ministers, in not removing the wine from Villa Nova.

Villa Flor wishes to resign. Don Pedro refuses to accept his resignation. Desertion among the Queen's troops Movements of Admiral Sartorius. Actions between Sartorius and the squadron of Don Miguel. Flight of Don Miguel's squadron. . . . . Page 43

CHAPTER V.

Count Villa Flor attacks the Miguelites on the south of the Tagus. Panic among the Queen's troops. Retreat of Villa Flor. Alarm in Oporto. Don Pedro is advised to reembark. Admiral Sartorius puts to sea. His dispute with Captain Minns. Indecisive action with the Miguelite squadron. Error committed by the captain of the Rainha. Don Pedro dissatisfied with the admiral. English and French troops refuse to work on the entrenchments. Bravery of Bernardo da Sa. The Miguelites attack the Serra convent. They are defeated. They make a second unsuccessful attack. Texeira takes the command of Miguel's army. Miguelite battery destroyed. Major Staunton is killed. The south bank of the Douro neglected by the Queen's generals. The Miguelites prepare to attack Oporto. Absurd expedition of the Queen's troops to Aveiro. Page 57

CHAPTER VI.

The Miguelites attack Oporto. Delay in despatching reinforcements to Colonel Hodges. Arrangements of Colonel Hodges. Hot contest between the French auxiliaries and the Miguelites. Intrepidity of six Portuguese. Combat between the British auxiliaries and the Miguelites. Death of Lieut.-colonel Burrell. Instances of personal courage. Blunders committed. Failure of an attack on the enemy. The Miguelites take flight. Calumnies against the English and French troops. Offensive treatment of Colonel Hodges's brigade. Count Villa Flor resigns, and

CONTENTS.

is created Duke of Terceira. Don Pedro assumes the command. Attacks on the Serra repulsed. Sir John Milley Doyle arrives. Bad treatment of the British. Colonel Bacon arrives. Operations of the Miguelites. Colonel Hodges resigns. Sir J. M. Doyle commands for two days. . . . . Page 71

CHAPTER VII.

Successful attack on Villa Nova, by the troops of Don Pedro. Useless sally from Oporto on the north side of the Douro. Serious loss sustained. Visit of General Mina. Mission of the Marquis of Palmella to England. Diminished interest felt in England for the cause of the Queen. Failure of the Marquis of Palmella's mission. Incapacity of Don Pedro's council. A new ministry is formed. Proposal made by the author to Palmella. Sally from Oporto. Heavy loss on both sides. Inhabitants of Oporto active in the constitutional cause. Attempt to reinforce Sartorius. Dissentions in the squadron. Trial and acquittal of Captain Rose. Mutiny in the squadron. Cholera in it.

Page 101

CHAPTER VIII.

Oporto strictly blockaded. Difficulty of obtaining provisions. General Solignac appointed to the command of the Queen's army. Attack on Villa Nova by the Queen's troops. Slaughter made by the Miguelites. Fire at the Custom-House in Oporto. Arrival of General Solignac. Arrival of reinforcements at Oporto. Indecisive attack on the enemy. Arrival of Generals Saldanha, Stubbs, and Cabrera. Scarcity in Oporto. Cholera. The author's plan is adopted. The command of the squadron offered to the author. Blame attributed to Marshal Solignac. Count St. Lorenzo appointed general of the Miguelite army. He attacks the

CONTENTS. xi

Serra without success. The Miguelites are defeated in an attack on the Pasteleiro. Bad situation of the squadron. Admiral Sartorius dismissed, and Captain Crosbie appointed in his place. Intention to arrest Sartorius. Interview between Admiral Sartorius and Sir J. Doyle. Sir J. Doyle is put under arrest. Sartorius is restored. Propriety of his conduct. . . . . Page 118

CHAPTER IX.

The Miguelites are foiled in an attack on Oporto. Death of Major Sadler and Captain Wright. Monte de Cavallo carried. Mutiny in the squadron. The author is invited by the Chevalier de Lima to concert measures. Plan of the author for an attack on the Algarves. It is adopted. Exertions of the Duke of Palmella and M. Mendizabal. Order restored in the fleet of Admiral Sartorius. The Admiral determines to resign. Bad management with respect to the Algarves expedition. Mutiny among the recruits. The author joins the expedition at Portsmouth. The mutiny is renewed at Falmouth. Arrival at Oporto. Meeting of the author with Sartorius. The author lands at Oporto. Attempt to bring about an arrangement between Don Pedro and Don Miguel. Description of the Foz and the neighbouring works. . . . . Page 139

CHAPTER X.

Reception of the author at Oporto. Unsatisfactory conduct of Don Pedro, and of General Solignac. Cause of Don Pedro's strange behaviour. The author's second interview with him. The author submits various plans to him. Worthlessness of the ministry. Narrow escape from a shell. Measures for forming a new ministry. Don Pedro's dislike of Palmella. Discussion in a council of war. The author gives in a written opinion. Don Pedro resolves to make a dash on Lisbon. He changes his mind. A smaller expedition decided upon. The author appointed Vice-Admiral and Major-General. He embarks. Admiral Sartorius gives up the command to the author. Part of the seamen quit the service. State of the squadron. Order issued to the squadron by the officer. Delay in sending troops. Marshal Solignac resigns, and Don Pedro takes the command of the forces in Oporto. Letter of Don Pedro to the author. The troops are embarked. . . . . Page 156

CHAPTER XI.

Difficulty in obtaining water. The expedition sails. Undisciplined state of the seamen. Alarm felt by the Miguelite ministry. Don Carlos favoured by Don Miguel. Intrigues carried on at Lisbon by the Carlists, &c. The expedition arrives on the coast of Algarve. The troops are disembarked. Faro taken. Lagos taken. The Miguelite fleet appears in sight. Miguelite order of battle. Errors of the enemy. Cowardice of the steamers. The author's dispositions for the battle. Commencement of the action. Proceedings during the battle. The enemy's flag-ship carried by boarding. Complete defeat of the Miguelite squadron. Loss sustained in action. How the enemy's fleet was bought.

Page 179

CHAPTER XII.

The Queen's fleet anchors in Lagos Bay. Burial of the slain officers. The captured ships officered and manned. Operations of the Duke of Terceira. All Algarve in possession of the Queen's forces. Naval blockade of Lisbon established. The author sails for Lisbon. The author created Count Cape St. Vincent. The cholera breaks out in the Queen's fleet. Movements of the Duke of Terceira. The Miguelites abandon Lisbon. The Queen's fleet enters the Tagus. The author lands at Lisbon. State of the city. Blockade of the Miguelite ports. Terceira marches on Almada. Setubal taken. The Miguelite general, Telles Jordaõ, routed. Surrender of Almada. Telles Jordaõ killed. This defeat causes the evacuation of Lisbon. . . . . . Page 207

CHAPTER XIII.

Folly of Don Miguel's ministers. Joy caused in Lisbon by the flight of Don Miguel. Few excesses committed. March of Palmella compared with that of Napoleon from Cannes. Lisbon might have been defended by the Miguelites. Cascaes and Peniche evacuated by the Miguelites. Splendid naval arsenal at Lisbon. Faulty state of the naval department. Proceedings in the naval department. Tricks of the workmen. Delay in providing for the defence of Lisbon. Captain Elliot appointed to command Don Miguel's non-existent fleet. Marshal Bourmont takes the command of Don Miguel's army. The Miguelites attack Oporto and are defeated. Cause of this defeat. . . . . Page 230

CHAPTER XIV.

Don Pedro arrives at Lisbon. His splendid reception. The author graciously received by him. Don Pedro visits the admiral's ship. Enthusiasm of the people of Lisbon. Don Pedro reviews the army. Description of the Ajuda palace. Don Pedro not a bigot. Impolitic conduct of Don Pedro's advisers. System of conciliation unwisely rejected. Plan to get rid of the marine director. No risings in favour of the Queen. Cholera in the Algarves Military arrangements in Lisbon. Errors of the Miguelites. The Miguelites relinquish the siege of Oporto. Lord William Russell sends intelligence of Bourmont being on his march to Lisbon. Delay in fortifying Lisbon. Activity of Don Pedro.

Page 249

CHAPTER XV.

Description of the entrenchments of Lisbon. Stations of the shipping. Insubordination in the fleet. Disposition of seamen. The Queen recognized by the British government. Lord William Russell appointed ambassador. Decree summoning the Cortes. The Queen's ministry is disliked. Lord William Russell vainly counsels an amnesty. Sir John Campbell taken prisoner. The British minister at Madrid unfavourable to the Queen's cause. March of Bourmont's army. General Saldanha arrives from Oporto. Reinforcements despatched from Oporto. Scarcity of horses. Success of Miguelite guerilla parties in the south. Lagos saved. The troops take their positions in the lines of Lisbon. The Miguelite army appears before Lisbon. General Bourmont attacks the lines and is defeated. Death of Larochejacquelin. Skirmishes. Negotiations. . . . . Page 271

CHAPTER XVI.

General Macdonnell replaces Bourmont as commander of the Miguelite army. Arrest of Mr. Luckraft. Anger of Lord William Russell. The Queen and the Empress arrive at Lisbon. Their reception in England. Anger of Don Pedro at the Duke of Leuchtenberg being ordered from France. Meeting of Don Pedro, his wife, and the Queen. Description of the Empress and the Queen. Landing of the Queen and Empress. Presentations. Grand review. Deputations received. The author dines with the royal family. The City of Waterford steamer is wrecked with the Queen's suite. Arrival of the Marquis and Marchioness of Loulé. Their characters. . . . . Page 296

APPENDIX.

I. Proclamation of Don Pedro to the inhabitants of the Azores	313
II. Proclamation of Don Pedro to his army	315
III. Representation made by the crew of the Donna Maria to the Captain	316
— Reply of the Captain of the Donna Maria	317
IV. Proclamation of Gaspar Texeira	319
V. Thanks of Marshal Solignac to the army	320
VI. Portuguese offer, to Captain Napier, of the command of the squadron	321
— Letter from B. Sa Nogueira to Captain Napier	322
VII. Reply of Captain Napier to the offer made by the Portuguese government	324
VIII. Letter of Admiral Sartorius to Captain Napier	326
IX. Instructions of Don Pedro to Sir J. M. Doyle	328
X. Resolutions of the officers of Admiral Sartorius's squadron	331
XI. Letter of Admiral Sartorius to the author, announcing his resignation	333
XII. Reference to Captain Wilkinson's letter	334
XIII. Letter from the Chevalier d' Abreu e Lima to the author, with respect to the author's taking the command	335
XIV. Commission of Don Pedro, appointing the author to the command	338

XV.	Appointment and instructions of the Duke of Terceira	339
—	Letter of Don Pedro to the Duke of Palmella	344
—	Instructions to the Duke of Palmella	345
XVI.	Letter of the author to the Marquis of Loulé	350
XVII.	Proclamation of Villa Flor to the inhabitants of the Algarves	352
XVIII.	List of killed and wounded	353
XIX.	Decree appointing the author Admiral of the Royal Navy	354
XX.	Letter of Don Pedro to the author	357
—	Letter of the Marquis of Loulé to the author	357
XXI.	Proclamation to the inhabitants of Lisbon	359
XXII.	Declaration of the inhabitants of Lisbon in favour of Donna Maria	361
XXIII.	A list of the Portuguese navy	361
XXIV.	Proclamation, of the Duke of Terceira, to the inhabitants of Lisbon	362
XXV.	Letters of the author to General Bourmont	363, 368
—	Answers of General Bourmont	365, 369

WAR OF SUCCESSION

IN

PORTUGAL,

ETC. ETC.

CHAPTER I.

When Dom John of Portugal died, Dom Pedro, the Emperor of the Brazils, abdicated the crown of Portugal, and presented to that kingdom his daughter Donna Maria de Gloria, a minor, and a constitutional charter, which was brought to Lisbon by Lord Stuart de Rothesay. The princess Isabel Maria was appointed Regent. Dom Miguel had been banished from Portugal for having conspired against his father, and had resided for some time at the court of Vienna. During Isabel Maria's regency, a rebellion broke out against the government, at the head of which was the Marquis de Chaves, supported by the court of Spain.

Mr. Canning, then minister, at the request of the Regent sent a small army to Portugal to defend that kingdom from foreign aggression. This demonstration checked the rebellion, and put an end to Spanish interference. Shortly after this Donna Maria was affianced to Don Miguel, who was created Lieut.-General of the kingdom, and proceeded to Lisbon from this country, having pledged himself to the Emperor of Austria and the King of England to preserve the charter, and marry the young queen, as had been settled by his brother Dom Pedro.

This faithless prince had hardly set his foot on Portuguese ground ere he began to pave the way for usurpation, by displacing all the constitutional officers, and appointing creatures of his own in their places. This was followed by dissolving the constitutional Cortes, and assembling the old Cortes of the kingdom, who proclaimed him absolute king. Mr. Canning in the meantime died; the Duke of Wellington came to the head of the administration;

and the British army remained tame spectators of the treachery of Miguel, with orders even to protect his person, and finally embarked for England, leaving suffering Portugal to be ruled by the iron hand of despotism.

The troops at Oporto declared against the usurper, and the chiefs of the constitutional party, who had withdrawn from Portugal, now returned, and put themselves at the head of the army, who were near Coimbra; they were defeated, and retired to Oporto, from whence many embarked; others retreated on the Minho, crossed over to Spain, and laid down their arms. Neither talent nor energy was displayed by the constitutional party, and they became an easy prey to the absolutists. The regiments stationed in the island of Terceira remained faithful to the Queen, and to that bulwark of Portuguese liberty many of the Constitutionalists repaired.

Saldanha, and a part of the refugees who had taken shelter at Plymouth, in endeavouring to get to Terceira, were driven back by two frigates sent by the existing government, who fired into one of his transports, killing one or two men, and obliged them to proceed to Brest. Terceira, nevertheless, remained faithful. The Count Villa Flor proceeded to that island, and arrived in time to defeat a formidable force sent by Don Miguel to reduce it to obedience; he was followed by the Marquis Palmella and many respectable officers; and a regency was formed, consisting of Palmella, Villa Flor, and Guerreiro. The island was fortified, and by great exertions, and with the assistance of their friends in France, England, and the Brazils, they managed to keep up a respectable force, always looking forward to some happy occurrence in their favour. The French Revolution in July, 1830, was the first light that dawned upon them: this was followed by a change of ministry in England.

The obstinacy of Don Miguel, in refusing an amnesty, had prevented his being recognized by the Duke of Wellington's administration: in a despatch from Zea Bermudez to Count Montalegre, found in the Foreign Office at Lisbon, he relates a conversation with his grace, in which the latter distinctly stated that it was quite impossible for the powers of Europe who had already acknowledged Donna

Maria as the rightful Queen of Portugal, to recognize Don Miguel, unless he granted an amnesty without any exception, as the adherents of the Queen had relied on the justness of her cause in consequence of her being acknowledged, and to abandon them to the mercy of Don Miguel was quite impossible; but that, in the event of a full amnesty being granted, a minister would be shortly sent to Lisbon in a ship of the line, accompanied, if necessary, by two frigates, and a corvette to Oporto. His grace further warned them of the danger of delay, and pointed out the regency of Terceira as the quarter from whence a blow would be struck, which might throw the whole peninsula into a state of anarchy and confusion. The sequel has proved what a true prophet the duke was.

Previously to the change of ministry in England, several British vessels had been most unjustifiably captured off the Western Islands, and I was sent to Lisbon in the Galatea, with orders to the consul-general to insist on restitution, and two frigates proceeded to the Western Islands to restrain such lawless proceedings. In 1831 fresh insults were offered to England and France: the former sent a force to the Tagus, and obtained redress, but it was refused to the French, till a squadron forced the river, dictated terms to the usurper, and deprived him of the ships that were at that time considered serviceable. A frigate was also sent to the Western Islands, and one of the two Portuguese corvettes on that station was captured. These events were not looked upon with indifference at Terceira: great exertions were made to equip an expedition, two small schooners were armed, forced loans had recourse to, the bells were melted down and converted into money, and every means that a government reduced to despair could think of, were employed to profit by the present circumstances and extend the Queen's authority over the Azorean Archipelago.

Representations were made by the British inhabitants that their lives and properties would be endangered in the event of an attack, as they were, generally speaking, disliked by the Miguelite party, who would profit by the confusion and make them suffer for their favourable feelings towards the Constitutionalists. The English in all foreign settlements are extremely sensitive of danger, and generally cry out before they are hurt. Nevertheless the government determined on affording them protection. I still commanded the Galatea, had just returned from the West Indies, and was sent upon this service. On my arrival at St. Michael's, early in June, I found the Druid lying there; she had been ordered to touch at that island on her way to the Brazils, and to await my arrival. The expedition from Terceira had already sailed and taken possession of the islands of St. George and Pico, and were making preparations to attack Fayal.

After consulting with the consul-general, Mr. Reid, and paying my respects to Vice-Admiral Prega, the captain-general, (who, though a Miguelite, was a worthy man, and had refrained from all unnecessary cruelties to those who differed with him in politics, though fully authorized by Miguel's government to be summary in his proceedings with his enemies,) I proceeded to Terceira, and was received with great kindness by the Marquis Palmella and Mr. Guerreiro, two of the regency: the Count Villa Flor, the other member, was absent with the expedition. I at once explained to the duke the purport of my visit, that my orders were to be perfectly neutral, and that I trusted he would take care not to oblige me to interfere with English vessels employed in his service, as complaints had already been made by the owners of one that had been impressed by the regency and lost. I gave him to understand that I should not prevent either party from hiring English vessels, but that no warlike operation could be carried on with them under the sanction of the British flag.

After this interview I proceeded to Fayal. The governor and garrison were in great alarm, as an attack was hourly expected, and the corvette had been driven from her anchorage by bad weather. I also learned that Don Pedro had touched at Fayal in the Volage, on his way to England, having abdicated the imperial crown of the Brazils. This intelligence gave fresh vigour to the hopes of the Constitutionalists, but still they hesitated long and were extremely dilatory. In the meantime the governor became more alarmed, and on the arrival of the corvette abandoned the island, leaving more than half the garrison behind him, becalmed in an American brig, which was captured by the

Count Villa Flor in his passage across. After arranging the government of Fayal, the Count returned to Terceira, organized another expedition, and took St. Michaels on the 2nd of July, and subsequently the whole of the islands. The cause of the Queen now began to brighten, and the regency already talked of fitting out an expedition to attack the usurper in Portugal. My opinion of how that attack ought to have been made is to be found in the United Service Journal of 1832, and was as follows:—

" The only sure manner of settling the Portuguese question, is by dashing right up the Tagus, and carrying the capital by storm. The defences of the river are no doubt strong, but with a fair wind and strong current, they would be soon passed. The Portuguese artillery, though of high reputation in the Peninsular war, have not had much practice lately; every shot does not hit, and every shot that hits is not between wind and water; and if the guns on shore were divided between all the ships that form the expedition, there will not be more than half a dozen for each. It must also be remembered, that, in the event of a check, any number of ships may anchor in the Tagus out of shot from all sides; and with a squadron before the town having 8000 troops on board, the inhabitants of Lisbon do not rise *en masse*, they cannot be favourable to Donna Maria; if unfavourable, that force on shore in any part of Portugal could never dethrone Don Miguel. With a larger force they could not carry on a defensive war in the provinces of Minho and Douro in the first instance, it is not likely they can carry on an offensive war with a smaller one now."

Shortly after the capture of the islands the marquis Palmella came to England, and concerted measures with the Emperor for attacking the Usurper. Captain Sartorius voluntered to command the naval expedition, and two indifferent frigates were purchased and fitted out in the Thames as far as the Foreign Enlistment Bill would permit; but notwithstanding all their precautions, they met with many difficulties, and one was seized in the Downs and detained for some time, but on reference to the proper authorities she was given up. Several naval officers accompanied Captain Sartorius for a summer cruize, as they expected; and the frigates proceeded to Belle Isle, there to be equipped as ships of war. Men were forwarded from this country to that port, and after a series of blunders, bad management, and bad faith to the crews, the queen's agents succeeded in manning them; and on the 10th of February the Emperor embarked on board the Rainha with Sartorius, who was made a vice-admiral, and arrived at St. Michael's on the 22d. Colonel Hodges, who commanded the English auxiliary force, accompanied the Emperor; the Donna Maria, and several vessels with men and stores followed.

A loan had been negotiated in England, and M. Mendizabal, a Spaniard by birth, was charged with the financial arrangements. Few men possessed more talents for raising money than this active-minded individual, and few men knew less how to take care of it, or were more liable to be imposed upon by the numerous agents he was obliged to employ. The very nature of the service required the assistance of charlatans and intriguers, who distinguished themselves by the honourable name of friends of the cause, and in this capacity they risked much, and robbed more.

The Emperor, in his passage to the Western Islands, had not shewn any particular partiality to his British auxiliaries; in short, he had been persuaded by those about him that his presence in Portugal was only necessary to the success of the Queen's cause, and Portuguese jealousy of foreigners and consequent intrigue began with the expedition, and continued throughout the arduous struggle. At St. Michael's the Emperor was well received by the inhabitants, and much pleased at the military appearance of the eighteenth regiment and fifth caçadores, who formed the garrison of the island, of which Count D'Alva was the governor.

A few days after the landing of the Emperor, the rest of the expedition arrived; and on the 4th of March they all rendezvoused in Angra roads, in the island of Terceira. The Emperor immediately landed under the salutes of the squadron and castle, was received with every mark of joy and respect, and proceeding to the palace, took the constitutional oath and assumed the regency, which was ceded to him by the Dukes of Palmella, Terceira, and Guerreiro. He afterwards heard mass at the cathedral; salutes and fireworks had been going off all day; and in the evening the town was brilliantly illuminated. Although the island of Terceira had been the seat of government, it was far from being a constitutional island: indeed the heavy contributions levied upon them by the regency had cured their constitutional feelings, if they ever possessed any. St. Michael's and Fayal, on the other hand, who had been ruled by the usurping government, cherished tolerably strong feelings in favour of the Queen's cause.

CHAPTER II.

Don Pedro now formed his administration, which consisted of Palmella for Foreign Affairs and Interior; Freire, War and Marine; Mouzinho de Silveira, Finance and Justice. The former, well known in Europe as a statesman, had been the rallying point of the Constitutionalists, and head of the regency; the second had been President of the Cortes, an ultra-liberal, was a man of neither military genius or talent, had every thing to gain and nothing to lose: he had lived quietly at Paris, free from danger and responsibility. The latter had been confined in St. Julian's, and was a man highly respected in his native country. Besides the ministers, there were several influential men around the Emperor:—Candido Xavier, his first aid-de-camp and private secretary, a cunning old fox, who preferred that place to a portfolio : he had served in the French army against his country in the Peninsular War, and had been Minister of War before the return of Miguel. He had bad health, bad manners, and was altogether a bad-looking man ; but with all these imperfections, he was a first-rate favourite of the Emperor's. Silva Carvallo had been Minister of Justice, was apparently frank, fancied he knew a great deal of the feeling of his countrymen, and was of opinion that not a hostile shot would be fired on Portuguese ground. The Duke of Terceira was appointed commander-in-chief of the army, and M. Guerreiro, the other member of the regency, remained unemployed and neglected. The Marquis Palmella was much blamed for associating himself with Freire, and either ought to have refused office or insisted on the formation of his own ministry; and the sequel will shew this was not the only error committed by the Marquis.

The first political act of the ministry was

abolishing the lay-tithes, which obliged every peasant to pay the government a tenth of his poultry and other domestic property. This was a wise measure and very acceptable to the poor. The tithe of fish to the clergy was also abolished: this also was another popular act with the people, but necessarily the contrary with the clergy. Then followed the dismissal of the friars from the monasteries, and the seizure of their property, allowing them a small pension, the payment of which was very uncertain. The convents were also thrown open, and the nuns so inclined were allowed to return to their families, an annual stipend being allowed them. One nunnery was permitted in each island, for those whose religious feelings induced them to remain. That both monasteries and nunneries in these islands required reforming, is beyond a doubt; but taking this opportunity of disgusting the clergy, and wounding the religious feelings of a bigotted people, at a moment when they ought to have been conciliated, pretty clearly proves the impolicy and incapacity of the Emperor's advisers: their whole energies should have been employed to render the expedition perfect, leaving reform till the Queen's authority was established in Portugal.

The English auxiliaries, as might be expected from the nature of their composition, on their arrival at Terceira broke out into every sort of irregularity; and Colonel Hodges very judiciously obtained permission from the Count Villa Flor to remove them to Praya, a distant part of the island, and there he was indefatigable in reducing them to order, and bringing them to a proper state of discipline, which, considering the inefficiency of the greater part of the inferior officers, was a matter of no inconsiderable difficulty. This was augmented by the want of clothing and shoes, which had not yet been supplied.

One of the first plans taken into consideration by the ministry was the propriety of immediately sending an expedition of three thousand men against the island of Madeira. This was supported by Palmella, and opposed by Freire, and with reason. The acquisition of Madeira, could it have been immediately obtained, would have added to the resources of the constitutional party, but if successfully defended, as there was every reason to expect, the whole summer would have been lost, and the little money they possessed frittered away. Winter would have left the squadron without a harbour; discontent would have got into both services; and the Queen's cause would have been lost. Had it been thought advisable to attack Madeira, it ought to have been done with the whole naval and military force on their way to the coast of Portugal: this would have rendered success certain, and saved time.

An expedition of this sort was, however, never contemplated by the minister, but one of the most ridiculous nature was decided upon, and orders were actually given on the 6th of March to carry it into execution. This was no other than for Admiral Sartorius to embark in the Donna Maria, Villa Flor brig, and Terceira schooner, Hodges's unclothed, unarmed, and undisciplined battalion, and proceed off Madeira to summon the garrison to surrender, and in the event of refusal to land his men on the barren rock of Porto Santo, where there was neither food, raiment, or shelter. The proposition was made to Colonel Hodges by the

Marquis Palmella, who was soon convinced of the folly of such an enterprize. Freire, however, was not so easily persuaded, and as he had before opposed an expedition of three thousand men, I verily believe this sapient minister of war, impressed with the idea that Portugal was to be gained without difficulty, actually conceived this plan to get altogether rid of the English, whom he thoroughly detested; for I am convinced, had he entertained the least idea that this expedition would have led to the surrender of Madeira, he never would have allowed the foreigners to have reaped the honours of the enterprize.

Another council was held in the evening: the Quixotic expedition was given up, and admiral Sartorius was ordered with the Donna Maria, Villa Flor brig, and a company of caçadores, to make a demonstration off Madeira, and was accompanied by Mouzinho de Albuquerque.

From the moment the Emperor arrived in the island, he evinced the most indefatigable activity in making preparations for the expedition. The force at Terceira consisted of the third, sixth, and tenth of the line; the volunteers of Donna Maria, in which Don Thomas de Mello, a member of one of the oldest Portuguese families, and many others served as privates; the second and third caçadores; a corps of about two hundred students from Coimbra; and the artillery. The greater part of the troops as well as officers wore long beards, with which custom the Emperor also complied.

The men were well clothed and appointed, with the exception of the British regiment, who were nearly naked, and when their clothing arrived from England, it was actually refused to be delivered to them till a duty of fifteen per cent. was paid upon it; and although the general as well as Colonel Hodges remonstrated with the minister-at-war, the only answer they could obtain was, that the British being an auxiliary force, paid by the commission in London, they must also pay the duty, and the British regiment was actually kept four weeks naked before the minister-at-war would consent to clothe his own troops. This was a beginning of the follies of that most incapable minister.

In the beginning of April the Emperor visited

Fayal, where the squadron was refitting. In this island he was received with much enthusiasm. Balls and parties were given, at all of which he made a rule of attending, and danced continually, that being his favourite amusement.

After reviewing the troops and examining the arsenal and ships, which required four days, he returned to Terceira. On the 15th he reviewed the English battalions, which now had a very military appearance, expressed himself satisfied, but did not give out the usual complimentary order he had been in the habit of issuing to the native regiments.

The foreign corps were certainly not favourites with the government; they made no allowances for the dissolute habits of British soldiers, nor did they reflect that it was impossible to establish the same discipline over auxiliaries, as can be done over regular troops, particularly when the agreement made with them was frequently unexecuted. Want of pay led to discontent, and selling their necessaries; the soldiers became dissatisfied with the government, and the government in their turn with the soldiers, without reflecting that breach of faith was the cause of the soldiers' irregularity. A battalion of five hundred French now arrived. Amongst them were many old soldiers decorated with the Legion of Honour, and the medal of the July Revolution. After a long voyage they were unwisely ordered to St. Michael's, thereby occasioning a great deal of discontent, indeed mutiny; and the Emperor, who had gone on board to inspect them, was glad to get on shore, much less pleased with the behaviour of the French than he had been with the English. Neither the pay nor the allowances of the French were equal to the British, which was another cause of discontent.

On the 20th of April Admiral Sartorius returned in the Villa Flor, having left the Donna Maria and Terceira schooner off Madeira, and the company of caçadores under the command of Mouzinho de Albuquerque at Porto Santo. The governor having refused to surrender, as might have been expected, Admiral Sartorius was of opinion, had a force of two thousand five hundred men been sent there, the island would have been given up; but from the steady manner in which the governor held it to the last, assisted by the inhabitants, who were almost all Miguelites, I am disposed to think he was mistaken.

The Emperor having decided that the whole of the expedition should collect at St. Michael's, Admiral Sartorius proceeded to Fayal, and the necessary orders were given for that purpose. The Donna Maria and Terceira schooner, together with the company of caçadores, were recalled from Porto Santo, and on the 7th of May, the Emperor, his ministers, and suite proceeded to that island in the Superb Steamer, the Count Villa Flor and his staff having preceded him.

The greater part of the troops from Terceira were already there. The British, the Sacred battalion, composed of officers of all ranks old and young, the corps of Guides, and the artillery remained at Terceira, waiting for transports. On the 24th the Emperor returned to that island, highly dissatisfied at the tardiness in embarking these corps, and having given positive orders for their immediate embarkation, proceeded to Fayal for the same purpose ; it was not before the 29th of May that the whole of the armament was collected at St. Michael's.

During the stay in the Western Islands, the Emperor's activity was unabated: he was regent, general, and admiral; sometimes he did good and sometimes harm; but he knew his countrymen; and with all his faults, had it not been for his activity, the expedition never would have left the Islands.

The army was now organized under their respective chiefs. Colonel Brito commanded the first division; Fonseca the second; Swalbach the light division; brigadier Cabreira the artillery; major Serra the engineers; and Count D'Alva the cavalry, that is to say, when they were to be found, for none embarked from St. Michael's.

On the 6th of June the Emperor reviewed his forces, consisting of six thousand five hundred men. The park of artillery consisted of 3 nines, 6 sixes, and 4 three-pounders, with three five-and-a-half-inch howitzers, well organized. This little army was certainly well-appointed in every respect, and well-officered; but the troops of which it was composed were not entirely to be depended upon;

one half had been recruited in the islands, and taken from the different Miguelite garrisons who had surrendered.

On the 20th of June the army was assembled on parade, and high mass performed in the most imposing manner. This finished, the embarkation commenced, and was completed the following day. The Emperor had embarked on the 19th on board the Amelia yatch, fitted out for his reception, and was most active in assisting Admiral Sartorius in his arrangement. He was the only Portuguese I ever saw who did not understand *Amanha* (to-morrow), the common answer of Portuguese, even on the most pressing occasions, when decision is necessary; indeed, do nothing to-day that can be done to-morrow is the leading feature of the Portuguese character, and never will they become a nation till that word is banished from their dictionary.

General Vasconcelles was appointed governor of the Azores; General Saraiva prefect, with sous-prefects in the other islands, the French system of civil government having been adopted; and on the 26th the signal was made to weigh, which was joyfully received by the whole fleet. On embarking and taking leave of the islands, the Emperor issued two heart-stirring proclamations to the inhabitants and troops.

<small>Appendix I. and II.</small>

CHAPTER III.

The sojourn of the army had been so long in these islands, that it is natural to suppose great intimacies had been formed with the inhabitants of both sexes, and their now leaving them on a hazardous expedition, which many would never survive, called forth the warmest feelings of their nature. The amiable Countess Villa Flor, who had accompanied her husband in all his adversities, felt most deeply, as did the Marchioness of Palmella: her grief was heightened by the recent loss of her eldest son, a young man twenty-two years of age, of great promise. He died at St. Michael's of a consumption. The ladies were to retire to Paris under the protection of the Count Villa Real, who had not been invited to accompany the Emperor. The Count was a nobleman of consequence in Portugal, and an experienced officer; he had served with Lord Beresford in the Peninsular war, and certainly his services ought not to have been rejected: he was a man of moderate principles, and some intrigue had probably been on foot against him.

On the 27th Admiral Sartorius, having made his arrangements, bore up for the coast of Portugal with his convoy, composed of forty-two sail of transports under the protection of the Rainha de Portugal, of forty-six guns, commanded by Captain Crosby, and bearing the vice-admiral's flag; the Donna Maria, forty-two, Captain Mins, (Bingham); the Amelia, the Emperor's yacht, Captain Bertram (Pryce); Villa Flor brig; Terceira, Liberal, Bon Esperansa, and Eugenia schooners. The Stag, commanded by Sir Thomas Troubridge, had arrived from Lisbon, and accompanied the expedition for four days. On the 7th of July the land was seen, and in the evening the whole convoy was close in shore with Villa de Conde. The Emperor and his advisers were so sanguine of meeting a favourable reception from the army and people, that Bernardo de Sa was sent on shore, at day-light on the 8th, with a flag of truce to Villa de Conde to summon the governor either to surrender or join the liberating army. He was received with shouts of " Viva Don Miguel!" " Viva el Re assoluto!" and conducted to the head-quarters of Brigadier-general José Cardoza, who threatened to shoot him as a rebel and traitor, and only allowed him fifteen minutes to return to his boat, which he regained with considerable danger, amidst vivas for Don Miguel and hisses for himself. This had some effect in opening the eyes of Don Pedro's advisers, particularly Candido Xavier, who opposed the landing of the Emperor and staff to the last moment.

It was, however, too late to recede, and the admiral pushed the men-of-war and small craft within musket-shot of the beach abreast of the village of Mindella, the transports anchoring outside. There had been no previous arrangements made for landing by divisions, and Colonel Hodges having anchored his transport close to the flagship, got the grenadier company, with the staff and colours, into the men-of-war boats, and had the honour of being the first on shore. He was followed by the light company under Captain Shaw, who did duty as marines on board the flagship. He immediately took possession of a windmill, situated on some high ground. Captain Staunton was detached on the right and front, and the remainder of the battalion now landing, Colonel Hodges marched them up to join Staunton, at the same time sending a detachment of forty men into a wood that stretched as far as Villa de Conde.

Count Villa Flor now landed with his staff, expressed himself pleased with the disposition of Hodges to cover the landing, but informed him the emperor was much dissatisfied at his precipitation, very naturally wishing the native troops to land first. The rest of the army were soon on shore. Colonel Schwalbach, with the second and third caçadores, moved rapidly on Lessa, while Major Xavier and the fifth caçadores menaced Villa de Conde on the left. At sunset, the greater part of the troops having disembarked, the Emperor landed.

Every thing as yet had favoured the enterprize; fine weather and a favourable breeze had brought them to the coast; the water was smooth, and the landing easy,—a rare occurrence on the coast of Portugal, which is almost continually protected by a heavy surf. No enemy appeared to oppose the landing, which was effected without the loss of a man: it was indeed unaccountable that General Cordoza, who commanded an imposing force at Villa de Conde, should have remained there a quiet spectator of the disembarkation, and still more unaccountable that a rapid movement was not made on Villa de Conde, and the army of Cordoza overturned before they had recovered from the panic with which they were struck at the appearance of so large a fleet, which they supposed contained at least 20,000 men.

I am convinced, from what I had before and have since seen of Villa Flor, that had he been left to himself, he would not have hesitated one moment; but, unfortunately, the Emperor had timid, incapable, and intriguing counsellors about his person, who thwarted Villa Flor's operations, and he was of too mild and kind a disposition to act independent of them, and shew the Emperor that, now he was in the field, it was to his general and not to his advisers that he ought to intrust the military operations. If, however, Cordoza shewed no activity, the priests did, and they were indefatigable and successful in persuading the country people that Don Pedro was at the head of a band of brigands for the purpose of plundering the inhabitants, and returning to the Western Islands: the whole country was in consequence abandoned by the people.

Cordoza, seeing there was no intention of attacking him, moved with great celerity on Penafiel, and General Santa Martha, who commanded the province of the Entre Minho and Douro, where were stationed twelve thousand men, abandoned Oporto in the night, with his garrison, about four thousand strong. Here began the Miguelite blunders. Santa Martha ought to have held firm at Oporto, and Cordoza should have hung on Villa Flor's rear, if he marched on Oporto, or defended Villa de Conde should he take that direction, while Santa Martha would have advanced from Oporto.

The Emperor, on landing, proceeded to Parafita, where he found the British under Hodges. They were directed to remain there till the army had passed and form the rear-guard. At three in the morning the whole of the troops had defiled and collected at St. Pedro D'Avroga, with the exception of Schwalbach's division, which had moved on the road of Lessa.

The news of the evacuation of Oporto reached the Emperor at nine o'clock in the morning of the 9th, and he immediately put the troops in motion; and after a severe march of five leagues, under a burning sun, the liberating army entered Oporto, the second city of Portugal, at four o'clock in the afternoon. Their reception was by no means what was expected; a few vivas were given, and a few flowers strewed upon the Emperor's head as he passed to his quarters, which commanded a beautiful view of Villa Nova and the adjacent country. The troops were quartered in the different barracks and convents, all of which had been abandoned by the friars, who took up arms in Don Miguel's cause. The enemy occupied Villa Nova on the opposite side of the river, and very much annoyed the inhabitants in the lower part of the town.

On the 10th, the admiral anchored in Oporto roads, and pushed the small craft into the Douro, losing a few men by the fire of musketry from Villa Nova; and it was not before the afternoon of the 11th that Schwalbach, with the light division, was ordered to drive them out of the town at the instigation of Admiral Sartorius, the Emperor and his ministers being still impressed with the idea that not only the army, but the whole country were so attached to the cause of Donna Maria, that it was most advisable to avoid collision with the Miguelite troops. The capture of Villa Nova and the Serra convent, which the enemy abandoned and never afterwards recovered, inspired the inhabitants of Oporto with more confidence, and in the evening the town was brilliantly illuminated.

The Emperor had now been three days in Oporto, and no ulterior operations were decided on. Villa Flor, who was the most competent judge, was for pushing on at once for Coimbra, being morally certain that nothing but a foreward movement would give them the smallest chance of success. No deserters had come in; there was no appearance of defection in the army; and every hour's delay gave the Miguelites time to recover from their panic and ascertain the weakness of the Emperor's forces. The incapable minister-at-war was crying out for delay and organization, had no soul to advise a forward movement, was looking towards the provinces of the Minho and Douro and Tras-os-Montes for support, where the inhabitants were all Miguelites, and gave his opinion that in a week the army would declare for the Queen;—Lisbon would be revolutionized, and the Emperor would then march in triumph to the capital. Before this gentleman had presumed to thrust himself into such an office as minister-of-war, he ought to have read the account of Buonaparte's march from Cannes; and if he had neither head nor heart to have advised the Emperor to follow his example, he ought to have remained at Paris, and allowed his place to be filled by a bolder man.

On the 12th the light division advanced a league and a half on the Coimbra road, and Brito occupied Villa Nova with his division. The ministers amused themselves in framing laws for the government of a kingdom they did not occupy. General Cabrera was appointed governor of Tras-os-Montes, and a battalion of the 15th regiment of the line was sent to Guimaraens to support his authority, and collect provisions and stores for the army. Don Thomas de Mascarenhos was appointed governor of the town, M. Van Zellar corregidor, and all the inferior offices were filled up with the Emperor's friends. The principal inhabitants of Oporto showed no disposition to undertake offices in the town, and the people in general seeing the weakness of the Emperor's force, and putting no confidence in his advisers, were afraid to compromise themselves. This feeling extended even to the British merchants, who were very shy in noticing any of their countrymen in Don Pedro's service.

The inactivity of the troops in Oporto restored confidence to the Miguelites, who now crossed a force over the Douro under the command of Cordoza and the Viscount Montealegre; and at one o'clock on the morning of the 17th Colonel Hodges marched with the first battalion of the fifteenth, the British battalion, and thirty mounted guides on Carvoeiro, to reconnoitre the enemy. He there learnt that they occupied Penafiel with three companies of the line and a battalion of royalist volunteers. He then returned to Valongo, and was reinforced by the regiment of volunteers of Donna Maria of four hundred strong, under the command of Lieutenant-Colonel Luis Pinto de Mendosa Arraes, and two six-pounders, with orders to drive the enemy out of Penafiel if not too strong, and there wait for further directions. At three o'clock on the morning of the 19th he put his force in motion and halted at Baltar. Both in this march and that of the day before the most perfect indifference was shewn by the peasantry; they followed their usual occupations without caring, and probably without knowing, whether the troops were in favour of the Queen or Don Miguel, and very likely were not even aware that an expedition had landed at Oporto. Pushing on from Baltar, they were fired on from the surrounding heights, and the peasantry showed themselves inimical to the advanced guard; and as they approached Penafiel, the resistance became more pronounced. One friar alone presented himself; he brought intelligence that the Miguelites were in position at Penafiel supported by bands of guerillas, and were determined to fight. This gentleman brought two horses as a present to the Emperor. At Valongo, a little in advance of where the Miguelites were posted, the guerillas opened their fire and, after discharging their pieces, fled. On the left of Penafiel the enemy were posted, resting their right on a convent; another convent in front of the town appeared fortified; the baggage-carts and mules were placed on some high ground to the right, and appeared ready to retreat; and a party of guerillas were stationed at the convent of Bostello. Through Valongo ran a deep stream with considerable volocity, having a bridge over it, and further down a ford practicable for infantry.

Hodges now showed the heads of his columns, and threw forward his artillery; Donna Maria's volunteers attacked the enemy's right, and the fifteenth the convent in front. The British battalion moved through a valley to gain the hill, to cut off the mules and baggage, and keep the guerillas at Bostello in check; the artillery covered the attack with a brisk and well-directed fire; the conflict lasted half-an-hour; the enemy were driven from their position and retired in disorder on Amarante, closely pressed by the Queen's troops. About two miles to the right of the town they made a stand to cover the retreat of their baggage, but were charged and driven from their position by Donna Maria's volunteers. The loss of the Miguelites was about two hundred killed and wounded, amongst whom were seven friars. There were several women in this fray, who made themselves useful in carrying off the wounded. Our loss was three killed in taking possession of the convent of Bostello, and nine died afterwards from the effects of heat and fatigue. The fifteenth regiment burnt the convent in Penafiel, and Bostello was sacked notwithstanding all Colonel Hodges' efforts to prevent it. The friars had it well stocked with all sorts of provisions and wines; but the fatigue of the troops was so great that many were absolutely incapable of enjoying the fruits of their conquest. At five o'clock Penafiel was occupied, but with the exception of about twenty persons it had been abandoned by the inhabitants, who left their houses barricaded. Strict discipline was observed, and the soldiers bivouacked in the streets.

The enemy had now passed the Douro in force, and were moving on Amarante; and at eleven at night Colonel Hodges retired on Valongo, agreeably to the orders he had received from the Count Villa Flor. Having reached Ponte Ferreira, a strong position, he there halted for a few hours, and got to Valongo at eight on the morning of the 19th, after thirty hours hard service. At four they again marched, and arrived at Oporto at eight in the evening. The fifteenth of the line had also retired from Guimaraens. Thus terminated the duties of the governor of Tras-os-Montes.

<small>Hodges' Narrative.</small>

On the 22d of July, at one o'clock, the fifth caçadores, the volunteers of Donna Maria, the three battalions of the eighteenth regiment, and the British battalion with four field-pieces and a howitzer, under the command of Colonel Fonseica, marched on the Valongo road, on the heights of which they arrived before day-light. The enemy were strongly posted in front of Ponte Ferreira in great force. The first battalion of the fifteenth and British battalion were in reserve on the heights of Valongo, and the fifth caçadores and

Donna Maria's volunteers, supported by a six-pounder and a howitzer, attacked the enemy, and were repulsed, losing two guns. Hodges moved the light company of the eighteenth and the British grenadiers to watch the enemy, who were in motion on the left, rapidly advancing to the point where the light troops had attacked, and who were now retiring on the Valongo road; and he fell back on the reserve. The enemy's force now advanced on the Oporto road. Here the Count Villa Flor came up, and ordered the column to halt. An aide-de-camp from the Emperor also arrived, and ordered the column to retire on Rio Tinto, where he was posted with another division. Colonel Brito and Schwalbach had also been called from the south, and joined the main body of the army, removing the bridge. The armed volunteers were left in Oporto to defend the town.

What object was expected to be gained by this foolish attack it is not easy to conceive; if it was meant as a reconnaissance, that would have been accomplished without attacking a very superior force strongly posted and unsupported by the main body. The Queen's troops were few enough, and they should not have been risked where no object was to be gained. This check had a bad effect on the troops, as well as the inhabitants of Oporto.

CHAPTER IV.

THE whole army being now assembled at Rio Tinto, dispositions were made for a general attack the following day. The light division under Schwalbach was placed in the centre; Brito's division was on the right; the battalion of officers, a battalion of artillery with muskets, the third battalion of the eighteenth regiment, the French and British, composed the left wing under Hodges; the Count de Bemposta and Monsieur Lasteyrie, the Emperor's aide-de-camp, accompanied their countrymen. The whole moved from the bivouack at three in the morning. The Miguelites were posted behind the river Souza, their left protected by the high ground on the right bank of the Douro, and their right by a sugar-loaf hill, occupied by a considerable force, and one field-piece.

Hodges' Narrative.

Major Checar, who commanded the French, was ordered to cross the ford; he was closely followed by the British under Shaw; two companies of the eighteenth, under Major Miranda, acted as light troops, and cleared the road in front; the eighteenth was ordered to turn the enemy's right; and the battalion of officers and artillery were held in reserve. The British and French soon drove the enemy from their position, and the eighteenth, instead of turning the enemy, ascended the hill unmolested.

Major Checar with a part of his battalion advanced too far in the plain, and was followed by some of the British; a body of cavalry, hid by a hedge, now charged, and killed the major and a considerable number of the men who advanced with him. The main body of the French and British were formed under a wall skirting the wood; the cavalry, flushed with success, rode gallantly up, and received a volley which threw

Hodges' Narrative.

them into confusion, but not before several had actually attempted to leap the wall, and were bayonetted while endeavouring to clear it. Brito's division had been ordered to attack the enemy's left, and three several times orders were sent to that purpose by Villa Flor; but by some unaccountable mistake he did not move, and it was alleged the Emperor had ordered him not to advance, as he was menaced by the enemy's cavalry. The enemy, seeing his left was not attacked, advanced two columns to retake the position Hodges had gained, supported by clouds of guerillas on his left and in his rear. Lieutenant Mitchell was sent to the Count Villa Flor to request a reinforcement; this was supported by another request made by the Count of Beinposta; but it was not till some time had elapsed ere the Emperor sent the third battalion of the eighteenth to his support. The hill had been abandoned, the French and British were now placed in reserve, the reinforcement was ordered to regain the hill at the point of the bayonet; at the same time Hodges led the third battalion to turn it on the left; this was done with great gallantry, many of the enemy were killed, and some prisoners taken. Thus ended the battle of Ponte Ferreira, which led to no consequences; the attack on the enemy's right was not followed up by a simultaneous movement on their left; and with the exception of the light division in the centre having driven in their outposts, no further fighting took place.

Villa Flor was not to blame; his orders were interfered with by the Emperor and those about him, who disconcerted all his plans, and prevented him reaping the advantages that he most probably would have gained, had the movements of the army been left entirely to his management. This was not the only evil, for some one of his staff sent an order to the governor of Oporto to embark the treasure and the Emperor's baggage. This order, instead of being kept secret, was publicly known, and created a great sensation in Oporto, which was increased by general Povoas taking possession of Villa Nova, and collecting boats above the Serra convent, threatened to cross over and attack Oporto, under cover of a heavy fire of musketry on the lower part of the town; and although there were three schooners in the river keeping in check the fire from Villa Nova, it had no effect in quieting their fears. Crowds of people of all ages and sexes were hurrying to the Foz, and the governor had even given orders to pull up the paving stones and barricade the streets in the lower part of the town, and many of his friends to whom he had communicated the orders to embark the Emperor's baggage were the first to take to flight. On the return of the Emperor to Oporto, Mascarenhos was superseded, and the governorship of Oporto conferred on Bernardo de sa Nogueira, a gallant officer and one of the Emperor's aide-de-camps.

After the battle of Ponte Ferreira the enemy retired two leagues. The Queen's troops did not advance, but returned to Oporto at four o'clock on the following day, carrying green boughs in their caps as an emblem of victory. An order was issued next morning, not to thank the troops for their behaviour, but to praise Doctor Tavares for his attendance to the wounded, Padre Marco, and Paul D'Almeido, the Emperor's chamberlain. *Hodges' Narrative.*

The battle of Ponte Ferreira put an end to the hopes of gaining the Queen's cause by any thing short of hard fighting. The Emperor's eyes were now opened to the perilous situation he was in; and he at length saw how little reliance was to be placed in the knowledge his advisers had of the feelings of the army. The green boughs in the caps of his troops did not blind the inhabitants of Oporto; there were neither rejoicing nor vivas for the constitution; all seemed to have awakened from a dream, and despair was deeply depicted in their countenances.

The unnecessary retreat into Oporto after the battle of Ponte Ferreira, which ought to have been followed up by vigorous measures, as the only chance of repairing the errors already committed, was rendered still more pernicious by an attempt to destroy the whole army by setting fire to their barracks when the troops were asleep, exhausted with the fatigues of the two previous days. This infamous project was supposed to have been undertaken by three priests, who set fire, at one o'clock in the morning of the 25th, to the convent of St. Domingo, where were quartered the fifth caçadores. The flames broke out with great violence; the alarm was given, and happily the men escaped, only three losing their lives, and the colours of the regiment burnt. One of the friars was instantly put to death by the soldiers, and the other two were imprisoned, but never brought to trial, though the evidence against them was so strong as to leave little doubt of their guilt. It was reported that an attempt was intended to have been made against the life of the Emperor, should an opportunity offer, by a Capuchin friar, who presumed that his Majesty, with his usual activity, would be forward in assisting to subdue the fire. This, however, was only conjecture, and it never could be traced with any certainty.

The intention of offensive operations was now abandoned, and it was decided to fortify Oporto, and wait the course of events. In this undertaking the Emperor showed his usual diligence, and in this *undertaking* he was unanimously supported by all parties; there was no intriguing here: the first law of nature, self-preservation, came home to all, and perhaps this is the only instance in the whole war in which honest men and intriguers perfectly agreed. The fortifications began at the Quinta de China, touching the river, and extended all round Oporto, including the light-house and the Foz. Redoubts were thrown up on the commanding hills, the whole connected with ditches; and although of no great strength, they were sufficient, when defended by the Queen's troops, to baffle all the attempts of the Miguelites to penetrate them. Villa Nova was not included in the defences; many were of opinion that it ought not to be neglected, but the Emperor resisted all importunities on this head, and limited himself to the defence of the Serra convent; and here he was right, for with the small force he commanded, it would have endangered the whole, had both sides of the river been garrisoned. The defence of the Serra was intrusted to Brigadier Torres, a brave old man, with Bravo for his second.

Although the Emperor was in my opinion perfectly right in not attempting to defend Villa Nova, his ministers ought to have been suspended on a gallows fifty cubits high for not removing the immense quantity of wine in the stores. It was arranged that Palmella should proceed to London to negociate a loan, and the only security he had for that loan were the wines at Villa Nova. It had been decided in council that they should be immediately removed; and before his departure he pressed on the ministers the absolute necessity of immediately commencing the operation; but the more than incapable ministers put it off from day to day, until the whole fell into the hands of the enemy, and with the wines the last hope of raising money for the exigencies of the war was lost; and yet those ministers, instead of being hanged or banished from Oporto with disgrace, were still allowed to direct the Emperor's councils.

It must not, however, be supposed they were idle; far from it—they were sitting in their offices distributing orders and promotion to their friends, pleasing some and disgusting more, and intriguing against the general, who had, when left to himself, been successful in all his undertakings. The moment this came to his knowledge, he tendered his resignation to the Emperor, and offered to serve his country under any commander he thought proper, with the exception of his majesty's aid-de-camp Candido Xavier, who, it was supposed, was to be appointed chef-d'-etat major, in the event of the Emperor himself taking command of the army. His Majesty became alarmed at the determination of Villa Flor, refused his resignation, and assured him that no change should take place. The count in consequence retained the command on condition that Colonel Battiste, the chief of his staff, and Captain Pimentel, the quarter-master-general, should be removed. Brigadier Valdes was appointed adjutant-general, Major Lourerio quarter-master-general, and Major Mendez secretary. Colonel Battiste was appointed to command the artillery, and Pimentel made aide-de-camp to the Emperor.

Up to the present time there had been some desertion from the enemy's ranks, which now very much decreased, probably owing to the precautions taken by the Miguelite general, as well as the Miguelites losing confidence in the Queen's cause; and the latter reason seems the more likely, as desertion about this :me became considerable from the Queen's troops, particularly in the fifteenth regiment, which more than once lost a whole picquet. This regiment had been largely recruited from the Miguelite prisoners taken in the Azores, and they corrupted the young soldiers raised in the islands. There was little desertion from the other corps, none from the French, and only two from the English.

On the 18th of July Admiral Sartorius sailed for the Tagus with the Rainha, Donna Maria, Villa Flor, Amelia corvette, and Eugenie schooner, and on the 19th anchored in Cascaes Bay, where he found Admiral Parker and a British squadron. A remonstrance having been made by the governor of Cascaes to the British admiral, the Queen's squadron moved to the south passage of the Tagus, from whence they could plainly perceive Don Miguel's ships at anchor between St. Julian's and Belem. On the 23d Admiral Parker weighed, and passing close to Admiral Sartorius's squadron, hoisted Donna Maria's flag, and returned his salute. This species of acknowledgement of her flag by a British admiral was most annoying to the Miguelite government, and proportionally agreeable to Admiral Sartorius. The Tagus was strictly blockaded, and several vessels of value captured: amongst them was the St. John Magnamino, store-ship from India, carrying thirty guns, captured by the small corvette 23d of July, Captain Morgal, and Eugenie schooner.

On the 3d of August Miguel's squadron,

consisting of a ship of the line, a frigate, three corvettes, and three brigs, commanded by Commodore Joao Felix, put to sea. Sartorius weighed and recalled the Donna Maria. At ten, the admiral, being to windward of the enemy, made the signal to prepare for battle and bore up. I believe the Rainha ran through the squadron, but not being followed nothing decisive took place. On the 5th the Amelia, who sailed bad, was considerably astern. Two corvettes chased her; she tacked, the signal being made to provide for her safety, which she did by proceeding to Oporto: her appearance there without knowing what had become of the squadron caused great consternation. The corvettes soon gave up the chase; the squadron kept close together till the night of the 10th, and at half-past eight Sartorius bore up and ran through the enemy's squadron, passing under the frigates' stern, and then hauling his wind, engaged them to leeward. In about half an hour the Don John tacked, which finished the action. Both ships suffered considerably in their masts and rigging, and lost two or three men killed, and about twenty wounded. Next morning the enemy's squadron were still in sight, the Don John having lost her main-topmast.

Nothing further took place till the 12th, when both squadrons appeared off the bar of Oporto. The Miguelite squadron to windward, bore up and made all sail, the frigate and a corvette considerably ahead. Sartorius did all he could to separate them from the rest of the squadron ; they were, however, too cautious, shortened sail, and hauled their wind. In the evening it fell calm, and there was every prospect of bringing on a decisive action. The Rainha lashed the steamer alongside of her, took the Donna Maria in tow, and steered towards the enemy, who now appeared in perfect dismay. They were much separated, and were hoisting out their boats, the small craft using their sweeps. In half an hour they would have been in action, and probably the Miguelites would have been annihilated, but unfortunately a breeze sprang up, and another steamer and corvette joining Sartorius, so alarmed Joao Felix that he made sail, and was seen by the Amelia, who joined on the 17th, steering for Lisbon. Sartorius returned to Oporto, repaired his damages, and completed his water and provisions.

It does not appear that the Miguelite commodore had any serious intention of bringing Sartorius to action; it is most probable that he wished to draw him off the land to enable stores to be sent up to the army before Oporto, and in this manœuvre he succeeded. The Emperor and his ministers do not appear to have been much satisfied : they expected nothing less than the capture of the squadron, without once reflecting on their superiority, or considering the state they would have been in at Oporto, had Sartorius lost the day or been so disabled as to have obliged him to seek a port to refit in either France or England.

CHAPTER V.

AFTER the battle of Ponte Ferreira, no movement took place on either side till the 7th of August. The emperor had been fortifying his lines, Don Miguel collecting troops to attack them. At three in the morning of that day Villa Flor marched with the first and light division on Souto Redondo to reconnoitre Povoas' force; they were driven from the village of Feira with some loss. Villa Flor was following up his success with great boldness, when Captain Rebosa, who was in advance, either seeing or fancying he saw the enemy's cavalry, sounded the retreat, exclaiming at the same time that the horse were upon them. The fifth caçadores, who till now had always distinguished themselves, were seized with a sudden panic, and fled in the utmost confusion; the other troops caught the alarm, and ran for Oporto without giving themselves time to look behind. In vain did Villa Flor attempt to stop their flight; nothing could induce them to halt. The Miguelites, themselves astonished, could not believe the flight was serious, and did not profit by the panic. This hesitation gave Villa Flor time to collect his staff and a few men, who kept in check the enemy's sharpshooters and a few cavalry, until his troops, probably fatigued with the celerity of their retreat, halted at the entrance of Villa Nova, where they were met by the Emperor. The loss of the enemy in the early part of this affair was considerable; that of the Queen's troops about three hundred in killed, wounded, and missing, and two field-pieces. Passou was cut down at his guns. Schwalbach was wounded early in the action, but did not quit the field. Mascarenhas, the late Governor of Oporto, was also severely wounded; he accompanied Villa Flor as a volunteer, anxious to wipe off the stain he had undeservedly incurred in the battle of Ponte Ferreira.

This affair created great alarm not only amongst

the inhabitants of Oporto, but in the councils of the Emperor; and the very men who had led him to believe he would meet with no opposition in landing in Portugal, were the first to advise him to reimbark his arms and give up the contest. This was strongly opposed by Villa Flor and Palmella; but it was not till after forty-eight hours' deliberation that their pusillanimous councils were rejected. Rebosa was tried and condemned to be shot, but his punishment was very improperly commuted to degradation and hard labour for life. This disaster strengthened the enemies of Villa Flor, and it is generally believed that Palmella, who went to England after this affair, had instructions to treat with some British officers either to take the command of the troops, or to act as chief of the Emperor's staff.

Hodges's Narrative.

On the 22d of August the squadron again sailed: they now consisted of the Rainha, Donna Maria, Coquette schooner, twenty-third of July brig of 18 guns, Eugenie schooner, and a couple of steamers. On the 25th they were off the Tagus. They there learnt that the Miguelite frigate had lost eight men killed and thirty wounded, and shifted her foremast. The Don John and a brig had been a good deal cut up, but were now refitted and expected shortly to put to sea.

On the 10th of September they sailed : their force was a line-of-battle ship, a frigate, two corvettes, two brigs, and a steamer. The following day one of their brigs lost her fore and main-topmasts, and was in tow of a steamer. This steamer was so overloaded with heavy stores that she herself went down before the brig was ready, which was not before the 14th, both squadrons then in sight of each other. There had been for a long time some dissension in the fleet, particularly between Admiral Sartorius and Captain Minns. I shall not enter into the cause of these dissensions, but I cannot omit publishing a most extraordinary letter addressed by the petty officers of the Donna Maria to her captain, and Captain Minns's reply, neither of which were creditable to her discipline. On the 23d the Donna Maria parted company, and did not join the admiral till the 30th off Oporto, where was now assembled the whole of the squadron, consisting of the Rainha 46, Donna Maria 42, Portuense 20, Villa

Appendix No. III.

Flor 16, 23d of July 18, Regencia 18, Constitution 13, Mindella 13. The admiral was much dissatisfied at the Donna Maria having parted company, and thinking all was not right, shifted his flag to that ship, and on the 2d of October anchored at Bayonne Islands: the enemy were then lying in Vigo Bay.

At day-light on the 10th of October the enemy's squadron quitted Vigo and passed through the South Channel. Sartorius followed through the same passage, and at half-past one on the morning of the 11th brought them to action. It appears to have been the admiral's intention to attack the Don John with the two frigates, leaving his corvettes and brigs to fight the enemy's frigate, and keep their smaller vessels in check, but from want of wind or other causes the smaller vessels did not get to their stations, and the brunt of the action fell on the Donna Maria. At half-past two the Rainha ran between the line-of-battle ship and the Donna Maria, and then took a station on her weather-bow, where she was of little service. Her running between the two ships was most injudicious; but had she afterwards put her helm up, and ran athwart the Don John's hawse, she would necessarily have been supported by the Donna Maria running alongside, and the Don John would have inevitably been captured. The small vessels at the same time should have mobbed the frigate, who could have easily been carried, and the corvettes would have saved themselves by flight. This was not done, and the consequence was the Donna Maria was dreadfully cut up, having eighty shot in her hull and being otherwise damaged; and the enemy escaped. The loss on this occasion was ten killed and forty wounded.

On the 20th the squadron anchored in Oporto Roads, and the Miguelites returned to Lisbon. Admiral Sartorius landed, and took upon himself the duties of major-general; and a large proportion of the seamen were landed to occupy the Eoz batteries. Shortly after the weather became unsettled, and the squadron took shelter in Vigo Bay.

Little consideration was shewn to the admiral on his landing either by the Emperor or his ministers. They had buoyed themselves up with the hope that the whole squadron would be captured, and never took the trouble to reflect that in no one instance had even a well-manned and well-disciplined British frigate taken a line-of-battle ship.

During the time the naval operations were going on, the opposing parties were not idle at Oporto. The former appearance of the enemy's fleet off the bar had frightened a little activity into the Emperor's ministers. The troops were employed night and day on the fortifications, and the Emperor himself was indefatigable. The English and French, much to their shame, declined working in the trenches, although three vintims a-day were offered to them. Faith had not been kept with them in the first instance, which was probably the cause of this refusal, as well as of the disorders that frequently took place.

Heavy fogs had been hovering over Oporto for many mornings, which was most favourable for attack, and the troops were kept under arms from two in the morning till they cleared away; but the enemy's attention seemed to be entirely taken up with preparations for attacking the Serra convent, and on the 8th of September a strong column was seen advancing from Grijo by the Bandeira road. Passou's* horse artillery was placed at the Seminario, which commanded the road by which they were advanicng; and many of the inhabitants of Oporto armed themselves and crossed over to assist Major Marcelli and a battalion of the sixth infantry in the defence of so important a post, which, if lost, would have rendered the town untenable.

Bernardo da Sa, the governor of Oporto, led out part of the garrison to oppose the enemy, who were rapidly advancing, and received a severe wound in the arm, which was afterwards amputated. This officer had a particular *penchant* for fighting, and was never willingly absent wherever a shot was fired: and he was generally successful in his undertakings.

The enemy advanced to the attack with great gallantry, led by the lieutenant-colonel of the Tondella militia, and were severely harassed by the

* The nephew of the one who was cut down in defending his guns at Souto Redondo.

guns and musketry from the Seminario. Torres, the commandant of the convent, reserved his fire till they actually began to storm, when it was poured in with such effect that they could no longer hold their ground. Their gallant leader fell in attempting to scale the wall. A second attack was made at another point, which was also repulsed. This affair cost the enemy two-hundred and fifty men in killed and prisoners, besides the wounded. The garrison only lost five killed and twenty wounded: amongst the latter were Major Marcelli and Count St. Leger. Two days afterwards another attack was made, which met with no better success.

On the north of the Douro the enemy had nearly completed a battery opposite Monte Pedral, which on the 16th of September Villa Flor decided, if possible, to destroy. A detachment of eighty-six men under Colonel Burrel had landed on the 12th, and though small it was considered of great importance. Gaspar Texeira had assumed the command of Miguel's army, having Santa Martha for his second, and issued a proclamation worthy of the cause he served. [Appendix. No. IV.]

General Brito commanded the sortie: the force employed was thirteen hundred men. They sallied out at two P. M., and gained the heights of Cobello and Paranhos without being discovered. The fisrt piquet was surprised, and the greater part taken or killed. Brito then completely destroyed the works and retired. The enemy by this time were under arms, and showed a strong force on the centre, menacing the left at the same time with two squadrons of cavalry and some light troops. Colonel Fonseca advanced from the Foz with five companies of caçadores, and the enemy retired. An attack on the outposts of Carvalhedo was also repulsed.

Three strong columns now advanced on the heights in front of the Antas. Major Shaw commanded the piquet and retired, placing them behind some walls, from whence he opened a fire, which, together with the batteries of the Captivo and the Fojo, kept the enemy in check. Colonel Hodges sent two companies of the twelfth caçadores to support Shaw. Major Staunton with the British grenadiers, and a company of the twelfth caçadores was ordered to move on the enemy's left, but by some accident took the road on their right, ascended the hill with fixed bayonets, and the enemy fled; they were, however, rallied by an officer, were again charged by Staunton, and again routed; but the gallant Staunton fell, and his subaltern, Lieutenant Jenkins, was shot through the thigh. Of the British, two were killed and seventeen wounded; of the Portuguese, one lieutenant killed, one wounded, and nine privates.

No attempt had been made to disturb the enemy on the south bank of the Douro, though two batteries for the attack of the Serra and the bombardment of the town were rose under the very muzzles of our guns, without any serious endeavour to molest them. Villa Flor, Palmella, and the British merchants, who were anxious to get possession of their wines, were loud in their representations to attack Villa Nova. Palmella, when in England, had contracted a loan of £200,000, pledging the wines as a security, and when these wines were lost, the loan was not completed; and although the ministers saw ruin staring them in the face, they were not to be moved.

About this time Colonel Sorrel was appointed consul at Oporto. British property had not been much respected by the Miguelite general, and he sent a flag of truce with a severe remonstrance. Lieutenant Elliott, who was the bearer of it, was well received and invited to dine at head-quarters. Promises were given to be more circumspect, but so ill kept, that Lieutenant Elliott was again sent over. This time he was not received by the Miguelite general, and treated with little politeness. In both his visits he saw Sir John Campbell, who was with the Miguelite army.

On the 27th the London Merchant arrived with fifty-four horses, and cavalry appointments for two hundred men, and more were on their way to Oporto. For several days rumours of an approaching attack were afloat, which was supposed would take place on the 29th, Miguel's Saint's-day. Loaded mules and a good deal of baggage was passed over to the north side, together with four battalions and some field artillery. The officers in command in various parts of the line made every preparation for defence. To the right, where the foreign brigade was stationed, were many houses and garden-walls outside the lines, which Hodges had repeatedly applied to have cleared away, but without effect; and on the 28th, when he saw an attack would certainly take place, he took the responsibility on himself and levelled them with the grouud.

When a position, not strong and feebly garrisoned, is expected to be attacked by a numerous army, it has been the custom both in ancient and modern times to concentrate the whole force for its defence; but Don Pedro's minister-at-war, despising all these rules, actually sent away, two days before the expected attack, the twelfth caçadores in the London Merchant steamer, to make a descent at Aveiro—a port extremely difficult of access at all times, and so uncertain, like all the bar-harbours on the coast of Portugal, that you may get in one day, and perhaps be detained a week before the bar be again passable. This alone ought to have forbid an expedition, unless there was a moral certainty of success, which was not the case here. The pilots knew nothing of the passage of the river; one hundred and twenty men were put into boats to reconnoitre; the enemy showed themselves in force; and it was with the greatest difficulty, owing to the strong tide, that the boats regained the steamer; and it was even no easy matter for the steamer to repass the bar. Thus ended this foolish expedition, which might have caused the loss of Oporto.

CHAPTER VI.

The attack of the 29th is so well described in Colonel Hodges' Narrative, that with his permission I shall employ his own words.

" On the morning of the 29th, two hours before daylight, we distinctly heard columns moving in different directions. This fact I communicated to the Count de Villa Flor, with the intimation that unless I received a reinforcement of five hundred men, as an equivalent to those withdrawn from me on the 27th, I could not answer for the maintenance of the position which the French then held. The position referred to was that from the St. Cosme road to the Quinta da China, touching the river, which important range I had assigned to the charge of the French battalion under the Count de St. Leger.

" At half past five, whilst I was at the Bom Fin Battery, (in the centre of my line, on the main road to Valongo,) I received notice from the Count de St. Leger that the enemy was rapidly advancing upon him both by the river side and the St. Cosme road. Proceeding immediately to the Count's quarters, and finding that no reinforcement had arrived, I directed the officer of the Quarter-Master-General's department attached to me, Don Fernando de Almeida, to present himself to the Emperor with all speed, and demand the required succour. I also detached the Cadet Valdez to the General-in-Chief, to point out the perilous situation the extreme right of my line was in, from the want of a reserve, and to request urgently that a battalion of five hundred men might be sent with all possible dispatch. At the same time, I assured the General that I would maintain my ground while I had a man left to enable me to do so. The Count de Villa Flor stated in reply, that he had ordered the fifth Caçadores to my support, and that I might expect their arrival within a few minutes. No reinforcement, however, did arrive until nearly three hours afterwards, and then only one hundred and twenty men, with a captain and three subalterns.

" I had charged Lieutenant-Colonel Burrell with the defence of the Quinta and gardens of the *Praça das Flores,* while Major Shaw was placed at the barrier and redoubts in front. Both these officers had instructions to maintain their respective posts against all skirmishers, and only to retire within the lines on the enemy's advancing in column. The Portuguese troops furnished on this morning the picquets for the heights on the *Lugar das Antas;* an arrangement which I made for the purpose of enabling me to concentrate my little band of English, and to have them disposable for any required point.

" The enemy's first effort was directed on the Quinta da China and the St. Cosme road. Their columns of attack on the Quinta were conducted by the identical Balthazar, the Count de St. Leger's favoured, but double-dealing spy, already spoken of.

" The numerical force of the French battalion in position at this time was but three hundred and seventeen bayonets, while the two brigades

of Miguelists which attacked them mustered about
two thousand five hundred. The French picquets
on the St. Cosme road were charged and driven
in by cavalry; and the hostile columns were enabled, through the treachery of the inhabitants of
the neighbouring houses, to advance within half-
musket shot of our trenches and batteries, without
our being able to discover the heads of them.
This contrivance exempted them from the effect
of the instructions I had given to the various
batteries, not to fire until the enemy were within
the range of grape, and then only to pour it in
on the heads of their columns. Favoured by the
concealment they had obtained, and by the brisk
impetuosity of their own movement, the Miguelists
reached our very lines, and actually brought up
their pioneers to cut down the fir-trees we had
placed as a stockade in our front. Their over-
whelming superiority of number, and the loss
occasioned by their fire, created a momentary
sense of alarm in the heroic little band of Frenchmen, who had, however, rallied together for the
defence of the battery in their rear, when I
came up.

" Seeing the Count de St. Leger dismounted, (his horse having been shot a few moments before,) I called upon his gallant corps to retake the stockade at the point of the bayonet. He himself led them to the attack *au pas de charge*, and they retook the post with all the dashing spirit so much noticed among French soldiers. This point regained, (although I regret to say, not without a severe loss,) I ordered the men to expose themselves as little as possible—to place the muzzles of their muskets through the interstices of the stockade, and only to fire when they were sure of bringing down their men.

" Seeing the description of foe they had to contend with, the Miguelites abated somewhat of their impetuosity, but kept up a sharp fire from the neighbouring houses and sheltered gardens. They next made a bold attack on the barrier placed on the St. Cosme road, a hundred yards in front of the house of Baños Lima. A mine had been laid there, but proved unserviceable, owing to the previous rains. Here also the Miguelites made a momentary lodgment, and got possession of the barrier, just as the long-expected but scanty reinforcement arrived. The men of this latter body were not disposed to retake the barricade at the point of the bayonet, and the consequence was, that between one and two hundred Miguelites actually got within our lines. They were, however, promptly charged by a detachment of the mounted corps of guides, (commanded by Colonel Joao Nepomuceno de Macedo,) who cut some down, made a few prisoners, and obliged the remainder to retire across the trench, which had been filled up with the furniture from the contiguous houses.

" With the exception of this spirited charge, the French corps had received no assistance up to that moment, in defending their ground (no inconsiderable portion of our line) against a force of two thousand five hundred men. The Count de St. Leger, a short time before this charge, was severely wounded, and obliged to quit the field. The brave young Lasteyrie, who was throughout the day forward in all danger, (having relinquished the comparative security of the Emperor's staff,) was also wounded, but was not compelled to quit his post.

"Seeing this part of my position apparently secured, I repaired with all haste to the Fojo battery, immediately in the rear of the *Praça das Flores*,* and from thence I perceived the British battalion to be warmly engaged—they having been also attacked by greatly superior numbers. The enemy having gained the heights of the Antas, which were abandoned without resistance by the picquet of eighty men from the eighteenth regiment, that had been placed there, the British

* " Previously to my leaving the extreme right, Lieut. Colonel Pacheco, with the battalion of the tenth infantry, garrisoned the batteries that had been momentarily in the possession of the enemy, as well as that part of the external line fronting the battery of Lombo, and touching the Bom Fin Church. A fine trait of intrepidity was exhibited before the arrival of Pacheco, by six of a body called the *Corps of Academicians*, who, on seeing the enemy repulsed from the St. Cosme barrier, rushed forward from the Lombo battery, and retook the fort immediately in its front. In this fearless and successful attempt, two brothers out of the six assailants were killed. The other four maintained their acquisition until Pacheco's arrival. Throughout the protracted struggle which I am recording, the little corps of Academicians distinguished themselves honourably by their courage and devotion to the cause."

became exposed to imminent danger. This small corps, retiring from the barricade on the Valongo road, (but not till they had made an obstinate resistance there,) got within a house that had been prepared for defence, and barricaded its doors and windows, which were loop-holed for the use of musketry. While Lieutenant-Colonel Burrell, with the right wing of the British, was defending this house, Major Shaw commanded the left wing, for the defence of the garden. Here the Miguelites made a desperate attack, having rapidly pushed a large body of troops into the neighbouring houses immediately in front, by which means they were secured from the fire of our batteries, and enabled to scale the garden-walls, and in part to surround the house in which Lieutenant-Colonel Burrell was. He, however, perceiving his danger, made a bold sally, and at the point of the bayonet charged them, and caused them for a brief interval to retire. Scarcely had he thus far succeeded, when he himself received a musket-shot which killed him on the spot. With him fell twelve of his men. The remainder then joined Major Shaw, who with marked obstinacy disputed every inch of ground, until such of the officers and men as were wounded were brought within our lines; after which he, with the remainder of his body, retired in good order into the battery of the Captivo.

"In the course of this attack on the garden of the *Praça das Flores*, some remarkable evidences of personal courage were given on both sides. Some of the enemy's light troops had the hardihood to attempt single combat with the British, being elated with the show of success attending their onset. Nor were these individual rencontres among the privates alone. One of the Miguelite Caçadores made a rush towards Lieutenant Burton, who at the moment was standing near to Major Shaw. The Lieutenant, with characteristic coolness and precision, took up a stone and flung it at his assailant with such effect that it struck him in the face, and knocked off his cap. He in return levelled his rifle, and shot poor Burton dead, at so close an approach to him that his coat was singed by the powder. The Caçadore himself presently paid the forfeit of his life for his temerity. Major Shaw, too, was struck by the spent shot, which, for a few minutes, rendered him insensible.

Captains Mitchell and Chinnock, and Lieutenant Walsh, were badly wounded, and carried to the rear.

"When I saw the remnant of this valiant little band within the battery, and perceived, by the thinness of their number, the slaughter that had been made in their ranks—when I beheld, likewise, their gallant Major insensible through the hurt he had received on his breast, and only two of the junior subalterns, (one of whom carried the colours,) left for duty, my feelings, it will readily be supposed, were of no enviable nature. I was directing the Adjutant to take charge of the battalion, and addressing a few encouraging words to the men, when Major Shaw recovered, and I had the satisfaction to hear from his own lips that he was able to return to the field. Suiting the action to the word, he got up and assumed his position of command, to the great joy of the men under his orders.

"The British, on going into action, had numbered only two hundred and eleven bayonets. They were attacked by a column of two thousand men in front, while the fire from clouds of skirmishers, who were placed on the heights of the Antas, did them destructive mischief.

" As the action proceeded, much inconvenience was sustained in regard to our *matériel*. A field nine-pounder in the Captivo battery was damaged in its carriage, so as to render the guns unserviceable. Unfortunately, too, there was a lack of ammunition in all the batteries under my command, although, from the commencement of the day's business, I had appointed an intelligent Portuguese officer to attend to this important service. To repair the first accident, I ordered up Captain Pasos, with a six-pounder from his brigade, to take the charge of the Captivo battery; and to remedy the second, I sent urgent demands to Colonel Battiste, the commander of artillery, for fresh supplies of ammunition for the several batteries, as well as for the use of the battalions, whose reserve ammunition had become exhausted.

" I then proceeded to the Fojo battery, which the enemy was now advancing upon, having brought three nine-pounders to bear upon it from the Antas heights. The fire of musketry on this battery was extremely heavy. Within twenty minutes six artillery-men were shot dead, while working an eighteen-pounder. Their places were speedily and efficiently filled up from amongst the Academicians, and the brave Volunteers of Oporto, who, although only incorporated a few weeks since, vied with the best of the veterans in fearless self-exposure. Still no ammunition arrived for the batteries, so that I was compelled to use nine-pound shot for the eighteen-pounder. When the supply did arrive, there had been such ignorance or negligence in its distribution, that the eighteen-pound shot was sent for the use of the nine-gun batteries, and *vice versâ!*

"Another evil lay in the fact that the men's muskets (which, when new, were none of the best) were so hot from incessant use as to be unsafe in their hands. I therefore made a pressing requisition for two hundred stand of new arms to be issued, flinted from the arsenal, and specified the several points they should be sent to. With the strangest absurdity, these much-needed weapons, instead of being sent to the lines, were forwarded, together with a supply of ammunition for the infantry, to *my* quarters, a large house situated a quarter of a mile in the rear of the lines.

" Such blunders and delays as these were a considerable obstacle to our operations. It so chanced, however, that I had a supply of Congreve rockets in the Captivo battery; and these came into serviceable application. By directing only two of them against the heights of the Antas, we checked the advance of the enemy's fresh columns, although it was visible that their superior officers were using all their efforts to induce their men to the attack. Just at this time there fortunately arrived a *small* supply of suitable ammunition for the use of the Captivo and Fojo batteries. Directing two shots from the eighteen-pounder on the enemy's guns on the heights of Antas, we dismounted one of them. Presently some cavalry, and (as we afterwards learned from the prisoners) Sir John Campbell himself, who had directed the entire attack on this quarter, appeared on the heights. A discharge of grape soon sent them about.

" The Miguelites now evinced no desire to

renew the attack. They kept up, indeed, a sharp fire from the front on our head-quarter battery of the Congregadors, to the extreme right; but this was plainly with the object of keeping us in check until dark, when they might retire without risk.

" At this juncture I despatched an officer to the Count Villa Flor, requesting his Excellency's permission to attack the enemy's left from the St. Cosme road, and suggesting that a similar movement should be made from the centre of our line, with a view to secure that portion of our opponents that had occupied the houses and cottages in front of our position. I was speedily informed that the Count approved of my proposal, and that he had directed Brigade-general Henrique de Silva da Fonseca to detach a force from under his command to attack the enemy's right as soon as I should be engaged. Accordingly, taking with me forty men of the British battalion under the command of Adjutant Brown, and sixty Frenchmen, commanded by the chef-de-bataillon, Gentil, (an old officer of experience in his own service,) I directed at the same time two companies of the third caçadores to advance along the ravine to the right of the Bom Fin, while Major Shaw was simultaneously to make a rapid movement upon his old quarters and gain possession of them; and three companies of the fifth caçadores from the left of the Fojo battery were to recover the heights of the Antas. I also gave direction that as soon as a bugle should be sounded for the advance, Lieutenant-colonel Pacheco, and the battalion of the tenth infantry under his command, should break from their lines, and support the attack of the British on the *Praça das Floras.*

" On our first sortie upon the road from our lines, we were received with a heavy fire of musketry. The French detachment, which headed the attack on the road, while the British inclined to their left, were also exposed to a deadly fire, by which Major Gentil and two subalterns were killed, and Major Bourso de Carbonette, and three other officers, were severely wounded. Of the English, we lost six men, while the adjutant and many others were wounded.

" Finding that Pacheco did not advance as he had been directed to do, that our force was inadequate to the intended object without such aid, and that the brave Captain de Montenegro, who commanded the companies of the third caçadores, was added to the number of the killed, I was constrained to order the men to retire.

" I was afterwards given to understand that the cause of Pacheco's not advancing was attributable to the minister-of-war, though I was never able to clear up the matter satisfactorily. However it may be, no doubt remains on my mind that Pacheco was not only willing but anxious to grapple with the enemy in the open field, and that he would generously and nobly have seconded French or English at so important a crisis, when all were contending alike for the emancipation of his country. If, therefore, the fact is to be attributed to Senor Freire, it is but in keeping with the rest of his conduct towards the foreigners in the Queen's service.

" I now proceeded to the Captivo battery, and had the satisfaction to behold the enemy in disgraceful flight. They had thrown away their arms, and were ascending the heights of Antas in crowds, while a few remaining red jackets and the fifth caçadores were in full pursuit.

" On the attack of the British on the Praca das Flores, a frightful massacre took place; for seeing many of the bodies of their comrades mangled in a most disgusting manner, their feelings of revenge could not be controlled. They gave no quarter. At the barrier on the Valongo road sixty Miguelites were bayonetted."

" While the enemy were ascending the heights, I again brought grape and Congreve rockets to bear on them, so that the slaughter was very considerable, and their cries were distinctly heard within our lines. The whole scene, however animating to the victors, was still shocking to humanity. We made two hundred and sixty prisoners on this point alone; and had the attack on the right been seconded with all due vigour, it is a reasonable calculation that two thousand prisoners would have crowned our success on that day. As it was, we made but three hundred and fifty, with two-six-pounders, and a howitzer captured in front of the position held by the French. The two former of these guns had been previously taken from us on the 22d of July, the day before the battle of Ponte Ferreira.

"The enemy made no attack or considerable demonstration during the day, either on our left or our centre. His whole efforts were directed to the right; and it has been asserted that Sir John Campbell boasted of his intention to annihilate the French and English battalions posted in that quarter. It is true he had nearly succeeded; but the determined resistance he met with, and his final utter failure on the point of attack, will compel the gallant general, when party feeling shall have lost some of its bitterness, to acknowledge that the valiant little band nobly upheld the honour of their respective nations.

"Our Portuguese fought admirably throughout the day, and too much praise cannot be bestowed on the new levies of volunteers raised among the heroic inhabitants of Oporto. After this day I could never bring myself to believe that a "Carcundo" (or Miguelist) could be found within the walls of that noble city. The old men, the women, and children, were active in various ways in supplying our wants, and aiding the public service. Nor must I fail to acknowledge the kindness of the ladies of various English families in the town, who were most assiduous in their attendance at the hospitals, and liberal in their supplies of shirts, sheets, and linen for the wounded. The wounded officers too are not likely to forget their delicate attentions, particularly those whose wounds were most dangerous, and to whom such attentions were most especially important."

The brunt of the action fell on the foreign brigade. The French and English rivalled each other in daring, and well maintained their military reputation: they had often fought against each other on Portuguese ground, but here they fought for the first time side by side: no jealousy or animosity subsisted between them; their only feeling was admiration at each other's determined bravery, and no little credit is due to Colonel Hodges for creating such a good understanding. After the action was over and Oporto safe, Portuguese jealousy and intrigue went to work against them. It was asserted that the English were drunk, and that the French had abandoned their position. On this being reported to Hodges, he immediately applied to Villa Flor, and was by him informed that the Emperor had made the assertion through the Marquis of Loule, and that he had contradicted it. Hodges then wrote to the Count, and requested that his letter might be laid before the Emperor, which was done; but no explanation was given to Villa Flor by the Emperor further than that it was a mistake, and that he himself would speak to Hodges on the subject, which, however, he never did.

The foreign hospital was much exposed to the enemy's fire, and ill provided in every respect. Application was made for another, and even two empty houses pointed out where they might be well accommodated. The usual answer, "to-morrow," was given by the minister, and when to-morrow came, after much delay they were thrust into one house with little bedding and no accommodation, and so small that both stairs and passages were crowded with sick and wounded men.

On the 1st of October Hodges' brigade was replaced by the light division, and they were ordered to form the reserve. This change was nothing in itself, had it not so closely followed the reports that had been in circulation, or had it been accompanied with some mark of approbation, or even a simple notification that they were relieved in consequence of the hard duty they had performed, or the severe loss they had met with. Count Villa Flor felt this, and represented it to the Emperor; he was, however, overruled at the palace, and in consequence absolutely refused to convey the order to Hodges, and the Emperor was himself obliged to send orders by Major Loureiro to give up the post to Schwalbach, who was already on his march to occupy it.

<small>Hodges' Narrative.</small>

This affair, together with many other annoyances, determined Villa Flor to resign the command, which was exactly what the Emperor's advisers wished. The minister-at-war never had the manliness to openly dismiss an officer whose services he did not wish; his system was to disgust and oblige him to resign. I speak more particularly of the minister-at-war, because it was his department; he was the responsible man, and if the acts were the Emperor's, and disapproved by him, it was his duty to resign.

The Emperor now assumed the command of the army. Candido Xavier became military secretary; Loureiro, one of the best officers in Portugal, was dismissed without ceremony, and Pimentel appointed quarter-master-general. The Count Villa Flor was created Duke of Terceira, with one hundred contos of reis when he could get them, and his military appointment, first aide-de-camp to the Emperor; such were the empty rewards bestowed upon Villa Flor, who had performed such eminent services to his country. There is not in Portugal a better or milder man than the Duke of Terceira, and it was to be regretted that in these dangerous times he had not assumed a higher tone: had he held up his finger, he might have driven the Emperor's imbecile advisers not only from his presence, but from Oporto, and had he done so, his conduct would have been applauded by all right-thinking men.

On the evening of the 9th of October the Serra was again attacked, and the enemy repulsed with considerable loss. Works were now in progress in various parts of the Miguelite positions, and the town was cannonaded every night. The Emperor was driven from his quarters, which were much exposed, and many families were obliged to quit their homes, and seek shelter in less exposed parts of the town.

About this time Sir John Milley Doyle made his appearance, with a suite of twenty gentlemen; what were his views and prospects, or how these gentlemen were to be employed, it was difficult to say. Already were there officers more than sufficient for the few remaining British troops. The gallant officer probably expected the command of the army, and had taken the precaution to bring out his état-major; but the Emperor having assumed that command himself, Sir John was obliged to put up with the appointment of orderly officer. A few English and Belgians now arrived for the British and French regiments, and two subalterns and eighty men for Bacon's lancers, and he was shortly expected himself; the horses that had preceded the men, for want of proper care, had fallen into a wretched state, and when the evil was done, they were consigned to the charge of Colonel Hodges.

The new comers unfortunately brought money in their pockets, with which they regaled their countrymen; and till it was gone, there was much disorder in both the French and British regiments, which did not escape the observation and the severe remarks of the Portuguese.

On the 14th the Serra was again attacked with the most bold and determined courage; a battalion of caçadores was the first to attempt to scale the walls, the commanding officer himself carrying a ladder: they were received with vivas by the garrison, and repulsed with great loss. Again and again were they brought up by their officers, but the Serra was not to be taken. The enemy lost in these attacks five hundred men, killed, wounded, and prisoners. Batteries were now established against the Serra at four hundred yards distance, which damaged the walls and buildings, but did little harm to the garrison. Towards the end of this month two steamers arrived from England with troops. Major Sadleir brought with him about one hundred men and officers: another body of two hundred and forty men, under the name of Cochrane's Battalion, commanded by a gentleman of that name, but his services and several of the officers were rejected by the Emperor. This order was communicated to Admiral Sartorius by the minister of marine, (the British having been formed into the regiment of the Armada, were now under his orders.) About this time Mouzinho de Albuquerque resigned the marine department to Bernardo de Sa, and was appointed minister of the interior, and the British returned to the war department. They were now without clothing, shoes, and were not even entirely armed, and had never been supplied with bedding. This was repeatedly represented to the quarter-master-general, who referred Hodges to the minister-at-war; and though there was clothing of every description in store sent out expressly for the British troops, this minister, from some unknown cause, (I believe hatred to foreigners,) would not supply them. Hodges appealed to the Emperor by letter, which was read by Palmella in presence of the minister, and all grievances were promised to be redressed. A trifle of pay was issued to the men who were much in arrear, and clamorous. Indeed M. Freire had taught them, that mutiny was the only means of getting their grievances redressed, for he made a rule of never paying them till that took place. It has been alleged, and with some justice, that the British were constantly selling their clothing, which the Portuguese never did; but let it be remembered, that the Portuguese were regularly paid—the British never; and I am satisfied, had faith been kept, or even had a reasonable pay been regularly given them, there would have been no difficulty in keeping them under proper control. It is true the military chest was low, but it is difficult to make the soldiers understand that question. They agreed to come to Oporto to fight in the Queen's cause, and to receive a certain pay, and that pay ought to have been insured to them; and if not, the Emperor himself ought to have honestly explained to the foreign troops his position, and treated them with some degree of kindness or even flattery, which I really believe would have had the desired effect.

Colonel Bacon, a few cavalry officers, and one hundred horses now arrived from England, and a regiment was formed, called the Queen's Lancers; they consisted of four squadrons, composed of French, English, German, and Portuguese, and it is astonishing with what celerity that active officer brought them into an efficient state. They consented to serve on Portuguese pay, on condition that their arrears should be paid up on their arrival in Lisbon. This was no doubt most generous on their part, but it had a bad effect, as many, if not almost all the infantry officers were without private fortunes; and to keep themselves respectable on £2 : 10 a month, the pay received by all the Portuguese officers from the highest to the lowest, was perfectly impossible, and they in consequence did not follow the example of the cavalry, which much displeased the Emperor's ministers.

Shortly after the arrival of the cavalry, Sartorius, who was now refitting at the Bayonne Islands, sent the marines to Oporto, which increased the British to seven hundred and fifty strong.

The enemy were not idle : they constructed two batteries, the Cabodello and the Sampayo, which blocked the river completely against the ingress or egress of merchant ships. They were in consequence obliged to anchor in the roads and watch favourable opportunities of sending their boats in at night either over the bar, or in a small bay to the northward of the Foz. Both operations were attended with difficulty and danger, and the inhabitants soon found out that in the winter it would be quite impossible to provision the city. This added to the uneasiness of all parties, both civil and military, as they foresaw the possibility of being obliged to capitulate from starvation. Provisions rose in price in consequence, in about the same ratio that the means of purchasing decreased; and to add to this, Don Miguel arrived at the head-quarters of the army with a reinforcement of four thousand men. Gaspar Texeira was replaced by Santa Martha, and a severe attack was anticipated.

Little respect had been paid to the British vessels in the Douro, and the Childers, Orestes, and a steamer were ordered into the river for their protection.

The British battalion were still without necessaries, accoutrements, or shoes, the greater part of which had fallen into the enemy's hands on the 29th of September, and the new-comers were without arms or clothing. Hodges made another strong demand on the minister-at-war, and with the same success: he seemed determined to get rid of him, would not honestly say so, but followed his system of annoyance to obtain his purpose.

The sick and wounded were still without a proper hospital, though there were two empty houses in the same street; they were without either comforts, necessaries, or bedding, though it was known that both had been sent to Oporto from Liverpool by some friends of the British, and addressed to Hodges or Shaw, and appropriated to other purposes.

On the 8th of November the French regiment and the second battalion of Portuguese in Hodges' brigade were removed from under his orders, and he was reduced to the command of his own regiment. To put up with this was impossible, and he decided on sending in his resignation to the Emperor, which was accepted. This was followed by resigning the order of the Tower and Sword, which had been conferred on him for his conduct at the battle of Ponte Ferreira. On Hodges' resignation, Sir John Doyle was appointed to command the British, and they were ordered to occupy the post they formerly did in the proximity of the enemy. This appointment so disgusted Major Shaw and several other officers that they sent in their resignations, which were not accepted; but Sir John was removed from the command, which he only held forty-eight hours. During that time he had been liberal in promises; and after Hodges embarked for England, four hundred of the British got under arms, marched to the Emperor's quarters, and demanded their pay, which was promised as usual.

CHAPTER VII.

THE first military event that marked the assumption of the command of the army by Don Pedro, was the attack on Villa Nova on the 14th of November. Schwalbach passed the Douro above the Seminario, at the head of one thousand five hundred men; his orders were to destroy the batteries of St. Christovao, Bandeira, and that of the Pinery if possible, while two hundred seamen pushed over to the Cabedello to destroy it, and the Sampayo battery. Captain Hill commanded the gun-boats, and landed Schwalbach with great promptitude. The Miguelites were prepared for the attack, swept the landing-place, and pounded the town from their various batteries. Schwalbach advanced at a charge, carried their bivouac, and the two batteries, which were destroyed; the guns were disabled as well as they could be done without either spikes or sledge-hammers, which had been forgotten. The enemy now advanced two heavy columns, and Schwalbach, who knew his art well, retired in good order and embarked under cover of the fire from the Seminario and Serra Convent. The gallant Captain Morgal with his sailors carried the Cabedello, but he too was unprovided with implements to destroy the guns, and could only upset them and break the carriages. His men had only ten rounds of ammunition, and when that was expended, they were obliged to retreat.

Captain Morgal and Lieutenant Haward, a volunteer from the British regiment, and six men, were killed and fourteen wounded. The success these sorties met with, proves how much it is to be regretted a larger force was not employed. The Serra Convent ought to have been well re-inforced the night before, and as Schwalbach landed, they ought to have made a sally. The seamen should also have been supported by troops; they are always active, but never ought to be employed in shore expeditions, unless properly assisted; they are liable to fall into disorder, and not being accustomed to act together, when attacked by regular troops are easily cut up.

The troops behaved with great courage, and lost two hundred men in killed and wounded, which could ill be spared from the Queen's little army. The enemy, it is supposed, suffered considerably more.

On the 17th of November another sortie was decided on, under the command of Schwalbach. The British, now divided into three battalions, were commanded by Brigadier Bento de Franca; they marched out on the Valongo road, supported by a battalion of the sixth regiment, and forty mounted guides. The French and the third caçadores, commanded by Lieutenant-Colonel Sequeira, advanced from the Captivo battery, and the second caçadores on the St. Cosme road. The fifth caçadores were in reserve on the Antas. The enemy's piquets at St. Roque fell back on Rio Tinto, where the main body was stationed. Before they had time to form, Lieutenant-Colonel Soares, with two hundred of the second caçadores, seized the bridge of Campanhan, and destroyed the barricade: those of St. Roque were also destroyed by Captain Barreiros. The enemy were in great force, and by no means backward to engage; their main attack was on Schwalbach's left and centre, as well as on the Antas. Shaw reinforced this point with the second battalion of the British, was shot through the thigh and obliged to quit the field early in the battle. Lieutenant-Colonel Williams, with the first battalion of the British, being menaced by half a squadron of cavalry, was ordered to retire, which he did in close column in good order, but was not followed.

Schwalbach, being hard pressed, was obliged to retire within his lines, with a loss of three hundred killed and wounded. The French suffered considerably, the Miguelites giving no quarter either to French or English. There appears to have been no object whatever in this sortie: a few barricades were destroyed, which could be more easily replaced than the men who were killed. The Miguelites were supposed to have lost five hundred men, but their army in Portugal consisted of nearly one hundred thousand men of all arms, and they had the whole country to recruit from, while Don Pedro could with great difficulty procure either men or money; and all the exertions and resources of Mendizabal were inadequate to keep pace with the losses attending these ill-digested attacks.

Desertion now became a heavy drain on Don Pedro's force; the rations of his troops had been much reduced; and not only Portuguese, but both French and English went over to the enemy. A private of the third caçadores was shot, and it was with great difficulty Don Pedro could reconcile himself to permit his execution: this was the second that had taken place at Oporto. The Emperor had a great antipathy to the punishment of death, and yet I have heard this man accused of every species of cruelty.

The Duke of Palmella and Mouzinho de Albuquerque left Oporto in the London Merchant on the 22nd of November, and were nearly lost in passing the bar. On board this vessel General Mina was also embarked: he had been examining various parts on the coast of Spain and Portugal in disguise, had visited Lisbon, and landed in

Spain, and been some time in Oporto undiscovered, and only made himself known to Colonel Hodges, who was his old friend. His disguise was so complete that discovery was impossible, and in this manner he remained unknown even in the steam-boat, though he was well acquainted with the Marquis of Palmella. The British government had insisted on Don Pedro not permitting any Spaniard connected with the Spanish liberal party to come to Oporto as the price of their preventing Spain from meddling with Portuguese affairs; and had it been known that Mina was in Oporto, it would have placed the Emperor and his ministers in a very awkward predicament.

The object of Palmella's mission to England was to employ his influence to raise money, and to obtain, if possible, the direct interference of France and England in Donna Maria's favour. Unlimited powers were granted to Palmella, but he insisted on Mouzinho de Albuquerque being associated with him in his mission. The marquis had no confidence in the Emperor's advisers, and suspected they would sacrifice him at the earliest opportunity. The ministers, on the other hand, were pleased to get rid of him, and would have objected to nothing he proposed provided it removed him from Oporto.

On the Marquis's arrival in England, he found that the interest in favour of Donna Maria was fast subsiding: her friends had lost all hopes of her cause; many of the officers coming home in disgust at the manner they had been treated, and the little thanks they got from the minister-at-war for their services, together with sick and wounded men appearing in London totally unprovided for, had very much cooled those interested in Don Pedro's success. Added to this, rumours were afloat of discontent and mutiny in the squadron, and disagreements between the admiral and several of his officers. These occurrences were necessarily reported to the French and English governments, and it is not surprising that they should be extremely cool in their reception of Palmella; being a minister, he necessarily became mixed up with all the faults, follies, and intrigues that had been so long going on at Oporto. They were not to know that the Emperor was completely in the hands of Freire and Candido Xavier,

On an exposé of the state of affairs at Oporto being laid before the cabinets of France and England, it is believed, (though I have had no means of getting at the fact,) that they both refused to interfere even in negociations with Spain, unless the two princes and their ministers should retire from Portugal and Oporto. This stipulation, as regarded Don Pedro, was absurd to ask, and equally as absurd to consent to. The Emperor, with all his faults, was the heart and soul of the cause; he was active, determined, and obstinate to a degree; and though that obstinacy often did harm, it was the cause of the splendid defence of Oporto. As for his advisers they were totally incapable; they had neither military talent nor military firmness; they had persuaded Don Pedro that he was a great general, and had driven from his military councils the best and wisest men in Oporto; and had they been moved from his person affairs would have gone on well. The Marquis and Albuquerque were, however, supposed to consent to this, and Sir Stratford Canning proceeded to Madrid. Zea Bermudez was now minister, and it was hoped he was less hostile to the Queen's cause than his predecessor. Palmella without loss of time communicated the arrangements he had made to the Emperor, and as might have been expected from a man of his temperament, was dismissed from office, his conditions rejected; had he been himself the bearer of them, he would have most certainly been imprisoned by his former colleagues, and executed if they dared go that length.

A new ministry was formed: the Marquis of Loulé succeeded Palmella, Silva Carvalho took the Finance and Justice, two most irreconcilable portfolios at the present moment, for money was wanted, the portfolio of finance was widely opened to receive it, while that of justice was securely locked up in the minister's bureau. Carvalho was, however, not to blame. The troops and fleet were in arrears, provisions scarce, the town besieged by a powerful and revengeful enemy; and as long as there was a shilling in the town, he was right to take it either by fair or foul means. Had Oporto fallen, the Miguelites would have respected neither property nor persons; the plunder of it had been promised to the troops, and the peasantry even came from afar to share the spoil. The sacking of Badajoz would have been a trifle to what would have happened at Oporto.

Candido Xavier became minister of the interior; Bernado de Sa remained; and the only excuse for him doing so, and for the Marquis of Loulé, who was an honourable man, accepting a portfolio with such colleagues, was their desire to serve the cause, and prevent Pedro's other ministers from doing as much harm as they would had they been left to themselves.

I still continued to be much interested in the affairs of Oporto; I had a sincere regard for many of the Portuguese officers, with whom I became acquainted in the Azores; and on the arrival of Palmella in London, I proposed to him, in the event of its being possible to embark the army at the Foz, to hire a dozen steam-boats, run up the Tagus in the night, land at Black-Horse Square, and settle the question at once. The best part of Miguel's army, consisting of at least thirty thousand men, was round Oporto; and the continual sorties made by the Queen's troops was a useless waste of life, and could not in the least advance her cause. This was evident to every one except those who had the management of military matters; and it was also evident that unless some daring measure was adopted, the army in Oporto must inevitably lay down their arms. There was a British steam-vessel of war at Oporto, to carry off the Emperor in that event; and I suppose his advisers looked for a passage in her. Had their retreat been out off, as was the case with the army, I suspect that the capacity of the minister-at-war would have been a little quickened; and as long as the danger lasted, he would have forgotten the word "*Amanha*," and even treated the foreign troops with justice.

The rage for making sorties had in no way subsided; and on the 28th of November two columns of a thousand men each, under General Brito, assembled at Carvalhido. The intention of this sortie was to surprise Telles Jordao, who commanded the right of the Miguelite army, extending from the neighbourhood of the Foz to Matazinhos. Here, then, was a decided object in view, sufficient to countenance an attack: we shall see how it was executed. The left column under

Hodges' Narrative.

Brito took the Ramalde road; Queirioz headed the other on the road of Padrao de Legoa. Fonseca, with a hundred and fifty men from the Foz, menaced the enemy's right; while Bacon, with a squadron of lancers, was in reserve in advance of the Lordello.

Xavier, with the fifth caçadores, commenced the attack with his usual impetuosity, surprized and bayonetted the enemy's picquets; he then carried their entrenchments, where the surprise was complete, and the greater part of the enemy destroyed. Santa Martha now advanced with a large force to support Telles Jordao. Xavier was reinforced by Colonel Mariana Barossa, by which he was enabled to destroy the enemy's encampment, and carry off a considerable quantity of cattle and grain. Brito was now ordered to retire, and in his retreat was attacked by Santa Martha, and suffered considerably. Colonel Williams's battalion, under the orders of Barossa, formed the rear-guard, and behaved well. The loss of the Queen's troops was about three hundred killed and wounded; the enemy were supposed to have lost nearly eight hundred men, fifty prisoners, and about fifty deserters came in, and three hundred were said to have deserted to their homes.

The French on this occasion met their old antagonists the royalist volunteers, who had refused them quarter on the 17th, and bayonetted two companies of that blood-thirsty corps.

This sortie, like the other two, led to no results: it did not succeed in cutting off Telles Jordao's division, and the Miguelites could better afford to lose men than Don Pedro; but it made a strong impression on the Miguelite troops. They found they had to contend with a desperate enemy, and it inspired the inhabitants of Oporto with much confidence. They had now taken up the constitutional cause with great vigour, and on every attack or sortie old and young were seen armed with every species of weapon they could lay their hands upon: even the women on many occasions showed their enthusiasm for the cause of the Queen.

The squadron continued in Vigo in consequence of the danger of the anchorage off Oporto; they were far from being provided with stores, either to keep the sea, or ground-tackle to keep the anchorage. The crews were without pay, clothing, and provisions. At first they were well received at Vigo. The Donna Maria was stripped and allowed to refit; but on the Don Pedro, an Indiaman mounting fifty guns, arriving from France to reinforce the squadron, the governor requested Captain Mins to send her to sea. This ship had been purchased in England in September, and the Marquis Palmella, then in London, requested me to assist in getting her fitted out as expeditiously as possible.

Sartorius, conceiving that his force was not sufficient to cope successfully with the Miguelite squadron, had written to Mendizabal to procure a ship of this description. The funds at that time at his disposal were very scanty, and the friends of the cause had purchased this ship. She was not of a sufficient size to insure a decided superiority over the enemy; and assisted by M. Da Sylva, now the Baron of Lagos, who took a great interest in the affairs of the Queen, I endeavoured to induce them to fix on an Indiaman of twelve hundred tons, a much more effective ship; but hundreds of reasons were against this selection. The friends of the cause had already purchased the Don Pedro, and it was indispensable that they should force her on the Queen's agent: he had no means of resistance; and the Don Pedro, a small ship of eight hundred tons, was taken up. She was well and expeditiously fitted out in Mr. Young's yard: none of her old rigging, anchors, or stores were thought sufficiently good; every thing was landed; and, what is rather singular, the Queen's friends actually sent out her anchors to the Bayonne Islands, though they were not supposed good enough for her in the Thames; and one, marked with her former name, the Lord Wellington, found its way afterwards as new stores on board the Don Pedro.

The Foreign Enlistment Bill prohibited the arming of this ship in England, and she was in consequence sent to Cherbourg, where, after the usual blunders and the usual want of faith to the crews, she was equipped.

The Rainha sailed shortly after the Don Pedro, which had proceeded off Oporto; and in the beginning of December the Donna Maria was again ready for sea. Shortly after this Admiral Sartorius arrived from Oporto, where he had been since the action, attending to the duties of major-general, and the Rainha coming in he hoisted his flag on board his old ship. The rest of the squadron, with the exception of the Don Pedro, had also arrived. On the 9th the governor of Vigo, who had as yet been very kind, invited the officers of the squadron to a ball.

The dissentions in the squadron had not subsided; on the contrary, they had increased. It is not my intention to enter into their causes. Captain Mins has published one account; Captain Boyd has replied to it, and I have every reason to believe that Admiral Sartorius himself intends favouring the public with an account of his proceedings when in command of the squadron. I shall merely observe that Captain Rose was brought to a court-martial on various charges, and acquitted. The discretion of the admiral may be here questioned; troublesome times are not favourable to court-martials. If the admiral was dissatisfied with his officers, and was of opinion they were plotting mischief and intriguing against him, they ought to have been superseded, and sent to Oporto; or one might have been selected and punished without the ceremony of a court-martial.

This trial did not at all tend to improve the discipline amongst the seamen. No great pains were taken to prevent the disagreements between the admiral and the officers from being known to the ships' companies, and on the 20th of December, when the Donna Maria was ordered to carry stock to Oporto, the men refused to weigh till they were paid, and no persuasion or threats of the admiral could induce them to change their resolution. Upwards of two hundred left the squadron, forfeiting their pay and prize-money. Had the admiral been supported by his officers as he ought to have been, whatever was their cause of complaint, this mutiny would not have taken place; and if it had taken place, strong measures would have put it down.

Shortly after this the cholera broke out in the squadron, and the Spanish authorities took this opportunity of ordering the ships out of Vigo, and, ill provided as they were, they had no other place of refuge except under the Bayonne islands.

CHAPTER VIII.

As the winter advanced, the provisioning of Oporto became more difficult, and the force of the Miguelites kept increasing, which enabled them to establish a very strict blockade by land; while the difficulties of the bar rendered the provisioning of the town very uncertain. On the 7th the Lord of the Isles steamer crossed the bar under English colours, wearing a pendant, and was not fired at. She brought stores and three hundred ragged recruits from Boulogne. A French schooner also attempted to cross the bar, but was sunk. Soon after this the brig 23d of July was sunk, and ultimately the small vessels of war, with the exception of the Liberal, who was most gallantly brought out of the river by Lieutenant Souares Franco. Keeping them so long in the Douro was a great mistake; they were of little or no use there, and it could not be supposed that the Miguelite batteries would allow them to remain unmolested.

As the danger increased, the ministers became wiser. General Solignac, a French officer, who had served with much reputation under Massena, was invited to take the command of the army, which he accepted, and his arrival was daily expected. The government, not yet satiated with sorties, decided on another, and Villa Nova was the part fixed where more constitutional blood was to be needlessly shed. It will be remembered that through the procrastination of the ministers in not removing the wine from Villa Nova, it had fallen into the enemy's hands. An attempt was now to be made to obtain a supply for the inhabitants and the army. On the 17th of December detachments from the different corps were passed over to Villa Nova; the enemy opened a fire from the Quinta de Cavaco, from whence they soon after retired. The convent of St. Antonio was occupied by the Queen's troops, who were also stationed on the neighbouring heights to cover the removal of the wine. The stores were to the right of the convent near the water's edge. The boats which conveyed the troops were quickly loaded and returned to Oporto. In the meantime the third caçadores foolishly set fire to the convent, which they could easily have defended. The Miguelites, perceiving this, immediately advanced with a strong force; a panic seized the Queen's troops, and they fled to the river side. Few of the boats had returned from Oporto; those few were crammed with troops, and a scene of confusion not easily to be described took place. Those who could swim threw away their arms, took to the water, and endeavoured to reach the shipping, where they clung to the ships' sides and cables. Many were shot in the water, others were drowned, and not a few bayonetted in the quay. Here there was no respect shown to the British flag; some of the unfortunate wretches, thinking they would be safe, made for the British ships, and were shot hanging on their cables and sides.

On the 30th of December the Custom-house took fire, and the Miguelites, who now amused themselves in daily pounding the town, eagerly seized this opportunity of doing as much injury as possible. The flames were a good mark, and that part of the town suffered considerably.

On the 1st of January, General Solignac arrived, and was named marshal and major-general of the army. He was well aware of the intriguing spirit of the various people about the Emperor, and it is believed he was very plain and frank in his language to Don Pedro on assuming the command of the army.

He examined with care into its state, as well as into the material; proper regulations took place with respect to rations, and he steadily set about reforming many existing abuses, and met, no doubt, with much opposition from those interested in their continuance.

On the 5th of January nearly two hundred Scotch arrived, and were put under the orders of Major Shaw, who was much pleased with having the command of his countrymen. Six hundred had been recruited in Glasgow, four hundred of whom were wrecked on the coast of Ireland, and every soul perished. This was a severe blow to the cause at a time when both men and money were so much wanted at Oporto. On the 15th a reinforcement of two hundred Portuguese arrived from the islands, and four hundred French; the whole were safely disembarked under the lighthouse, where provisions continued to be landed, though frequently interrupted by the surf.

On the 20th of January the squadron anchored in Oporto roads; and on the 24th the marshal, having made his arrangements with Admiral Sartorius, determined to attack Monte Castro and the castle de Quejo. At one o'clock in the afternoon the French marched by the road leading from the Foz, and drove in the piquets; while Major Brownston with the second British charged the enemy, drove them from Monte Castro, and advanced by the beach to the Quejo. They were to have been supported in their attack on that battery by the squadron, but the crews refused to weigh till they were paid; and it was with the utmost difficulty that Sartorius could induce them to get the anchor up, and then it was much too late to be of any service.

General Brito had advanced with a division from Carvalhido to attack the enemy's left, but was halted, as it has been alleged, by the Emperor himself. This left the Marshal without support, and he was obliged to retire. The order of the day given out by him looks as if he was not satisfied with what took place. _{Appendix, No. V.}

The loss on this occasion was eighteen killed and ninety-five wounded; that of the enemy considerably more. The marshal called this affair a reconnaisance; and it is probable he intended it as such, and also to ascertain by personal observation what dependence he could place on his troops when brought into contact with the enemy.

A great deal had been expected from the marshal by the Emperor, the inhabitants, and the army; but he was cautious, and I have no doubt he soon perceived that, with the small force under his command, continual sorties were not advisable; and a forward movement with the whole army, with any prospect of success, extremely problematical. This caution was displeasing to the military as well as to the ministers, and the personal activity of the marshal not being conspicuous, they soon lost hope of any thing brilliant being undertaken, and became discontented.

On the 27th Generals Saldanha, Stubbs, and Cabrera landed at the Foz. Their services had been declined in the early part of the expedition, but they had since been called upon by the Emperor; and, although the cause was desperate, they obeyed the call with alacrity, and directed their best energies to serve the Queen and constitution. Saldanha and Stubbs had fought with distinction in the Peninsular war; the latter had been long governor of Oporto, and was highly respected by the inhabitants; he now resumed that post, and Saldanha took the command of the left, having his head-quarters at the Foz, the hottest part of the whole line of defence.

The weather had now set in bad; the squadron had returned to the Bayonne Islands; and the landing provisions was entirely cut off. The allowance of rations had been much reduced, and what they got was of bad quality: salt-fish and rice were the principal articles of diet. The

Portuguese were patient under their deprivations; but the French and English, being accustomed to better fare, were not so easily pleased; and there were occasional disturbances and demands for pay, which, as usual, were complied with as far as circumstances would permit. Fresh provisions were not to be had, and dogs, cats, and rats were in considerable requisition. The inhabitants suffered much; many had laid in stores in time; but the poor, who were not in a situation to provision themselves, were in a starving state.

In addition to this scarcity of provisions, an almost constant fire was kept up on the town, and many of the inhabitants were killed. The cholera also broke out with violence and carried off immense numbers. Thus was this unfortunate city subjected to war, plague, pestilence, and famine, all of which evils they bore with Christian fortitude: indeed the inhabitants had become desperate, and sooner than surrender, seemed determined to perish in the ruins.

It has been asserted, and I believe with truth, that orders were given to the marshal fully authorizing him to break out of the city with the whole army, and try the fate of a battle. The marshal, on the other hand, accused the ministers of preventing him from executing those orders, when he had made dispositions so to do; and it is true that when the bar again became open, and reinforcements were expected, his orders were countermanded.

The plan I had proposed for removing the army from Oporto and attacking Lisbon, had been submitted by the Duke of Palmella to the Portuguese government; and on the 1st of February, Rodrigo de Magalhaes arrived in London from Oporto, with orders to carry the plan into execution.

Here I must correct an error, fallen into by the ministers-at-war and finance, who in their reports take the credit of having planned this steam-boat expedition, which they do not appear even to have thought of till my plan was forwarded by the Duke of Palmella, which will be seen by Bernardo de Sa's letter in the Appendix.

The only part they had any thing to do with was sending one of their party to London, unprovided with either means, money, or credit, to carry it into execution; and M. Mendizabal, who was no great admirer of the Emperor's ministers, seemed little disposed to have any transactions with Rodrigo Magalhaes, the gentleman entrusted with the mission.

He was also bearer of a letter to M. De Lima, desiring him to offer me the command of the squadron; and one from the minister of marine, begging me to concert measures with M. De Lima and Mendizabal. The date of these letters was the 31st of January. It was reported that there were disagreements between Sartorius and the Emperor's ministers, but no open rupture had taken place; and I was not aware that Admiral Sartorius had resigned the command; and as there was an article in his contract by which no officer could be put over his head, I did not see my way at all clearly, and consequently sent to the minister the conditions on which I should take the command, and wrote to Sartorius at the same time. It had been rumoured, though I do not pretend to say with justice, that it was the intention of the government to invite Admiral Sartorius to Oporto, and to take that opportunity of

Appendix, No. VI.

Appendix, No. VII.

removing him, and I thought it right to put him on his guard.

No attempt was made to procure the steamboats for the projected expedition; it was altogether impossible. The friends of the cause were much cooled; they entertained no hope of ultimate success; and indeed a great disaster was anticipated. The merchants in London were well aware of the difficulties of provisioning the city, and the news of its surrender was expected by every packet.

After the reconnoissance of the 24th January no further movements took place on either side for some time. The enemy continued, however, to strengthen their lines and bombard the town. Marshal Solignac was blamed by some for want of activity, and for not sufficiently examining into the defences and obstructing the enemy; and, above all, for not possessing himself of Monte Castro and fortifying it, which would have greatly facilitated the landing of stores. I was not sufficiently long at Oporto to form any opinion on those subjects, and I have not seen documents sufficient to assist me in judging how far he was right or wrong; it would, therefore, be great presumption in me to criticise the acts of a French general of his experience.

Monte Castro was certainly a desirable position to possess, but it would have too far extended our already extensive lines, and cost many men in defending it; and be it remembered, how many had been already lost in ill-judged attacks. Moreover, if the marshal entertained any serious intentions of marching his whole army out of Oporto, he was right in not diminishing their numbers. I must, however, observe that as the minister-at-war opposed a forward movement on the first landing at Oporto, before the Miguelite army was collected and entrenched, I cannot understand how he should afterwards approve or advise it, unless the provisions were so reduced that there was no alternative left but a desperate attack or surrender. He states, however, in his report to the Cortes, that at different times the government insisted on the Marshal undertaking offensive operations as the only means of saving them; and in the same report the troops at Oporto are stated to amount to nearly eighteen thousand men of all arms, not half of whom, however, were fit to take the field. The same minister states that the enemy's force at that time round Oporto consisted of upwards of thirty-nine thousand infantry and fifteen hundred horse.

Figures are awkward things, particularly when they are officially stated by a minister; and Mr. Freire may explain to the Portuguese nation how he could expect Marshal Solignac to attack such a force strongly entrenched, when it was by his councils that an immediate advance was not made from Oporto after the Emperor landed; he was minister-at-war, and was responsible for the military operations.

Santa Martha had been lately deprived of the command of the army, which was conferred on the Count St. Lorenzo; and on the 3d of March, he attacked the Serra without success. A serious attack being expected next day, the troops were kept under arms all night; and at day-light a cannonade was opened from all parts of the enemy's lines, and the Serra was again attacked. Torres still commanded there, and as usual reserved his fire till the enemy approached, and drove them back with loss.

The Pasteleiro had been fortified by General Saldanha, but the works were not finished, and to this point the enemy directed their attention, making a feint at the same time on the defences of the city. Colonel Pacheco, with the tenth infantry commanded by Major Carneiro, and a battalion of the Minho under the orders of Colonel Ozorio, was charged with the defence of the redoubt of Pinhal, to the left of the Pasteleiro. Major Cabral, with a part of the third infantry, defended the latter position. A detachment of the third and tenth were stationed in the curtain that connected the two redoubts. Colonel Fonseca occupied the light-house with the first moveable battalion, commanded by Major Rangel. The communication between the Pasteleiro and the Lordello was confided to the Scotch and the English rifles under the orders of Shaw; and a battalion of the ninth occupied the Lordello. The columns of the enemy, preceded by their skirmishers, attacked those positions and the communication between them; while another column endeavoured to penetrate between the Pinhal and the light-house. The latter was vigorously charged by a company of the third regiment under Captain Meniz, supported by two companies of the tenth under Major Magalhaes, and were driven back with great loss.

The attack on Shaw was gallantly repulsed at the same time by the Scotch and rifles. In the two attacks two officers and thirteen men were killed; Pacheco and ten officers and thirty-four men were wounded. The enemy were reported to have lost three hundred men killed, and one thousand five hundred wounded: their loss must have been considerable, as they were exposed in their advance to the fire of the redoubts, but I think it was greatly exaggerated. This defeat was, however. a severe lesson to them, and inspired much confidence in the inhabitants and troops, and they began to believe that Oporto was not to be taken.

Since the marshal's attack on the Quejo, the squadron had been lying under the Bayonne islands, without pay, provisions, or clothing, cut off from all communication with Vigo, and even threatened to be driven out by a Spanish squadron;

the crews discontented, or, rather, in a state of mutiny, and every day expected to rise and take possession of the ships. The admiral had been ordered to Oporto, but having suspicions of treachery declined complying with their wishes. The St. Vincent was in Vigo to watch the movements of the Spanish squadron.

In this state of things the Emperor's ministers were mad enough to deprive Sartorius of the command of the squadron, and confer it for the time being on Captain Crosbie. The decree was dated the 13th of March. A few days previous to this, the admiral received my letter, which prepared him for a coup-d'-état. This letter he replied to under date of the 14th. Appendix, No. VIII.

Sir John Doyle was the bearer of the decree, accompanied by Captain Crosbie, to whom he was to deliver up the squadron; and Captain Bressane Lieto was charged with the settlement of their accounts. In the event of the admiral declining to give up the command, he was instructed to arrest him, for which purpose he was provided with a party of caçadores. Appendix, No. IX.

Will posterity believe that, in a town besieged

by a powerful force, without means either to pay or provision an army, a squadron in a state of mutiny, on the brink of starvation, unprovided with anchors, cables, stores, or clothing,—I say, will posterity believe that a set of men, calling themselves statesmen, were to be found capable of such unparalleled folly? The decree was signed by the Baron de Sa, but I have reason to believe that he, as well as the Marquis of Loulé, was overruled in the cabinet by Freire, Carvalho, and Candido Xavier.

It was not before the 23d that Sir John Doyle arrived at Vigo. The admiral was in some degree prepared for his reception, and, indeed, had read the decree in the Chronicle, which was the first intimation he had of being superseded.

An officer was sent from the flag-ship to make enquiry who the passengers were, and returned with a request that a boat might be sent from the flag-ship, to convey the gallant officer on board, with his despatches and instructions. This was of course complied with as far as Sir John Doyle was concerned; but Captain Crosbie was put under arrest, and Captain Bressane, and two officers who accompanied him, were ordered to remain. Sir John, in full uniform, and decorated with his various orders, now appeared on the Rainha's quarter-deck, and offered his hand to the admiral, which, however, he declined until informed of the nature of his mission, and requested it might be communicated to him on the quarter-deck. The general produced the Carta Regia, and, not being an expert diplomatist, also produced his instructions, which the admiral read, rather against the ambassador's will, and, as he might have expected, he was placed under arrest and deprived of his sword. He attempted to address the officers and ship's company, and to assure them that all promises made to them should be fulfilled, but was stopped by the admiral. Captain Goble and the other captains now came on board, and retired with the admiral to his cabin, leaving Sir John on deck, under custody of a lieutenant of marines. In half an hour the diplomatist was summoned to the cabin, and then Captain Goble communicated to him that the crews of the different ships had determined that neither the admiral nor captains should quit their respective ships until they were entirely settled with; and, in fact, the Don Pedro's ship's company, who were now becoming mutinous, had drawn up resolutions to that effect.

The admiral required Sir John to pledge his honour that he had no money or other public documents, which he did. A boat was sent for Captain Bressane, who declined coming on board the Rainha with either money or documents, as his instructions were to settle the accounts of the squadron only when it was delivered to Captain Crosbie.

Another boat was sent, to bring him on board. On appearing on the Rainha's deck, he protested against their proceedings, but delivered the money and papers. Sir John and Captain Bressane now returned, under escort, to the vessel which brought them to Vigo. Several letters passed between the admiral and Sir John, which it is unnecessary here to publish. They were shortly after released, and permitted to return to Oporto, to make their report to the ministers.

When the services admiral Sartorius had rendered to the cause are considered, together with his preserving the squadron under the most trying circumstances, and under every deprivation, it is not to be wondered at that the officers should feel indignant at this treatment. They now came to certain resolutions relative to their future proceedings, which were forwarded to Oporto. The ministers, seeing the danger their folly had brought on the Queen's cause, restored Sartorius, and complied with the demands of the squadron. Bernardo de Sa, who had opposed the proceedings in the first instance, thinking they betrayed weakness, resigned his portfolio.

Appendix, No. X.

The Portuguese government have endeavoured to persuade the world that the admiral was a traitor to the cause he served; but, taking all circumstances into consideration, had he acted in any other manner, the squadron would have been lost. The crews had been long discontented, being neither paid, victualled, nor clad. The admiral had so often promised them a settlement of their claims, that they had lost confidence in him; and nothing but his seizing this opportunity of placing himself at the head of the revolt restored confidence and saved the squadron. The crews wished to carry the ships to Flushing, and abandon the cause altogether. It was their idea that the admiral was ill-treated, and would support them, which again restored his authority. The only error Sartorius committed was not proceeding immediately to Oporto, and insisting that Messrs. Freire, Carvalho, and Candido Xavier should be consigned to his charge, thereby ridding the Emperor of three men who had done all they could to ruin the Queen's cause. I do not accuse them of treason; but had they been the vilest traitors that ever drew breath, they could not have taken a more decided part to serve Don Miguel and ruin the Queen.

Besides, it was a gratuitous insult to a man who had performed great services, and made great sacrifices; and had they signified to Admiral Sartorius that he no longer enjoyed their confidence, he would have been too happy to have resigned the command, with which he had been thoroughly disgusted for a considerable time.

CHAPTER IX.

On the 21st Oporto was again attacked on the side of the Antas by a column of three thousand men; the half-constructed redoubt was destroyed, and the piquets stationed there driven in. During the day there was a good deal of skirmishing, and at two o'clock the marshal ordered the fifth caçadores, part of the third infantry, and the first and second British battalions, supported by two squadrons of lancers, to attack the position in front, while Schwalbach's brigade advanced on their left; Major Sadler's battalion charged up the hill, and the major was mortally wounded. The men fell into confusion and retired. Major Brownston, who commanded the other battalion, rallied them and carried the hill at the point of the bayonet. Here the Queen's lancers endeavoured to break a spear with the Miguelite cavalry, who showed themselves on the hill, but retired on the approach of the lancers. Schwalbach gained the height on the left and made fifty prisoners. Twice the army attempted to regain the position, and were driven back.

Our loss on this occasion was one hundred killed and wounded: amongst the latter were Major Sadler and Captain Wright, who both died. Mr. Woldrige behaved with great courage on this occasion and was wounded. Two strong redoubts were now constructed on the Antas without having been molested by the enemy.

The weather now became more moderate, and the landing of provisions comparatively easy. For two months Oporto had been in the utmost distress for want of provisions and ammunition; and it was even contemplated to make propositions to the enemy. The marshal had been instructed to move out, but this order was contradicted, further reinforcements having arrived, and more expected. The Emperor was so well aware how precarious his tenor of Oporto was, that he wrote to the Empress about this time to say that nothing but a miracle could save them.

On the 9th of April, Monte de Cavallo, where the enemy were constructing a redoubt, was attacked and carried with great gallantry by the third, tenth, and fifth caçadores; this hill was maintained and fortified.

About this time Mr. Sandford, the commissary-general of the fleet, arrived at Vigo, with a small sum of money, from England, which assisted Sartorius in quieting the people, and persuading them to relinquish their intention of carrying the ships to Flushing. A reinforcement of seamen also arrived in the Edward transport, and finding the squadron in an unsettled state, they made an attempt to carry her off, but were stopped by the Rainha. She had also a main-mast on board for that ship, which Mendizabal had taken the precaution to send out: it had been once before at Oporto, and had been sent back by the minister.

The Don Pedro had been cruizing off Oporto, and arrived about this time at the Bayonne Islands. Her ship's company, thinking they were as much entitled to mutiny as those of the Donna Maria and Rainha, rose and sent their officers out of the ship. The other crews, were, however, of a different opinion. She was not so deeply in arrear of pay; and they most willingly supported the admiral in bringing them to reason. This was an opportunity that ought not to have been lost, and had a severe example been made of the ringleaders, there would have been no further disturbance in the squadron.

The news of the revolt of the fleet, which arrived in England in the beginning of April, aroused some of the Queen's friends; and they were determined to make a last effort to rescue suffering Portugal from the grasp of Don Miguel and his wicked advisers. The Chevalier de Lima, knowing that I was a well-wisher of the Queen, requested me to come to town and concert measures with him and Mendizabal to save her cause.

At this time I had received no answer from the Portuguese government to my proposals, and considered the affair at an end. Rodrigo Magalhaes was still in London, but had made no progress in in his mission about the steam-boats; indeed it had been entirely given up. It was now necessary to do something, and we cast our eyes towards the Algarves.

We had been assured that they were favourable to the Queen, and that a respectable force landed there would insure the revolt of the whole kingdom. Mendizabal engaged to provide twelve hundred Poles at Rochefort for the purpose, and two or three steam-boats to carry them; to this point we directed our attention.

I had been in the Algarves during the Peninsular War, and retained a very good recollection of the Guadiana; and it appeared that, by forcing the entrance of that river, and steaming up to Mertola, a rapid march might be made on Beja; and if the people were really favourable to the cause, a general rising might be anticipated throughout the Alemtejo; but this ought to have been accomplished with native troops, and I hesitated undertaking such an enterprise with the motley crew I had reason to suppose would be engaged for this forlorn hope; but the persuasions of Mendizabal, and my own sincere desire to serve the cause of the Queen, which had much interested me when in command of the Galatea in the Western Islands, overcame my objections, and I consented to undertake it, provided I was accompanied by the Duke of Palmella and Mendizabal, who had long been enthusiasts in the Queen's cause.

The zeal of the Duke, though no longer minister, was in no way diminished, and he left his amiable wife and large family in Paris, and consented to embark in this hazardous undertaking. The sum of ten thousand pounds was necessary to fit out the expedition; Mendizabal had exhausted all his money and all his rhetoric; and most of those who had already advanced large sums, looked upon the cause and their money as lost, and refused further aid. Others, also deeply engaged, were willing to come forward with a small sum, and make a last effort for suffering Portugal. M. Da Sylva, now the Baron Lagos, was the first to engage his father-in-law, Mr. Pratt, Mr. Humphreys, Mr. Wright, Mr. Easthope, and Mr. Pitta, to advance the necessary sum, on condition that the troops were not to land at Oporto; and the security they required was an assurance from me that an expedition would actually take place. Secrecy was necessary, but we were obliged to communicate our plan to those who advanced the money; and, as all were interested in being silent, I have every reason to believe the secret was well kept.

Mr. Pratt had always been a sincere friend to the Queen, and, through the influence of the Baron Lagos, had lent her Majesty twenty-five thousand pounds on her departure from Portsmouth for Rio de Janeiro, which was the salvation of the Terceira regency.

A few days after these arrangements were made, letters of a more favourable nature were received from Admiral Sartorius. The ministers, having failed in their unworthy attempt to arrest him, had annulled their ordinance depriving him of the command of the squadron, and restored him to his rank. This apology and a small sum of money to the crews restored order, and the squadron consented to weigh and proceed to Oporto. The Admiral, however, had determined to relinquish his command, and only waited the arrival of his successor; and he had written to this effect to the Portuguese minister in London and myself. The expedition now assumed a more

Appendix. No. XI.

respectable appearance. The hopes of the Queen's friends revived, and through the influence of the Baron Lagos and M. Mendizabal a sum sufficiently large was obtained to send five steamboats, with an English battalion of four hundred men, commanded by Colonel Dudgeon, an old Peninsular officer, and a Belgian of like number: four hundred seamen were to be entered, and several distinguished naval officers consented to accompany me.

This expedition, like all others sent to Portugal, was ill managed in the details, which led to much inconvenience, loss of men and money, and well nigh to a total failure. Instead of the steamboats at once receiving their men in London, some rendezvoused at Portsmouth, others at Falmouth, and small steamers at an enormous expense conducted the seamen and troops to the different ports. The Mendilla Portuguese corvette was lying in the Thames, and little or no difficulty was thrown in the way of entering men. Upwards of two hundred had been obtained by the usual method of crimping, and the usual method of cheating them was carried on to a shameful extent. They received nominally two months' wages, the greater part in bad and dear slops supplied between the crimps and the Jews. In this manner they were shipped on board a steamer to be conveyed to Portsmouth. On the passage from London, spirits were obtained from the steward, and a scene of drunkenness, insubordination, and confusion took place, not easily to be described. By the great exertions of Captain Wilkinson and the other officers order was restored; and on their arrival at Portsmouth they were turned over to the City of Waterford steamer, destined to convey them to Oporto. At night, the men, having had time to reflect, found they had been imposed upon, and instead of quietly submitting their case to the officers, broke out into a general mutiny. Some rushed aft with open knives, and threatened to massacre Captain Wilkinson and all the officers; others lowered the boats down, and as many as they could contain went on shore. One boat, which was crowded to excess, upset, and several men were drowned. As we were all embarked in the face of the Foreign Enlistment Bill, caution was necessary in endeavouring to suppress

Capt. Wilkinson's letter, Appendix, No. XII.

a mutiny. Had lives been lost, the authorities would have interfered and stopped the expedition; and how the officers would have been protected by the law was not very easy to foresee.

The loss of life by the upsetting of the boat, together with the impossibility of getting on shore, brought them a little to their senses; and the prudent, temperate, and firm conduct of the officers restored peace. Before daylight all was quiet, and they appeared ashamed of their conduct. In the afternoon I got quietly on board without its being generally known at Portsmouth, gave the men a severe lecture, heard their story, and promised to redress their grievances, and on the same evening, 22d of May, we left Portsmouth in company with the Britannia steamer, having on board Dudgeon's regiment, where a similar scene, but less violent, had occurred. Every precaution was taken to prevent a recurrence of these evils at Falmouth, and an allowance of one sovereign was given to each man to make up for what they were supposed to have been defrauded of; but the volcano, though smothered for the moment, was not extinct, and the day after our arrival there was much grumbling and discontent: in short, they had received their money and were determined to proceed no further; they kept quiet, however, till after midnight, when, the moon going down, the boatswains' mates very coolly piped all hands on shore. A rush was made to the boat tackle falls, which were cut, and as many as the boats would contain took French leave and went on shore.

Before leaving Portsmouth I had taken professional advice how to act in a similar case, and was informed that the only legal manner of resisting was by the captain of the vessel calling upon the officers to prevent the men taking away his property. Our captain, however, was a poor devil, and instead of taking any steps, very quietly took himself into a small boat at the beginning of the row, and came on shore to report the circumstance to me. Fortunately the steamer's boats were only capable of containing a few men, and none others being allowed to come alongside, the remainder of this unruly crew were obliged to remain. Next morning, I embarked, in company with the Duke of Palmella and M. Mendizabal, thinking ourselves fortunate in getting out of Falmouth with only one hundred and thirty-seven men instead of four hundred men, which were wanted to complete the squadron. All this might have been prevented had honest and proper people been chosen to carry on the details, and had our friend Mendizabal been less active in mind, and had found out that one head, be it ever so clever, is incapable of managing every thing. The steamers should have started from their different ports, and have rendezvoused off Ushant, which would have given the men no time for reflection, and put it totally out of their power to get on shore; the very sight of which, particularly when they are unoccupied, is too much for so unprincipled and thoughtless a set of men as undisciplined British seamen generally are.

The auspices at starting were unfavourable; nevertheless we were not discouraged, and, much to the annoyance of some of the authorities at Falmouth, we got clear off on the 28th, with five steamers, containing about one hundred and sixty officers and seamen, and an English and Belgian regiment; and, after a pleasant passage, arrived on the 2d of June at Vigo, where we found another steamer from Rochefort with twelve men instead of four hundred Poles, that part of the armament having completely failed.

A few hours sufficed to make arrangements for completing four of the steamers with fuel and water, who were left there for that purpose; and the City of Waterford pushed on and anchored in Oporto roads after dark : the usual night salutation of shells was going on with great vivacity on both sides, and appeared to us novices a serious attack.

Admiral Sartorius was lying there with his flag on board the Rainha, together with the Don Pedro, Donna Maria, Villa Flor brig, and a numerous convoy of merchant-vessels waiting favourable opportunities to land provisions and stores for the army and inhabitants. The landing had been effected during the last two months with tolerable safety, though frequently interrupted by the surf; and the town was now well supplied with every species of provision with the exception of live stock, which was not easily obtained. The Duke of Palmella and Mendizabal accompanied me on board the flag-ship, where we were received with the greatest kindness and sincere welcome. He was quite disgusted with the service, and indignant at the conduct of the ministers towards him.

It appeared pretty certain that, when he was invited to come on shore at Oporto, it was the intention of the government to have kidnapped him, and the letter he received from me was the first intimation he had of their intention to supersede him. This having failed, the Quixotic expedition of Sir John Doyle followed.

Sartorius hastily recounted the various events that had taken place, and by all I could collect from him, the prospect before me was by no means brilliant. The Miguelite fleet was fitting out in great force, and shortly expected to sail. Our force was very inferior in numbers and material, and no dependence was to be placed on the men who had the direction of the war. They were on bad terms with the marshal, and were pretty generally despised by the Portuguese officers.

The civil war in Portugal was unlike other wars. Don Pedro's and Don Miguel's ministers vied with each other in intrigues and follies; but, fortunately for the cause of the Queen, Don Pedro was more active than his brother; his ministers could do less harm, and the cause of liberty triumphed.

After remaining a few hours with Sartorius, the despatch boat came off; and as the beach was good, no time was lost in getting on shore,—a task attended with considerable danger. The entrance of the river is little more than pistol-shot across; the north side, where the Foz is situated, was possessed by the Queen's troops; the opposite by the Miguelites. To the north of the Foz there is a small bay under the light-house, where the boats landed when the surf permitted; this bay was commanded by the enemy's musketry, which, however, at night did little damage, as they were kept in check by the light-house battery; and it is to be presumed that the piquets stationed to annoy the landing got careless and kept under cover, firing their muskets at random over the parapet. In this bay we landed, and received a tolerable good salutation of musketry, happily without effect. Crossing the bar is attended with considerably more danger, which shall be described in its proper place.

We were received with great kindness by General Saldanha, who commanded at the Foz; and during the time the mules were preparing, he gave us some insight into the affairs of Oporto. Our arrival had been talked of, but little known. The army was tolerably well supplied, and desertion, which had got to an alarming height, had ceased.

A meeting had taken place on board Lord Henry Paulet's brig between Saldanha and the Count Torre Bello, one of Miguel's officers, to endeavour to bring about an arrangement, which failed. Different opinions have been given about this meeting, and about the proposals made by Saldanha; but as they are not supported by proof, it is unnecessary here to state them. I believe the Count Torre Bello gave him to understand that nothing short of Don Miguel marrying the Queen would be listened to.

The marshal was highly incensed at this meeting, and told Saldanha that had he been in the French service, he would have been shot: but it soon passed over. The intentions of Saldanha, I am convinced, were good; but an unauthorised meeting of that description at such a critical time was decidedly improper.

No fresh enterprise had been undertaken on either side, and with the exception of the batteries exchanging shot and shell, all was as quiet as if nothing was going forward. The Foz was much exposed both to the north and south, and was nearly destroyed; but still, though protected only by a few redoubts connected with ditches, certainly not strong, there seemed to be little apprehension on the part of the constitutionalists.

The Castle is situated at the entrance of the harbour. On the opposite side of the river were placed the Miguelite batteries, threatening destruction to any vessels that had the hardihood to force the passage. On a hill to the north of the Foz is placed the light-house battery within musket-shot of the enemy's lines, composed of strong redoubts connected with ditches extending from the Foz all round Oporto. The Foz, on the other hand, is connected with Oporto by a chain of redoubts and ditches, which were never forced, but which could have been forced by a strong and determined enemy.

CHAPTER X.

AFTER partaking of the hospitality of Saldanha, we mounted our mules, and proceeded to the town. The weather was fine, the country beautiful, and the scenery enlivening to a degree. On the left were the enemy's batteries, with their flags flying, sufficiently close to observe their centinels: on the right, at a little distance, the river with its high-rising banks well wooded, and the opposite heights crowned by the Miguelite batteries, occasionally sending their shot and shell from either side into the Queen's lines, distinguished by the blue and white constitutional flag. Nearly twenty years had elapsed since I had seen an enemy: the sight of flags, the noise of guns, the sound of drums and bugles, soon awoke me to a recollection of the scenes of early life, and conveyed a sensation which will be well understood by those accustomed to the bustle of war and camps. The road was tolerably well covered, being dangerous only in a few places, and we passed without molestation.

At six we entered the besieged and heroic city of Oporto, and proceeded to the Duke of Terceira's quarters, where we were greeted with the greatest joy by the duke and his staff,—Palmella as a sincere friend and colleague, and myself as an old acquaintance in the Western Islands. A few minutes sufficed to explain how we came and what brought us, and the whole party were rejoiced at our arrival. They now looked forward to active measures and to the termination of the intrigues that had been so long going on at Oporto.

The house in which we were had been frequently perforated by shells; nevertheless the inmates seemed quite at ease, and we sat down to a most comfortable breakfast; and after making ourselves acquainted with the situation of affairs, we waited on the Marquis of Loulé, the Emperor's brother-in-law and minister of marine, and were rather surprised to learn from him that all was not quite right at head-quarters: he even cautioned me to say nothing about the projected expedition. I shewed him the Chevalier de Lima's letter, and at once gave him to understand that I should not take command of the squadron unless an expedition was immediately decided on. We had all calculated on a welcome reception from the Emperor, and the Duke of Palmella had proposed to proceed at once to the palace, which I objected to, not being exactly in a costume to appear before royalty, having suffered much from a nervous affection of the face, and my head being wrapped up in flannel, like a respectable old lady. The Marquis of Loulé conducted us to the palace, and ushered in the Duke of Palmella, who soon returned, not well pleased at the very cold reception he met with. I came next, and was received at the door of the apartment by the Emperor, who stood with his hands behind him, looking very angry, and speaking as roughly as he looked. Not being accustomed to such company, I began to consider whether this was

<small>Appendix, No. XIII.</small>

an uncivil or only an imperial manner of receiving a person who had come out to render him a service. My meditations were soon disturbed by his Majesty, in rather a brusque manner, asking me if I wished an expedition immediately; to which I replied, I had come out for the express purpose. He then referred me to Marshal Solignac, and dismissed me rather abruptly. My interview with the marshal was not much more satisfactory; when I shewed him the letter of _{Appendix, No. VI.} the late minister of marine about an expedition of six thousand men, he at once told me it was out of the question, as he had not more than six thousand bayonets altogether, and he invited me to accompany him next morning to the Emperor, which I declined unless expressly sent for. I added that I felt much hurt at the reception I had met with, and if something was not immediately decided upon, I should return to England forthwith; and this I communicated to all my Terceira friends. During the course of the day we found out that some evil-disposed persons had put it into Don Pedro's head that we had brought the expedition out to displace him; for which reason it had been got up secretly, without communicating with his government. The latter part of this was quite true, and the reason plain,—secrecy was necessary; and that word was nowhere to be found in the Portuguese dictionary at Oporto. Next morning I accompanied the marshal to the Emperor, at his particular request, and was most graciously received; he had got the better of his ill-humour, and I suppose had been told that I was not satisfied the day before.

I told him at once the view I took of his situation, that he had no choice but to lay down his arms or take a decisive step; the shortest was to force the Tagus, if we could get a good breeze at night, and land in Black-Horse-square or close to Lisbon, make a rapid march on the capital, or send a force to the south; the three different plans being subject to the troops he could spare. I recommended him at once to commence the embarkation of troops, which was difficult and required time, and pressed upon him the necessity of dispatch, as the Miguelite fleet were fitting out in great force, and would, if ready, check all our operations. The interview, however, ended without any determination; the Emperor and the marshal would consider. The delay caused considerable discontent among the general officers, and they were anxious to go to the Emperor, and request him to put Palmella at the head of the administration, and go to work at once. Palmella, however, thought it advisable to wait, being of opinion that the ministry would fall from their own weakness, but in this he was mistaken.

No person had confidence in the present ministers. Freire was idle, incapable, and an intriguer; Candido Xavier a worn-out old man; and Sylva Carvalho unpopular, though certainly clever, and the only one who could have found funds to have kept the army together at Oporto. This day the Duke of Terceira gave a grand dinner to the ministers and superior officers; every thing was talked of; Mendizabal, impatient at delay, could hardly contain himself, and no one was pleased. In the middle of dinner a shell burst against a wall, within a few feet of the window of the room in which we sat; but neither guests nor servants seemed much disturbed, though a little more powder would have pitched it in the centre of the dining-table, and in all probability sent marshal, admiral, generals, and ministers to their consultations in another world. This was an every-day occurrence in Oporto during the siege in one house or another, and scarcely a day passed without loss of life.

Next morning the marshal called upon Palmella, and after talking a good deal about expeditions, &c., asked if he was willing to form an administration, to which the Duke readily assented, provided he was at liberty to choose his colleagues. Next morning at ten we were appointed to meet the Emperor: there were assembled Mr. Freire, minister-at-war; Candido Xavier, foreign affairs; the Dukes of Terceira and Palmella; the marshal and myself. I was still very ill, and could hardly articulate from an inflammation of the tongue and face, which was still bound up, and in this plight, for the first time in my life I attended a cabinet council; the expression of Oxenheim to his son flashed across me when I saw some of the councillors. The marshal made an exposé of his force, which amounted to nine thousand men fit to take the field; various points were discussed, but nothing decided, and we were all invited to dine with the Emperor. Palmella was to return at four o'clock, and the marshal told him he would then be desired to form an administration; but alas! between twelve and four the Emperor changed his mind, and the interview ended in some trifling conversation.

It is difficult to know who was at the bottom of all this indecision. It was clear the Emperor did not like the Duke of Palmella, who he fancied had lent himself to an intrigue to displace him; whether this is true or not I never learnt. The Emperor liked his present ministers, from whom he had nothing to fear, and they cordially hated Palmella. The marshal was not partial to them, and with great reason, for one of their colleagues had been a short time before turned out of office for surreptitiously getting hold of his papers; perhaps also he feared Palmella, who had the reputation of being a good statesman, and was probably afraid of losing the influence he had with the Emperor, which appeared considerable, though at the same time his majesty did not appear very placid under it.

I was very ill and out of temper, and did not go to the Emperor's dinner. In the evening Palmella, Terceira, Saldanha, and several of our old friends came to see me; a good deal of discussion took place relative to the causes of all this procrastination: we were totally in the dark, and knew not whether to blame the Emperor, the marshal, or the ministers; but as there was a council of war next morning, we hoped it would lead to something decisive.

At the council were assembled about twenty generals, ministers, and officers, and the Emperor prepared four questions for discussion.

1st. Is it advisable to embark as many troops as can be spared, and make a bold attack on Lisbon?

2d. Is it better to embark between two and three thousand, and make an attack on some distant point?

3d. Should Villa Nova be attacked by landing in the rear?

4th. Should an attack be made in the rear of the lines to the northward?

The marshal again made his exposé, gave us

to understand we were to state our opinions, and the Emperor should decide.

I was so ill I could hardly speak one word, and gave my opinion in writing:—that the Emperor was placed in a critical position, and nothing but an immediate and decisive step could save him. The squadron of Don Miguel was to be ready by the 20th, consisting of two line-of-battle ships, a fifty-gun ship, a fifty-gun frigate, and five or six corvettes and brigs; he had three frigates, one corvette, and one brig to oppose them. Should they come out before we sailed, and beat his squadron, he must lay down his arms; if we beat them, we should probably be too much disabled to undertake an expedition, and he must still lay down his arms. Should the battle be a drawn one, we had no place to refit; they would return to Lisbon, refit, and blockade him, and he must eventually submit. I therefore advised him to contract his lines, give up the Foz and the communication, and defend Oporto, which was provisioned for three months,—embark all the men he could spare, and make a dash on Lisbon; if we succeeded, Don Miguel's game was up, and his troops in Oporto delivered; if he failed, the Oporto troops must share the fate of the Lisbon division.

There were various opinions about this. The marshal opposed, as fatal to the cause, sending a small force to a distant part of the kingdom, and preferred an attack either on the enemy's lines to the north or south. I could see no advantage in this. We were led to suppose Don Miguel had from thirty to forty thousand men round Oporto; their lines were strong, and could not be forced without great loss; and even should we be victorious, it would be quite impossible to advance with so small an army, and must eventually return to Oporto with diminished numbers. Should a landing be effected to the north or south of the Douro, and the enemy taken in the rear, some of their works might be destroyed; but from the difficulty of landing on all parts of the west coast of Portugal, nothing certain could be calculated upon, and the division, if landed and unsuccessful, would be entirely cut off. There were various opinions on these plans. Saldanha agreed with me, as did the majority. He was of opinion that Lisbon was

Portugal, and once in possession of the capital, the war was at an end. The sequel, however, proved he was mistaken as well as myself, and had our plan been put in execution, we should certainly have taken Lisbon, but Oporto must have fallen before we could have organized a sufficient force to relieve it. Had the Foz and the line of communication been given up, Oporto could certainly have been defended, but it was only provisioned for three months, and would have ultimately been reduced by famine. Had the lines of communication with the Foz been preserved, Bourmont must have forced them on the 25th of July.

The whole of the proceedings were reduced to writing, and I was desired to attend on the Emperor next morning, who was to decide. I had seen so much indecision and vacillation that I still expected nothing, and was most agreeably surprised, at the meeting with the Emperor and Marshal Solignac the following day, to find he had decided on embarking five thousand men, making a dash on Lisbon, and playing double or quits. The Emperor asked where I should place him; I told him the royal standard must fly on board the

Rainha de Portugal. All this was to be kept secret—I was desired not even to communicate it to Palmella.

Two hours afterwards I again met the marshal, who told me the Emperor insisted on having a steam-boat for himself. I explained the impossibility of complying with this; our means were so circumscribed, it would be with the greatest difficulty we could embark five thousand men; that the Emperor must come on board the flag-ship with the marshal and his staff, and leave his ministers at Oporto, where they could do little harm. I also pointed out the bad effect of the Emperor placing himself in a steam-boat, as people would suppose, in the event of a failure, he was ready for a start. I also spoke to the minister of marine, who quite agreed with me and promised to mention it to the Emperor. I begged to be allowed to communicate with the Duke of Palmella, as we had gone on together from the beginning, and my silence would appear as if there was a wish to detach me from him and create want of confidence. I also recommended him to tell the Emperor that a great deal depended on who his ministers were, and that he had better put Palmella at the head of the administration.

In the course of the day all was changed. The Emperor and the marshal were to remain at Oporto, and a smaller expedition sent to land where was most advisable. I was permitted to communicate this to the Duke of Palmella, but not to the marshal, as he was known to be entirely opposed to it. I now received my commission as Vice-Admiral and Major-General, with authority to appoint my officers, took leave of the minister, and embarked at the Foz after dark. I had not proceeded many yards when the Miguelite batteries, which we were obliged to pass within pistol-shot, opened their fire of round, grape, and musketry, throwing fire-balls at the same time to point out more clearly the position of the boats. The castle of the Foz and the adjacent batteries returned the salute, and between the two fires, which to a person in safety would have been very beautiful, but to one in danger very unpleasant, I managed to get safe through the surf with a boat's crew half of whom did not know how to pull their oars, and could not have been worse had they

Appendix, No. XIV.

been selected by Don Miguel himself. I was followed by about five hundred men of the first division, and though they were peppered most confoundedly, not a man was hurt. The landing and embarking, both from the river and the bay, had been going on upwards of six months, yet no improvement had taken place. There were no capstans to haul the boats up, no discipline amongst the boatmen, no classification, yet there was no want of naval officers. They had, however, more confidence in Providence than in their own genius, and Providence most singularly assisted the Queen's cause, and brought it to a happy termination.

Early on the morning of the 11th I got safe on board Admiral Sartorius's ship, who gave up the command of the squadron on having received letters of thanks from the ministers in the name of the Emperor, and I was assured that his accounts should be settled forthwith, and a title conferred on him as a reward for his services. How those promises have been fulfilled, he will probably inform the public. To the Marquis of Loulé, who was minister of marine, no blame can be attached; he was an honourable man, and Sartorius must look to the other worthy gentlemen who advised his dismissal, and I believe opposed the settlement of his claims to the last.

My flag had not been long up ere I found I was not reposing on a bed of roses. Promises had been made to the oldest seamen that they should be allowed to return to England with the admiral, and no persuasions would induce them to remain. I was thus deprived of one hundred of the best men the day I took command of the squadron. I had brought out one hundred and thirty-seven, who were barely sufficient to complete the crews of the frigates. The Villa Flor was chiefly manned by Portuguese, the Portuense entirely so; the latter was in such a state of disorder that she was paid off, and the officers and men landed. Captain Blackstone, late of the Rainha, was appointed to her, and a mixed crew of one hundred men got together. Captain Wilkinson took command of the Rainha, with the rank of commodore; Captain Charles Napier was appointed principal adjutant, and Mr. Pearn master of the fleet, both with the rank of commander; Lieutenant Peak was appointed to command the Donna Maria. Captain Goble remained in command of the Don Pedro, and Captain Ruxton in the Villa Flor. Captain Mac Donough took charge of the steamboats, and Captain Pryce of the naval transport, with directions to complete her with water and provisions, and be ready to move where required.

Those changes very much tended to re-establish discipline, which from want of pay, food, clothing, and other causes, was much relaxed; indeed the crews had been in open mutiny; many of the officers had been intriguing against the admiral; an attempt had been made to arrest that admiral on board his own ship, by a weak and foolish government; some of the officers had been dismissed, and others had gone home.

The ships were badly furnished in every species of stores, had hardly a boat that could swim, and could not average two anchors and cables for each ship. The men were almost naked, and there was no means of clothing them. In short, it was impossible to see a more inefficient squadron, and how Admiral Sartorius got through the winter and kept them together, is difficult to understand.

The Don Pedro mounted fifty short eighteen-pounders and thirty-two carronades; the Rainha forty-six eighteen-pounders, long and short; the Donna Maria forty-two eighteen-pounders and thirty-two-pound carronades; the Villa Flor eighteen eighteen-pounders; Portuense twenty thirty-two-pound carronades. The crews consisted of about one thousand men and officers.

With this force, and in this state, we had to conduct an expedition to rescue Portugal from the tyranny of Don Miguel, and place Donna Maria on the throne, against one hundred thousand men in arms, and against the will of the nation, as had been repeatedly asserted and believed by the Tory party in this country; and this was to be done in face of a squadron of two line-of-battle ships, one fifty-gunned ship, a fifty-gunned frigate, three corvettes, and four or five brigs, ready for sea in the Tagus; and the troops to go on this expedition were to be embarked at night, and pass over a dangerous bar, within pistol-shot of the enemy's batteries, who had full warning of our intention, and had made every preparation to destroy them.

On hoisting my flag I issued the following order :—

" On taking command of the squadron of Her Most Faithful Majesty, I feel proud in associating myself with so many gallant officers and men, who have already so nobly distinguished themselves in the cause of freedom and the Queen.

" The squadron must have seen that a large force of steam-boats are now here to co-operate with them. Should the enemy put to sea, you will know what to do with them; should they remain in port, attacks will be made on various parts of the coast, and a general rising of the people against usurpation and tyranny is anticipated. My lads! we have battles to fight, and great exertions to make—preserve discipline and look up to your officers, and we shall succeed. The eyes of all Europe are on you—your countrymen, aye, and countrywomen also, are longing to welcome you to England; and when the battle is won, and you return to your native homes, you will be hailed as men who rescued suffering Portugal from tyranny and oppression."

The steam-boats were ordered in shore to receive

the troops, and boats sent to assist in towing them off; we received, however, only one cask of water and five soldiers. Next morning I telegraphed—" That was not the manner to gain the cause of the Queen;" and suspecting that there were dissentions between the government and the marshal, I again telegraphed—" Are soldiers coming off or not ? I shall act accordingly"—and I wrote to say that if troops were not immediately embarked, I should haul down my flag, and return to England forthwith. I had been most explicit with the minister, and I knew, from the vacillation and intrigues that were going on, that nothing but taking a high tone would put an end to them.

In the evening I received an intimation by telegraph to send boats on shore for troops, and a dispatch by the guard-boat, informing me that another council had been held, in which it was decided that five thousand men could not be spared, and that two thousand five hundred were to be embarked under the Duke of Terceira, and Palmella was to accompany the expedition as civil governor of the provinces who declared for the Queen; that Marshal Solignac, who disapproved of this entirely, had resigned ; that the Emperor had taken command of the army, and appointed General Saldanha chief of his staff.

It is due to the marshal to observe, that though he disapproved entirely of sending so small a force to the south, he offered either to accompany an expedition of five thousand men to Lisbon, or, if the Emperor went, to remain and defend Oporto. This measure, however, did not square with the timidity of the Emperor's advisers. They neither cared to go with the Emperor on so bold an enterprize, nor liked to remain with the marshal with so small a force, and, consequently, they succeeded in persuading His Majesty to choose the smaller enterprize.

The appointment of the officers seemed to be very satisfactory, and all began to look forward to a happy change of circumstances. I also received the following letter from the Emperor.

" *Oporto, June* 11, 1836.

" My Dear Admiral,

" I hasten to communicate to you that a decision was yesterday taken to send an expedition of two thousand six hundred and seventy-two men to the south, of which four hundred and ninety are already on board, one thousand four hundred and seventeen will embark to-night, and to-morrow the rest, by which means the expedition will be ready, I think, to sail in the course of the following day. You may be assured that I will contribute all my energies that there shall be no delay.

"I should have wished to have written this with my own hand, but too much business hinders me. Go away then, my dear admiral. I follow you with my vows, and I hope to see you return to me covered with glory and the blessings of a grateful nation, to whom you came in the generous intentions of performing brilliant services. Receive, my dear admiral, the assurance of the consideration with which I am,

"Your affectionate,
"D. PEDRO."

"I send you the detail of the troops embarked."

On the night of the 15th the Dukes of Terceira and Palmella came on board with a numerous and brilliant staff, and brought me a copy of their instructions. They were received on board the Rainha, the upper cabin being occupied by the two dukes and myself, and the fore-cabin provided with a sail for the staff. This was rough accommodation for counts and marquisses, but the best we had; and I never saw in any service a finer set of young men, or officers more ready to put up with every inconvenience. I must not omit to mention that a company of students, serving as volunteers, had no other accommodation than a sail under the half deck, and ship's provisions, and yet I never heard a grumble from them; they were all devoted to the cause they served, and were ready to put up with any hardships to advance it. Together with the duke came a division of troops, and by the 18th all were on board.

Appendix No. XV.

CHAPTER XI.

At the time the troops began to embark, we had only ten days' water in the squadron; the steamers less, and they had not completed at Vigo, though left there for the express purpose. They had also neglected to take in fuel, all of which was to be done at Oporto in an open road with a constant swell. The difficulty of getting off water was great and expensive, and when you add to that difficulty the want of arrangement, it is astonishing we ever got any from Oporto at all. The water ought to have been sent before the troops; but after the latter came on board, it seemed to those intrusted with the embarkation that all was right; and as for water, I suppose they thought there was a good supply alongside.

Day after day and hour after hour telegraphs were made for water, and on the 15th—" tell Emperor if water is not sent off expedition will fail." This was communicated to him, and it appears that a great exertion was made; for on the 19th we received a sufficient supply to enable us to proceed.

Too much praise cannot be bestowed on the fishermen and watermen of the Douro: night after night were those men employed under a heavy fire in bringing off troops and water, and disembarking provisions and stores; and too much blame cannot be given to those employed at the Foz to superintend it; there was neither energy, zeal, ability, nor arrangement, and the only exception I can make is in favour of Lieutenant Salter, who was indefatigable: he crossed the bar every night, and was at last wounded. Strange to say, in the whole of this embarkation there were not more than half a dozen killed and wounded, and amongst the latter was Marshal Solignac, who was obliged to return to Oporto, having received a severe contusion in endeavouring to pass the bar.

On the 20th I wrote to the minister and took leave by telegraph, having failed in weighing and lost an anchor the day before, as did the Don Pedro and Portuense in consequence of the heavy swell, and the want of proper messengers, nippers, &c. The steamers got away the day before, joined in the morning, and with a fine breeze we stood to the southward, our hearts leaping with joy at the brilliant prospect before us.

<small>Appendix, No.XVI.</small>

At noon we reconnoitred Figueras, and for the first time in my life I felt what it was to be in an undisciplined ship. The people were at dinner as we closed the land. The breeze was fresh, and as it would be necessary to reef top-sails when we hauled off, the hands were turned up for that purpose and to trim sails ; but such was the want of zeal and exertion on the part of the ship's company, that there was no getting them on deck under half-an-hour ; and had we been in a difficulty, we must have either lost our spars, or ran ashore before we could get the men to their stations. This state of things could not last, and the commodore who had a good deal of firmness and tact, made a severe example the first good opportunity, which soon convinced them of the necessity of turning over a new leaf.

I had intended to have anchored the expedition in Cascaes bay, and to have been guided by the information we might receive; but the want of discipline of the squadron, and the little zeal and energy displayed by the people, or I may say the perfect indifference with which they did their duty, obliged me to relinquish that intention as fraught with danger in the event of the enemy putting to sea. The ships were also much crowded with troops, which was a great obstacle to exercise and improvement of discipline.

After showing ourselves off Peniché, we shaped our course a few leagues outside of the rock of Lisbon, abreast of which we lay to till sunset, with the view of distracting as much as possible the attention of Don Miguel's ministers, who had no idea where the blow was to be struck: indeed, at this time we did not know ourselves, which after all was the best way of keeping the expedition secret.

The government at Lisbon, seeing us on the coast, were by no means at their ease. Great exertions were made to get the squadron ready, and they were anchored in a line reaching down to Belem for the defence of the town. On the 12th of June orders were given that no vessel of any description was to be permitted to enter the Tagus at night, and on the 23d the merchant-vessels were ordered to move up the river to be out of the line of fire, and the British squadron were held in readiness to slip their cables.

Previously to my arrival at Oporto, Don Miguel's cause began to be considerably mixed up with that of Don Carlos, who was residing at Cintra. General Cordova, the Spanish minister at Miguel's court, was instructed to demand a categorical answer from Carlos, whether it was his intention to proceed to Madrid and be present at the meeting of the Cortes to take the oath to the young Queen. This he declined to answer, but promised to write to his brother.

Shortly after this the king of Spain gave him a peremptory order to quit Portugal and proceed to Italy; and on the 25th of May a Spanish frigate arrived at Lisbon to convey him there. On this he suddenly quitted Cintra, and proceeded to Coimbra, where he was received by Miguel, who evidently came to meet him. On the day Cordova arrived at Coimbra, Miguel, wishing to avoid him, suddenly quitted it on horseback, leaving his suite and baggage to follow.

Cordova had been refused admission to Carlos's presence, but was quite ignorant of his intention to leave Cintra. The Portuguese ministers also declared their ignorance of his project to depart, and expressed their disapprobation of his conduct. When Cordova returned to Lisbon, he ascertained that both the Viscount Santarem and the Duke of Cadaval had had interviews with Carlos at Cintra, which they concealed from him. The Spanish minister, enraged at this treachery, and annoyed at being duped by Carlos, expressed his indignation in strong terms, accused the ministry of giving offence to the king of Spain and of ingratitude to him, who was and always had been a great friend to Don Miguel.

Zea Bermudez disapproved of Carlos's proceedings, but pretended to believe that he only meant to pay a compliment to Miguel, and continued to protect him notwithstanding the insults to the Spanish minister.

The king of Spain was now in rather an unpleasant situation. Should Miguel succeed, he had every thing to fear from the Carlists; should the Queen's cause triumph, he was in danger from the Constitutionalists. Spanish troops were consequently ordered on the frontier to be ready to check either party.

Miguel, on the other hand, was afraid of offending Ferdinand, lest he should become liberal in opposition to Carlos and to favour his daughter, and equally afraid of offending Carlos, lest Ferdinand, who was in bad health, should die, and his party should be strong enough to place him on the throne.

At this time there were many Spanish refugees in Portugal, who were well received, and even employed in Don Miguel's army. A communication was in consequence made to Cordova, that if that practice was continued, the English government would no longer prevent Don Pedro employing the Spanish constitutionalists, and that

Mina and many others were both ready and willing to join his cause.

While those intrigues were going on in Lisbon, the expedition was sailing quietly to the southward, and preparing to cut the Gordian knot. Many speculations were afloat in the squadron about the issue of the enterprize: on board the flag-ship the opinion of a successful result was predominant. Our party was large, and I may say the flower of Portugal were embarked. In addition to the Dukes of Palmella and Terceira, the Marquis Fronteira, Count Ficalho, and Don Thomas Mascarenhas accompanied the expedition. Colonel Loureiro was quarter-master, and Colonel Mendez adjutant-general: both were old Peninsular officers, and well versed in their art. M. Mozinho, the chief engineer, was also a man of talent, and the first poet in Portugal. In addition to those were four or five aide-de-camps; and last not least our impatient and restless friend Mendizabal. Our party consisted of about twenty, and a happier one I never saw collected together: we were well supplied with every thing except water, and the days passed merrily away.

On the night of the 23d we rounded Cape St. Vincent, which was well lighted by the friars in the convent, who have on certain nights a brilliant fire on the promontory. On the 24th we passed Lagos, Faro, and Tavira, and at five o'clock in the afternoon anchored in the bay of Cacellas, two leagues to the westward of the Guadiana, having decided on the previous day to make our descent there, push the steam-boats up the river, and make a rapid march on Beja. A battery of one gun, which was soon silenced, was the only defence, and notwithstanding the caution of the captains of the steam-boats, who were very unwilling to approach the land, the troops were all on shore together with their stores and ammunition before midnight. The enemy had collected a force in front of Tavira, on which point the Duke marched at day-light, having relinquished the line of the Guadiana. After a slight skirmish, he drove the enemy across a small river, and entered the town at noon, the squadron anchoring at the same time. Our reception was none of the best; in fact the inhabitants being given to understand we were robbers and murderers, had abandoned the town to a man. The Duke of Terceira issued a proclamation, and in the evening the inhabitants began to return to their homes. A deputation was also received from Villa Real, who declared for the Queen, and a small detachment under Colonel Breyner was sent there, with arms to organize a force. The following morning the duke marched on Olhao, where he was received with great enthusiasm by the inhabitants, and on the morning of the 27th entered Faro, the capital of the Algarves, the squadron moving there at the same time.

Appendix, No. XVII.

At Faro we were tolerably received, but confidence was by no means restored. Our force was small, and the inhabitants were under apprehension of again falling under the government of Don Miguel, and were most cautious in taking a decided part. The Duke of Palmella landed, established a provisional government, and the principal inhabitants signed their adhesion to the Queen. Abundance of ammunition and stores were found in the arsenal; the engineer marked out redoubts for the defence of the town; and after halting two days to refresh and organize the division, the

Duke of Terceira marched on Loulé, leaving the French regiment, who were composed of raw and undisciplined men, in garrison, to secure the town and neighbourbood from any guerilla parties that might be formed. About two hundred of this regiment, composed of the worst of characters, were sent back to Oporto: I fear that the conduct of the remainder in the sequel was far from good. The duke had as yet formed no plan of operations, which could only be fixed after feeling his way, and ascertaining the force and position of the troops under the Viscount Mollelos, governor of the kingdom.

The squadron was well supplied with fresh provisions and water, which was most acceptable to the crews: they had long been without refreshments, and the inhabitants, finding every thing paid for, felt no disinclination to supply them. In Faro the squadron was augmented by a schooner of war, and one or two armed vessels were sent up the Guadiana to open a communication with Mertola, which had declared for the Queen.

On the 30th I anchored in Lagos Bay, the enemy having abandoned that city the day before.

Here we were better received than either at Faro or Tavira, and perhaps the fact of the squadron being composed of English officers and men brought back former recollections to the inhabitants, who had been accustomed in days gone by to see British men-of-war constantly in their port, and had no doubt profited by their sojourn. The authorities and principal inhabitants were assembled to take the oath of allegiance to the Queen, and this they willingly did, but showed very little disposition to form themselves into corps either for their own protection or for the advancement of her cause. With considerable difficulty I got together a party of about twenty, who marched a few leagues to re-capture the military chest, which had been removed; and I believe a small sum was secured. The enemy had now retired from the whole line of coast; a few deserters came in, but principally men belonging to the different towns we occupied; and I doubt much whether the division of the Duke of Terceira was augmented by five hundred men. Officers wearing uniforms and swords were in abundance, but they were chiefly old worn-out men, and showed no disposition to make themselves useful. No horses were to be found, and the detachment of lancers was kept in garrison at Faro.

From Lagos the City of Waterford steamer was despatched to Oporto and thence to England with the news of our first success; and after organizing the government and completing our supplies, on the evening of the 2d of July we sailed from Lagos, leaving the steamers to take in fuel and follow us along-shore to Lisbon. At this time we knew nothing certain of the movements of Don Miguel's squadron. A vessel from the Tagus had brought intelligence of their having dropped down to Cascaes, and returned the following day; but this must have either been fabricated by the master, or she had been sent to throw us off our guard.

At eight o'clock on the morning of the 3d of July, the officers of the watch reported two sail, then three, then four, and so on till they counted nine. I was surprised, and, as Sir Richard Strachan said, delighted; but the delight was accompanied with a disagreeable sort of feeling, just resembling the sensation of your heart coming up into your mouth, and requiring a tolerable gulp to keep it down. We were standing on the starboard tack under courses and top-gallant-sails; the enemy were on the larboard, broad on the lee-bow under their top-sails: one alone, which we took for the fifty-gun ship, had her courses and top-gallant-sails set, and sailed bad. The Villa Flor was immediately despatched to Lagos for the steamers, and after nearing the enemy to three or four miles, we tacked. They were formed in two lines, having the Don John, bearing a commodore's pendant, to windward, supported by the Rainha of the line, the Martin Freitas, and Princess Real. The three corvettes and two brigs formed the lee division opposite the open spaces,— all well painted, sails well set, and lines compact. It was a majestic sight, and I turned the hands up to shew the crews how well they looked, and to exhort them to pay attention to the management of their guns as the surest means of success. I had never been in a general action, and although delighted at the prospect before me, I could not but feel appalled at their great superiority, and the magnitude of the enterprize I was about to undertake.

Both squadrons stood in for the land, and I was apprehensive they meant to prevent the junction of the steamers, who were in Lagos Bay, and considerably to leeward. At two I tacked and stood towards the enemy. This manœvre had the desired effect; they tacked also, and left the bay open. At five the Villa Flor and steamers joined, and we took our station about a mile and a half on their weather-beam. The breeze was strong, and the sea too rough to attempt to board with success,—the plan of attack I had decided upon.

Here the enemy committed a great error: they ought to have stood boldly on, and either forced me into Lagos Bay to protect the town and steamers, and risk an action at anchor, or oblige me to fight under the disadvantages of wind and weather, one of which I must have done, or abandoned the town and steam-boats, which was impossible.

During the night the hostile squadrons kept within musket-shot,—the Miguelite fleet in a compact line, my squadron in two, ready to take advantage of any favourable opportunity that should offer of bringing on a general action or cutting off any of their ships who might drop astern during the night. At day-light one of the corvettes was about three miles in the rear of the body of the fleet: we bore up in two divisions. She was under her topsails, but whether from indolence, or trusting to her superiority of sailing, she did not increase sail till we were within musket-shot. The Don John then tacked, and there being no possibility of cutting her off without risking a general action, we hauled off, neither ship firing. This brought us considerably to leeward. By noon we regained our station on their weather-beam: neither party showed any disposition to engage.

There was a good deal of impatience manifested by the crews to come to blows, and they expressed their concern that this might be delayed some time longer, or entirely given up. I instructed the different captains to assure them, that the moment a favourable opportunity offered, they should have their fighting propensities indulged to the fullest extent, and recommended them to profit by the delay in improving the men in the gun-exercise, particularly fighting both sides, and working the alternate guns. Both squadrons wanted practice, and although we necessarily improved, it was natural to expect the enemy would improve also. They shewed no disposition to bring us to action: we dared risk nothing till the weather became sufficiently fine to make one desperate effort to save Portugal or lose the cause. There was no medium : all must be gained, or all lost. A partial action could only prolong for a few weeks the fate of Oporto and the division in the Algarves. A victory might save both ; a defeat would end the civil war at once. I was very anxious to draw the enemy under the land, but this they avoided ; and I became apprehensive that a convoy might have sailed from Lisbon with troops to take the Duke of Terceira in the rear ; at the same time the enemy wished to draw me to sea and thus leave the coast open. This is what ought to have been done, and for that very reason it was not ; and more experience shewed me, that the war ministers of both parties were only gifted with the talent of acting wrong, and in this the Miguelites had the advantage.

We kept our station close to the enemy during the afternoon and the following night, and towards morning there was every appearance of a calm, which eventually took place about nine o'clock. The steamers were now ordered to close, and to our astonishment and disappointment, the captains, engineers, and crews to a man, refused to take us in tow, with the exception of Captain Wilson of the William the Fourth, who with great difficulty persuaded his men to act. The Pembroke had parted the night before under pretence of her engines being out of order.

Officers and seamen came forward with all the money they possessed to bribe the cowards to act, which they refused to do unless two thousand pounds were laid down on the capstan-head for each engineer. This being impossible, they were dismissed the ship with the hearty curses of officers and men.

It had now been calm two hours: had the steam-boats taken the frigates in tow, we should have chosen our position, and in all probability have gained a bloodless victory; or had the ships been fitted with paddles similar to those in the Galatea, the effect would have been the same. Never did I before see an occasion where they could have been so triumphantly employed.

Towards noon cats'-paws here and there indicated an approaching breeze, and the swell had completely subsided; the men went to dinner, and the captains came on board to receive their final instructions. I had at first intended to have laid the Don John on board with the flag-ship, leaving the other line-of-battle ships to the Don Pedro, and the Princess Real frigate to the Donna Maria; but the uncertainty of getting alongside of her without being disabled in passing the sternmost ships, and the possibility of a repulse, induced me to relinquish that intention, and content myself with throwing the flag-ship and Don Pedro on board the Rainha of the line, which I calculated on carrying ere the Don John could come to her assistance. This effected, if not too much disabled, we should be ready to attack the commodore, whom it was important to secure. At all events we were pretty certain of holding our prize, and I felt quite satisfied that Captain Peak in the Donna Maria would carry the Princess Real, while the Portuense, Villa Flor, and Faro schooner, should make the most they could of the Martin Freitas, leaving the three corvettes and two brigs in the hands of Providence, who was sure to be on the side of the good cause. At the same time the steamers took their station to windward, ready for a bolt should the day be lost.

About one the breeze became steady; the people were at quarters, determined to fight to the last, and I sat down to a hasty dinner with Commodore Wilkinson, Captains Goble, Blackstone, Pearn, Charles Napier, Ruxton, and Macdonough, who had quitted the steamers in disgust. We talked over the approaching battle with great confidence, little thinking that in half an hour three of the party would cease to live or be mortally wounded, and two more dangerously. At two the captains returned to their ships; the signal was made for battle and close order; the boats were lowered down; and the squadron, led by the Rainha, displaying the constitutional flag at each mast-head, gradually edged away under their courses and top-gallant sails. The enemy (with the exception of the Martin Freitas, who had her courses and top-gallant sails set) were under their top-sails, and as we approached, the lee line closed up in the intermediate spaces, but a little to leeward, thus forming a sort of double column of two line-of-battle ships, a fifty-gun ship, a fifty-gun frigate, three heavy corvettes, two brigs, and a xibeque. Previous to this, the frigate being to leeward tacked, and had all the appearance of coming over; but after fetching in the wake of the fifty-gun ship, she again tacked and took her station. The breeze was good, the water smooth, not a cloud in the heavens; the enemy looked well and firm, and they were plainly seen training their guns as we approached. It was a trying and awful sight, and accompanied with a considerable degree of dread, (at least I can answer for myself.) Officers and men were calm and determined, though aware of the danger of the enterprise, the success of which mainly depended on the state we should be in after the first broadside.

The enemy kept their line close, and reserved their fire till well within musket-shot; the frigate then threw out a signal, which we concluded was for permission to fire: the moment was critical, and we all felt it.

The commodore's answer was hardly at the mast-head ere the frigate opened her broadside, which was instantaneously followed by the whole squadron, with the exception of the Don John, whose stern and quarter guns could only bear. Poor Rainha! I looked up, and expected to see every mast tottering; but the cherub was sitting aloft, and notwithstanding the most tremendous fire I ever witnessed, which made the sea bubble like a boiling cauldron round her, the smoke, clearing away, discovered to the astonished Miguelites the Rainha proudly floating on the waters of Nelson and St. Vincent, with her masts erect, her rigging and sails only shewing the fiery ordeal she had gone through.

The men were lying down at their quarters, few were struck down on the main deck, but the three foremost guns on the quarter-deck were nearly cleared, and Lieutenant Nivett, of the marines, received a mortal wound. At this time we had not fired a shot, and I ordered a few

BATTLE OFF CAPE St VINCENT between THE PORTUGUESE SQUADRONS.

Plan of Attack

Donna Maria's Squadron

A	Rainha de Portugal	46	D	Pernicieuse Corvette	18
	Fregate Vigo's Flag	46	E	Vilar Flor Brig	10
B	Don Pedro formerly	46	F	Four Schooners	6
C	Wittington Indiaman	36			
	Brazil Statesman	44		total	176

Don Miguel's Squadron

1	Don John	74	6	Isabel Maria	26
2	Rainha	74	7	Fagos	20
3	Martin Freitas	44	8	Principe Real Corvette	22
4	Principe Regent	36	9	Audaz	20
5	Zeberque		10	Ophelia	26
				total	372

to be thrown on board, to check as much as possible their taking a deliberate aim. Our example was followed by the Don Pedro, and we soon passed the frigate and Martin Freitas, the latter losing her fore top-mast. At this time the sternmost line-of-battle ship luffed to; our helm was put up to avoid her broadside, and the Don John bore up across her bows, intending to place us between the two line-of-battle ships. This was just what I desired, and when she had passed too far to leeward to recover a weather position, our helm was put suddenly down. The frigate flew to, grazing the Rainha's stern with the flying jibboom; the foremost guns were poured into her, crammed to the muzzle with round and grape; the helm was then shifted, and we ran alongside under a very heavy fire, which struck down my secretary, master, and many men. The ships were lashed with the main-sheet, and Commodore Wilkinson and Captain Charles Napier, heading the boarders, passed from the bower anchor to her bulwark, driving the men across the forecastle along the larboard gangway.

I had not intended to board, having enough to do to look after the squadron; but the excitement was too great, and I found myself, without hardly knowing it, on the enemy's forecastle, supported by one or two officers. There I paused, till several men jumping on board, we rushed aft with a loud cheer, and either passed through or drove a party drawn up on the break of the quarterdeck. At this moment I received a severe blow from a crow-bar, the owner of which did not escape unscathed, and poor Macdonough fell at my side by a musket-ball; Barradas, the captain of the ship, came across me wounded in the face, and fighting like a tiger. He was a brave man: I saved his life. The second captain came next, and made so good-natured a cut at me that I had not heart to hurt him: he also was spared. Barradas took up arms again, and was finally killed in the cabin.

The commodore and Captain Charles Napier, after driving a whole host before them, fell severely wounded on the larboard side of the quarter-deck; the former with difficulty regained his ship; the

Position when boarding

1. Don John
2. Ruzader
3. Martim Freitas
4. Princeza Reyal
5. Zebecque
6. Izabel Maria
7. Tagus
8. Princeza Real Carvalho
9. Audax
10. Orwlito

A. Rainha de Portugal
B. Don Pedro
C. Donna Maria
D. Pertinence
E. Villa Flor Brig
F. Faro Schooner

latter, being stunned, lay some time, till the noise of friends coming to his assistance, roused him from his stupor.

The quarter-deck was now gained, but the slaughter still continued notwithstanding the endeavours of the officers to stay it. The main and lower deck were yet unsubdued; and as the Don Pedro ranged up on the opposite side to board, both ships fired. I hailed Captain Goble to desist, as we had carried the upper deck, and desired him to follow the Don John, who had made off: at the same moment a ball from the lower deck struck him, and in a few minutes he was no more.

Lieutenant Edmunds and Wooldridge jumped down with a party on the main-deck, which they carried, but both fell under mortal wounds. In a few minutes all was quiet; the lower deck gave in, and many of the Portuguese seamen rushed on the quarter-deck for safety, with white canvas on their left arms, having discovered that was the badge worn by our men in boarding. Others got on board my ship, amongst whom several little boys found their way into the gun-room, and employed themselves wiping glasses.

The men were now ordered back to the Rainha, with the exception of those appointed to remain, and in the hurry the ships separated, leaving me in the prize. I, however, soon got back to the flag-ship. The fore-top-sail, which was cut to rags, was shifted;* all sail was set, and we were fast approaching the Don John, the Don Pedro being still nearer, when, seeing no chance of avoiding an action, she luffed-to and hauled her colours down.

The Don Pedro was directed to secure her, and I followed the Martin Freitas, who had been too strong for the Portuense,(whose captain, Blackstone, was mortally wounded,) and Villa Flor, and though much disabled, was making off: by ten she was in my possession. The Princess Royal corvette, coming across a steamer, surrendered also. A little after I got alongside the Rainha. Captain Peak, in the Donna Maria, passed under the fifty-gun frigate's stern, raked her, luffed-to, and after firing a few broadsides, ran his bowsprit into her mizen rigging, and carried her in gallant style.

* The main-sail was also useless, and we were in the act of shifting it.

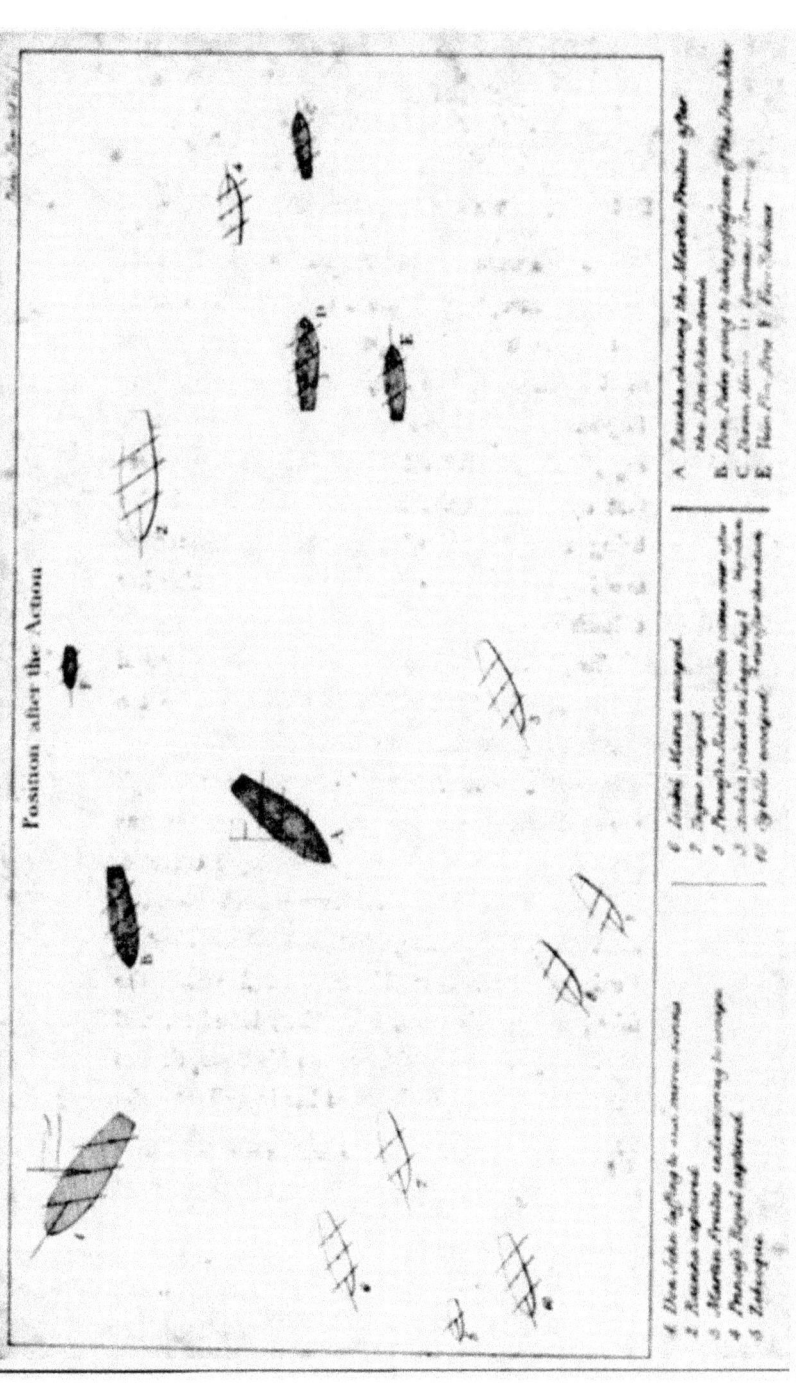

Thus finished the action of the 5th of July, leaving in our possession two ships of the line, mounting eighty-six guns each, including four forty-eight pounders for throwing shells; one frigate of fifty-two guns, a fifty-gun ship, and a corvette of eighteen guns. Two corvettes and two brigs escaped; the two former arrived safe in Lisbon; one brig joined the following day, and the other got to Madeira. The enemy were amply found in every species of warlike stores, and mounted stern-guns, in addition to the full complement on their broadsides.

The loss of the squadron was about ninety killed and wounded. The enemy lost between two and three hundred. [Appendix, No. XVIII]

It is not for me to comment on this action; I shall leave that to the world; simply observing, that at no time was a naval action fought with such a disparity of force, and in no naval action was there ever so severe a loss in so short a time.

It has been said by our detractors that the fleet was bought; I answer that they were, but with the same coin that Earl St. Vincent bought the Spanish fleet, viz. British powder, British shot, and British steel, wielded by the hands of British officers and seamen, with the disadvantages of a long peace, an ill-found and ill-disciplined squadron, and many of the officers totally unacquainted with naval habits and discipline. I must also do justice to the Portuguese officers and men who were in the fleet, all of whom behaved most courageously.*

* It is a singular coincidence that a strong reconnoisance was made on Oporto on the day of the action, and the news of it arrived on the day twelve-month Don Pedro landed at Oporto.

CHAPTER XII.

By midnight the prizes were manned, their crews were secured, and after a hard day's work, both of body and mind, we were in full sail for Lagos Bay, where we arrived in triumph next morning, and were received with the greatest joy by the inhabitants, who vied with each other in showering down blessings on the people they were pleased to call their deliverers from the most unheard-of tyranny that ever oppressed a nation.

Next morning detachments were landed to pay the last tributes to the officers and men who had fallen. Poor Goble, Blackstone, and George were buried in the same grave, and they were followed to the tomb by all the principal inhabitants, who vied with each other in providing comforts and accommodation for the wounded officers and men.

The Donegal, Castor, and Leveret, who had been sent to demand an apology from Don Miguel's commodore for having fired at the latter, appeared in the offing, and Captain Fanshaw sent his commander to ascertain who were the victors.

The Duke of Palmella and M. Mendizabal arrived in the afternoon from Faro, half mad with joy at this unexpected event, and assisted me in the arrangements that were necessary to be made with the ships and crews. To hold them as prisoners would have been both impolitic and impossible; the Queen's service was offered and accepted by a few of the officers, who were known to be constitutionalists; the commodore and rest, who declined, were sent prisoners to Faro. The crews to a man declared for the Queen.

On examination it was found necessary to leave the flag-ship and the Martin Freitas to refit, and I shifted my flag into the Don John, and manned her from my late ship and the Don Pedro. The captain of the Princess Real corvette was appointed to the Don Pedro and manned from the Don John; the captain of the Martin Freitas, Marcel Pedro, who defended his ship well, was appointed to the Rainha, and as many of her crew had deserted at Lagos, she was completed from the Don John and Martin Freitas, and the rest were sent to my old ship. Captain Ruxton, of the Villa Flor, was appointed to the frigate; Lieutenant Leot, my first lieutenant, to the Villa Flor, and Captain Napier to the Portuense. These arrangements having been made, every exertion was used to refit the squadron, and Pedroites and Miguelites vied with each other in repairing damages, and getting their respective ships ready for service.

The Duke of Terceira had marched from Faro on the 28th of June; he united his divisions betweeen Loulé and Silves; he there learnt that the garrisons of Albufeira, Lagos, Sagres, and other small towns, having united at Silves, with several pieces of artillery, were rapidly marching on St. Bartholomew de Messines, to join the Viscount Mollelos, who had already abandoned that post, and was retiring on Santa Clara by St. Marcos de Serra. On the 30th he arrived at St. Bartholomew, and found that the enemy had already passed that town, having abandoned three pieces of artillery, which were destroyed, and a considerable quantity of ammunition.

Thus in six days from the time the division disembarked, the whole province was cleared, and a considerable number of officers and soldiers, principally artillery, had joined the Queen's standard. All the coast artillery and the material of the province had also fallen into our possession, and the whole of the enemy's force on this side of the Serras de Monchique and Caldeirao were disorganized. The rapidity of his movements had rendered it impossible to bring up his artillery and ammunition, and he was consequently obliged to halt at St. Bartholomew till its arrival. During this halt two officers with an escort were sent to reconnoitre St. Marcos de Serra, and were surprised by the Viscount Mollelos' ordinenzas, who afterwards retired before a company of caçadores, taking with them the whole of the inhabitants of the village.

On the 3d the duke learnt that Mollelos had retired on St. Martinho das Amoreiras, where the roads meet that lead from the Algarves to Almodovar and Ourique, by Santa Clara, having devastated the whole country in his line of march. He also received information that Colonel Breyner, with his volunteers and fifty of the Queen's tirailleurs that the Duke of Palmella sent from Faro, had advanced to Mertola, and joined a guerilla party from Serpa and the neighbourhood, and were moving on Beja. This determined him to return to Loulé on the 4th, as the best point of departure to cross the Serras, and being nearer Faro he might more easily unite the artillery, ammunition, and provisions necessary to pass the mountains : that done, he had the choice of three movements, which must be decided by the operations of the enemy; the first was to penetrate into the Alemtejo by Almodevar, the second by the road of St. Marco, the third, to gain the banks of the Guadiana, and advance by Mertola on Beja; but this required a retrogade march on Tavira, being the only practicable road between Loulé and Mertola. This last movement, I am of opinion, would have been fatal to the cause of the Queen; it would have had the appearance of a retreat, and encouraged the enemy to return into the Algarves.

The line of the Guadiana, which was the original plan, was in my opinion the best and safest, because the steam-boats could have pushed up the river; and in the event of a reverse, the division was safe, and the squadron could have probably secured Faro and Tavira, but certainly Lagos, without any assistance from the army. Mollelos never could have united his troops in sufficient force to have arrived at Beja before the duke, and in all probability the presence of the squadron on the coast would have kept him in the Algarves. The retrogade movement to Loulé, together with the long halt there, certainly had a bad effect, which, however, was dissipated by the victory of the 5th of July.

The news of the action brought the duke to Lagos on the 8th, and I need hardly say he was delighted at the great success we had met with. All dangers and difficulties now disappeared. I spared him a couple of hundred of the Portuguese marines, who volunteered to join his division, and he at once decided on entering the Alemtejo by the road of St. Marcos and Santa Clara; and having united his forces and provisions at St. Bartholomew on the 12th of July, he marched on the 13th on St. Marcos, where I shall leave him and return to the squadron.

Captain Peak, being ready, sailed on the 9th with the Princess Real corvette and Villa Flor to establish the blockade of Lisbon. The corvette, having parted the following night from the Donna Maria, returned to Lagos, her captain not having sense to proceed ; and the Villa Flor came in on the following day with the loss of her bowsprit. On the evening of the 13th, I sailed for Lisbon, with the Don John bearing my flag, and the Portuense manned with English;—the Rainha, Don Pedro, and Princess Real frigate, manned by the same officers and men we had fought and conquered the week before, all sailing better than the flag-ship. That there was great risk in this is beyond a doubt; they might have again tried the fate of war, or walked off to Lisbon, but there was no alternative. To leave them behind was impossible ; it was necessary to make an imposing appearance before Lisbon; I therefore decided on taking them with me and forcing the bar with the very ships who had sailed a fortnight before to bring my squadron to the Tagus. This war was unlike any other I had been engaged in. I took up a desperate cause, and it was necessary to fight a desperate game to the last; and fortune never left my side, except in the melancholy instance I shall shortly relate.

The day after leaving Lagos, we fell in with the Marquis of St. Iria, who was appointed governor of the Algarves; he brought letters from the minister, informing me that the Emperor had promoted me to the rank of admiral, and ennobled me by the title of Viscount Capo St. Vicenti; all this was very gratifying, but I should have preferred the latter part to have been left alone. During the time the squadron lay in Lagos Bay, the men had worked hard, and had fallen into the irregularities very common in harbour, and more particularly after an action. Symptoms of cholera made their appearance before we sailed, and the late master of the Don Pedro had died of the disease. On the 14th off Cape St. Vincent, it broke out with the greatest violence; men were seen walking about apparently in perfect health, and in a moment they were struck down, and before sunset nearly a hundred were in the

<small>Appendix, No. XIX.</small>

hands of the medical officers; they were lying about all parts of the ship in the agony of collapse. Their messmates employed friction and every means they could think of to alleviate their sufferings, but in vain: seven died the first night.

The attention of Dr. Fraser and the medical department was beyond all praise; but the disease marched with such rapid strides, that their exertions were quite inadequate to keep pace with it: it frequently happened that while they were administering to some patients, others were taken below and fell into a state of collapse before any assistance could be rendered.

A gloom came over the crew: they became stupified with fear, not knowing at what moment they might be attacked. The same men, who a fortnight before had fought and conquered the Miguelite fleet, were now unmanned and unfit for any exertion. After the action they had shifted a topsail from the store-room in less than half-an-hour, and were ready to fight a second ship of the line: they were now upwards of twelve hours shifting the Don John's main-topsail. This state of things lasted for a week, when no less than two hundred passed through the surgeons' hands, and about fifty into the next world. As we stood to the westward, it gradually disappeared.

On the 19th I received a communication from the Duke of Terceira, to the effect that Viscount Mollelos had on the 15th made a flank movement on Beja, which town had declared for the Queen, thus leaving the road to Lisbon open; and that, having gained two marches on him, he had decided on marching on the capital at all risks, and would arrive at Alcacer de Sal on the 22d, and St. Ubes the 23d. The bad sailing of the squadron and the northerly winds delayed us so long that we did not make Cape Espichel till that day, when we were joined by a steamer, with letters from the Emperor begging us to show ourselves off Oporto, to convince Don Miguel's army that his fleet was captured, the ministry very foolishly supposing that our appearance there would induce the army to declare for the Queen: and indeed they had actually sent a letter to the enemy's camp acquainting them with

<small>Appendix, No. XX.</small>

the circumstance, and calling upon them to submit.

On the morning of the 24th, I despatched a corvette and steamer to Setubal, who brought me the intelligence that the duke had passed through that day and marched on Almada. The wind was still light and to the northward; and our anxiety for the safety of the duke was great. We knew he was followed by four thousand men; Almada was strong; and there was every reason to expect that a large force would be sent there from Lisbon. The usual sea-breeze had not blown for three days, and to attempt to force the bar without a strong wind was impossible. I looked upon the duke as lost, and without having the power of saving him. Every exertion was made to get to Cascaes, which I intended to have attacked in order to make a diversion in his favour; when abreast of the entrance of the Tagus, a British brig of war brought us the welcome intelligence that Lisbon had been abandoned by the Miguelites the night before, and was now occupied by the duke's troops. Thus by the cowardice and imbecility of Don

Miguel's ministers was Lisbon lost to Miguel and the Duke of Terceira saved.

The wind was still light; we made little progress with the squadron, and were obliged to anchor at the mouth of the river. As yet it was not known whether St. Julian's and the Bougie had been abandoned, and it was difficult to believe it possible that such an unpardonable folly could be committed; but nevertheless it was so. That night those forts, together with the whole of the defences of the Tagus, were deserted and the river left open to the squadron. We weighed at day-light, and were obliged to anchor at noon abreast of St. Julian's, which we occupied, lest the enemy should recover from their panic and return.

Several hundred persons, who had been confined in subterraneous cells for five or six years, were restored to their families, and many of them came on board the squadron to thank us for their deliverance. The Duke of Palmella and myself left the ships at the entrance of the river, and rowed up the Tagus. Our first visit was on board the Asia, where we were received in the warmest and handsomest manner; Admiral Parker saluted, and cheered us on taking leave. This was followed by the rest of the squadron as we passed; nothing could be more gratifying to my feelings than receiving such honours from the officers of a profession to which I had so long belonged, and was a convincing proof that though removed from the naval list* by the infuriated howlings of an enraged and disappointed party, who by such a step might glut their revenge, but could not save Don Miguel, I was not removed from the good opinion of naval officers, who on this occasion did not allow their political feelings to depreciate the service I had performed.

From the Asia we proceeded to the arsenal, where the concourse of people was immense. Nothing could exceed the reception we met with; the whole population were drunk with joy; they had been for five years kept in the most abject state of slavery; all friendship and sociability was at an end; one family was afraid to trust another; the streets were patrolled night and day by horse and

* It is singular that I received an order to appear at the Admiralty the day the action was fought.

foot; thousands of people were in prison for supposed political offences; and more than half of Lisbon was under the surveillance of the police; and yet Englishmen were to be found who regretted that such a horrible system was on the eve of being destroyed, and maintained in their places in Parliament that Don Miguel was the choice of the people.

At the arsenal we found the splendid equipage of the Baron Quintella waiting for us. Himself, the Duke of Terceira, and the authorities had gone down to the bar. We were conducted through the principal streets, where the greatest enthusiasm prevailed, and were finally put down at the Baron's house in the square of the same name, which now became the centre of attraction. All Lisbon seemed crammed into this place, and the vivas for the Queen, Don Pedro, Palmella, and myself were loud and continued beyond description.

In the afternoon, the breeze favouring the approach of the squadron to the city, the river was covered with boats containing the beauty and fashion of the capital. The ships were so crowded, that it was with difficulty they could be managed.

Many came to welcome their friends and relations back under a new flag, and many returned in affliction for the loss in battle of fathers, husbands, brothers, and sons.

The two line-of-battle ships were anchored abreast of the arsenal, and the Don Pedro was pushed up as far as Aldea Gallego to prevent the crossing over of Mollelos's troops, who had arrived there in a state of disorganization. Three brigs, who had gone up the Tagus, came down and joined the squadron, and were stationed in various parts of the river. The Donna Maria, Princess Royal frigate, (now the Duchess of Braganza,) and Princess Real corvette, (changed to the Cacella,) were sent to Oporto, together with several small craft, to be at the Emperor's disposal, and blockade the various ports on the coast. The Spanish frigate, which had been waiting for Don Carlos, left Lisbon the day we entered.

I had, under date of the 9th of July, at Lagos, four days after the action, declared all the ports of Portugal, which had not proclaimed the Queen, in a state of blockade; and on that day Captain Peak sailed from Lagos with the Donna Maria and Cacella to enforce it, the rest of the squadron sailing on the 13th. Yet Lord Londonderry, who I do not apprehend knew much about sea blockades, in his speech on the 31st of July, declared that it was quite impossible to blockade fourteen ports and a line of coast of four or five hundred miles from Cape St. Vincent to Viana. If his lordship had consulted a chart, he would have found an extent of coast of only three hundred and twenty miles, which, with all due deference to his lordship's judgment, could be well blockaded with two sail of the line, three frigates, two corvettes, two brigs, and two schooners, which was the force of the squadron when the blockade was declared. The Duke of Wellington was also of opinion that after an action we could not be in a state to blockade the whole coast of Portugal; but had his Grace reflected that the action was fought by boarding, he would have known that the ships must have suffered little in their masts or rigging. In short, the whole was a party question, and although supported by a majority in the House of Lords, the Commons took a more correct view of the subject, and supported ministers by a large majority.

In the evening I met at dinner the duke and his gallant staff, and he gave me the following account of his unprecedented march. When the squadron left Lagos, the duke was at Gravao, where the news of the revolt of Beja was confirmed; and he learnt at the same time that Mollelos had marched upon and occupied that city, his troops committing the greatest horrors, Colonel Breyner's detachment being obliged to retire on their approach, and leave the city to their vengeance.

On the 17th he arrived at Messejana, and there he called a council of war, and communicated to the members that Mollelos, having committed the great error of leaving the road to Lisbon open by his occupation of Beja, thereby giving his division two days march a-head of him, he had determined on gaining the banks of the Tagus, and putting every thing to the hazard of a die. He did not conceal the difficulties and dangers of such an enterprize, and that it must must either terminate in immortal glory or a halter. Fortunately he was addressing as gallant a band as ever drew a sword, and his determination was received by acclamation. Their enthusiasm extended to the troops, who, forgetting the fatigues they had undergone, and setting at nought the dangers and privations they must incur in such a march, rent the air with cries of 'to Almada and Lisbon!' On the 19th they arrived at Bairros, and on the 20th the head-quarters were at Val de Ferreira. On the 21st, after dispersing a few royalist volunteers, they entered Alcacer do Sal, where they were received with the greatest enthusiasm. After halting a few hours, they took up a position near the Quinta de Palma. On the 22d they encountered the enemy in position in front of Setubal, who shewed every disposition to give battle. The column advanced in double quick time, their flanks being covered by a few sharp-shooters; the enemy immediately fled and were pursued through the town, leaving a considerable number of prisoners behind, as well as many deserters, who came over. The column halted at the Quinta of Esteval; and the castle of St. Philip and the town of Oritao opened their gates, and displayed the Queen's colours.

Here prudence would have dictated a halt till the position of the squadron could be ascertained;

but the duke, having thrown away the scabbard, pushed on to Azeitao, detaching a company of infantry by the road of Palmella, with orders to join him at the former place. By this time the news of his arrival at Alcacer, and of the rout of the force of Brigadier Freitas in front of Setubal, was brought to Lisbon by the fugitives. Then, and not till then, did the Duke of Cadaval open his eyes.

A strong detachment of infantry, with three squadrons of cavalry, were crossed over to Almada under the command of Telles Jordao, a staunch Miguelite and a great barbarian; and there he was destined to receive just punishment for all the cruelties he had committed when governor of St. Julian's. A plain of three leagues, which separated Azeitao from Lugar d'Amora, and where the enemy ought to have been posted, was passed on the 23d. Their advanced posts were then discovered, but they retired on the duke's approach; and the peasants brought information that the enemy were in position on two hills which commanded the road leading to Almada. Here they had established a line of tirailleurs. The duke threw out his caçadores on each flank of his column, and continued his march, the enemy's tirailleurs retiring from height to height, to the entrance of the defile, which, by the barrier of Alfeite, opens into the Valle da Piedad. This valley, extending to the borders of the Tagus behind Cacilhas, is bounded on the south by the heights of Almada, and opens into a small space, which is entered on one side by the road the duke advanced, and on the other by the roads of Pragal on the left, Almada on the centre, and Cacilhas by Murtella on the right.

Here the enemy, knowing his superiority in cavalry, endeavoured to draw the column, in order that he might profit by that arm. The duke, being acquainted with the ground, foresaw and was prepared for this manœuvre, which was confirmed by the little resistance as yet opposed to his march. He persevered, however, and scarcely had his flankers, which were extended in the valley, dislodged those of the enemy, and the head of the column entered by the road of Alfeite, when the distant noise of cavalry was heard, and shortly after two squadrons, by the road of Cacilhas, charged him with an impetuosity that ought to have insured them victory.

The Portuguese infantry have a horror of cavalry, and began to waver; but the duke and his staff being at the head of the column, by their noble example and exhortation to be steady, restored confidence; and as they approached the column, a volley brought down the leading men and horses, and the survivors fled in great confusion.

The duke followed up his success with vigour, and leaving the sixth infantry to cover the roads of Pragal and Almada, advanced with the rest of his troops direct on Cacilhas to cut off their retreat, having occupied the avenues leading to Almada with several companies of the third infantry. At the entrance of the square of Murtella the enemy had two field-pieces; but the second and third caçadores, despising their fire, charged bayonets and captured the artillery, and pushing on the head of the column, penetrated after dark to the Caes de Cacilhas. It is quite impossible to describe the disorder that now took place. Infantry, cavalry, artillery, and baggage,—generals, officers, and soldiers, precipitated themselves into boats. The darkness of the night increased the confusion; the conquerors and the conquered became mixed; and much to the honour of the former they spared the enemy no longer resisting; and in half an hour after both parties were friends.

As the fortress of Almada had not yet surrendered, the duke countermarched his troops, leaving a guard on the Caes de Cacilhas, and marched to the entrance of that town; and wishing to spare his troops and the conquered enemy as much as possible, and to avoid the disorder inseparable from a forced entry into a town in a dark night, he there halted, and General Schwalbach, who commanded the head of the column, sent his aide-de-camp, Alfius Jorge, with a flag of truce to summon the fortress. He unfortunately fell in with some of the Miguelite cavalry, and by them was mortally wounded. The duke remained in his position, and at day-light in the morning Almada surrendered, and the garrison laid down their arms on the esplanade.

The loss of the enemy in this action could not have been less than a thousand in killed, wounded, and drowned; amongst the former was Telles Jordao, who commanded; he well deserved his fate. The Spanish ambassador Cordova was taken prisoner: he had frequently been over to Almada giving advice to the Miguelite commander; and, instead of being dismissed, he ought to have been sent to the castle, which would have been the shortest manner of obliging Spain to withdraw her minister from the court of Miguel.

The news of this victory had such an effect on the nerves of the Duke of Cadaval and Don Miguel's other ministers, that at midnight the troops and police, consisting of upwards of six thousand men, assembled, and the capital was abandoned without a struggle, which no one who read Cadaval's fiery proclamation could have expected. Appendix, XXI.

CHAPTER XIII.

It is incomprehensible that with all the devotion Don Miguel's ministers had for his cause, in which they were so deeply implicated, and though danger was staring them in the face, of which they were warned by Marshal Bourmont, who gave them excellent instructions for the defence of the Tagus, and to guard against the advance of Villa Flor; and although they had seen an insurrection take place at Punhete, which marched into Thomar, carried off the public money and a considerable quantity of cattle, and crossed into the Alentejo, still nothing could rouse them from their lethargy. On the 9th of July a few troops had been passed over to Aldea Gallego to reinforce Mollelos; but not till the Duke of Terceira was close upon them, was any energy displayed.

During the night all was quiet in Lisbon: indeed it was not generally known that the ministers and troops had evacuated the capital. They managed, however, to press carriages of every description, and carry off their baggage and families.

The Queen's colours flying on Almada was a signal for rejoicing. The whole population now poured into the street, and declared for the Queen; Appendix XXII, salutes were fired in all directions; and the blue and white flag was displayed in every quarter of the town. Boats, crowded with the inhabitants, pushed across to Cacilhas, received the troops with open arms, and conducted the duke and his gallant band across the river in triumph to the capital.

It may easily be supposed how great was the excitement in a city which had for five years groaned under the most abject slavery. Imprisonments and executions had been innumerable, and even the very night before the evacuation two unfortunate wretches were executed in the public square. Nevertheless few excesses were committed; the most obnoxious of the Miguelites, particularly the judges, took shelter in the houses of foreigners, and in few instances were their habitations plundered. Only one or two lives were lost.

When the size of Lisbon is considered, and the facilities that the various streets afford for every species of disorder and murder, with no police to keep order, the greatest credit is due to the inhabitants for their forbearance. After a cruel usurpation of five years, it may easily be conceived how many injuries were to be revenged on spies and informers, and even on the families of the police and other public functionaries who had been left behind; but the minds of the people were more occupied in rejoicing at their deliverance than in revenging the injuries they had received.

The march of Napoleon from Frejus to Paris has been thought the boldest and finest enterprize recorded in history; but when we consider that Napoleon was the idol of the French army, I may say, personally known to almost every officer and soldier in it;—a general who had fought and conquered in a hundred battles, and who had planted his eagles in almost every capital of Europe;—an emperor who came to rescue France from the imbecile government of the Bourbons, and who came to meet his comrades in arms and reward them for their fidelity;—I say his enterprize sinks into insignificance in comparison with that of the Duke of Terceira. He had been shut up in Oporto for nearly a twelvemonth, surrounded by a large army, many of whom knew him, and had served with him; yet there was no reason to suppose they would join his colours: indeed, on the contrary, there was every reason to believe that they would not desert the standard of Don Miguel. Yet the duke, with a division of less than fifteen hundred men, threw himself into the heart of Portugal, and though followed within two days' march by a division of four thousand, with a garrison in Lisbon of eight thousand more, pushed boldly on, fought and defeated double his number, and placed the Queen's colours opposite to Lisbon; and he accomplished all this without knowing that a squadron was at hand to support him, for he had received no communication from me, nor was it in my power to send him any till he had left Setubal.

The ministers of Don Miguel of course knew by telegraph that I was at hand, and they also knew that almost always a strong breeze blows into the Tagus during the day; and I dare say they had a shrewd suspicion that I would force the river, which no doubt operated on their fears; but this takes away none of the duke's laurels. Had the governor of Almada stuck to his post, and the ministers to theirs, and acted with vigor, it is more than probable the duke would have been lost. Mollelos was at hand; he might have been reinforced from Lisbon. St. Julian's, the Bougie, and the numerous batteries on the Tagus were in excellent order and well manned; the duke would have been hemmed in, and owing to the light winds I could not have got into the Tagus before the 27th. Had he maintained himself, and I had succeeded in approaching the town, which would have been attended with great loss, I could then have passed him across to Lisbon, and probably pounded them out; but had I failed, there was no retreat, and I should have been obliged to burn the fleet, join the duke with the sailors and marines, and then God only knows how the war would have ended. However, it was much better as it was, and in the sequel I shall show that Don Pedro's ministers were as capable of taking a nap as Don Miguel's; and that, had it depended upon them, Lisbon would have been lost as easily as it was gained.

The Duke of Cadaval was still in the neighbourhood, and 1 was under considerable apprehension that after ascertaining the smallness of our force, he would have returned and turned our joy into grief and mourning. In point of fact, had he shewn the least degree of enterprise, he would have called over Mollelos's division, and either driven us out of Lisbon, or blockaded us in the Castle St. George, in less than forty-eight hours; for though there was great enthusiasm amongst the people, they had not the most distant idea of being attacked; and instead of the authorities immediately barricading the streets and cutting traverses in every direction, nothing was thought of but eating, drinking, and rejoicing.

The arsenals in the first instance had been broken open by the populace, who provided themselves with arms; and it was with great difficulty that they could be collected together to arm the corps the duke was assembling. I found it quite impossible to convince my friends of any danger; in fact, they knew their opponents better than I did, and they happened to be right. I, however, did all I could to render things secure. The George IV. steamer, who was seized in the Tagus, was sent up the river on the side of the Alemtejo towards Salvaterra, where Mollelos's head-quarters were established; and my officers had actually been in his quarters passing themselves off as British, and counselling him to come over to the Queen. There was great confusion in his army; they had neither outposts nor piquets; and a regiment of caçadores might have captured or destroyed them in their beds; but the duke had few troops, and those few were fatigued, and Mollelos's division was allowed to cross the river at Vallada and form a junction with the garrison of Lisbon, who had retired on Leiria and Pombal.

Immediately after the occupation of the capital, noblemen, gentlemen, and people of all colours of politics waited on the Duke of Palmella, who held out to all parties conciliation, forgiveness, and oblivion of the past. The same line of conduct was followed by the Duke of Terceira and myself to military and naval men; and the Miguelites began to think they were free from persecution and retaliation; and every thing was settling down to peace and quietness.

The occupation of Lisbon was followed by the evacuation of Cascaes and Peniché, the latter a strong fortress. A detachment of disorderly troops had been sent to the Burlings to get rid of them, and the commanding-officer, profiting by the panic, summoned the governor, who marched out, and it was quietly taken possession of. A detachment of marines was sent to reinforce the garrison, and they were followed by the Don Pedro, which placed it in security.

On the 27th, having formed my staff, I took possession of the office of major-general at the naval arsenal, which is the most complete and compact establishment I ever saw. It was built like most of the other splendid establishments by Pombal. The store-houses are large, well constructed, and well arranged, with splendid rigging-lofts, sail-lofts, and one of the finest mould-lofts in the world, in which the young gentlemen intended for the navy study. The ordnance and victualling departments are included in the building.

There were two slips; one occupied by a corvette nearly finished, and the other by a ship of the line in considerable progress: the latter had been laid down upwards of ten years, and the first part begun bids fair to rot before the latter part is finished. There is also a splendid dock half full of mud; and the gates, which had been lately made, were too feeble to resist the pressure of the water, and had been left in that state for several years. The store-houses had been cleared to fit out the fleet, and they, as well as the victualling stores, were empty. The Sibyl and Isabella Maria, the two corvettes who escaped, were dismantled. In addition to those were four store-ships, a prison-ship, sheer hulk, and several rotten craft, making a navy of about thirty sail.

Appendix, XXIII.

The strength of the arsenal was upwards of two thousand, including the lame, the blind, and the lazy, who formed the principal part of the establishment. The principal officers have naval rank, and were seen attending their duties dressed in cocked hats, swords, and epaulettes. There were builders and builders' assistants in abundance; some of the latter not bred to the business: but in this arsenal ability was not considered a necessary qualification.

On taking my seat, I was waited upon by all the naval officers and others connected with the department. Amongst the former were captains, commodores, and lieutenants, several of whom had never been at sea. This was no unusual occurrence; and, indeed, Don John had in one instance transmogrified a bishop into a naval captain. Those ceremonies over, I inspected the different departments, all of which were good in theory, but nothing could be worse in practice. The navy of Portugal had long been neglected, and, except the late Marquis of Viana, no major-general ever had influence to make it better. The minister of marine and colonies is superior to the major-general, and as the least influential minister is generally in this department, it is always the last provided for; in addition to which there was no unity between the two offices. I vainly flattered myself I should be enabled to remedy those evils, but I was most egregiously mistaken.

The first thing necessary was to put the squadron

in order; the larger ships for the defence of Lisbon, and the small craft for blockade. The Portuense and Villà Flor required repair; the two corvettes replaced them. Captain Charles Napier and an English crew were placed in the Sibyl (now the Eliza); and the Isabel Maria was commanded and manned by Portuguese. The officers who joined the Queen's party at Oporto were, of course, employed in preference to any others.

Great objections were made to the late captain of the Martin Freitas, whom I had appointed, in the hour of need, to the Rainha; he had given offence to the Emperor, and I was obliged to replace him by Commodore Bernardine, and refit the ship for temporary service. The Don John, which I intended for the permanent flag-ship, was ordered to be arranged in the same manner as an English ship of the line, and got ready for permanent service; and the corvette on the stocks to be finished forthwith. This employed the whole of the arsenal establishment, who were certainly neither the best nor the most industrious artizans.

The former defect is accounted for by the system

of allowing an immense number of apprentices in the different trades, who are not obliged to find tools; and after playing about, sleeping, and pilfering for a certain number of years, are admitted as workmen. The latter fault was owing to the irregularity of the payments. They had now been many months in arrear, and they proportioned their labour to their pay. I found it necessary to pass over for the present those arrears, and begin a fresh score from the date of the occupation of Lisbon. I promised them regular pay, and I exacted regular work or their dismissal from the arsenal. Under the old system they worked when they liked; some came three, some four, some five days in the week: half-days were also admitted, which led to all sorts of abuse. Fellows would be found sleeping about in all directions, and if detected, it was probable they did not work that day, or, at all events, said so. The system of mustering led also to every species of irregularity: those present were checked, and the absentees left blank, so that the clerks could introduce their names at pleasure, and in all probability went shares with the absentees. I am much inclined to think this was the case from the great opposition I met with in changing it. A table, signed by the inspector, was presented to the major-general every morning, of the number of men at work and where employed; but though this was the neatest thing possible (the Portuguese are famous for making out tables), it did not contain one word of truth; and myself and all the department laboured for full three months before we could obtain a correct statement. I could not have believed it possible that such a strong fight on the part of the inferior clerks could have been made to preserve the old system; and except my own officers, who I must do the justice of saying were indefatigable in their labours to assist me, I met with obstacles at every step I took, both from the superior and inferior departments.

Appendix, XXIV. Proclamations were now issued by the Dukes of Palmella and Terceira, and orders given by the latter to unite the old corps in their former quarters; but nothing further was done for the defence of the city, and I looked forward with great anxiety for the arrival of the Emperor, whose activity in constructing the lines of defence at Oporto led me to hope he would be equally active in the capital. In the evening the news of the defeat of Bourmont before Oporto added greatly to our joy, as considerable apprehensions were entertained that he might succeed in penetrating the lines.

It appeared by the correspondence of Saraiva to the Viscount Santarem, that great exertions had been making in London by the friends of Don Miguel to support his cause, and the very people who were crying out against interference were doing all in their power to assist him. Captain Elliot, of the Royal Navy, had been in Lisbon, and made arrangements with Don Miguel's ministers to assume the command of his fleet, and had actually embarked on board the United Kingdom, five hundred seamen and a host of officers, accompanied by bands of music, &c. to keep up their spirits on the passage; and promises had been made that the fleet should not sail till his arrival. The government, however, trusting in their strength, very naturally sent the squadron out, to prevent us, if possible, from carrying all before us in the Algarves; and the 5th of July saved him and his officers the reproach of coming out to fight their own countrymen—and the disgrace of a defeat, which, in all probability, they would have met with, for it is not to be supposed that the junction of English officers and men with Portuguese, unacquainted with each other's language and customs, could have constituted a force sufficiently fit to take the sea in less than a month or six weeks, and the nature of the service they were on would not have allowed them as many hours. Be that as it may, the news arrived in London the day previous to that appointed for their sailing, and their cruise finished at Gravesend instead of in the Castle of St. George.

Marshal Bourmont and a numerous staff had sailed previous to this, and fell in with the Britannia off Viana, carrying the news of the defeat of the fleet. Nevertheless he pursued his course, landed at Villa de Conde on the 12th, and joined Don Miguel's army the 13th. He immediately endeavoured, and partially succeeded, in discontinuing the cruel system of firing into the town, which had long been found to be useless, as far as intimidation went; on the contrary, it had made the inhabitants warriors, and determined them to defend it to the last extremity. Colonel Sorrel, the British consul, had before this represented to the Count St. Lorenzo the total inutility of firing into the town, and recommended a cessation of hostilities of that nature until the fate of the expedition was known. This, however, was not attended to: he also notified the probability that a larger naval force might be sent into the Douro, which was strongly objected to by the Miguelite general.

On the 15th the Lordella was reconnoitred, and considerable apprehensions were entertained for the safety of the town. The Miguelite force was now commanded by an able general, assisted by numerous French officers; and it was not probable that the same miserable system, which had so long marked the incapacity of the Miguelite general, would be persisted in.

Colonel Badcock and the British consul recommended the English church and its vicinity as a fit place of security for their countrymen, as it was not probable that much favour would be shewn to them in the confusion of an assault; but there was little or no union amongst them, and each family trusted to the protection of their own houses. On the 14th the Miguelites reconnoitred in various directions; there was very little firing, but troops were seen passing over to the north. From that time to the 25th both parties were fully employed, Don Pedro in preparing for defence, and Don Miguel for attack. The disparity of force was so great, that, according to every rule of war, Oporto ought to have fallen; but, according to every other rule, it was defended, and defended with success.

At daylight, on the morning of the 25th, the Miguelites attacked the Lordello and the Quinta of Vanzeller in great force. In the former place they met Colonel Shaw's Scotch; they had leapt a stone wall, and were pushing forward to gain the road in gallant style, when their commander, a French officer, was killed, and they were beaten. The infantry, after driving the Pedroites from a work, were also repulsed, and the work retaken. The attack at the Quinta Vanzeller was most vigorous, and though repulsed, they again and again renewed their attacks, and again were beaten back with great loss. Bomfim was attacked at nine by a strong column, who reached the entrance of the place; but Saldanha, putting himself at the head of his staff and a troop of lancers, vigorously attacked the column, and drove them back with great slaughter. The firing continued on both sides till two, when Bourmont gave it up as a bad job, and withdrew his troops.

In this attack Don Pedro lost between three and four hundred men, and many brave officers: amongst them were Alexander Almaida, one of Saldanha's aid-de-camps, and Colonel Cotter, of the Irish, and his brother-in-law. The Miguelites lost between one thousand and fifteen hundred men.

The failure of this attack must be attributed to the great dislike the Miguelite troops had to attack intrenchments. The heads of the columns, instead of keeping firm and filling up the spaces, become vacant by the killed and wounded, and, marching boldly up, invariably broke into skirmishing parties, securing themselves as well as the nature of the ground would allow, thereby exposed to a desultory fire, probably from its duration more destructive than the bolder and more decided attack of the bayonet would have entailed upon them. During this action there was no confusion in the town; every body capable of bearing arms was in the lines: even the women displayed great firmness, and in many cases were seen carrying water and ammunition to the troops.

CHAPTER XIV.

On the night of the 26th the news of the occupation of Lisbon arrived at Oporto; next day the Emperor reviewed his troops, and communicated his intention of proceeding to the capital. He was well received by the soldiers; indeed I should say his kindness and affability made him a great favourite with the army. After dark he embarked with his staff, minister, &c. and got safe on board the William IVth, leaving Saldanha to command the army at Oporto. Next day he arrived in Lisbon, where he was received with the greatest enthusiasm. The moment the salutes from St. Julian and the Bougie announced his approach, the news spread rapidly through the town; every vessel and boat was put in requisition; and before the steamer with the royal standard had passed Belem, the now peaceful waters of the Tagus bore on their surface all the beauty and fashion of Lisbon, decked out in blue and white colours, hastening to meet and welcome the Emperor to the capital of his ancestors. It was indeed a brilliant sight, and what with rockets, fireworks, and salutes from the batteries and ships, there was more powder burnt than would have fought a general action.

I was the first on board, and was met on the gangway by the Emperor, who fairly pulled me out of the boat, and embraced me in the warmest Portuguese fashion. He repeatedly thanked me for the services I had performed, and very flatteringly gave me the credit of having placed the Queen on the throne.

This meeting was very different from the first I had with him. He was frank and kind, and I ever found him so to the day of his death. He begged me to speak always openly to him, and he would do the same by me, and I never had reason to think he deceived me. I was complimented afterwards by the ministers and his personal staff in the most flattering manner; they all seemed rejoiced at having at last got out of Oporto, and no doubt were longing to find themselves comfortably fixed in their homes and offices, where they could actually play the game of minister, which they had been so long rehearsing at Oporto.

Shortly after I got on board, the Dukes of Palmella and Terceira arrived, and were also warmly received by the Emperor, who embraced them and thanked them for their eminent services. Sir William Parker and the captains of the British men-of-war came next, and were treated with great attention.

When the steamer got abreast of the arsenal, the Emperor and his principal officers accompanied me on board the Don John, and were received by the gallant crew with three hearty cheers. The commodore was still confined to the cabin by his wounds: to him and to all the officers and through me to the crews, he returned thanks for their brilliant conduct, and repeatedly acknowledged that the Queen owed her throne to the squadron.

From the Don John he proceeded to the arsenal, which was crowded to excess; and no king or emperor ever met so warm a reception. It is in vain to talk of Lisbon having been attached to Don Miguel: the people's feelings had been stifled for some years, and they burst forth like a volcano. The Emperor in his joy drew, and, I believe, threw away his sword, thinking he should have no further occasion for it; nor in all probability would he had he been blessed with good advisers: but this we shall examine into in its proper place.

The crowd in the arsenal was so great that to move out was impossible, and the Emperor was glad to take refuge in one of the store-houses till horses could be procured to carry him through the town. This delay gave an opportunity of collecting a few cavalry and soldiers to keep the arsenal and the adjoining streets sufficiently clear to allow the cortege to proceed. As soon as horses could be procured, the Emperor, accompanied by the Duke of Terceira, myself, his aid-de-camp, and as many as could procure conveyances, proceeded through all the principal streets of Lisbon, amidst the acclamations of a numerous and delighted population. The windows were adorned with flags and the most ornamental carpets and coverlids that the houses afforded ; and there was no want of white handkerchiefs in the hands of the fair sex to welcome his arrival. After visiting the Necessidades, he proceeded to the magnificent palace of the Ajuda, which was still unfinished, and unfinished it ought to remain as a memento of the folly of Don John commencing such a structure in the small kingdom of Portugal. Had the same money, in addition to what Mafra cost, been expended in making roads and improving the country, Portugal for its size would have been one of the richest nations in Europe.

In the square in front of the Ajuda, were drawn up the gallant troops who had marched from the Algarves and occupied Lisbon. The Emperor, on coming on the parade, clapped spurs to his horse and galloped towards them : they in their turn broke out of their ranks, and flocked round him, and he seemed to take great delight in the affectionate manner they met him. After talking to whoever came first, they fell into line, and he passed them in review, repeatedly thanking them for their gallant conduct.

The Ajuda stands in a most commanding position above the Castle of Belem, and about three miles from Lisbon. The front with the great entrance looks to the city; the north, south, and east fronts are nearly completed. The building is quadrangular, three stories high, having four projecting square towers somewhat higher than the centre building: the two eastern ones only are finished. In the centre is a splendid court, and the apartments are approached by a magnificent staircase. The rooms are large and well proportioned, but badly furnished; they command beautiful views of the river, sea, and city. There are no good paintings in this palace: those in fresco on the walls are complete daubs, and Don John is represented in various places in all his native ugliness: the painter certainly cannot be accused of flattering him.

After slightly inspecting the palace, the Emperor proceeded to the chapel and heard high mass: it was performed by one of the inferior clergy; the services of the Patriarch were declined in consequence of his having preached against the rights of Donna Maria.

I had the honour of being placed in the Emperor's tribune, and on his right hand. The minister, generals, and the other officers, with the exception of two aid-de-camps behind his chair, were in the body of the church. This was a great compliment to me, but the same attention ought to have been shewn to the Dukes of Terceira and Palmella. During the service he made several remarks on the ceremonies, and asked whether I did not think a man might be a good Catholic and a good Christian without so much mummery. He was certainly a very religious man, but no bigot, as he has clearly proved by the reform he carried through in the church.

After the ceremony the Emperor returned to Lisbon, and took up his quarters at the Palace of the Bemposta. Next day he held a court, which was numerously attended. Few of the nobility appeared, as they had not as yet ascertained how they would be received. In the evening I dined with the Emperor and met the ministers, the Dukes of Palmella and Terceira, and the principal people of his court. The following day the Duke of Palmella was relieved from his authority by a Carta Regia. I have already stated that the policy of Palmella was conciliation, and the Miguelite party had a considerable degree of confidence in his character, and none whatever in the Emperor's ministers. They considered the war at an end, and conciliation unnecessary. Many of the nobility who remained in Lisbon, were desirous of paying their respects to the Emperor, and Lord William Russell, who was most anxious for kind measures, enquired of the minister for foreign affairs how they were likely to be treated. He recommended them not to appear, and many of those noblemen, naturally distrusting the government, left Lisbon and joined Don Miguel.

Now I am satisfied, had the Emperor given them a kind reception, taken them by the hand, excused their conduct on account of the difficulties of their situation, and the impossibility of abandoning their families and properties during the usurpation, it would have tended much to restore confidence; but the contrary line of conduct was followed. Decrees came out, depriving people of the places they had been appointed to during the usurpation, and replacing all those who had been superseded; thus creating a general confusion in every department of the state because it extended to the lowest and most subordinate offices. That it was necessary to purge the offices of dangerous men, there cannot be a doubt; but it ought to have been done with caution and judgment, and left to the officers at the head of each department, and not at one sweep send whole families into a state of starvation. Many had risen in their places by seniority without having any political bias; and others were constitutionalists; those who remained in their situations during the usurpation were not meddled with, although they were surely as criminal as those appointed by the usurping government. Had the ministers been endowed with the least common sense and prudence, they must have seen the impossibility of several thousands of clerks refusing posts during an usurpation of five years having probably no means of subsistence.

In addition to this, all naval and military officers promoted by Don Miguel were degraded, and in the most ungracious manner. This might be just; but when there was an army of thirty thousand men in the field, besides militia and royalist volunteers, opposed to Don Pedro, it was impolitic and unnecessary. Those arrangements ought to have been left till the end of the war, and every encouragement held out to men to abandon the standard of the usurper.

It is true the Emperor had a difficult game to play, as his officers would not submit to serve under those of Don Miguel; but they might have been promoted without degrading the others, which would have satisfied both parties. But all this was unheeded by the Queen's ministers. Paper, pen, and ink were rife, and their inclinations were willing. Bouyed up with success, they thought the war at an end, and conciliation useless.

Palmella and myself had urged Admiral Parker to land the British marines for the protection of the town; the British merchants had also petitioned for protection under the plea that it had been abandoned by the Miguelite government carrying off the whole of the police, and in the event of an attack their lives and properties would be endangered. We of course were all anxious to commit the English government, and the admiral was as anxious to avoid doing so, unless circumstances authorized it, which he was of opinion was not the present case. The Emperor and his ministers, however, fancied the victory their own, and were displeased at the very mention of foreign assistance.

In the marine department I did every thing in my power to soften the decree: it was inexecutable and dangerous, and the officers with few exceptions were reappointed in a few days. In one instance the minister succeeded in outwitting me by the most unjustifiable means ever adopted by any government. The director of the marine unaccountability had been in office many years. He was a respectable old man, and I had never heard of his entertaining any violent political feelings. His place was wanted, and as I had reinstated him in office, it was necessary to concoct a plan to get rid of him. This was easily managed. A barber was found to swear he was engaged in a plot against the life of the Emperor. On this information two files of foreign soldiers were sent to the inspector's office without consulting me or the minister of marine (as he said), and he was conducted to prison, and his place filled up. I remonstrated with the minister of marine and justice on the cruelty and indecency of this proceeding, but the latter assured me that the proofs were so strong it was impossible to act otherwise: but that if his accuser did not make good his charges, he should be sent to Cape Verd. The old man remained in prison about three weeks, had a sort of trial, and was acquitted for want of proof; but nothing was done to his accuser. He lost his place, returned to the arsenal as a clerk, and shortly after died. I mention this as a fact that came under my own observation, and I have no doubt many similar cases occurred.

The Pope's Nuncio was recommended to quit the kingdom, and a ship of war was offered to convey him. The patriarch was ordered not to appear at the palace, and the Jesuits were sent out of Portugal. The English judge conservator was removed, but reinstated on a remonstrance from Mr. Hopner, and Madame Juramenha was sent to a convent and shortly after released. Precipitation and want of thought was the order of the day as far as administration went: imbecility and procrastination were conspicuous in military preparations.

The occupation of the capital made no impression on the country. Santarem alone declared for the Queen, and the towns through which the Duke of Terceira had passed were again occupied by the Miguelites. Forty-two prisoners were murdered at Estremos; and had the governor of Elvas not sent away the royalist volunteers, the prisoners there would have shared the same fate. All was quiet in Lisbon, but every thing without indicated a long and bloody civil war.

The cholera, which had been raging in Lisbon, Setubal, Coimbra, and Leiria, considerably subsided after the occupation by the Queen's troops, and shortly after entirely disappeared; while, on the other hand, it broke out in the Algarves, and carried off many thousands: that unfortunate province was likewise overrun by guerillas, and little respect was paid to property or persons whatever were their political opinions.

On the 7th of August Colonel Guyot, a French officer, arrived from France with orders to protest against Marshal Bourmont and the French officers being employed on Don Miguel's service, but no attention was paid to his remonstrance.

It will naturally be supposed that as the government were so active in creating internal enemies, they would have been equally active in making preparations to resist external ones, who might be expected shortly at Lisbon. This, however, never entered their heads. The minister of finance was certainly most active in raising money, and did wonders; but the minister-at-war never contemplated the possibility of the Miguelites marching on the capital; and he contented himself with issuing out decrees for the formation of moveable and fixed battalions. All persons from the age of eighteen to fifty, with few exceptions, were obliged to join those battalions; the young unmarried men formed the moveable, and the married men the fixed. The government found arms and rations; they clothed themselves.

The artizans of the naval and military arsenals and public works were also formed into battalions;

and it is astonishing what progress they made in the drill, and with how much good-will they submitted to it. This was the extent of the exertions of the minister-at-war; no other proposition was made to meet the enemy. As for lines of defence, though a plan had been submitted to the government the very day they arrived, they were never thought of; and they seemed determined to lose Lisbon with the same facility we got it.

Officers were much wanted in the new regiments; many had arrived from Oporto, and others were appointed from amongst those who had been confined and persecuted by Don Miguel; but whether they had been worn out by confinement, or had never been good for any thing, in few instances could they be compared to those of the liberating army. Arms were wanted, as were clothing and horses; and much time was lost in sending for, and much time lost in procuring them. Orders were sent to England and Belgium to enlist men for the British and Belgian regiments, and, I fear not much to the credit of the agents employed, not the best description were picked up, and abundance of promises made which were never kept. Young gentlemen were fairly kidnapped with the offer of commissions by people who had no authority to give them; and on their arrival in Lisbon, instead of finding themselves officers, they had the choice of carrying a musket and a pack, or of returning to England, in many instances without having the means of doing so.

Had a bounty of four or five moidores been offered, I am of opinion that abundance of native troops would have been raised for the regiments of the line, much more efficient than the moveable and fixed battalions. That sum would also have brought many from the opposite party, who were both badly fed and badly paid, and who would have been superior to the description of men and boys brought from England, Ireland, Scotland, France, and Belgium, who were generally unruly, addicted to drinking, averse to discipline, and clamorous for pay, which was rarely forthcoming.

After the attack of the 25th on Oporto, and the news of the capture of Lisbon was known in the Miguelite army, it was supposed that many deserters would have come in, but in this we were mistaken. They showed no disposition, however, to renew the attack, and contented themselves with occasionally firing into the town. Here the Miguelites committed a great error; they ought either to have marched to Lisbon immediately, where they would have found Mr. Freire asleep, or have concentrated the whole of their artillery before the Foz and Serra Convent, which they would have levelled to the ground, and ultimately taken Oporto. This would have required time, but its success was certain, and Don Pedro would have lost his army. Bourmont might then have marched on Lisbon with his whole force; the Emperor's resources would have failed; and he must have finally capitulated. A middle course was pursued after a considerable delay, and Don Miguel lost his crown.

On the 2d of August the guns began to disappear from the Miguelite batteries, and on the 6th their troops were seen to move off, which was confirmed by deserters who now came in in considerable numbers. On the 9th, cattle and provisions of all descriptions entered Oporto, the whole country between Matozinhos and Lordello being free from the enemy. On the 12th General Saldanha occupied the Monte Castro, Ervilha, and Seralva batteries, and convinced himself of the immense strength of the Miguelite lines. In fact Oporto was hemmed in on all sides, and had the plan of attacking either from the north or south been adopted, instead of sending a force to the Algarves, the army of Don Pedro would have been defeated and Oporto taken.

On the 16th of August the Conde D'Almer, who had been left in command at Villa Nova, having failed in making arrangements with Saldanha relative to the wines, set fire to the stores, and destroyed about twenty thousand pipes of port wine. Captain Glascock landed with a party of seamen, and fortunately saved from destruction the British stores.

Badcock's Rough Leaves.

On the 18th General Saldanha moved out from Oporto, and drove the enemy from their positions on the north of the Douro, and made many prisoners. On the 19th vessels entered the river, and on the 20th the Miguelites retired from Villa Nova, leaving Oporto free after a siege of eleven months, in which the Queen's party lost sixteen thousand souls, including seven thousand troops, — a siege that, with an enterprizing enemy, ought not to have lasted eleven days.

So little apprehension was entertained by the Emperor or his ministers of the approach of the Miguelites, that Mendizabal had been sent home to bring out the Queen and Empress. Admiral Parker made an offer of a frigate for that purpose, which was declined, with many thanks by the Emperor for his attention: but a British steam-ship-of-war was requested might convoy the Queen, who was herself to embark in an English steam-boat fitted up for the purpose, and bearing the constitutional flag of Portugal.

On the 11th of August I received a communication from Lord William Russell, that Bourmont was in full march on Lisbon, having left from eight to ten thousand men to watch Oporto and cover Braga. The advanced corp consisted of five thousand men, composed of their best troops, in which were placed upwards of one hundred French officers.

They were followed by eight thousand more, commanded by Gaspar Texeira. This intelligence ought to have been known to the minister-at-war, who should also have been acquainted with the force of the Duke of Cadaval and Mollelos's troops; but still no order was given to fortify Lisbon.

On the 12th I rode round the ancient defences of the town, waited on the minister, and pointed out the absolute necessity of beginning the fortifications, and offered to superintend them myself. At the same time I wrote a strong letter to the Emperor, pointing out the situation he was in, and calling upon him to save Lisbon by the same activity he had displayed at Oporto. I had before applied to Admiral Parker to land the marines for the protection of the town, in which I was supported by Lord William before he was minister, but his task was difficult; he was tied down to strict neutrality; but such scenes had been acted in the defenceless towns in the Algarves by the Miguelite party, that he at last consented, for the protection of the English, to land at St. Julian's and

Fort St. George, after the enemy had passed Leiria, provided the ministers requested it; and he could perceive they were exerting themselves for their own defence. This I communicated to the minister-at-war, and to my astonishment thanks were not even tendered for his assistance; and the enemy had absolutely passed Coimbra before a spade had been put into the ground. Who was to blame for this apathy it is difficult to say; but it is evident the minister-at-war ought to have known of the approach of Bourmont, and have given directions for the fortifications; but I verily believe he knew as little of the movements of the marshal as the Duke of Cadaval had known of Terceira's.

Next morning the Emperor came to the arsenal, and assured me he had begun the works of defence, and that he would himself attend till they were completed; and he kept his word. From daylight till dark he hardly ever quitted the workmen; and I feel quite convinced, had he not been in Lisbon, his minister would not have awoke until Don Miguel had rapped at the gates of the town, and the Queen's cause would have been lost, by the same indolence that Don Miguel's was, a fortnight before.

CHAPTER XV.

THE fortifications began at Alcantra, where a deep ravine separates Lisbon from Jonqueira. The ground here is strong, and easily fortified, as far as Lourical and St. Sebastian. It then becomes flat to the Pena de Franca; from thence to the Tagus it is again strong. Redoubts were thrown up on all the commanding heights, connected together with breast-works and ditches. The position was not extensive, and when finished and well defended, was not to be forced.

The frigate Rainha, of Portugal, flanked the right of the position; a brig was stationed higher up, and the Liberal at Villa Franca. The Don John was placed below the Necessidades to flank the ravine. The Miguelite Rainha (now Cabo St.

Vicenti) took her station above Belem; and the Don Pedro, (which had returned from Peniché,) below, both ships flanking the approach to that castle, which was an important point, as it commanded the river, and it was necessary either to defend or destroy it. Old Torres, who had so well preserved the Serra at Oporto, was in command here. The Donna Maria was at Sines, and the Isabel Maria at Setuval; the rest of the squadron along the coast, to prevent the introduction of stores and ammunition.

The spirit of insubordination still existed in the fleet. Between the Rainha and Don Pedro's ship's company, (who manned the Dohn John,) there was a great deal of bad blood and jealousy, which arose to such a height that it was impossible to carry on the duty. They were clamorous to be sent home, pretending that they had received promises to that effect. Their wishes were immediately complied with, under the understanding that all pay and prize-money was forfeited. About seventy of the most mutinous gave in their names; the remainder cooled, had time for reflection, and went quietly below.

A transport was ready for the malcontents, and they were sent on board forthwith, many of them heartily repenting of their conduct; but this was no time for trifling, and they had full warning that if they left the transport they should be imprisoned. Of this they were regardless, broke out into open mutiny, threatened to cut the captain's throat if he attempted to take them out of the Tagus, lowered down the boats, went on shore, and committed every excess; were arrested agreeably to my promise, and sent to Fort St. George, where a regimen of bread and water brought them to their senses, and they were shortly shipped off for England.

From that moment every thing settled down quiet in the Don John. The commodore became sufficiently well to do his duty, and in a short time she was as well-disciplined as any ship in the British Navy. Seamen, like boys, when left to themselves, soon run wild, and are capable of going to any excess; but, provided severity is tempered with justice, they are easily subdued, and become sensible of their folly, and soon discover that there is more happiness and comfort in a well-disciplined ship than a privateer, and I had an opportunity of observing that a few severe examples are much better than the niggling punishments now in practice in the British service; and if our naval rulers would hold out more encouragement to the petty officers, by giving the first class double the seaman's pay, and the second class one-half more, they would soon find that such a system would tend more to abolish corporal punishment, and preserve discipline, than any means that have been as yet adopted.

On the 14th a steamer brought the welcome intelligence of the recognition of the Queen, at the same time accrediting Lord William Russell as minister; but this was done with so much caution, that it was only on condition that her affairs continued prosperous. The next day was appointed for his reception, it being the Queen's name day. Lord William was well received, and the Emperor expressed himself much satisfied with the early recognition of his daughter by his oldest ally.

The decree for the summoning the Cortes for the 1st of October also appeared on this day.

Nothing could shew the state of ignorance in which ministers were, with regard to the feelings of the country, than issuing this decree. Did they expect the war to finish before the 1st of October? Did they still believe that Bourmont was not marching on the capital? Or did they think Don Miguel was coming to lay down his arms? They must have believed either one or the other, or they never could have issued a decree which every one saw could not be put in force, and knew they would afterwards be obliged to rescind.

The appointment of Lord William as minister was much approved of; he had been some time in Lisbon watching the movements of the Spaniards, and was well known to be a friend to the cause of liberty. His name alone was a sufficient guarantee for his principles; Lady William was supposed to lean the other way, and for no better reason than because she afforded occasional protection to a Miguelite, who fancied himself in danger; but be it remembered, when Miguel's party ruled in Lisbon with an iron sceptre, and that red-hot, her house was always open for the protection of the unfortunate constitutionalists.

Admiral Parker was also looked upon with suspicious eyes, because, although decidedly in favour of the Queen, he was scrupulously neutral in his conduct; no man could have better maintained the dignity of a British admiral, or conducted himself with more propriety; and I am happy to be able to bear witness to this fact, and to state that during the whole time he commanded in Lisbon we were on the best of terms.

Lord William, being now in an official capacity, was entitled to give advice. Old Candido expected interference, and was prepared to resist. Advice he was willing to receive, but, I much fear, not to follow. Lord William was favourable to the Palmella party, and to conciliation, which was always promised, but never performed. The Emperor's ministers had committed so many errors in former times, that they inspired little confidence; they were not liked by the Queen's party, and hated, feared, and detested by the Miguelites. When shut up in Oporto, they had promised indemnity to the Queen's friends at the expense of their opponents, and still they expected the country would be in their favour. They had abolished the tithe (a great part of which went to the state) without substituting another tax, and otherwise alarmed the Church, which they had no power to reform, and still they expected the priests would become constitutional. They were detested by the Miguelite nobility, and took no pains to conciliate the few peers who had sacrificed all, and remained faithful to the Queen. They degraded the Miguelite officers, yet expected the army to declare in their favour. They issued a decree to confiscate the property of the Miguelites absent from Lisbon, and actually began selling their moveables, which nobody but Jews and brokers would buy. In fact one species of tyranny was substituted for another; there was a change of men, but none of measures; they were rulers of a party, not of a kingdom. One half of Portugal had been confiscated by Don Miguel's ministers, and the other half by Don Pedro's. They thought themselves masters of the kingdom, and took no pains to conciliate.

Those acts satisfied a few hot-headed men, who looked forward to enrich themselves by confiscation; but the sensible men, and those who had lost most by the usurpation, saw the impossibility of pacifying the country by such a system.

Lord William pressed for an amnesty, which was promised on the arrival of the Queen: that of Palmella at Terceira had been already published with the same exceptions, but it had no effect.

As the enemy approached Lisbon the government became alarmed; and on the 19th the minister of foreign affairs officially asked for the armed interference of England, and yet a few weeks before they had taken no advantage of the admiral's offer, and had neglected for three weeks to commence the fortifications. The interference was refused, accompanied with a recommendation to exert themselves.

Don Carlos was still at Coimbra: he had been repeatedly ordered to quit Portugal by the king of Spain, who was in declining health, and now positively refused. The Princess de Beira, a clever woman, exercised much influence over both Carlos and Miguel. The Portuguese government were most anxious to get the whole of Carlos's family

IN PORTUGAL. 279

out of the kingdom. An English frigate was in consequence offered to convey him to Italy, which he declined. Don Pedro was much dissatisfied with the Spanish ministry not withdrawing their minister from Miguel's court. He however refrained from remonstrating, in hopes England would insist on his being withdrawn.

A Spanish courier, with a passport from Cordova, on coming into Lisbon was detained and his despatches seized; against this the Spanish consul remonstrated, and received for answer, that Spain had no right to keep a minister at the usurper's court, and that his passport would not be respected. At the request of Lord William Russell the despatches were given up, with an intimation that no more couriers would be permitted to enter Lisbon when in a state of siege.

The Spanish government was much offended at this, as well as the detention of another courier named Texugo; he had been a notorious spy, and now passed for Sir John Campbell's secretary; both were taken in the Queen, an English vessel who had broke the blockade at Figueiras, and were sent to the castle of St. George. Sir

John remonstrated against his seizure and claimed the protection of the English minister. It was quite notorious that he had been with the Miguelite army, and, although not employed, assisted them with his advice, and had now retired, disgusted at the little attention he received from Miguel.

Under those circumstances Lord William declined interfering, and on reference to the British government his conduct was approved of, and Sir John remained a prisoner.

The Spanish government complained to the English minister at Madrid of the seizure of their couriers, and threatened, if instant reparation was not made, to take the matter seriously up, expressing at the same time that they had no wish to quarrel with the Queen's government. The British minister at Madrid took a wrong view of the subject, and thought taking a spy out of an English vessel who had broke the blockade was an insult to England. This minister was not very favourable to the Queen's cause, and rather encouraged the Spanish ministry in making frivolous complaints of her government. This came with a peculiar bad grace from Spain, at the time she had a minister at Miguel's court, and permitted the Madrid gazette to be filled with false accounts of what was passing in Lisbon.

Lord William had requested Mr. Addington to insist on the recal of Cordova, which he declined, not conceiving he had a right so to do, but promised his good offices, and Cordova was finally ordered to watch Carlos, and not accompany Miguel's court.

It is difficult to understand what was the policy of Zea Bermudez at this time. Though Carlos had constantly refused to quit Portugal, and Miguel had taken no steps to compel him, on the contrary had countenanced his remaining, probably foreseeing the death of Ferdinand, and afraid of a constitution in Spain, yet a Spanish minister had till now been kept at his court. Ferdinand, it is very evident, did not like the constitution in Portugal; but he liked the presence of Don Carlos less. Zea Bermudez, on the other hand, was no friend to the Portuguese constitution, which he feared might be imported into Spain on the death of Ferdinand, and probably encouraged Carlos to remain, preferring him and absolutism to a queen, a minor, and a constitution.

On the 10th of August the Miguelite army entered Coimbra and joined the troops who had retired from Lisbon, Bourmont and the French officers were indefatigable in reorganizing the army, which was ill-appointed, but nevertheless enthusiastic in Miguel's cause; and it was not before the 14th he could put his troops in motion.

Count San Lorenzo had been dismissed from the office of minister-at-war, and Bourmont filled that office as well as commander-in-chief; but about this time San Lorenzo again received the portfolio.

The army was divided into three columns. The first, under De Larochejaquelin, was directed on Abrantes, there to pass the Tagus, and occupy Salvatierra; the second, under General Lemos, marched direct on Santarem. Don Miguel accompanied the marshal with the third column, who marched on Leiria. The three columns consisted of from fourteen to fifteen thousand men. The troops were ill off for shoes, and were obliged to halt two days at Leiria and three at Caldas.

On the 21st of August the Duke of Terceira marched with a division of from four to five thousand men on Villa Franca, where the Liberal schooner was anchored. On the 25th General Saldanha arrived from Oporto. He had little confidence in the activity of the ministers, and thought it advisable to leave the command at Oporto in the hands of Sir Thomas Stubbs, to act upon the defensive, and proceed at once to Lisbon without waiting for leave; and fortunate it was he took such a decided step; for although the Emperor was extremely active, he required the head of his staff at his elbow, and I know he was delighted to see him, as were the generality of the people in Lisbon.

Saldanha, at one time, was no favourite with the Emperor, but he soon found out his merits, and I believe gave him all his confidence. He also liked the Duke of Terceira, but was jealous of the glory he had acquired by his rapid march, and rather appeared to keep him in the back-ground; at least I have every reason to believe so, for certainly, after the Emperor's arrival in Lisbon, the Duke had little power, and only the command of his own division.

Terceira was a good unobtrusive man; when sent on service, no one would perform it better, as he often proved; but he was not a person likely to push himself into notice; and both he and the Duke of Palmella repeatedly told me, when I spoke to them on the subject of fortifying Lisbon, that they had no power since the arrival of the Emperor and his ministers. The position of Saldanha was different; he was chief of the Emperor's staff, and could direct every thing in his name without exciting jealousy.

He took up his quarters in a large house above the Quinta of Lourecal, from whence he could view the whole position. The fortifications went on with great activity, as well as the organizing and disciplining the new levies, who were divided, as I have already stated, into moveable and fixed battalions. As the enemy approached Lisbon, considerable reinforcements arrived from Oporto; amongst them were Bacon's lancers, two hundred and fifty strong, the fifth caçadores, and ninth and fifteenth of the line. Two additional squadrons of cavalry had been formed from deserters, and infantry soldiers who could ride; but there was much difficulty in mounting them Requisitions had been made in Lisbon for both horses and mules, but many were sheltered by the

English, who took them under their protection. Men escaped the levies by the same means.

The situation of the Queen's party at this time would have excused setting momentarily aside many of their privileges; but they had been so long accustomed to their abuse under all circumstances, that it would have been considered next to robbery; and as the generality were not particularly favourable to the Queen's cause, a great outcry would have been made.

I, however, strongly recommended the Emperor to prevent the abuse of privileges, and requested him to make me inspector of horses and mules for twenty-four hours, and order them all to be paraded in Black-horse Square without any distinction. I should then have requested the English to point out their own horses on their word of honour, and the rest should have been sent to the depôt. This would have had the desired effect; for although the English from good-nature might have lent their names to protect the horse of a friend without reflecting on the consequences, they would never have publicly given protection to horses not *bonâ fide* their own property. The

Emperor, however, felt delicate about any interference; my advice was not followed, and we were in consequence badly off for cavalry.

During the time the enemy were marching on Lisbon, priests and friars were not idle in stirring the people up to arms: large Guerilla parties were forming in the Alemtejo and the Algarves under the command of a notorious brigand, Ramochin, who drove the small detachment of the Queen's troops out of Mertola, Villa Real, and Castel Marino; and finally obliged them to retreat to Faro. The Audaz brig and gun-boats also quitted the Guadiana: these disasters were followed by the abandonment of all our posts in the Algarves with the exception of Faro and Lagos.

I had collected together about five hundred English and Portuguese marines with the intention of seizing Figueiras, when despatches were received from the governor of the latter place, demanding immediate assistance. The steam was already up to proceed to Peniché: her destination was changed to the Algarves, and she arrived in time to save Lagos from capture. The guerillas were driven from before the town, and about two hundred Portuguese marines were left in garrison.

On the 30th the Duke of Terceira retired from Villa Franca, the enemy having made their appearance in force. The Liberal schooner was withdrawn, and the troops occupied their different positions in the lines, bristled with upwards of one hundred pieces of artillery. Saldanha was on the left; the Duke of Terceira on the right; and the Emperor commanded the whole.

A few days before the enemy appeared, I ascertained that the greater part of the guns on the Tagus as far as Cascaes were still mounted. I had repeatedly urged the minister-at-war to have them removed, and it is probable he had given orders to that effect; but no one looked to their execution, and they remained in *statu quo*. It was now too late to remove the guns, but the boats of the squadron brought away the carriages, thus depriving the Miguelites of the means of besieging St. Julian's and Belem, and of strengthening the positions they would occupy in front of our lines.*

* When the Emperor landed in Portugal, Santa Martha left guns enough in Oporto to arm the lines.

On the 3d the enemy appeared before Lisbon, and occupied Campo Grande, Campo Pequeno, and the adjacent villages. The Miguelite flag was seen flying in all directions, and the water was cut off, which caused much inconvenience, although arrangements had been made to receive a supply from the south.

The force of the Queen's troops was about eight thousand, including five hundred cavalry, as many artillery, and about the same number of moveable and fixed battalions. The lines were not finished, and in many places much exposed. The three weeks of idleness was now felt.

There were upwards of one hundred pieces of cannon mounted. The force returned by the minister-at-war was twenty-nine thousand three hundred and seventy-seven, and one hundred and eighty guns; but that was on paper, and probably exaggerated to make the Cortes believe he had been most active in his exertions for the cause; but Marshal Saldanha, I am certain, did not bring half that number equipped into the lines.

On the morning of the 5th General Bourmont, having made his dispositions, pushed forward his light troops from the Quinta Lourical close up to the redoubt which commanded it, not far from the aqueduct; taking advantage of a wall which ran from the Quinta to the angle of the redoubt, and by some unaccountable neglect had been left standing, together with many houses in the neighbourhood, probably from a desire to injure the proprietors as little as possible. From those houses, and wall, a very destructive fire was kept up for several hours on the redoubts, as far as St. Sebastian, where stands a house at an angle where two roads meet leading into Lisbon. From the Quinta of Lourical an avenue of trees led up to the redoubt before mentioned.

About seven o'clock a strong column, well covered by light troops, pushed up this avenue to the right of the redoubt with great courage, were met and overthrown by the fifth caçadores, who followed them down the hill to the very Quinta itself, inflicting on them a heavy loss. Don Thomas Mascarenhas was killed, the Duke of Terceira had a horse shot under him; and the poor Marquis of St. Iria lost a son, being the second killed in this war. The Emperor had a narrow escape a little before the attack from a cannon-ball, which killed a man close to him. The loss of the caçadores was not heavy in driving the enemy, but many were killed and wounded in the redoubts. I never saw a heavier fire than was kept up on St. Sebastian: the house was completely covered with round, grape, and musketry: and the approach through the court-gate to the garden where the battery stood, was just as hot as any amateur could wish it. Here I think General Bourmont should have made a simultaneous attack. Two roads led from the enemy's lines on each side of St. Sebastian's, meeting in a broad street. On each of those roads should have been placed a strong column between stone walls. Another column should have advanced in the open space in front: they would have probably broken into skirmishing parties, as the Miguelite troops generally did; but the other two being confined, must have either pushed on or remained to be shot in mass, which, if well led, would not have been the case, and, in all probability, they would have entered the town.

It may be presumptuous in my giving an opinion on military matters, but I should always prefer leading soldiers boldly up to an attack, than through a cover; for they in general dislike as much leaving it to come under a shower of musketry, as people in civil life do to leave a portico and get into a shower of rain.

About two the enemy made dispositions for a second attack, and collected a strong column in a field to the left of Lourical. In the redoubt in which I was, we had neither powder nor shot, and the guns were very imperfectly manned ; and had they pushed boldly up and kept steady in column, it is more than probable they would have forced that part of the line ; but this the Miguelite troops never did ; they invariably, when under a sharp fire, broke their ranks and spread out as caçadores.

After remaining a short time in column they were withdrawn, and in half an hour a squadron of cavalry, led by Louis Rochejaquelin, made a desperate attempt to gallop into the redoubt under cover of the wall I have already mentioned. Their gallant leader, who deserved a better fate, was killed close to the ditch, where many men and horses fell, and the rest retreated in confusion. A party of fifteen or sixteen came by mistake on the wrong side of the wall close up to the redoubt; and though a heavy fire was opened on them, they only left two men and horses behind.

It is difficult to conceive the object of this daring enterprize. They were not supported by infantry; and had they succeeded in entering the battery, they must have been driven back or destroyed before any assistance could have been given them. It is possible that this gallant youth, impatient at the inactivity of the general commanding the column, had rushed up either to ascertain the nature of the defence, or, if he succeeded in entering, to strike a panic into our troops, and preserve it till he received succour. Such things have succeeded before; and in armies there are always aspiring spirits who will risk every thing to obtain renown; and in most instances their valour is crowned with success. Here the brave youth perished in a foreign land, and lies in a common grave with others, without even a monument to record his gallant bearing.

The firing from behind the wall and the redoubts lasted till dark; but no further attack was made by the enemy. In the night they were driven from behind the covering, which was razed with the ground. Our loss in this affair was from three to four hundred men; that of the enemy could not have been less than a thousand.

Next morning the ground occupied by the Miguelites previous to the attack, was taken possession of by the Queen's troops, and the adjacent houses, which had much annoyed the lines the day before, were destroyed. For several days after, there was occasional skirmishing and moving about troops; but no further attack took place, unless the reconnaisance of the 14th could be called one. Indeed, from this time General Bourmont appears to have given up all idea of taking the town by assault, and probably hoped to do it by blockade. To accomplish this required a greater force than he had at his disposal, as supplies could be thrown in both from the south and by sea. Had he got possession of the numerous heavy guns which had been removed from the batteries on the Tagus, he might have possibly possessed himself of St. Julian's and Belem; this would have rendered our situation less pleasant, but could not have prevented supplies being thrown in. In the mean time the new levies were getting into a better state of discipline, and were rapidly increasing; and an expedition of three or four hundred men, under Captain Ruxton and Colonel Raboca, were sent to Samora to bring over a quantity of forage and grain in store there and at Benevento. A strong detachment of militia was surprised and driven from thence, a good many killed and wounded, eleven or twelve prisoners taken; and several boats brought away with grain. The enemy in their turn surprised our detachment two days after, captured our boats, and drove the troops to Baroca d'Alva; at least they marched there as fast as they could, but without waiting to ascertain the force of their opponents.

At this time several communications went on between Admiral Parker and General Bourmont relative to the protection of British property, and

I took advantage of this circumstance to endeavour to bring about an accommodation with the Miguelite general, but without success. This was winked at by the Emperor, but not authorized; and indeed, as the *sine-qua-non* was the retirement of Don Miguel from Portugal, it was at once refused.

<small>Appendix, No. XXV.</small>

CHAPTER XVI.

On the 21st of September, Marshal Bourmont resigned the command of the army. It is supposed he wished Don Miguel to withdraw the army from before the lines, assemble the Cortes, and change the ministers, to which he would not consent. Desertion also became considerable at this time from the Miguelites, but more went home than came over to the Queen.

Marshal Bourmont was succeeded by a General Macdonell, who had formerly served in Spain. He had arrived a few days before at St. Martinho, in the Lord of the Isles steamer, afterwards captured by a gun-boat fitted out by the governor of Peniche. He was accompanied by several French officers; and Captain Elliott, Don Miguel's admiral, or rather naval adviser. He was still sighing for an opportunity of serving his worthy master's cause. One of his officers, Mr. Luckraft, a master in the navy, had been sent to Castle St. George for holding communication with the Miguelites at Belem. Information had been received of the proceedings of this gentleman, but the proof was not sufficiently strong to arrest him. I therefore determined to have it out of his own mouth, and he was requested to attend at the arsenal; as he had been captured in the Lord of the Isles steamer a few days before, he made no objections to this. I represented to him the danger he had incurred in going to Belem, and observed that, had the Miguelites known it, he would certainly have been hanged as a spy. He fell into the snare and acknowledged he had been frequently there. He was in consequence arrested by the orders of the minister of marine. At this Lord William Russel took fire, and made a strong representation to the Portuguese minister of foreign affairs, observing that such a proceeding struck at the very root of the English privileges. Now I apprehend Lord William was wrong, for it never could have been contemplated by the

Methuen treaty, that in the event of Lisbon being besieged, it should be necessary to consult the judge conservator before a man who had confessed himself to have been in the enemy's camp could be arrested. Be this as it may, he was released a few days after, and sent out of the country, not a little satisfied at his escape. He was under the name of Williamson, and it was not till after his departure that his real name was ascertained, and that he was a master in the navy. Had that circumstance been known, he certainly would have stood a very fair chance of exaltation.

The change of generals made no change in military operations. The Emperor continued to fortify his lines and discipline his troops; the opposite party remained in front of Lisbon without undertaking any enterprise on either bank of the Tagus.

On the 22d, the Queen and Empress arrived in the Tagus in the Soho steamer, bearing the Portuguese colours and standard, escorted by an English steam ship-of-war. Their Majesties had been residing in Paris, watching the progress of events. When the troops in Oporto were reduced to the last extremity, the Emperor had written to the Empress that nothing but a miracle could save them. After the capture of the squadron, he again wrote—" the miracle has been worked, the fleet is taken, and we are safe."

On receiving the Emperor's invitation to come to Lisbon, they proceeded to Havre, where they embarked in a steamer and landed at Portsmouth. Their Majesties were remarkably well received in England, and invited to pass some days at Windsor. Don Pedro was much pleased at the attention of the King of England to his wife and daughter, and highly indignant at the King of France for having ordered the Duke of Leuchtenberg, the Empress's brother, out of the kingdom; he considered it a personal insult to himself, and could not allude to the subject without expressing his indignation.

The moment the signal was made from St. Julian's, Lisbon got into motion; blue and white flags were flying in all directions, and blue and white dresses were generally displayed by the ladies. Boats were put in requisition, and long before the steamer passed Belem, the river was covered.

The Emperor had prepared a magnificent boat of twenty-four oars and forty-eight men painted blue and white, the men dressed in the same manner, in which he embarked at the arsenal with a couple of aid-de-camps and myself to receive the Empress and Queen; and so impatient was he to meet them that he pushed off without either court or ministers. I never saw him so gay or pleased; he got on board a little above Belem, was received at the gangway by the Empress, who embraced and kissed him with great affection. The Queen was much affected, and could not restrain her tears. The little Princess Amelia, his youngest child, occupied much of his attention: she was rather alarmed at the appearance of his beard, and was not very grateful for his caresses. After the first salutation, the Emperor presented me to the Queen and Empress, from both of whom I received much attention and sincere thanks. She expressed her regret that there had not been sufficient accommodation for my family, but they might be expected every day in a steamer who was shortly to follow.

After the steamer anchored, Admiral Parker with his captains and Lord William Russell came on board, and shortly after all the ministers and principal people of Lisbon. The marshal and officers of the army were prevented from coming off, least the enemy should seize that opportunity of attacking the lines. It was arranged that the landing was to take place next day at twelve.

The Empress is above the middle stature, handsome, and extremely pleasant and agreeable; by no means proud, though perfectly acquainted with her station; in fact she is an accomplished lady. The Queen is fair, has a plump and handsome face, about the middle size, and a great deal of *embonpoint*. She was about fifteen, very shy and retired, and said little. Both spoke English: the Empress discoursed with great affability, and seemed highly delighted. About five o'clock, the visitors having retired, dinner was announced. The Emperor handed down the Queen, and at his desire I had the honour of handing the Empress and was invited to dinner; and I do not think I ever saw a more happy party. There was no form or stiffness whatever. The company was small, consisting of the Emperor, Empress, Queen, two ladies of honour, and two or three gentlemen and aid-de-camps. Several toasts were drunk after dinner, and about eight o'clock the party went on deck, took coffee, listened to a very good band, and enjoyed the beautiful evening in that delightful climate.

At ten the Emperor went on shore, and guard-boats were placed round the steamer to prevent any surprise in the night.

Next morning at half-past eleven I went on board the Soho in the Queen's barge: the Emperor, the principal officers of the court, and the minister, were already there. The royal barges, about a dozen in number, were appropriated to carry different persons of the suite, and attend the disembarkation, forming themselves in a line on the starboard quarter of the Queen's barge. Admiral Parker and the captains of the English squadron were on the larboard quarter, and the boats from the

Portuguese squadron took their stations outside of each line. At noon the Queen, accompanied by the Emperor and Empress, the ministers, officers of the court, and myself, shoved off in the state barge. This was the signal for manning yards and for a royal salute from the ships and forts. Innumerable boats, under sail and rowing, floated on the river. The windows of the houses were crowded to excess, as also the different quays, with well-dressed people wearing the Queen's colours. The streets from Black-Horse-square to the cathedral were lined with the fixed battalions, and the army on the lines kept under arms to prevent surprise; the officers were strictly forbid to quit their posts.

At half past twelve the Queen landed in the square, which was announced by another royal salute. There General Saldanha was presented, and on this occasion was made a marshal. She took the Emperor's right arm, the Empress the left, and prompted by the Emperor she called out " Viva la Carta Constitutional !" This was re-echoed by the public, together with cries of " Viva Donna Maria ! The Emperor and the Empress !"

A state carriage was in waiting, which conveyed the royal personages to the cathedral, where Te Deum was sung. This finished, they proceeded to the palace of the Necessidades, followed by an immense concourse of people. No court was held this day, though many kissed the Queen's and Empress's hands. After remaining a few minutes in the palace, the Emperor bowed to the company, who took the hint and retired, leaving the royal party to their own domestic circle.

On the 24th there was a grand review in the lines. The Queen, accompanied by the Emperor and Empress in a carriage and four, passed before the troops, the bands of the different regiments playing the constitutional hymn. The troops looked well, and the sight was altogether imposing. The generals and principal officers were presented on passing. On the 25th a court was held at the Bemposta. The Queen sat on the throne for the first time, the Empress on her left; the Emperor stood below. The company was numerous, and sufficiently brilliant; the show of nobility small; independent of those attached to the court in some way or other, there was only the Count Farobo, myself, and a youngster (whose name I forget). In Portugal the nobility, whether holding official situations or not, have the entrée to the throne-room before the levée begins, and occupy the right of the throne. The rest of the company remain in the other rooms, which are sufficiently large for their accommodation; and there is no necessity to squeeze them in between rails, as is done at St. James's.

At half-past two the door of the throne-room was thrown open, and the diplomatic corps introduced. They were followed by the foreign officers, who paid their respects to the Queen and to their Imperial Majesties. A deputation from Oporto came next; then the municipal body of Lisbon; a deputation from the Wine Company at Oporto, and several other public bodies: after them, officers of both professions, priests and civilians, who have the right of appearing at court.

In the evening I had the honour of dining at the Necessidades with the royal family, where I met the ministers and principal people of the palace. The dinner was plain, and by no means on an expensive scale. The Emperor was a great economist, and looked himself into all the expenses. There was no state at this dinner; indeed it looked much more like a family party than a royal one. The Emperor drank water only, and the wine was far from being good. This was the first and last dinner the Emperor gave after the arrival of the Empress and Queen; indeed he appears to have kept the latter much too back, considering the important post she was destined to fill.

The City of Waterford steamer, with the rest of the Queen's suite, had not made her appearance, and some apprehension was entertained for her safety; and a few days after the Queen's arrival, Saldanha came to my office much agitated, having learnt that she was wrecked on the coast; and his wife and family, with many of the Queen's and Empress's suite, were at St. Martinho, under the protection of a detachment sent from Peniché by the Baron de Sa. The guerillas had paid them a visit, but they were not aware who was in their hands, and Mr. Bell, acting with great presence of mind, convinced them she was an English steam-boat with passengers on board, and by those means they were saved from plunder, and probably from worse treatment. On receiving this intelligence from Saldanha, I took two companies of caçadores on board the Soho, and started in company with an English steamer of war, which Admiral Parker was kind enough to send with me, called at Peniché, took on board the Baron de Sa, and then proceeded to St. Martinho, where we found the Countess Saldanha and family, Madame Mascarenhas, and several of the Queen's and Empress's suite in safety. The greater part of the passengers saved their effects, but all the Emperor's, Empress's, and Queen's carriages and baggage were destroyed. I also lost the effects of my family, and only saved a horse with great difficulty. Two servants, who had charge of my things, amusing themselves gathering grapes, were made prisoners by the guerillas, and conducted to the enemy's quarters, but were immediately released.

After embarking the passengers and baggage, the caçadores were landed and marched to Peniché, and we returned to Lisbon. Poor Madame Mascarenhas had little idea that her husband was no more. Her brother accompanied me in the steamer, and we managed to keep her in ignorance till she got to Lisbon, to her mother, the Marchioness of Ficalho.

On the 2d of October the Superb steamer arrived, with the Marquis of Loulé and her royal highness the Marchioness, the Duchess of Terceira, my family, and the Swedish minister and family. I was in great hopes the Marquis would have resumed the portfolio of minister of marine; but he was so disgusted with the line of conduct of his former colleagues, that he declined having any thing to do with the administration of affairs, and took his station as one of the Emperor's aide-de-camps. The Marquis was an upright, honourable man, and an enemy to persecution; and the Marchioness a most amiable princess, the youngest sister of Don Pedro, very handsome and agreeable, and in private society she threw off the princess entirely and enjoyed herself; but no person knew better than she did how to assume it when necessary, or when she thought she was not treated with the respect due to her rank, and this not unfrequently happened at the Necessidades.

APPENDIX.

APPENDIX.

No. I.

(TRANSLATED COPY.)

RENOWNED INHABITANTS OF THE AZORES!

I HAVE passed more than three months among you, and throughout that time I have been filled with admiration at, and gratitude for, the services you have made, and for the adherence you have shown in behalf of the sacred cause of my August Daughter. I must now leave you: I go, at the head of my brave companions, to put down the usurper, to restore the throne to the Queen Donna Maria the Second, to assert the empire of the law, by establishing the government of the Charter, under the protection of which the Portuguese shall enjoy anew the blessings of union, tranquillity, and justice, of which, by the hands of barbarity and despotism, they have been too long bereft.

I leave you, then, faithful Azorians; but I carry with me a lively remembrance of your loyalty and patriotism. I likewise bear with me the important knowledge of the capabilities of your soil, and the industrious character and enterprising spirit of its inhabitants; and, if whilst here, amidst the difficulties with which the Goverament of Her Most Faithful Majesty has had yet to contend, I have provided, as far as circumstances allowed, for your necessities, you may rest assured, that hereafter, when the development of the projected institutions shall have taken place, the same Government will reckon it as one of its most sacred duties to extend, in a special manner, the protection and benefits of those institutions to this fertile country, and its useful and diligent inhabitants.

Farewell, then, brave Azorians! If a glorious undertaking obliges me to bid you adieu, I carry along with me the certainty that your love of justice, for which you have been ready to sacrifice yourselves, and your adherence to the new institutions, of which you begin already to experience the benefits, will preserve in security and in the full merits of all its acquired renown, this noble archipelago, the classic land of Portuguese loyalty, the illustrious cradle of the regeneration of the mother country.

(Signed)   DOM PEDRO, DUKE OF BRAGANZA.
25th June, 1832.

No. II.

SOLDIERS!

Your afflicted native country calls upon you, and offers to you, in return for your fatigues, your sufferings, and your loyalty, peace, gratitude, and reward.

Full of confidence in the visible protection of the Lord of Hosts, let us go, Soldiers, to finish the noble enterprise we have so gloriously undertaken. We are preceded by the renown of your incomparable courage and undaunted perseverance; we are accompanied by the unshaken love wherewith we have devoted ourselves to the Queen Donna Maria II., and by our enthusiasm for the constitutional Charter. We are followed by the ardent wishes of the suffering Portuguese nation. Europe anxiously attends the decision of the struggle betwixt loyalty and perjury, justice and despotism, liberty and terror. Finally, Soldiers, glory calls upon us to preserve our honour.

Come, then, let us march to the sound of " Long live the Queen, and the Charter, the palladium of Portuguese liberty !"

(Signed)   DOM PEDRO, DUKE OF BRAGANZA.
25th June, 1832.

No. III.

Her Majesty's Ship Donna Maria,
16th September, 1832.

HONOURABLE SIR,

We, the undersigned petty officers, in the name of ourselves and the crew of Her Majesty's Ship, beg leave most respectfully to solicit your interference with the Commander-in-Chief, in respect of redress to a general grievance, which is apparent to every man in the ship, *viz.* that our force is by no means adequate to meet the enemy to any advantage; and running, as we are at present, from any means of assistance, without our knowing to what purpose, is a general cause of discontent. Further, we do sincerely and solemnly protest, that this ship is by no means seaworthy: and in the condition she is in at present, it is at the risk of ourselves to be at sea in her, particularly when it comes to blow but half a gale of wind. That we shall, to the utmost of our power, when called upon, act as Britons ought, against the common enemy; but in the present state of affairs, we most sincerely wish for an explanation as to the course to be pursued.

We remain, Honoured Sir, with respect,
Your obedient Servants,

William Davie, ········ *Captain Forecastle.*
John Dawson, ········ *B. Mate.*
John Ryan, ··········· *Ditto.*
James Marshal, ······ *Quarter Master.*

APPENDIX. 317

William Davies, ······ *Captain Main Top.*
John Wood, ·········· *Quarter Master.*
William Parker, ······ *Captain Fore Top.*
George Mollay,········ *B. Mate.*
Adam Stow, ··········· *Quarter Master.*
William Brown, ······ *Gunner's Mate.*
Hugh Hughes, ········· *B. Mate.*
Joseph Rumble, ······ *Captain Fore Top.*
John Williamson, ······ *B. Mate.*
Alexander Surrey, ···· *Captain Afterguard.*
Thomas Wipshot,······ *Captain Main Top.*
James Palmer, ········· *B. Mate.*
Stephen Merryman,···· *Gunner's Mate.*
William Webb, ········· *Sergeant Marines.*
Patrick Hogan, ······ *Serjeant Marines.*
To Peter Mins, Captain.

Captain Mins, having received a letter from the seamen, stating that the ship was not sea-worthy, and the men dissatisfied, made the following remarks :—

" Whatever may be the opinion of the ship's company with regard to the Admiral's conduct, I will never, while I remain here as captain of this ship, allow any man on earth to question the Admiral's conduct in my presence. If his conduct is blameable, there are officers sufficient to judge whether he does his duty or not, and it is not by men, from whom the Admiral's motives must be necessarily concealed, that his conduct is to be estimated. With regard to the inefficiency of the ship in point of sea-worthiness, I am the responsible person, and on me (if any) the blame must fall. As to our ability for attacking the enemy, I will tell you, so far, that we have such and such ships (naming the number and force) expected by to-morrow night—a force sufficient to crush the enemy at once, which is an object of as much importance to the success of our cause, as the failure or the defeat of our fleet would tend to its complete ruin. The only part of your letter which I can at all approve, is the close, in which you say that whatever may happen, you will still behave with the spirit of Britons; and that I shall not be disappointed in this respect, I am (from your previous conduct) perfectly confident." To the remark in the letter, " That our force is by no means adequate to the enemy;" the Captain answered, " It is not the Admiral's intention to attack the enemy, until our other ships come down from Oporto; and as the steamers and schooners have been despatched for them, we may expect them here, if you keep a good look-out at the mast head, by to-morrow night. As for this ship, I can place so much confidence in her and my men, that by placing her against such a parcel of orange-fed rascals as the *Don John's* crew, I am certain we could knock her to pieces in a very short time."

Remarks made by Davie and Ryan:—" We will go into action with you, Captain Mins, with the greatest coolness; but the Admiral may do as he did last time, take us into action, haul his wind, and leave us to fight it out ourselves."

Another remark made by Surrey :—" I am sorry to say, Captain Mins, that the common seamen of the *Rainha* (flag-ship) knows more about what we are going to do than the captain of this ship."

No. IV.

PROCLAMATION OF GASPAR TEXEIRA.

Soldiers !—The rebels, dreading your valour and your discipline, have hidden themselves behind walls, not daring to shew themselves in the open field. Routed at Ponte Ferreira, obliged to fly precipitately at Souto Redondo, and driven from Villa Nova, they tremble at our arms.

Soldiers ! It is from Oporto, their last and vain refuge, that we must dislodge them; and it is on their own ground, in which they endeavour to hide their crimes, that it behoves us to chastise them.

Soldiers ! Let the day of attack be that of our victory ; *but, mark, that victory will not be complete so long as a single revolutionist remains in existence.* Swear, then, that you will not lay down your arms, and that you will never take repose, *until you shall have exterminated the rebels.*

The king and the nation expect this *great deed from you ;* their hopes will not be disappointed.

Soldiers! In the day of your greatest glory, one which you so anxiously and laudably expect, unite to your great courage and unshaken fidelity the most exact obedience to the orders of your superiors; because one negligence, one extravagance, even one incautious excess of valour, may be injurious to the brave themselves. The God of armies protects a cause so just; it is that of Portuguese lovers of their legitimate king and of their country.

Soldiers! Let us to battle; let us put an end to revolutions; and in the midst of our transports let our cry ever be, Live the Holy Religion of Jesus Christ! Live our King Dom Miguel the First! Victory and happiness to the Portuguese!

THE VISCONDE DE PEZO DE REGOA,
Commandant of the Corps of the Army
of Operations.

Head Quarters at Agoas Sanctas,
27th September, 1832.

No. V.

Agreeable to the orders of His Imperial Majesty the Duke of Braganza, Commander-in-chief of the Liberating Army, the Marshal Major-General yesterday made a reconnoisance on our left to ascertain the force and positions of the enemy on that side.

By extraordinary circumstances, none of which depended on him, he was obliged to remain in position with the small force he had on the heights of Pasteleiro for a longer time than he intended, or was convenient, which allowed the enemy to unite so superior a force, that, notwithstanding the devoted bravery and firmness of the army he had the honour of commanding, he found himself under the necessity of either abandoning the position and retiring, or suffering a great reverse.

In view of which the marshal thinks it is his rigorous duty to render to the officers and soldiers their well merited eulogies and praises, it not being possible to direct them in particular to any individual, in as much as all distinguished themselves with that intrepidity and bravery which characterises this devoted army, and which experience has just proved that it can be imitated, but never exceeded.

Qualities such as these guarantee to the marshal the complete and immediate triumph of the sacred cause in which he and the said army are engaged.

B. SOLIGNAC.

25th January, 1833.

No. VI.

Portuguese Legation,
36, Baker-street, 1st Feb. 1833.

SIR,

IN consequence of orders just received from my Government, I have the honour to propose to you the command of the squadron of Her M. F. M. Donna Maria II., on the same terms and conditions, and with the same rank as were granted to Admiral Sartorius, provided that you present yourself at Oporto on or before the 20th February instant.

Requesting the favour of your early reply to be communicated to my Government,

I have the honour to be, sir,

Your very obedient servant,

CHEV. D'ABREU E LIMA.

To Captain Napier, R.N.

Oporto, le 31 *Janvier,* 1833.

MON CHER CAPITAINE NAPIER,

JE vous ai dejà écrit en reponse à la lettre adressée par vous au Marquis de Palmella en lui proposant une expedition sur Lisbonne. Le projet d'entrer dans le Taje me parait impraticable, parceque si nos bateaux à vapeur échappaient aux nombreuses batteries de terre, il serait presqu' impossible qu'ils pussent échapper aux canons de plus d'une douzaine de batiments de guerre mouillés dans le fleuve. Je pense que la partie de la côte où il nous serait le plus utile de debarquer s'étend depuis Peniche jusqu'à Cascaes, qu'après vient la côte entre le Taje et le Sado: après cela nous avons Sines, la côte de l'Alentejo, peut-être la plus facile pour effectuer un debarquement, vu qu'il y a peu de ports et qu'on ne la garde point. Nous avons encore les belles plages de l'Algarve. Vous savez comme nous avons grimpé sur les rochers de St. George et de St. Michel. Et il vaut mieux avoir encore à grimper que d'être exposé pendant le debarquement à des batteries.

Il faut que chaque bateau à vapeur porte des canots pour le debarquement, ainsi que quelques échelles, qui pourront peut-être nous servir comme cela nous est arrivé à l'île de St. George.

Quant à votre engagement pour le service de la Reine et votre venue ici il faut garder le secret autant qu'on le pourra.

M. Magalhaes, porteur de cette lettre, est chargé par le gouvernement de s'entendre avec M. de Lima et Mendizabal sur cette affaire, et particulièrement avec vous.

Je vous dirai un mot de notre escadre. Nous avons en mer trois frégates et le brick Villa Flor, tripulés par des Anglais, ce sont des bons batiments, et deux corvettes, tripulées par des Portugais, de celles-ci la Portuense de vingt ou vingt-quatre canons est très bonne, la Constitution est mauvaise.

L'esprit des équipages Anglaises a été à la revolte, ou en partie du à cause d'arrérages de solde, partie du à des intrigues entre quelques officiers et Sartorius ; j'ai toujours soutenu celui-ci, pour soutenir la discipline, et je soutiendrai toujours celle-ci pendant que je serais chargé du departement de la marine.

La frégate Rainha est commandée par le Capitaine Blackeston, il a commandé longtemps des navires marchands. On le dit bon marin. La Don Pedro est commandée par le Capitaine Goble, il a été le second de

Sartorius dans la frégate Pyramus, on le dit bon officier. La Donna Maria est commandée par le Capitaine Massey, alias Evans, de la marine Anglaise. Cette frégate était auparavant commandée par le Capitaine Mins, alias Bingham, et la Rainha par le Capitaine Sackville Crosby, qui a été le second de Lord Cochrane.

Prenez vos informations, et voyez s'il vous convient de garder ceux-ci ou d'avoir d'autres meilleurs, choisissez donc.

Adieu, mon cher ami, croyez à l'estime avec laquelle je suis

Votre devoué
BERNARDO DE SA NOGUEIRA.

No. VII.

SIR,

IN reply to your letter of the 1st instant offering me the command of the squadron of Her Faithful Majesty, I have the honour of informing you that I shall not hesitate on taking the command on the inclosed terms.

1. Admiral Sartorius must be acquainted by the government of their intention to supersede him, if it has not been already done, or if he has not himself given it up, which I presume he has not done.

2. My passage, and that of the officers I may take with me, must be paid to Oporto.

APPENDIX. 325

3. Six months' pay must be paid in advance to myself and officers.

4. My life must be insured for a year for £10,000, which can be done at four or five per cent.

5. I am to have the same rank and advantages as Admiral Sartorius, and the officers I bring out are also placed on the same footing.

6. I am to have full power to appoint, promote, and discharge officers, without having recourse to courts-martial in the one case, or reference to the government in the other.

7. I am to have access to the Emperor when the service requires it.

8. The officers and ships' company must be paid up to the time I take the command.

I consider them indispensably necessary for my own security and the proper maintenance of discipline. I must also observe that my taking the command will be of little use to the cause, unless active operations are immediately commenced by the squadron. English seamen, when idle, are always discontented, and they become more so in a foreign service.—As I presume the force now assembled in Oporto is insufficient to make a forward movement without a rising of the people, steps should be immediately taken to force them to weaken their force before Oporto. Several plans present themselves to me; the first and grandest would be to hire ten steamboats, embark the whole army and carry them direct up the Tagus and land them in Lisbon. This would require funds; the second is, running the squadron into Lisbon with two thousand men on board; this could only be attempted if it was ascertained that the inhabitants were favourable to the cause. If successful, so much the better; if not, there is anchorage in Lisbon out of shot on all sides, and an enemy's squadron there would oblige them to raise the blockade of Oporto.

Should either of these plans be deemed unadvisable, from a thousand to fifteen hundred men should be embarked in the squadron, and descents should be made on different parts of the coast. Peniché, for instance, I have no doubt might be seized; this would draw men from Oporto. Attacks might be made in Lagos Bay in the Algarves, in fact the whole coast should be kept in hot water; the command of the sea is an enormous advantage, and it ought to be used, and should the people be favourable, men might be raised in the Algarves and armed, which would be attended with the most advantageous results to the cause. The fifteen hundred men might be the nucleus of an army that might march through the Alentejo, and create a powerful diversion.

No. VIII.

My letter missing, but merely to communicate to Sartorius that they had offered me the command, and my reply.

MY DEAR NAPIER,

Your conduct has been such as I expected from your strict and honourable character.

The —— have behaved in the most infamous manner to me; they commenced by intriguing with my officers ———— even at the islands giving each to understand that they should have the command. ——— went so far as to tell his officers that he was to hoist his flag before he left the Azores; his conduct ever since has been most atrocious. Although warned against him even then by many (particularly ————) I could not give credit to the existence of such gratuitous unmerited atrocity.

I have experienced a degree of wretchedness and misery I can hardly describe during the time I have been in this service, without pay, without clothing, without provisions for the last four months except what hazard presented, expecting every moment the ships to be taken from me, betrayed by ————, unsupported in action. I have notwithstanding kept Oporto free, have licked my opponents, and blockaded Lisbon, and if my advice had not been invariably neglected from the commencement, we should now have had Madeira, and a revolution in the south of Portugal.

I have advanced the little ready money I had to pay my men to quiet them, about £420; my bill for this has been dishonoured, and I am nearly five months in arrear, and many of my people nine months.

I gave up the money from the first they awarded to me for the risk of my commission, and have had no guarantee or reward of any kind, and yet see what is the conduct of these ————.

I shall however be very happy to give up the command

to you, if they fulfil their engagements to me, the officers, and people.

They were shaking hands with me and professing friendship during all the time this intrigue has been going on.

Yours, truly,
G. R. SARTORIUS.

Vigo, March 14th.

No. IX.

CARTA REGIA.

Sir John Milley Doyle, Marechal de Campo of the Royal Army, belonging to my Etat Major Imperial.

FRIEND,

I, the Duke of Braganza, Regent, in the name of the Queen, send you much greeting. It is for the good of the service, that you go on board the squadron of the same August Senhora, now at anchor in Vigo Bay, to put in execution the orders you have received. I direct you to embark immediately, and to be particular to fulfil all the instructions you have received of the same date as these. I have to assure you that I confide to your intelligence, zeal, and activity, in putting into effect the important mission with which you are charged.

D. PEDRO, Duke of Braganza.
(Signed) BERNARDO DE SA NOGUEIRA.
Written in the Palace of Oporto,
13th of March, 1833.
To Sir John Milley Doyle.

(Translations.)

MARINE DEPARTMENT.

Instructions given to Sir John Milley Doyle, Marechal de Campo, A. D. C. to His Imperial Majesty the Duke of Braganza, Regent of Portugal.

I.—Sir John Milley Doyle will immediately embark on board the *London Merchant* (steamer), and proceed to Vigo, or wherever he is likely to meet with Her Most Faithful Majesty's squadron, for the purpose of presenting to Vice-Admiral Sartorius the Royal Decree (Carta Regia), superseding him from the command in chief of the said squadron. For this purpose, Sir John M. Doyle will present the Vice-Admiral the Royal authority he has received, from His Imperial Majesty, the Regent, the important commission, as will be seen by the Royal Decree, which was delivered to him of the same date.

II.—Sir John is likewise charged to invest the Captain de Mar e Guerra S. Crosbie, with the temporary command of the squadron, in virtue of the decree, which to that effect has been passed, bearing the same date, and which will be delivered to him by the said Sir John M. Doyle.

III.—Sir John M. Doyle is directed to declare, and assure Vice-Admiral Sartorius, that the Government of Her Most Faithful Majesty undertake to satisfy all legal claims which can be made by the said Vice-Admiral Sartorius, officers, and crews of the squadron; but that it will only satisfy such claims, on the conditions that the command, *de facto*, be transferred to Captain de Mar e Guerra S. Crosbie; Vice-Admiral Sartorius being directed to return to Oporto, for the settlement of his accounts.

IV.—If (contrary to the expectations of Her Most Faithful Majesty's Government) it so happens that Vice-Admiral Sartorius refuses to deliver up the command of the squadron, Sir John M. Doyle, after having exhausted all means of persuasion, is directed to place him in arrest, and conduct him to Oporto, in consequence of his disobedience of these orders.

In all other occurrences which may take place in the present affair, Sir John M. Doyle will act conjointly with the temporary Commander of the squadron, and Captain Bressane Lieto, that the important commission may be terminated with the greatest brevity, and in the most amicable manner, so as to enable the squadron of Her Most Faithful Majesty to sail immediately for Oporto.

(Signed) BERNARDO DE SA NOGUEIRA.
Palace of Oporto,
13*th of March,* 1833.

No. X.

" The late conduct of the ministers, at present, unfortunately, conducting the affairs of Her Most Faithful Majesty, having shown (in spite of all our sacrifices and sufferings) a constant neglect, and positive refusal, to comply with the just claims of the auxiliary forces, naval and military, engaged under compact made with Vice-Admiral Sartorius; and by such conduct, so dishonourable, disloyal, and insulting, as must prevent the Vice-Admiral and his companions having any further reliance on their word, good faith, or honour; in consequence, the principal officers of the squadron, acting in the name, and for the interest, of the rest of the squadron, have come to the following resolutions, *viz.*—That they are ready to enter upon active service, on the following conditions:—

" *First,*—That £20,000 shall be immediately advanced, to pay the wages and claims of the squadron up to March 31st.

" *Second,*—That the ships of war, by a public decree,

be made over to the officers, seamen, and marines, acting under the compact, as a guarantee for the future payment of growing wages and allowances, and to provide against any claims that may arise for unpaid bills, drawn for the public service.

"*Third,*—That the payment of pensions for the wounded, and for the families of the killed, be put on a sure and satisfactory foundation.

"*Fourth,*—That, if the Admiral shall quit the service of Her Most Faithful Majesty, all those officers who wish to do the same, may have full permission of the Government, acting in the name of the Queen, to do so."

(Signed)

Captains GOBLET, BLACKISTON, AND GEORGE.
Commanders MASSEY AND WILSON,
Lieutenants LUDLOW, LIOT, ROBINSON, & FOX.
Surgeons BIRMINGHAM, FRASER, ACHESON,
   GILL, BELL, and a Portuguese.
Commissaries BEAUMOND, ROBERTSON, FISHER,
   AND BENSON;
and many others.

Additional Resolution, proposed by Captain MASSEY, *and adopted.*

"That the undersigned, in the name of the officers, marines, and crews, of the whole squadron, having entered into a determination, not to desert their Commander-in-Chief, after the just claims of the officers and men

APPENDIX. 333

are liquidated, require, that he shall be indemnified, in a pecuniary way, for the commission he so nobly risked for the cause of Portugal and the legitimate Queen Donna Maria, and which he has since been deprived of by his own Government."

No. XI.

Rainha de Portugal,
Oporto, April 24th, 1836.

MY DEAR NAPIER,

After the sparring I have had with this government, it is out of the question my remaining any longer than to give up the squadron to you. I have intimated this to them after they had reinstated me de facto and granted all my demands.

They are as follows,—the men to be paid up to the last farthing, officers also. The ships to be made over by a legal document (as a security for growing pay and pension) to the officers and crews, and those who wish to leave to have permission. Many talk of leaving, but I am sure of retaining sufficient with some Portuguese to make the squadron equally effective and more tractable than with all English, indeed it was my intention to have halved the crews, but all officers English. They are capital sailors, and mixed with our men they have shewn quite as much pluck.

I informed the government that had they honestly told me of their proceeding to replace me, and that they wished to have had you, that heart and soul I should have approved and concurred with them, both in having a most fit and competent officer, and for having done me a personal favour in giving me such an opportunity to retire.

When you come out, you had better bring with you some two or three hundred men, as several might wish to leave with me. The ships are in want of nothing of consequence; the masts, although badly strung, have been so well fished and so well tried that you have nothing to fear, the summer having set in.

Bring out a good captain and some good sailor men, as lieutenants are much wanted.

Very truly yours,
G. R. SARTORIUS.

No XII.

Captain Wilkinson's letter, giving an account of the mutiny, is unfortunately lost.

No. XIII.

Londres, ce 18 *Mai,* 1833.

Monsieur le Capitaine,

Il me semble inutile de vous rappeler ici tout ce qui s'est passé entre nous relativement aux ordres que j'ai reçûs de Sa Majesté Impérial Monseigneur le Duc de Bragança, d'abord en date du 19 Janvier dernier, pour vous offrir le commandement de l'escadre de Sa Majesté Très Fidèle, ce que j'ai fait par la lettre que j'eus l'honneur de vous adresser le 1er Fevrier suivant, et ensuite en date du 27 du dit mois pour vous consulter sur l'éxécution qu'on voulait donner au projet que vous aviez adressé à Monsieur le Marquis de Palmella en date du 8 du même mois, ce que je vous ai communiqué verbalement moi-même à Londres dans les premiers jours de Fevrier. Le 1er Avril je vous ai prié de venir encore ici, et le 3 nous eumes une conférence chez Mendizabal, à laquelle assista le Colonel Evans, et alors vous avez accepté avec un noble désinteressement, le commandement de l'expédition que l'on projetait de faire sur l'Algarve, en mettant la seule condition que Monsieur le Marquis de Palmella irait avec vous : mais non seulement vous vous êtes prêté de bon cœur à diriger la partie maritime de l'expédition, mais vous avez proposé d'aller à Vigo arranger l'affaire de l'escadre, et s'il le fallait vous placer sous le commandement de Sartorius, comme son second, si pour cela on vous fournissait un bateau à vapeur et £12,000 pour le payment des équipages.

Je n'oublierai jamais cette noble et généreuse proposition, qui seule doit inspirer pour vous les sentimens de la reconnaissance de tous les loyaux Portugais ; vous méritez tous les égards de Sa Majesté Impériale Monseigneur le Duc Régent, et l'estime de toutes les ames élevées. Vous savez comment et pourquoi l'expédition a changé de force et de projet ; maintenant elle se rapproche plus du plan que vous aviez suggéré, et que Sa Majesté Impériale avait approuvé.

Vous allez donc, Monsieur le Capitaine, commander la partie maritime de cette expédition, et vous voulez bien vous prêter à prendre aussi éventuellement le commandement de l'escadre. Il est cependant entendu que vous mettez à cet acte de devouement à la cause de la Reine, la condition que vous serez chargé de quelque entreprise particulière contre l'ennemi, et que vous ne presumez pas prendre le commandement de l'escadre, pour effectuer une simple croisière, ou un simple blocus. Il est toutefois entendu que vos plans et les opérations de l'expédition seront discutés et combinés à Oporto, sous les yeux de Sa Majesté Impériale, et soumis à sa haute approbation.

Je vous ai fait voir les lettres de Sartorius, et vous avez pu vous convaincre par vos yeux de la resolution où il est de quitter le commandement de l'escadre. Il m'a engagé fortement de solliciter votre prompt départ pour aller le remplacer, et c'est aussi sur cela que se fondent en grande partie les demarches pressantes que j'ai faites auprès de vous pour vous porter à prendre le commandement maritime de l'expédition prête à sortir.

Quant au poste dont vous serez investi dans la marine de Sa Majesté Très Fidèle, il est evident qu'il ne peut être moindre que celui qu'on a conferé au Capitaine Sartorius, votre *junior* officier dans le marine Britannique, et les conditions devront être celles qui se trouvent dans le contrat fait avec le dit Capitaine. En outre il n'est que juste que vous receviez six mois d'avance de la solde, qui vous reviendrait comme Vice-Amiral, pour subvenir à vos frais, et aux besoins de votre famille pendant votre absence. Votre vie sera aussi assurée pour la valeur de £10,000, afin de parer aux chances des dangers que vous allez courir dans le service de la Reine. Les deux conditions principales que vous aviez mises à votre engagement eventuel, et à votre départ pour Oporto se trouvent donc remplies, et je ne doute nullement que les autres ne le soyent également. Cependant tout ceci n'implique pas l'idée d'aucun engagement fixe et préalable, et il est entendu que vous allez à Oporto offrir vos services à l'Auguste Régent, et recevoir de Sa Majesté Impériale lui-même votre brevêt et votre commission.

Agréez mes vœux sincères pour l'heureuse reussite de votre noble devouement à notre cause, et croyez moi avec les sentimens les plus distingués,

Monsieur le Capitaine,
   Votre très humble et très obéissant serviteur,
    Le Chevalier D'Abreu e Lima.

Monsieur le Capitaine Napier,
De la Marine Royale Britannique,
   &c. &c. &c.

No. XIV.

Carlos de Ponza* (Napier), Vice-Admiral of the Navy of H. M. F. Majesty. I, Duke of Braganza, Regent in the name of the Queen, wishing you health. Taking into consideration your capacity, zeal, and intelligence, many proofs of which you gave in the service of His Britannic Majesty, and confiding in your love for liberty, that you will employ all your energies to terminate with glory the struggle in which I am engaged to restore the throne to the same August Lady, and the Constitutional Charter to the Portuguese nation,—I do, in the name of the Queen, charge you with the chief command of the squadron destined to assist in this noble enterprise, authorising you, on this occasion, to name and appoint the captains and officers to the ships of which the squadron is composed, in the certainty that the appointments you make will be legally confirmed. I communicate this to you for your intelligence and execution.

Given at the palace of Oporto, the 8th of June, one thousand eight hundred and thirty-five.
D. PEDRO, Duque de Braganca.
MARQUIS DE LOULE.

Para Carlos de Ponza.

---

* The name I assumed.

APPENDIX. 339

Carlos de Ponza, Vice-Admiral of the Navy of H. M. F. Majesty. I, the Duke of Braganza, Regent in the name of the Queen, wishing you health. Taking into consideration the zeal and intelligence you dedicate to the service of my August Daughter, and to the Portuguese nation, and wishing to give you a proof of the approbation you deserve, I, in the name of the Queen, name you Major-General of the Navy, whose duties you will at all times exercise when your service as the commander-in-chief of the squadron shall permit your residence near the government. I communicate this to you for your intelligence.

Given at the palace of Oporto, 8th of June, 1833.
D. PEDRO, Duque de Braganca.
MARQUIS DE LOULE.

No. XV.

His Excellency the DUKE OF TERCEIRA, Peer of the Kingdom, Lieutenant-General of the Royal Army,

Having taken the resolution of detaching from the army under my immediate command a divisionary expedition to aid the people in a free manifestation of their loyalty in favour of the cause of H. M. F. Majesty Donna Maria Secunda and of the Constitutional Charter of the Monarchy, and having unlimited confidence in your loyalty, honour, and patriotism : I have therefore thought proper to nominate you, in the name of the Queen, commander-in-chief of the above expedition, and to confide to you unlimited power for the execution of all military measures you may think necessary and useful for the accomplishment of the important commission with which you are charged, being regulated by the instructions sent you by the minister of war. Part of the civil duties will be discharged by the Duke of Palmella, according to letters patent and the instructions, of which a copy is enclosed; and I expect that with the Duke and with the Vice-Admiral Carlos de Ponza (Napier) you will maintain that good intelligence which is always conducive to the public welfare.

    (Signed) Dom Pedro,
           Duke of Braganza.
 (Countersigned) Augustinho Jose Freire,
Palace of Oporto, Minister of War.
15*th June,* 1833.

Instructions for the Duke of Terceira, &c.

ARTICLE I.

The divisionary expedition which is entrusted to the command of the Duke of Terceira is comprised of a light brigade formed by the second and third caçadores, and a brigade of the line, composed of the third and sixth light infantry and the first battalion of the first Queen's regiment, a detachment of lancers on foot, and another of artillery.

ARTICLE 2.

This division will be directed on a point which will afford the greatest probability of an easy landing, and the least opposition from the enemy, and the best reception from the inhabitants. Should there be found more than one place similar to the one before described, it will be preferable to land where from the operation may result a more prompt and decisive effect upon Lisbon or Oporto, or on both, taking particular care, should the enemy be able to detach a formidable force, not to enter into a disadvantageous conflict, or abandon the country.

ARTICLE 3.

There will be found along the coast many places which embrace all the conditions of the preceding article, but it is impossible to prescribe any thing with precision on this subject. A military council composed of the Dukes of Palmella and Terceira and the Vice-Admiral Carlos de Ponza will be assembled on board for the purpose of determining on what point the landing is to be effected, and in what manner the communication between the land and sea forces is to be maintained.

ARTICLE 4.

The troops when on shore are to be entirely and exclusively under the command of the Duke of Terceira; he may if he think proper secure some position for the purpose of establishing a depot or hospital, and at the same time maintain a communication with the sea, to protect a re-embarkation, if necessary.

The nature of the enemy we have to deal with makes us believe that any small fort, convent, or edifice well situated will answer the purpose, and along the coast many such are to be found.

ARTICLE 5.

The Duke, commander-in-chief, will receive with kindness all persons who may present themselves, without distinction of condition or class, or whatever may have been their past opinions or errors.

To the military men their rank must be allowed, even in case of their having acquired it during the usurpation; but no one is to be employed in an effective service without a certainty of his loyalty to the national cause, or without the guarantee of service lately rendered.

With respect to civilians that the Duke may want to employ in the absence of the civil government, he will always prefer such persons who by their virtues and qualities may have an influence over the people, and do credit to the situation entrusted to them and to the noble cause they serve.

ARTICLE 6.

The Duke of Terceira will use every effort to preserve the strictest discipline amongst the troops, especially foreigners, and to punish with rigour any breach thereof, and he is also authorized to confirm and put in execution all sentences of courts-martial.

APPENDIX.

ARTICLE 7.

The duke is also authorized to punish with severity all peasants and ecclesiastics who may be found in arms against the national cause, with such penalties as the law allows.

ARTICLE 8.

With regard to prisoners of war all those who can be depended upon may be admitted into our ranks; in any other case they are to be sent to Oporto or to any other place according to circumstances, being always treated with that kindness becoming a government of justice.

ARTICLE 9.

Particular care must be taken with regard to the employment of public money and the regularity of requisitions of every description, and finally, that all acts of authority should tend to shew in practice the difference between a legitimate government and one of usurpation and tyranny.

ARTICLE 10.

The commander-in-chief is authorized to promote to the rank of ensign those cadets and non-commissioned officers who shall distinguish themselves in action, and he may also propose to his Imperial Majesty those who shall deserve to be rewarded with the decoration of the Tower and Sword.

ARTICLE 11.

The duke commander-in-chief will take any other measures which may be suggested by his own observation, making reports of his progress through the department of the minister-at-war.

To his Excellency the Duke of Palmella.

Conceiving it for the interest of the cause of H. M. F. Majesty Donna Maria Segunda, my August Daughter, Queen of Portugal, and to the interest of the Portuguese nation, that a divisionary expedition should be detached to those parts of the kingdom which may be thought most appropriate, for the purpose of affording the people that aid that they so much desire to enable them to display that loyalty which force and the fear of a despotic power now stifle in their bosoms; I have nominated for the command of this expedition the Duke of Terceira, and have taken the resolution to choose a person, who by his loyalty and deep knowledge of the management of affairs may deserve that I intrust him with my confidence, and a part of the authority which I am exercising in the name of the Queen, during the necessary period for regulating provisionary both civil and judicial affairs in those countries whose inhabitants may declare their feelings in favour of the Queen and Charter, and consequently have nominated you civil and provisionary Governor, because I trust that in such an important commission you will be enabled to conduct yourself with loyalty and intelligence, which has distinguished you in many other commissions of high trust which have been confided to you, being regulated by the instructions which will be delivered to you with this letter patent.

(Signed)   Don Pedro, Duke of Braganza.

Countersigned by all the Ministers of State.

APPENDIX.

Instructions to accompany the letters patent of the 13th June, 1833. Addressed to the Duke of Palmella, member of the state council, peer of the kingdom, and provisionary civil governor.

ARTICLE 1.

The Duke of Palmella, &c. &c. will embark with the expedition under the command of Vice-Admiral Carlos de Ponza, with the purpose of accompanying the Duke of Terceira with the commission with which he is charged.

ARTICLE 2.

In a military council composed of the Duke of Palmella, the Duke of Terceira, and Vice-Admiral Carlos de Ponza, will be decided, (having first the information and the enquiries that they will think proper,) the point on which the landing is to be effected with the greatest probability of a good result, having in view the requisite means contained in the instructions given to the Commander-in-Chief the Duke of Terceira.

ARTICLE 3.

The civil divisionary governor, the Duke of Palmella, will land with the divisionary expedition, and will immediately proclaim to the inhabitants and acquaint them with the nature of the commission, and make known to them that the aim of the expedition is not to wage war against the people, but to effect reconciliation and peace; their only object being to encourage the manifestation of the Portuguese loyalty towards their legitimate Queen and towards the constitutional charter of the monarchy, that being the firm and unshaken intention of his Imperial Majesty the Duke of Braganza, Regent in the name of the Queen. What is expressed in the proclamation of the 2d January, 1832, has been always and ever will be executed with the greatest exactness, giving to the Portuguese nation and to the whole world an example of constancy and magnanimity.

ARTICLE 4.

He will make known to all classes of persons, as well by words as by actions, the immense difference existing between the legal government and that of usurpation and tyranny. He will cause to be published the laws about the extinction of the tithes, and will also publish all those laws (if he thinks it proper) with which the legal government of her Most Faithful Majesty the Queen has effectually benefited the people, making them free from all the tributes and vexations that have oppressed them.

ARTICLE 5.

He will take with him if possible a printer's press and the necessary persons to work it, in order that the convenient publication of the measures which have been taken and of the news should be made; periodical pamphlets should be issued with promptitude.

ARTICLE 6.

He will receive with kindness all persons who present

APPENDIX. 347

themselves, whatever may have been their past opinions or errors, but will not employ any person without conviction of his fidelity to the cause, or without a guarantee of his recent services.

The form of appointments shall be as follows:—

The Duke of Palmella, invested by his Imperial Majesty the Duke of Braganza, Regent in the name of the Queen, with a part of the authority which he exercises in that character, provisionally appoints you for that place which he will hold as long as he will merit it by his zeal, or until it shall please H. M. F. Majesty to employ him in any other way.

ARTICLE 7.

He will punish with severity by courts-martial all peasants or priests taken in arms, as well as the seducer of the troops and all others who shall continue to shew themselves obstinate and incorrigible in the perpetration of capital crimes, having always regard to shew by practice that the legitimate government is as lenient and paternal to all those who repent, as they are energetic and inexorable to those who deviate from the public spirit and the natural fidelity of the Portuguese.

ARTICLE 8.

He will nominate personally proper persons to the municipal commissions, and to all other charges of justice and finance, and adopting the denominations of the ancient legislature, to which the country is accustomed, and employ only persons who by their virtues and abilities are able to acquire public influence, and do credit to the noble and just cause which they serve. Immoral persons, without reputation or probity, are not to be employed in the public service, notwithstanding the sacrifices they may have made in the cause of the Queen. Such will be rewarded at a future time in another and proper manner.

ARTICLE 9.

He will collect with the necessary circumspection all the public revenues, ordering receipts to be passed, and taking care that the accounts be kept regularly; and in like manner will take possession of the wealth of the rebels, for the support of the army and navy.

ARTICLE 10.

He will provide the divisionary expedition with rations, transports, and all other necessary articles according to the requisitions of the commander-in-chief, and to which he may apply the civil revenues; taking particular care to do the least possible harm to the inhabitants, paying or giving bills at short date, to persons whose goods may be taken to furnish the army and navy.

ARTICLE 11.

He will take particular care to promote a friendly feeling with the inhabitants, not allowing the existence of any sentiments of private revenge, and will maintain firmly and with impartiality the force of the law, shewing that his Imperial Majesty's wish is to put an end to party feeling, and re-establish with the legitimate government of the Queen and of the charter, the complete reconciliation of all the Portuguese family.

ARTICLE 12.

He will maintain with the Duke commander-in chief and the Vice-Admiral, all the necessary intelligence and understanding for the good of the service.

ARTICLE 13.

He is authorized to enter into treaty with any individual of the enemy's party, but those treaties ought not to compromise the principles of the constitutional charter or the laws and decrees of his Imperial Majesty; being always aware that it is prohibited to enter into any treaty with the Infante Don Miguel, this being contrary to the glory of his Imperial Majesty and offensive to the honour of the subjects of H. M. F. Majesty Donna Maria Segunda.

ARTICLE 14.

He is authorized to promise and accord any rewards he may think proper, not including the persons named in the exceptions to the amnesty, published in the name of H. M. F. Majesty, and if any persons present themselves and will render service to the cause of the Queen, he can secure to them the pardon of H. I. Majesty in the name of the Queen.

ARTICLE 15.

The civil and provisionary governor, the Duke of Palmella, is fully authorized to take any other measures of political administration, civil and economical, which he may think most advantageous for the prosperous termination of his mission, reporting all circumstances to the proper ministerial departments with whom he will maintain a frequent correspondence.

   (Signed)   CANDIDO JOZE XAVIER,
           JOZE DE SILVAH CARVALHO.
           AUGUSTINO JOZE FREIRE.

Palace, Oporto,
13*th June,* 1833.

No. XVI.

Rainha de Portugal,
Oporto Roads, June 20*th,* 1833.

MY LORD,

We have at last received a good supply of water, cocoa, sugar, tea, and glass, and are now off.

I shall send the Liberal back, and put her under Captain Bertram's orders, who I have sent on board the Edward. I have also put the gun-boats under his orders, and all yachts with directions to send them to Vigo for water, he will apply to you for officers to command them, and men to man them. I recommend Your Excellency to put provisions for the squadron on board the Edward also, so that she may be ready to move about in any direction I may want.

Should the enemy put to sea in my absence, I have ordered her to proceed to the Bayonne Islands, where I presume she will be in safety. I have also directed Captain Bertram to establish some signals with you that he may communicate any news I may send you.

The Eugenie and Constitution have orders to join me the moment they arrive, and I hope that will not be tong as I expect seamen. The Pedro has parted her cable,—we are all infamously supplied. There are several men in prison who came out in the Edward, but never joined the squadron. I have no objection to their being sent on board, as they do not come under the head of mutineers. It will be necessary to send a large quantity of casks off to the Edward to fill the yachts with.

The news from Lisbon is favourable, several captains have resigned. An order of the day, dated at Coimbra, orders the troops in Lisbon in case of our approaching the coast to march there, and leave Lisbon in charge of the Ordenanzas—if we only could be sure of that, and a strong breeze, Black-Horse-square would be the place, but I fear our force is too weak for such an enterprize. It is, however, impossible to know what may happen when we are off Lisbon.

I beg you will assure the Emperor all that I can

do shall be done in his service for the cause of the Queen.

I have the honour to be, &c.
CARLOS DE PONZA.

His Excellency the Marquis of Loulé,
   Minister-of-marine.

No. XVII.

On landing in the Algarves.

PORTUGUESE,

The necessity of delivering you from oppression, in order that you may shew your fidelity to your legitimate queen, determined His Imperial Majesty the Duke of Braganza, Regent in the name of that august personage, to send an army amongst you, which I have the honour of commanding. Loyal Portuguese, come under my command to liberate Portugal; the arms we carry are formidable to your oppressors, unite yourselves to me and to my soldiers, and the legitimate queen shall be reinstated on the throne of her ancestors, treacherously usurped, and the constitutional charter and liberty restored to our country.

VILLA FLOR.

No. XVIII.

LIST OF KILLED AND WOUNDED.

RAINHA DE PORTUGAL.

Killed.
F. G. Macdenough, Capt.
Frank Wooldridge, Lieut.
and six Seamen.

Wounded.
James Wilkinson, Commodore, severely.
Charles Napier, Chief of the Staff, severely.
Lieut. Gidney, severely.
—— Knyvett, R.M. mortally.
—— Winter, Secretary, dangerously.
Lieut. Edmunds, mortally, and seventeen Seamen.

DON PEDRO.

Thos. Goble, Capt. and six Seamen and Marines.

Charles Stanhope, Capt. of Marines, severely; since dead.
John Powell, Mate, and twenty Seamen and Marines.

DONNA MARIA.

John More, Sailing Lieut. and three men.

Sixteen Seamen and Marines.

VILLA FLOR.
Five Seamen.

PORTUENSE.
Capt. Blackstone.   Lieut. Purver.
And four or five killed and wounded.

RETURN MISSING.

No. XIX.

Palace at Oporto, 10th July, 1833.

ILLUSTRIOUS AND EXCELLENT SIR,

His Imperial Majesty the Duke of Braganza, Regent in the name of the Queen, sends your Excellency the inclosed copy signed by Antonio Pedro de Carvalho, director of this secretariat, the decree of the 9th of this month, by which the said August Lord has in consequence of your brilliant services named your Excellency Admiral of the Royal Navy.

God preserve your Excellency,

MARQUIS DE LOULE,
Minister of Marine.

*To Carlos de Ponza,
Admiral and Major-General.*

*Office of the Minister of Marine.
Oporto, July 10, 1833.*

Seeing the renowned valour and great talent with which on the 5th of the present month, in the waters of Cape St. Vincent, the Vice-Admiral Major-General Carlos de Ponza, Commander-in-chief of the squadron of H. M. F. Majesty, gained with very inferior forces a complete victory over the rebel squadron, capturing by the most skilful manœuvres and intrepid boarding the greater and most important part of their ships, thus annihilating, with as much renown for himself as glory to the arms of loyal Portuguese, the whole maritime force of the Usurper: I do in the name of the Queen appoint Vice-Admiral Carlos de Ponza Admiral of the Royal Navy. The minister, secretary of state for foreign affairs, provisionally charged with the marine department, will so understand and cause to be executed with the necessary despatch.

Palace of Oporto, July 9th, 1833.

DON PEDRO, DUQUE DE BRAGANZA.
MARQUIS DE LOULE.

Carlos de Ponza, Admiral and Major-General of her Most Faithful Majesty the Queen of Portugal, and Commander-in-chief of the squadron of the said August Lady in the waters of the Algarves: Friend, I, Duke of Braganza, Regent in the name of the Queen Donna Maria II., send you greeting. Taking into due consideration the glorious victory which, on the 5th of July, you gained over the rebels in the waters of Cape St. Vincent by resolutely attacking the enemy by boarding with three frigates, a corvette, a brig, and a small schooner, the enemy's forces, composed of two ships of the line, two frigates, three corvettes, two brigs, and a xebeque, which gave them a great superiority not only in the number and force of the ships, but in their weight of metal, directing that bold attack with a talent that belongs to yourself, running the ship of the line Rainha on board with your own flag-ship, whose crew, notwithstanding their efforts, could not resist your impetuosity and that of the brave men who followed your example, and not satisfied with that brilliant result, after having obliged the enemy's admiral to haul down his flag, you gave chase to, and forced to surrender, the frigate *Martin de Freitas*, which fled before you and tried to save herself after the considerable damage she had suffered from the decisive attacks of the brig Villa Flor and the corvette Portuense, by which you not only acquired the glory of this brilliant enterprise and of so well executed a command, but in particular, that of the example you set in your own person of an activity and a valour which most especially distinguish you, the result of all which was the complete rout of the enemy, the capture of his ships of the line, and his frigates, scarcely allowing the smaller ships to escape, by running before the wind and thereby avoiding the certain fate that awaited them; and wishing to give you, in the name of the Queen and in my name, a further demonstration of gratitude for a deed so memorable in itself and of such vital importance in its results, I am pleased to name you Viscount of Cape St. Vincent, which I have thought proper to communicate to you for your information and satisfaction; and that you may immediately use the said title and enjoy in these kingdoms the honours and pre-eminence which thereby belong to you, I send you this. Given in the Palace of Oporto, &c.

D. PEDRO, Duque de Braganza.
CANDIDO JOSE XAVIER.

No. XX.

Porto, ce 24 Juillet, 1833.

Mon cher Vicomte,

J'ai reçu votre obligeante lettre du 22 courant; je suis bien faché de la contrarieté que vous avez eprouvée par le vent, ainsi que du danger que vous avez couru par la maladie : heureusement l'une et l'autre n'existent plus, et vous voila rendu au point essentiel, et au moment précis d'entreprendre ce que vous jugerez convenable. J' approuve les raisons, qui vous empechent de vous rendre dans ces parages ; des affaires encore plus importantes vous retiennent là ou vous vous trouvez. Je suis sur, Mon cher Vicomte, que vous ne manquerez pas l'occasion, si elle se presente ; et je suis encore plus sur que vous retrouverez le Cap St. Vincent partout ou il vous plaira de conduire vos braves à la victoire. Ci-joint le plan lithographié de la bataille, dont le grand honneur vous appartient en entier : c'est le moindre hommage que l'on puisse rendre à votre vaillance. Agréez, Mon cher Vicomte, les assurances de l'estime avec laquelle je suis

Votre affectionné et admirateur

D. Pedro.

A l'Amiral Vicomte du Cap Saint Vincent.

Oporto, July 14*th*, 1833.

Mr. Mendizabel landed here last night, and he gave me an idea of the state of the squadron and a general account of the Algarves. I am sorry that your Excellency has not forwarded any official letters to me, to give the government an exact account of the state of the squadron, the losses we have sustained, and those of the enemy, by which we might inform his Imperial Majesty, who now expects with great anxiety, every detail of so glorious and so important an action.

It is impossible to detach any forces from hence at present, because the enemy has been encouraged by the arrival of General Bourmont, who, having taken command of their army, intends to make an attack shortly.

The appearance of any vessel off here would be of service, for the purpose of convincing the rebel army, who are deceived by their government, and who think that the squadron of the Queen was destroyed on the memorable 5th of July.

The Don John is the best known, but perhaps your Excellency does not approve of this plan, and every thing is always left to your opinion and determination.

I must not conceal that General Bourmont has landed at Villa de Conde or Vianna in the George the Fourth steamer, which has been bought by the government of the Usurper. It would be excellent if that steamer could be captured, &c. &c. &c.

   (Signed)   MARQUIS OF LOULE.

Viscount Cabo St. Vicenti,
 Admiral of the Royal Navy.

No. XXI.

Loyal Portuguese inhabitants of Lisbon! Valorous soldiers, whom I have the honour to command!

Despair induced the rebels to land on the coast of Algarve, a party of adventurers, who, seeking in rapine the support which their country denies them, and avoiding the fifth division, directed their march to Setubal, relying on the asylum which their ships offer them.

General the Viscount de Mollellos with double their forces pursues their rear; and dispositions have been made that they should meet with a valiant resistance in front. The towns, &c. which they cease to oppress with their detestable presence, again with the greatest enthusiasm proclaim the King my Lord. There is nothing to fear; we have only to take measures against the evil-disposed, and against the persons abettors of the enemies of the altar and throne.

Honourable inhabitants of Lisbon! run to arms in defence of the holy religion which we profess, and the legitimate King we have sworn to. Let cowards disappear and traitors fly, and let honourable men alone present themselves to render their services to the justest of causes.

Soldiers! what have I to say to you? To recommend valour? You have valour superior to all the soldiers in the world. To recommend love and loyalty to the person of Don Miguel the First! Who is there among you who is not ready to shed his blood for him?

The most perfect discipline and subordination; you well know how necessary it is; with it, small forces overcome great armies; without it, great armies are destroyed by few enemies.

Soldiers! I am in your front, and I rely on the divine mercy that I shall not prove unworthy of the name I have inherited with my blood.

To obtain therefore the end which we all propose to ourselves and for the good of H. M. service, I determine the following.

1st. The city of Lisbon is henceforward to be considered in a state of siege by land and sea, and therefore the military authority superior to any other.

2nd. All those inhabitants of Lisbon who voluntarily wish to concur towards the defence and security of the capital, are to present themselves either at the quarters of the corps of royalist volunteers, or at those of the Urbans, in order there to be chosen for the service that may be most convenient according to circumstances.

3rd. Any person who by any act or seditious words promotes dismay or revolt, will be immediately seized, judged, and executed, if condemned to death, within twenty-two hours.

4th. Foreigners shall enjoy the protection of which the laws and treaties confer on them, and which shall be most scrupulously observed, provided that they interfere not with the political concerns of this nation, for in that case they shall be proceeded against according to the law of nations and to treaties, without scruple.

APPENDIX. 361

No. XXII.

On the 24th of July of the year of the birth of our Lord Jesus Christ one thousand eight hundred and thirty-three, the people in a large body, free from all influence either external or internal, without compulsion, the city being forsaken by the troops, being assembled in the hall of the council of this very noble and ever loyal city of Lisbon, with a free and spontaneous will, and with an unanimity never before seen, ordained and declared the Senhora Donna Maria the Second, daughter of the immortal Pedro the Fourth, for whom the people are ready to spill the last drop of their blood as all loyal Portuguese are ever ready to do, for their lawful sovereign and their legitimate Queen, and in order that this should be made known the present act was drawn up, which was signed by all present.

Signatures follow.

No. XXIII.

A LIST OF THE PORTUGUESE NAVY.

Don John ·········· 74   } the extra guns
Cape St. Vincent ···· 74 Sheer hulk. } were removed.
Duchess of Braganza 50
Don Pedro ········ 50
Rainha ············ 42
Donna Maria ······ 42

Fifth of July	50		
Eliza	26	Corvette	
Isabel Maria	24	Do.	
Cacella	20	Do.	Since sold.
Portuense	20	Do.	Since lost.
Audaz	18	Brig.	
Providenza	16	Do.	Since sold.
Villa Flor	18		
Third of July	10	Brig.	Since sold.
Liberal	8	Schooner.	
Faro	5	Do.	
Prince Don Pedro	20		Brought from Brest.
Schooner	10		Do.
St. John Magnanimo	30	East Indiaman.	
	30	Do.	
Eighth of July	24	Corvette.	
	50		On the stocks.

    4 store ships.
    1 Queen's yacht.
    1   do.   building.

At Brest, 1 good frigate, 1 corvette, and 3 bad frigates, all lying there rotting.

No. XXIV.

INHABITANTS OF LISBON !

A division of the liberating army intrusted to my command by H. I. M. the Duke of Braganza, to give you liberty, having passed through the provinces south of the Tagus, came to the banks of the river, and displayed the standard of the Queen and liberty. But this standard, under which the loyal supporters of the throne and the charter have served in the midst of persecutions, of exile, and of battles, was never the symbol of war or vengeance, but the sign of peace and concord, concord and reconciliation to the whole Portuguese Family, and of clemency and pardon for the deluded and unfortunate.

Therefore, inhabitants of Lisbon, I expect and exact order and respect to the rights of all, tranquillity and safety to the capital. I have given and will continue to give attention to arm you regularly, and to re-establish the same corps who formerly sustained the Queen and Charter.

With them, and with those I am about to organise, you will have an opportunity of sharing the glory in the restoration of the Nation, the maintenance of order, and the tranquillity of your homes.

DUKE OF TERCEIRA.

Head-Quarters, Lisbon,
　July 24*th*, 1833.

No. XXV.

LETTER TO GEN. BOURMONT.
Don John,
Lisbon, Sept. 18*th*, 1833.

MARSHAL,

You are a foreigner and command D. Miguel's

army—I am a foreigner and command D. Maria's navy—You are, I believe, a decided royalist—I am a decided liberal—Is it impossible, Marshal, to put an end to this unfortunate war in an honourable manner? When I took command of the squadron, I told the Duke of Palmella, the Duke of Terceira, and Count Saldanha, if I found the people opposed to the Queen and the Charter, I would haul down my flag and return to England. We landed in the Algarves, were received with open arms, and the Duke of Terceira marched through the country with fifteen hundred men and appeared before Lisbon. The government abandoned the capital and its defences, and the inhabitants proclaimed the Queen with the greatest enthusiasm. I captured D. Miguel's squadron, and with his ships, officers, and crews, in conjunction with my frigates, appeared at the same time off the bar.

Your Excellency has been obliged to raise the siege of Oporto, you have been repulsed before Lisbon, and you know our lines cannot be forced,—your army is discontented, are deserting, and wish to give up the contest. They are held together by foreign officers alone. The ports are either in our possession or they are blockaded, your resources are cut off, and your troops without pay or clothing. Your Excellency will perhaps answer that the greater part of the nobility, the priests and the peasants support you. I grant it; more than that, every robber and malefactor in the country is on the side of Don Miguel, and they are practising the most unheard-of cruelties, murdering even women and children. The nobles are fighting for their privileges, and the peasantry are excited by the priests. Are they, however, the intelligent people of Portugal? No!!! They are to be found in the large towns and in the middling classes, who are all for the Queen. Ought such a state of things to exist? I put it to your Excellency as an experienced soldier, as an honourable man, and above all, as a Frenchman, ought this unnatural war to be prolonged?

This letter is dictated by humanity alone.—Your Excellency knows we have nothing to fear. Should you even get possession of part of Lisbon, you would be driven out by the Castle and squadron.

France, England, and Sweden have already acknowledged the Queen—the other Powers will follow. Spain alone may hang back, but is she safe? Has she no fears for herself? Does she think a powerful squadron will be idle if she feeds the cause of Don Miguel and keeps an ambassador at his court?

I trust, Marshal, you will give this a patient consideration, and beg, Marshal, you will believe me to remain with the highest consideration your obedient servant,

CAPE ST. VINCENT.

Paço do Lumiar, 19 *Septembre,* 1833.

AMIRAL,

Assurément vous et moi sommes etrangers au Portugal; je suis certainement royaliste, et je vous crois très liberal puisque vous me le donnez l'assurance ; ni vous ni moi n'avons excité cette guerre dont je déplore ainsi que vous les tristes effets ; nous sommes je crois d'accord sur ces points.

Mais nous ne le sommes point sur les vœux des Portugais ; je crois que l'immense majorité des habitans repousse les institutions novatrices que vous voulez introduire dans le royaume, et qu'en servant le roi Dom Miguel, non seulement je défends les anciennes loix du pays, mais j'agis conformément aux vœux de la majorité de la nation ; vous la seriez convaincu vous-même si vous considériez ce qui vient de se passer dans les Algarves, où le peuple seul, sans l'appui d'aucune troupe, a chassé les garnisons et les autorités civiles que vous y aviez établies.

Je ne fais point la distinction que vous voulez établir entre Portugais : je suis chrétien, et je considère tous les hommes comme des frères, je leur souhaite du bien à tous, et je ne pense pas qu'il soit juste de ne s'interresser qu'à ceux qui tiennent le premier ou le dernier rang social, ni à ceux qui tiennent le rang mitoyen ; tous ont des droits fondés sur les loix de leur pays, tous sont des hommes de même nature que vous et moi, et je ne mépriserai jamais les vœux ni les besoins d'aucune de ces classes : un paysan, un laboureur est souvent plus homme de bien, et la raison de cela plus estimable, qu'un autre homme fort instruit et fort riche ; j'en ai eu plus d'une preuve dans ma vie ; cependant, vous m'assurez avoir reconnu que le plus grand nombre des prêtres, des nobles, et des paysans sont du partie du Roi, et je ne conçois pas bien l'application que vous voulez faire des principes libéraux, en opposition avec leur base établie dans les autres états de l'Europe, que *l'opinion de la majorité doit faire la loi.*

Mais je n'ai aucunement l'intention d'eclaircir ce point, qui ne regarde que vous-même.

Vous ajoutez, Amiral, que les voleurs et les malfaiteurs sont encore du parti de Dom Miguel; j'aurais préferé ne point trouver d'expression semblable dans votre lettre, elle ne peut servir à rien, et elle est peu conforme aux usages de politesse établis entre gens estimables; mais vous reprochez des cruautés inouies aux partisans du Roi; et cela me prouve que vous êtes bien malinformé des faits, car il me semble que s'il y en a eu malheureusement quelques unes de commises par le parti que je sers, celui que vous servez en a commis bien davantage, et qu'il la commet encore tous les jours à Lisbonne, où un système de confiscation et de vengeance est notoirement établi.

Les reproches, Amiral, sont au moins inutiles, et ne peuvent en aucun cas servir à diminuer les maux qu'entraine une semblable guerre; et comme la lettre que vous m'avez adressée se trouve sans conclusion, je ne veux, Amiral, que vous en accuser réception, et vous assurer que je suis avec une très haute consideration

Votre très humble serviteur,

Cte. De Bourmont.

A Son Excellence
Mons. l'Amiral Cape St. Vincent.

Lisbon, Sept. 20th, 1833.

Marshal,

I regret exceedingly that your Excellency should have taken offence at two expressions in my letter. They were intended to show the evils attending this unfortunate war, and not, I assure you, to give offence; but I frankly own on reading over my letter they ought not to have been used, and I sincerely beg your Excellency's pardon. I was also much irritated at the moment by intelligence of enormities committed at Alcacer do Sal, which will also plead my excuse.

If your Excellency disapproves of confiscations at Lisbon (cruelties there are none,) how much more must you disapprove of the executions, arrests, and confiscations that took place for five years before. Your Excellency cannot have forgot how your own countrymen were treated, and the chastisement that followed.

I wish your Excellency had seen Lisbon three months ago and could see it now; joy and happiness have taken the place of fear and trembling,—the high honour of a French general would induce him to immediately sheath his sword.

By putting an end to the war an immediate stop would be put to murder, rapine, imprisonment, and confiscation. So desirous is every man here to see it finished, from the Emperor to the common soldier, that I am certain if the " sine-quâ-non" of Don Miguel quitting Portugal was admitted, every difficulty would immediately disappear.

I beg, Marshal, you will believe me to remain with the highest consideration

> Your obedient humble servant,
>> VISCOUNT CAPE ST. VINCENT,
>> Admiral and Major-General.

COPY.

> *Paço de Lumiar,*
> 21 *Septembre,* 1833.

AMIRAL,

Je viens de recevoir la seconde lettre que votre Excellence m'a fait l'honneur de m'écrire. Je vous remercie de l'explication que vous avez bien voulu me donner relativement à quelques expressions contenues dans la première. J'en suis pleinement satisfait.

Le *sine qua non* dont vous parlez ne me semble pas pouvoir être accepté par le Roi; et par consequent ne peut servir à rien en ce moment.

> J'ai l'honneur d'être,
>> Mons. l'Amiral,
>>> Avec une haute consideration,
>>>> Votre très humble et obéissant serviteur,
>>>>> (Signé) CTE. DE BOURMONT.

A Son Excellence
L'Amiral Cape St. Vincent.

ERRATA.

Page 9, line 22, *for* there will not be *read* there would not be.
— 12, — 2, *for* and in this capacity *read* and in that capacity.
— 12, — 4, *for* had not shewn *read* did not shew.
— 16, — 18, *for* reforming *read* reform.
— 16, — 22, *for* proves *read* proved.
— 59, — 5, *for* arms *read* army.
— 111, — 8, *for* out off *read* cut off.
— 140, — 6, *for* army *read* enemy.
— 154, — 10, *for* Henry *read* George.
— 162, — 20, *for* Oxenheim *read* Oxenstiern.
— 164, — 13, *for* prepared *read* proposed.
— 171, last line, *for* Lieutenant Peak *read* Captain Peak.
— 173, last line, *for* intention, and had made every preparation to destroy them, *read* intentions, and had made every preparation to frustrate them.
— 175, line 17, *for* informing *read* informed.
— 178, — 5, *for* upper *read* after.
— 180, lines 2 & 3, tell *the* .... *the* expedition.
— 193, last line, *for* in a compact line *read* in compact lines.
— 197, line 11, *for* line-of-battle ships *read* line-of-battle ship.
— 200, — 3 from the bottom, *for* Lt. Nivett *read* Lt. Knyvett.
— 203, — 14, *for* Lieutenant *read* Lieutenants.
— 208, — 16, *for* the commodore and rest *read* the commodore and the rest.
— 217, — 4, *for* who brought me *read* which brought me.
— 221, — 10, *for* who had gone up *read* which had gone up.
— 222, — 12, omit " *which was*" the &c.
— 224, — 21, *for* town of Oritao *read* tower of Oritao.
— 242, — 15, *for* my own officers *read* my own office.
— 259, — 16, *for* unaccountability *read* accountability.
— 260, last line, *for* Hopner *read* Hoppner.
— 263, line 4, *for* proposition *read* preparation.
— 267, — 22, *for* corp *read* corps.

AN ACCOUNT

OF THE

WAR IN PORTUGAL

BETWEEN

DON PEDRO AND DON MIGUEL.

BY

ADMIRAL CHARLES NAPIER.

VOL. II.

The Naval & Military Press Ltd

CONTENTS.

CHAPTER I.

Captain Peak occupies Santiago. The Miguelites re-occupy Santiago, but are driven out with great loss. Stratagem of the governor of Lagos. The author garrisons Setuval. Value of the port of Setuval. Preparations to drive the Miguelites from before the lines of Lisbon. Positions of the Miguelites near Oporto. Fidelity of the Portuguese to their colours. Impolitic concealment of plans from the author. The Miguelites are compelled to retreat from before Lisbon. Errors committed by some of the Queen's officers. Fault committed by the Miguelites. The Miguelites retreat to Santarem. Saldanha establishes his head-quarters at Cartaxo. Consequence of not forming a plan. What might have been done by better management. . Page 1

CHAPTER II.

Reduction of the naval force. Wretched state of the Portuguese navy. Portuguese officers are scientific men, but not sailors. Merits of the seamen. Different classes of officers. Uselessness of the pilots. Fruitless efforts of the author to effect a reform. Indolence of M. Freire. Causes of the wretched state of the naval department. Dissatisfaction occasioned by the author's necessary promotions. The navy completely disorganized by a decree against officers who had served Don Miguel. Dismissal of the master-builder. The naval arsenal a mere receptacle of incapables. Attempt to reform it. Difficulty of keeping up the naval blockade. Reform of the marine corps. A council of state is formed. Don Carlos is ordered to quit Portugal. Shameful conduct of General Cordova. Death of Ferdinand VII. of Spain. Communication from the Queen of Spain's government. Don Pedro writes to the Queen-Regent of Spain. Death of Candido Xavier. Inefficient minister of marine appointed. Remonstrances of the British government. Don Pedro becomes unpopular. Reinforcements arrive from England. Shameful treatment of them. . . . Page 20

CHAPTER III.

Position of the armies of the Queen and Don Miguel in front of Santarem. The Miguelites make incursions on the other side of the Tagus. Probability that the Queen's army might have penetrated to Santarem at the outset. General Macdonald resigns the command of Don Miguel's army. Desertion from that army. Leiria declares for the Queen. Alcacer do Sal abandoned by the Miguelites. The Queen's troops defeated at Alcacer do Sal by General Lemos. Infamous conduct of General Lemos. The author throws succours into Setuval. The garrison withdrawn from Sines. Ill effect of indolence and neglect in various departments. The author proceeds to Algarve to secure that province. His arrival at Lagos. The mills at Pernes destroyed. Removal of Nepomuceno. Inactivity of both armies. Impolitic decrees. Angry discussion in the council. Spain offers its mediation. Negotiation with Don Miguel. It is broken off. Boldness of the Count de Taipa. Don Pedro consults Saldanha. Folly of the minister of marine. Audience of the author with Don Pedro. Affairs at Oporto. Skirmishes. Death of Colonel Pacheco. Sir T. Stubbs created Baron of Villa Nova de Gaya. He is removed. Cape de Verde Isles declare for the Queen. . . . . Page 43

CHAPTER IV.

Marvaõ surprised by a party under José Joaquim d'Abreu. Skirmishes between his troops and the Miguelites. Plan of operations in the south formed by the author. Movements of the Duke of Terceira. He advances on Leiria. Defeats the Miguelites. Leiria is fortified. Defeat of the Chaves cavalry. Inactivity of Don Miguel's army. The Miguelites are defeated at Pernes. Imperfect communication between Saldanha and Terceira. Danger which might have arisen from the expedition to Leiria. The author presses for a force to be sent to the south of the Tagus. It is resolved to send it. . . . . Page 72

CHAPTER V.

Lord Howard de Walden replaces Lord W. Russell as ambassador at Lisbon. He recommends a general amnesty. Confused state of affairs. Interference of Spain apprehended. Plans of Saldanha. Don Miguel publishes a general amnesty. He sends a force to the left bank of the Tagus. No result obtained from it. The Queen's army attacked by Don Miguel's at Santarem. Positions of the Queen's troops. Terrible slaughter of the Miguelites. Gallant charge made by Colonel Bacon. Excellent dispositions of the Miguelites. The army of Don Miguel is defeated. Expedition to the south abandoned. . . Page 90

CHAPTER VI.

Propositions for putting an end to the contest made by Lord Howard de Walden. They give offence. Don Pedro not well disposed towards Lord Howard. A negotiation opened with Don Miguel. Spain offers to send troops into Portugal. Error of Lord Howard. Decree depriving Don Miguel of his rank and property. Lord Howard objects to it. Counter-project of Freire. Meeting of Lord Howard and Lemos to confer about terms. Don Miguel refuses to abandon Portugal. Lord Howard's endeavours to bring about the abdication. Failure of the negotiation. Don Pedro is pleased with the failure. . . . . Page 105

CHAPTER VII.

Narrative of military operations resumed. The Miguelites acquire the ascendency in Algarve. Unpopularity of the French regiment. The Baron de Sa sent to Algarve. His activity. He marches to Castro Marim, and defeats the Miguelites in several encounters. He returns to Faro. The Miguelites repulsed in an attack on Faro. Reinforcements sent to de Sa. He defeats the enemy at Sao Braz. His repeated successes. He drives the Miguelite guerillas out of the province. The Miguelite guerillas a band of ferocious robbers and murderers. . . . . Page 113

CHAPTER VIII.

Don Miguel sends Louis de Bourmont with troops into Algarve. The author presses Don Pedro to let him seize the Miguelite sea-ports. Don Pedro consents. Misrepresentations in the minister-at-war's relatorio. The author sails to Setuval. He wishes to surprise Alcacer do Sal. Ordered to return to Lisbon. Declines. Baron de Sa advances into Alemtejo. He enters Beja. He makes a fruitless attack on Serpa. General Bourmont marches to attack him. Retreat of de Sa. Alcacer taken and lost by the Queen's troops. Don Miguel despatches a large force into Algarve. The author sails with the expedition to the north. Difficulty

CONTENTS.

of landing on the Portuguese coast. The author reconnoitres Caminha. Caminha described. The troops are landed at La Guardia. Caminha is taken by surprise. The Baron de Sa enters Beja. The author marches on Fifo. The Viana militia come over to the Queen's troops. Capture of Viana. The author marches on Valença. Motley nature of the force. Local situation of Valença. Dispositions made by the author for the siege. Valença capitulates. Bad conduct of the minister of marine. . . . . . . Page 124

CHAPTER IX.

Occurrences at Oporto. Torres marches against the Miguelite army. Skirmish at Lexa. The Miguelites are forced to retreat to Amarante. The Duke of Terceira is sent with reinforcements to Oporto. Proclamation issued by him. His military dispositions. The author returns to Lisbon. Abortive design of the Miguelites against Setuval. Painful situation of Don Pedro. Operations of the Baron de Sa in Algarve. He is worsted and compelled to retire to Silves. The Miguelites are repulsed at Faro. Operations of the Duke of Terceira. He drives the Miguelites from all their positions in the neighbourhood of Amarante. Lamego declares for the Queen. The Miguelites retreat before Terceira, and cross the Douro. They continue their retreat in Beira. They abandon Almeida. The two northern provinces are quite freed from the enemy. General Rodil offers to co-operate with the Duke. His offer is accepted.
Page 161

CHAPTER X.

The author sails to attempt Figueira. The Miguelites abandon the place. Coimbra taken by the Queen's forces. Error committed in allowing the garrison of Figueira to escape. General Cardoza, the Miguelite general, retires on

Vizeu. The volunteers of Beira are organized. The Miguelite army is compelled to retire from Vizeu by Terceira. Junction of the Spanish army with the Queen's. Halt at Coimbra to organize a government. Plan of operations concerted between Rodil and Terceira. Operations of the author. He joins Colonel Vasconcellos at Pombal. March to Ourem. Portuguese are easily made soldiers. The author's dispositions for the attack of Ourem. Ourem surrenders. Battle of Aceiceira. The Miguelite army is routed. Don Pedro arrives, and takes the command of the army. He issues a proclamation to the troops of Don Miguel. . . . . Page 185

CHAPTER XI.

The Chaves cavalry come over to the Queen. Abrantes abandoned by the Miguelites. Don Miguel retreats on Evora. Secrecy of his retreat. He is pursued by the divisions of Terceira and Saldanha. The author returns to Lisbon. Measures taken by him. Suspension of arms concluded between Don Miguel and the Queen's generals. Amount of the force collected at Evora by Don Miguel. Plan proposed to Don Miguel by General Bourmont. Another proposed by Don Carlos. The superior officers of Don Miguel are tired of the war. Treaty concluded between Don Pedro and Don Miguel. The quadruple alliance not the cause of Don Miguel's fall. Impolicy of that treaty. Danger of Don Miguel in embarking. Don Carlos is received on board of the Donegal. Mismanagement of that business. Don Carlos lands in England. Don Pedro's amnesty to the Miguelites excites dissatisfaction. Don Miguel ought to have been confined. Difference between his case and that of Don Carlos. Wrong system adopted by England with respect to the Spanish question. . Page 204

CHAPTER XII.

Causes which led to Don Miguel's downfall. His error in not subjugating Terceira; in not granting an amnesty; in not interrupting the passage of Don Pedro; in his violent proclamation against Oporto, &c. &c. Errors committed by Don Pedro's government. Want of vigour at the outset. Useless sorties. Ill treatment of the foreign troops. Misconduct of the ministry. It never had any military plans. Blunder in the negotiation with France respecting the Portuguese ships. Return of the author to England. He sails again to Portugal. Indecent haste of the Portuguese government to get rid of its auxiliaries. Bad faith of the government. Don Pedro in bad health. He meets the two Houses of Parliament. He is continued in the regency. His health grows worse. Political state of the House of Peers. The Queen is declared of age. A new ministry is formed by Palmella. The author resigns. Shameful conduct of the Portuguese ministry with respect to the widows and orphans of naval officers. Death of Don Pedro. His character. His burial. Letter of the Queen to the author. The House of Peers votes thanks to the author. Letter of Palmella. Promotions. The author leaves Portugal. Slight put upon him by the Portuguese ministry. Vote of thanks from the Chamber of Deputies to the author. . Page 220

APPENDIX.

I. Letter from the author to the minister of marine 249
— Letter to the director of the countability . . 250
— Letter from the minister of marine to the author 250

CONTENTS.

II. Letter from the author to Lord Palmerston	251
III. Reference to Don Pedro's letter to the Queen of Spain	253
IV. Letter from Captain Birt on the defeat of the Queen's troops by Lemos	254
— Letter of the author on the same subject	256
V. Reference to the decree against the Tobacco contractors	257
VI. Count Taipa's first remonstrance	258
VII. Count Taipa's second remonstrance	261
VIII. The Peers' protest, No. 1	271
IX. Carvalho's answer to the Peers' protest, No. 1	273
X. The Peers' protest, No. 2	273
XI. Letter of D'Aguiar to the Duke of Terceira in answer to the Peers' protest	278
XII. Letter of the author to the minister of marine	279
XIII. Letter of the author to Don Pedro on the state of affairs	280
XIV. Reference to an order of the day issued by Don Miguel	286
XV. & XVI. Reference to the project of Lord Howard and the counter-project of Freire	286
XVII. Proclamation of Baron de Sa de Bandeira to the Algarvians	287
XVIII. The author's proclamation to the inhabitants of Caminha	287
— Summons to the governor of the fort of Caminha	288
XIX. The author's proclamation to the inhabitants of Viana	288
XX. The author's summons to the governor of Valença	289
XXI. Letters between Don F. A. Caldas and the author	290

CONTENTS.

XXII.	Articles of capitulation of Valença.	291
XXIII.	Letter of the author to the minister of marine relative to Captain Cunha	292
XXIV.	Proclamation of the Duke of Terceira to the inhabitants of the north	294
XXV.	Proclamation of the author to the inhabitants of Figueira	294
XXVI.	Instructions given by the author to Captain Bertram	295
XXVII.	Summons of the author to the governor of Ourem	297
—	Reply of the governor	298
—	Articles of capitulation	298
XXVIII.	Proclamation of Don Pedro to the army of Don Miguel	299
XXIX.	Letters between the Duke of Terceira and General Lemos relative to a suspension of arms	302
XXX.	Convention of Evora	304
XXXI.	Farewell proclamation of Don Miguel to his army	309
XXXII.	The treaty of quadruple alliance between England, France, Spain, and Portugal	310
XXXIII.	Convention for the departure of Don Carlos from Portugal	314
XXXIV.	Speech of Don Pedro on opening the Portuguese parliament	316
XXXV.	Letter of the author to the minister of marine on the management of the naval department	332
XXXVI.	Letter of the author to the minister of marine relative to the widows and orphans of the slain	333

WAR OF SUCCESSION

IN

PORTUGAL,

ETC. ETC.

CHAPTER I.

During the inactivity of the enemy before Lisbon, and the festivities in consequence of the Queen's arrival, we were not idle in other parts. Captain Peak had possessed himself of St. Jago, a town twelve miles inland from Sines, but the guerillas having collected in great numbers, he was obliged to retire on the latter place, which was as well fortified as the nature of the ground would permit. Happily I had at my disposal a considerable body of English and Portuguese marines, and two steamers, and was enabled to give succour to all parts of the coast in danger without waiting for the dilatory arrangements of ministers. Captain Peak was reinforced by ninety English marines, under Captain Birt, of the Don John, and about two hundred Portuguese collected from Peniché and Lisbon, under Colonel Almada. St. Jago was again occupied, and the whole country for a considerable distance cleared; this done, Captain Peak sailed for Lagos, which was again in danger, and the English marines were embarked in the George IV. steamer for the same destination.

The frigate had hardly quitted the coast, when the guerillas again advanced in great force on St. Jago, which we were obliged to abandon for the second time. The English marines disembarked from the George IV., and joining the Portuguese, left Sines at night, and making a circuitous rout fell upon them at daylight, completely routed the whole party, who left one hundred and fifty on the field of battle. This example put an end to their depredations for some time, and the English marines proceeded to Lagos. The governor of that town Francisco Correa de Mendonca, had done wonders in its defence, and had been a long time left to his own resources. His applications for provisions and assistance had slumbered in the minister's bureau; and the place must have ultimately surrendered but for the assistance I was enabled to give him from time to time. He had been lately hard pressed, and resorted to a stratagem which completely succeeded. By means of spies it was communicated to the guerilla chief, that if he advanced at a particular hour to a given place, the town would be surrendered on making the preconcerted signal. Captain Peak arrived in the afternoon, and having made arrangements with the governor, stood out to sea, and returned after dark to the anchorage.

A little after midnight, on the 17th of September, the signal was made and answered, and the guerillas approached the walls. The garrison was under arms, and a profound silence reigned on the ramparts. They were allowed to come close to the gate, when a tremendous fire of musketry was opened upon them from all points. A sally was then made by the garrison, and the frigate's marines and seamen; and as they retreated in confusion, they were exposed to the frigate's broadsides, which flanked the road. The George IV. with the English marines arrived before daylight, were landed, and completed the catastrophe. The loss of the guerillas was very great; ours trifling. Excursions were made into the country, and the town was well stocked with provisions of every description, and got ready for another siege.

Setuval, the second best port in the kingdom, had been neglected by both parties; all I could do for its protection was stationing a corvette there, and I became apprehensive that the Miguelites, who had a considerable force in the south, would for once do right and seize it. Captain Peak was in consequence ordered there in the Donna Maria, and Fort St. Philip was garrisoned by the marines; the guns, which had been very improperly removed, were remounted, and a redoubt thrown up on a high point to the southward of the town, which, if in possession of the enemy, would have driven her from the anchorage. I went over for a day or two to examine the locality, and at once saw the importance of putting it in a proper state of defence; and here I may observe that it is quite inconceivable how Don Miguel's advisers and generals could have neglected occupying this port, and garrisoning it. Had they ever entertained the least idea of procuring a squadron, Setuval was a port capable of receiving them; it can be entered at all times, and would have been a safe place for receiving stores and ammunition from England, which facility no other port in Portugal offers during the winter, on account of their dangerous bars. On my return to Lisbon, a garrison composed of a few regulars and a regiment of Lisbon volunteers were sent there, and the town was put in a tolerable state of defence; a small flotilla was also organized for the protection of the trade, and to facilitate our future operations on Alcacer do Sal.

General Zegallo was also crossed over to Aldea Gallega with one thousand infantry and two hundred cavalry, a force fully sufficient to have advanced on Zamora, and probably on Salvatierra, supported by the force in Setuval, which could have moved out; but whether he had orders to remain there, or had not sufficient enterprize to advance, I do not very well know. After remaining there a few weeks, he was recalled with his men to Lisbon, and the whole of that part of the country exposed to the incursions of the enemy, which, with the command of the Tagus in our possession, never ought to have been permitted. I neither was acquainted with the intention of sending or withdrawing him, and could offer no cooperation; indeed there seemed to be no plan; every thing was carried on by chance, without either system or consultation, as must always be the case when there are so many masters, all pulling different ways. Had the whole command been left to one head, without any interference on the part of ministers, things would have been managed very differently. On the 29th of September the Baron de Sa took possession of Obidos after a short resistance, the garrison and inhabitants taking flight: his loss was only two men wounded.

There appearing no further prospect of any movement against Lisbon by the enemy, preparations were silently made by Saldanha to drive them from their position in front of the lines.

Steam-boats were sent to Oporto for the twelfth caçadores and the Scotch and English battalions, the greater part of whom were landed at Peniché. The only effective troops left at Oporto were the tenth and fifteenth regiments of the line, now completed to six hundred strong, and the original volunteers. In addition to these were the first, second, and third fixos, twelve pieces of field-artillery, and some smaller corps, amounting to about two thousand four hundred men.

This force was by no means sufficient for the defence of Oporto, and the Miguelites, by their constant movements, seemed to indicate an attack. They were established to the north at Santo Thirso, about four leagues from Oporto, and on the south at Olivares de Azameis to communicate with Coimbra, Lamego, and Vizieu. Had the Miguelites shewed any enterprize, they would have stood a very fair chance of taking Oporto, and it was equally inexcusable in them not attempting it, as it was in the minister-at-war weakening it to the extent he did. He looked at the returns, which shewed about eleven thousand of all descriptions, but never took the trouble to consider whether they were fit to contend against regular troops or not. Had Oporto fallen, which it ought to have done, the Miguelites would have gained confidence, and the war would have taken an entirely new turn.

At this time the enemy were supposed to have about twelve thousand men before the lines, including one thousand cavalry. Our force might be eight thousand regular troops and as many volunteers or moveable battalions, and not more than six hundred cavalry; in addition to this force there were about six thousand fixos and the three battalions of the naval and military arsenal and public works. The force of the enemy had very much diminished by sickness, desertion to their homes, and to the Queen's standard; though I must observe, to the credit of the Portuguese soldiers, that desertion to us bore no proportion to their losses by other causes, and yet Miguel's troops were ill-paid, ill-clothed, and ill-fed; but the Portuguese are generally true to their colours. The same praise is also due to the Queen's soldiers when suffering at Oporto under every privation. The desertion, though at once alarming, was nothing to be compared to what might have been expected. The regular troops on the Queen's side were certainly much superior to Don Miguel's, but little could be expected from the volunteer battalions, composed of all classes of citizens, badly officered, with little discipline, and totally unacquainted with war; nevertheless Marshal Saldanha contemplated driving the enemy from before Lisbon.

Independent of the troops within the lines at Lisbon, we had between two and three thousand men at Peniché, under General Nepomuceno and the Baron de Sa; and orders were sent there by the George IV. steamer to march upon Torres Vedras, and be ready to cooperate with Marshal Saldanha in the event of his succeeding in driving the enemy from their positions. On the evening of the 9th of October the minister-at-war desired that I might have the boats of the arsenal and the ships ready, in the event of their being wanted in the morning, to embark the troops at Almada under Colonel Raboca, but without communicating to me Saldanha's intention of attacking the enemy. Next morning he came to the arsenal, and for the first time I was acquainted with the marshal's intention, the minister observing at the same time that he was not himself aware of his plans till late the evening before. Whether this is true or not I cannot say, but it does appear that something must have been wrong in some quarter, if the marshal found it necessary to conceal so important a movement from the minister-at-war and marine, and in consequence from the commander-in-chief of the squadron.

Had the marshal contemplated making a reconnoissance, it was of less importance; but it ought to have been taken into consideration that that reconnoissance might cause the enemy to retreat, and every preparation should have been made to take advantage of circumstances; instead of which all that I could do to assist the marshal's movements was by moving up the flotilla, together with a brig and floating battery, and occupy the ground opposite Sacavem, to prevent a retreat across the river, and this at a considerable risk, because we knew nothing of the force the enemy had in that quarter, and the re-embarking, in the event of being attacked, was nearly impossible at low water. This, however, was done, and there we remained the whole day within hearing of the action, and without receiving any communication from the minister of what was going forward.

Towards the afternoon I passed the river, and moved down to the powder-mills at Veralles, to be ready to act on the enemy's flank next morning, should it be necessary; and at sunset returned to Lisbon, and repaired to the Emperor's quarters in a house outside of the town. There I learnt that the attack had succeeded at all points, and the enemy were driven from their position. During the night they retired on Loures, and next morning the Queen's troops followed them to that place, marching over the hills, the cavalry keeping the high road. At four o'clock the high ground above Loures was occupied by our troops, and the artillery came up. The enemy were seen making every preparation to decamp; in fact their baggage was already on the move, and their cavalry were drawn up on the plain to protect their retreat. Here the division from Peniché should have been in their rear, but from some unaccountable mismanagement they halted at Torres Vedras. It has been said that they received the despatch from Lisbon a day too late; they, however, heard the firing, and ought to have felt their way: indeed, if they had, this day would probably have finished the war.

As soon as I discovered the enemy in retreat, directions were sent to the flotilla to move up to Alhandra, and flank the road which passed close to the river, and by which road they were moving off. The Emperor came up at this time, and after remaining a few hours returned to Lisbon. No attack was made by us; but towards dark the Miguelites, I suppose to cover their retreat, attacked Saldanha's position, and were driven back with considerable loss. On the road to Lisbon I received a despatch from the marine head-quarters communicating the welcome intelligence that the inspector of the arsenal had anticipated my views, and moved part of the flotilla to Alhandra; and I naturally expected, on his receiving my orders, the the brig and floating battery would have followed. This was communicated to the Emperor, who was delighted at their activity, and actually gave orders to have it put in the gazette. On my return to Lisbon I found to my surprise and astonishment, that the inspector of the arsenal and the commander of the troops, after having landed on the road, and staid there a few hours, abandoned the position without having seen the enemy, and returned with all the gun-boats and troops to the arsenal, leaving the Miguelites and baggage a free passage, without the least annoyance. I ordered them to return forthwith; but next morning it blew so fresh that neither the brig of war nor floating battery could get up in time; and the enemy's army and baggage, who moved from Loures at two o'clock in the morning, passed without the least interruption.

Comments on this conduct are useless; and it is only to be regretted that the Emperor had not had a little more of the devil in his composition, and made examples where they were necessary. If such an unpardonable neglect, to say the least of it, was committed by us, the enemy at the same time shewed great want of enterprize. Before dark they had a full opportunity of seeing the positions we occupied, and instead of retreating by Alhandra, they ought to have made a daring movement to their left on Sacavem, got into the Lisbon road, which they might have done in the night, gained a march on the Queen's troops, forced the lines, which would have only been defended by the fixed battalions, and secured the capital.

It may be asked what they would have gained by this bold step, having Saldanha's army blockading them by land, and the fleet by sea. I answer, they would have regained the capital, captured the Queen and all the court, stores, arsenals, &c., which would have led to the entire disorganization of the army, and the probable return of every man raised in Lisbon. Besides, such a daring enterprize would have given confidence to their army, and struck such a terror into the Queen's troops that I doubt much whether they would have again followed them up to the capital. However, Don Miguel did not dare this, and lost his crown, as all princes ought to do who have not talent, courage, and enterprize, to put all to the hazard of a die to save it.

The Miguelites continued their retreat to Santarem, without even standing on the plain between Villa Nova and Azambuja, where from their superiority of cavalry, they ought to have risked an action. They entered Santarem on the 15th, without leaving a soul behind; indeed their retreat was conducted with great order and rapidity by General Macdonell, and was certainly not followed up with vigour by us. It must, however, be admitted that the discipline of our troops was by no means adapted for quick movements, nor were we prepared for so much success. Their cavalry was also infinitely superior to ours. On the other hand, the enemy were evidently frightened, and believed our force to be much greater than it was; and I have no doubt, had they been attacked at Loures, that they would have been totally routed.

General Nepomuceno arrived at Bucellas on the evening of the 12th, and at Sobral de Monte Agraco on the 13th. The same evening Saldanha halted at Villa Franca, and pushed his advanced posts on the roads of Rio Mayor and Santarem; and the flotilla went up to Villa Nova, where the enemy had halted, but retired on their approach. On the 16th Saldanha fixed his quarters at Cartaxo.

Driving the enemy from before Lisbon was certainly a bold measure; but I am sure the success we met with was not anticipated, nor do I believe any thing further than a reconnoissance was intended, for no preparations were made to follow them up; and here I think the Emperor, minister-at-war or Saldanha, whoever it was, committed a great error.

The moment Don Pedro was of opinion that his troops were sufficiently organized for a forward movement, he ought to have called to his council the two marshals and myself, and laid before us the state of his army and that of the enemy, which could have been easily ascertained. He ought to have informed himself of their dispositions, and above all of the state of Santarem, and the force in it. At that time I do not believe it was fortified, nor do I believe it was garrisoned. With this information before us a regular plan ought to have been laid down, and advantage taken of the great superiority the possession of the sea and the Tagus gave us over the enemy.

I have already said that a force of between two and three thousand men was collected at Peniché, who could operate on the enemy's left flank; and no two men could judge better than the Duke of Terceira and Marshal Saldanha how the military movements should have been executed; but neither the one nor the other knew any thing, or could be supposed to know, any thing of naval movements any more than the Emperor himself; and it certainly would not have taken any merit from them had I been consulted before the campaign was opened. Who is to blame for not forming a plan I really do not know, but certainly none was formed.

Had my opinion been asked, I should have advised that the three steam-boats we had should have embarked the battalions of the naval and military arsenal, the public works and the troops from Almada, accompanied by all the armed boats of the squadron, the brig, and the floating battery; and that the small craft on the coast should have been recalled. The day for opening the campaign should have been chosen when the wind and tide answered, an hour or two before daylight, or the wind need not have been considered at all. All this arranged, and the orders sent to Peniché, and a certainty that they had been received, the flotilla should have proceeded up the river before daylight, and the first intimation the enemy would have had of an intended attack would have been their seeing a force in their rear on the right, while the troops from Peniché were at the same time threatening their left flank. The flotilla at Setuval, and the troops there, should at the same time have made a movement on Alcacer do Sal. The Emperor would then have marched out of his lines at dawn of day, and if he could beat them without any plan at all, it is very evident how much better he would have succeeded with a well-concerted movement.

The Miguelites at this time were so dispirited that the probability is they would either have laid down their arms or made a hasty retreat, harassed on their left by the Peniché division, and the road cut and blocked up at Alhandra, and flanked by two or three brigs of war. They must have lost all their artillery and baggage at least, or even had they succeeded in holding together, and taking the road of Bucellas, timely notice might have been sent to me, and I should have moved up the flotilla, and occupied Santarem with the troops under my command. Had this been planned and well executed, the war would have been finished at a blow, and those employed would have had the credit of planning and executing the finest manœuvre that had taken place during the war.

This will no doubt be read by many naval and military men, who know the ground, and they will judge whether my observations are correct or otherwise. I have already said that who is to blame I know not. The minister-of-war had neither capacity to conceive, nor ability to execute such a combined movement; therefore he is not to be censured, and I suppose it must be attributed to the Emperor and Marshal Saldanha not expecting the success they met with. Be that as it may, they lost a fine opportunity of finishing the war, and I shall now leave both armies looking at each other along the Ponte D'Areca, and return to Lisbon and examine a little into the naval and political affairs of the country.

CHAPTER II.

When the enemy were before Lisbon, it was necessary to keep up a large naval establishment, both for its defence and in case of a disaster. That danger now over, the Cape St Vincent was paid off and fitted out as a sheer hulk. The Rainha de Portugal, my old flag-ship, and which by a decree of the Emperor was always to be in commission, was reduced to a lieutenant's command; and the Martin Freitas, now arrived from Lagos, paid off. The Duchess of Braganza had her masts shifted and was refitted; and the Don Pedro prepared to proceed to Angola to establish the Queen's authority in that colony. Store-ships were also sent to the Cape Verd Islands for the same purpose, and to bring home the political prisoners who had been sent there by Miguel's government.

On my arrival in Lisbon, a summons had been sent to Madeira; but the governor, having an excellent garrison, was determined to hold out, and we had not sufficient force to undertake an expedition against it, or even to blockade it.

No navy in the world can be compared to the Portuguese; they do manage to navigate their ships in the most extraordinary manner possible. There is not one ship in their whole service that would not be condemned in an English dock-yard. Their sails are only fit for summer; the greater part of their blocks are made of pine with wooden pins, and are constantly tumbling about your ears; there is no proportion in the strength of their yards to their squareness; they never have an anchor or cable that would hold a ship in a gale of wind in an open anchorage, or a capstan that could heave an anchor up in blowing weather; and should they spring a leak, they must go down for want of pumps; and to crown all, the greater part of their officers have not the least pretension to seamanship. The boatswain and his mates, who are always respectable men, are the only people in the shape of officers that are sailors; and indeed they manage the ships; yet with all these disadvantages they do stumble through their work in a most extraordinary manner. They can never be intended to keep the sea in bad weather, nor indeed do they ever think of doing so; and should they by accident be caught in a gale of wind, their sails are sure to be blown away, and they have nothing to do but put their trust in Providence.

Very few of their officers are conscious of their inefficiency; on the contrary they think themselves capital officers though not sailors: — in short, if you ask what sort of an officer so-and-so is, the answer is generally—' he is an excellent officer; he has completed his studies;' indeed, their studies are the only thing thought of; and they certainly are good navigators and good mathematicians; and I should say pass a severer examination at their college than is done at Portsmouth academy. There is no regulation about their age in going to sea, and many of them never go afloat till they are upwards of twenty, and indeed there are many second lieutenants who have never been at sea in their lives.

The seamen are good and capital riggers, and

when well treated and taken care of by their officers, which they never are, are capable of being made any thing of. They are sober, quiet, and easily led; their pay is good, *when they get it,*—about two pounds a month; but they are wretchedly fed. The boatswain's mates registered have double the pay of the seamen, and those not registered one half more. There are no other petty officers allowed by the law. There are admirals, vice and rear admirals, commodores and brevet commodores, captains and brevet captains, commanders and brevet commanders, lieutenants, second lieutenants, midshipmen, and volunteers, pilots, second pilots, and volunteers. The midshipmen and volunteers mess with the officers; the class of pilots are not provided for, nor could I ever find out what was their use; they are not seamen, nor required to know any thing of the coast, and their education is inferior to the collegians. I set to work to remedy all those evils, and was foolish enough to think nothing was more easy; but I soon found out from the minister to the lowest clerk in the establishment that I was opposed by every species of intrigue so well known and practised in Portugal.

Mr. Freire was minister of marine as well as of war,—a man much too incapable and indolent to fill one office instead of two; and the only recommendation he could possibly have to office must have been his subserviency to the Emperor, who, although a liberal, like most other princes was very fond of having his own way, and was pretty sure of not being thwarted by this minister. His office was filled by twenty or thirty clerks lounging over their desks; the two principal ones as great intriguers as were to be found in Lisbon.

Formerly there was a Board of Admiralty; but the Cortes of 1820 replaced them by a major-general of the Armada with a staff of two adjutants, and three or four clerks, to which I was obliged to add a secretary and another clerk for the correspondence in both languages. This constituted the whole of the head-quarter department; and as I insisted on an immediate reply to all letters and applications, and as every officer and man, both in the civil and military department of the navy are accustomed to write to the major-general, they certainly had no sinecure.

I have said that in the minister of marine's office, which is united with the colonies, there were about twenty or thirty employés. In former days the major-general was so completely under the minister, that, in order to preserve his place, he was obliged to submit to whatever he or his clerks thought proper; and as no minister had ever been acquainted with naval matters, it is easily to be supposed into what a deplorable state the naval department had fallen. The finances in Portugal had long been in disorder; and when the government was hard-pressed for money, the naval department was always the first to suffer. No stores could be obtained, except of bad quality and at exorbitant prices, as it was quite a lottery when the furnishers would be paid. They made their calculations, and charged accordingly, and those who had the most interest with the minister of marine, or probably who knew how to apply a douceur in the proper quarter, were the first paid. I could not permit such a state of things to continue, and the minister and his people very soon found out I was the most improper person to be at the head of the naval department: but the war was not over, and it was necessary to act with caution, and begin by gradually disgusting me, which is always the Portuguese fashion.

Agreeably to the law of the Cortes, the whole business of the navy ought to be carried on through the major-general; and the minister of marine, as far as I could understand the law, had no right to issue any orders to the inferior departments. Indeed, if he had been endowed with honest intentions, and really wished to benefit and improve the naval service, nothing was more easy. It was only necessary to divide his department into two sections, viz., the colonial, and marine, the clerks in the colonial office having nothing to do with the marine department, or the marine office with the colonial branch. At the colonial office, which is by far the most important, and requires a man of real talent and political knowledge, (if they wish to draw any advantage from their numerous and valuable colonies,) the minister himself should preside, leaving the naval department to the major-general, who should communicate with him in person, submit all papers necessary for his signature, and consult with him on naval affairs generally. Had such a system been followed, there would have been neither jealousy nor jarring between the offices, and the service would have been conducted pleasantly to individuals, and with advantage to the country. But neither minister nor clerks cared one sixpence about the good of the navy, if that could only be obtained by diminishing their importance, and taking away from them the means of persecuting the Miguelites, and doing mischief.

On first taking the command of the Queen's squadron at Oporto, I was authorized by the Emperor to promote officers, and I did not feel inclined to give up that power ; and shortly after my arrival in Lisbon, I selected and promoted a few of the most deserving who had been at Oporto, having already promoted the English officers who had served in the action. This alarmed the minister and his myrmidons, and my suspicions were first awoke by receiving a letter on the subject from the minister, which drew from

Appendix No. 1.

me a remonstrance, and finally an appeal to the Emperor, who ordered the officers to be confirmed, without, however, acknowledging my right to promote without the approbation of the minister. I referred his majesty to the Carta Regia he gave me on taking command of his squadron; but that he considered only temporary, and observed that he himself, as regent and commander-in-chief of the army, had not the power of promoting an officer on the field of battle without the concurrence of the minister at war. This was followed up by withdrawing the naval hospital from my control, and appointing first a commission and then a medical officer to attend not only to the professional, but also to the civil branch. This gentleman was a friend of Freire's, a very good man, and a good physician no doubt; but such an arrangement was placing a great deal too much power in his hands, and opening the door wider to the abuses I wished to correct.

The decree depriving all officers who had served Don Miguel of the rank they had obtained during the usurpation had completely disorganised the navy. Captains were sent back to be lieutenants, lieutenants to midshipmen, and midshipmen to volunteers, and so on; and this without any consideration whatever as to their political feelings, or whether their promotion had been obtained from favour, or from the common routine of the service. I laboured hard, but in vain, to shew the impolicy of this in the navy, as we were obliged to employ many of those officers; and sending them back to an inferior rank was certainly not the best means of making them faithful to the cause of the Queen. Few naval officers had emigrated to Oporto, and amongst these few several had served Don Miguel, and even commanded his ships when the French forced the Tagus, and took away the greater part of the squadron; and those men were by far the most violent against the Miguelites. Depriving officers of their rank who were notoriously attached to the usurper, and were of a sufficient age to judge for themselves, was perfectly correct, but visiting the same punishment on young men and boys whose parents had sent them into the service, and who had not the means of leaving Lisbon, and were obliged to serve if ordered, or go to prison, was consistent neither with justice nor common sense.

The captains of ships had great difficulty in finding officers fit for service, and in many instances I was obliged to give acting orders to those who had been turned back, until some definitive arrangement should be made ; but so intent was the minister on folly that all my good intentions towards them were frustrated, by the countability refusing to pay them higher than the rank they had been sent back to, and this no doubt by the directions of the minister.

There was only one man of talent in the whole shipwright department,—the master-builder. We really wanted his services, but he had committed an irreparable error in having done his duty in fitting out the Rainha, an old broken-backed hulk, and which no nation but the Portuguese ever would have thought of sending to sea. Nevertheless, what with doubling her sides and diagonal timbers outside of that doubling, she was rendered sufficiently strong for all purposes of war during the summer. This man was sent to the right-about, and as there was nobody competent to fill his place, I gave him an acting order, which was as usual counteracted by a refusal to pay him; he, as might be expected, got sulky, did little or nothing, and was ultimately sent about his business; thus we lost the services of the only native who had the least idea of ship-building.

No person who has not seen it can form an idea of the state of the naval arsenal at Lisbon; it was the receptacle for the blind, the lame, and the lazy. If a man was unfit for any thing else, interest was made to get him a place in the arsenal. The establishment consisted of between two and three thousand, certainly the worst artificers to be found in the whole country. There was hardly an officer in the establishment fit for his situation, and it was quite indifferent to them whether the men worked or not. In fact they were seen sleeping about in all directions, and even those who did work took especial care to do it in the manner most pleasant and agreeable to themselves, any thing like fatigue being quite out of the question. The inefficiency and indolence of the workmen in the naval arsenal was proverbial, and in the constitution of 1820 the workmen used to say the Cortes might reform whatever they pleased, but they never could introduce it into the arsenal; and they were not far wrong. The only efficient way of doing good would have been by paying off the whole establishment and beginning afresh; but that could not be done in troublesome times. The first thing necessary was to pay them regularly, which was no easy matter in the state of the finances; however, for the first few months they were seldom more than a fortnight in arrear.

A survey was held on all those unfit for employment, and they were discharged with pensions agreeable to their services. The workmen were divided into different gangs, and foremen placed at their head, who, however, were always afraid to report men who neglected their duty. In short I had the whole dock-yard to fight against,— officers and all; and by either suspending or discharging those whom I caught idling away their time, as long as I was present, things began to improve; but the moment my back was turned, they got into their old habits, and even used to place centinels in various places of the yard to give notice of my approach.

The Villa Flor, Portuense, and Liberal had been in hand four months, and little progress was made in their repairs; what with time lost in going on board, coming on shore, and idling, they cost more money than the purchase of new vessels. This was not the only inconvenience; as the season advanced, the difficulty of keeping up an effective blockade became greater; most of our vessels were crazy, and the officers had no idea of keeping the sea in bad weather. The Isabelle Maria, stationed off Figueras, quitted the blockade, and the captain reported that having only three weeks fuel on board, he had called his officers together, and they were unanimously of opinion that they ought to return to Lisbon. Such was the custom, and it was considered very harsh to supersede the captain and send her to sea. The first breeze brought in a couple of brigs, who were unfit to keep their station, and were condemned. This very much reduced our blockading force, and I found it necessary to quicken the operations of my friends the dock-yard men, by ordering them not to leave the ships in the river, till their repairs were completed. At first they laughed at this, but not finding themselves quite so comfortable as they were in their homes, they seriously set to work, remarking at the same time that treating them in that manner was not quite constitutional.

The marine corps had been sadly neglected, and I directed the commandant to send me a statement of the age, qualifications, and characters of the different officers composing that branch of the service, with the intention of carefully examining into its state, and putting on half-pay those who were notoriously attached to the cause of Miguel; but in my absence at Setuval, the report was sent to the minister of marine, and before my return the greater part of them had been reformed without any inquiry whatever, except the simple statement of the commandant, who thus got rid of all those senior to himself, together with many others. When any harsh measure was to be put in force, there was no delay in the minister of marine's office; it went through like lightning; and if any person was supposed to be a Miguelite, little or no inquiry was thought necessary.

A council of state was now formed, consisting of twelve. Palmella and eight members were named; the other three places were kept open for the ministers. This council appears to have been of no use. Had the ministers been obliged to follow their advice, it would only have clogged the wheels of government; and if not, they might just as well have staid at home.

The assembling of the Cortes was put off *sine die*, as every body foresaw would be the case, and the ministers were only laughed at for their childish precipitation in calling them together.

Don Carlos was again peremptorily ordered out of the kingdom, and Don Miguel called upon to insist on his leaving; but he appeared to have made common cause with Carlos, and took no step to oblige him to quit Portugal. On the contrary, he gave every encouragement to the Spanish Carlists, and had actually a corps of two hundred men under the command of a Colonel Serredo. Strong representations were made on this subject, but without effect. General Cordova said they were Carlist refugees, enemies of his country, over whom he had no controul; but it does not appear that he took any steps to insist on Don Miguel sending them out of the country, or even dismissing them from his army. In fact, the whole of the Spanish minister's conduct was inexplicable; he was a decided Miguelite in Lisbon, and I cannot conceive he can now be a constitutionalist in Spain.

It was also strongly reported that arms and ammunition were supplied from Badajos, and I thought it as well to accompany a remonstrance that was ordered to be made to Lord Palmerston, with a hint that the Portuguese squadron might probably take a trip to the southward.

<small>Appendix, No. II.</small>

On the 6th of October, the news of Ferdinard's death arrived at Lisbon, and the quiet succession of the young Queen, her mother assuming the regency. This event was most favourable to Portugal; on the thrones of the two peninsular kingdoms were now seated two queens, both minors;—the father of one queen, regent of Portugal, and the mother of the other regent of Spain. Each queen had an uncle, and each uncle was a pretender to the throne, and one a usurper in arms. It was evident that in opposition to Carlos the despot, the Queen must establish a constitutional throne.

Don Carlos having assumed the title of King of Spain, refused to hold any communication with Cordova, and proceeded to the frontier, in hopes of finding a movement in his favour. The generals commanding those provinces were constitutionalists, and took steps to prevent him crossing the frontier: indeed there appears to have been no movement whatever in his favour.

One of the first acts of the Queen of Spain's government was recalling the legation from Portugal, and expressing, through the British minister at Madrid, their wish to see the war in Portugal terminated, and hinting at the same time their desire to see some concession. This communication was well received by Don Pedro's government, who promised to take into consideration any proposition Spain might make, provided it was not injurious to the prosperity and honor of Portugal, and above all to the charter. Any proposal to meddle with it would not be listened to for a moment, and if listened to, would throw the whole country into a state of anarchy and confusion.

Don Pedro himself wrote a long letter to the queen-regent of Spain, which he requested Lord William Russell would forward to Mr. Villars, to be by him delivered to her Majesty; but though it was full of praises of the Queen, it reflected a good deal on the conduct of Ferdinand; and as Spain was well inclined to Portugal, he was afraid it would give offence, and very prudently declined presenting it.

<small>Appendix, No. III.</small>

On the 16th of October, Candido Xavier, the minister of interior and foreign affairs, died. Hopes were now entertained that a ministry would be formed composed of some of the leading men of the Queen's party, and who had a stake in the country; but Freire and Carvalho, thinking they possessed talent sufficient to carry on the government, appointed as their colleagues two men possessing neither talent nor property in the country. Majorchi, an astronomer, took the portfolio of the marine and colonies; he thought more of the stars than either of ships or colonies, in addition to which he was indolent and never thoroughly awake. It would have been as ridiculous to have appointed me archbishop of Braga as it was to place him at the head of the navy. Freire took the foreign department in addition to the war, and Aguiar, a professor of the university of Coimbra, the interior.

Those arrangements added nothing either to the popularity or respectability of the cabinet. Freire was bad enough in the marine, but this man was worse. Both were in the hands of their clerks, and I always observed, if I proposed any thing conciliatory or of use to the service, that my applications were unattended to; any thing, on the other hand, against a Miguelite officer or unpleasant to myself, was promptly executed; and as this man was still more indolent than Freire, he was still more governed by the people about him, and the annoyances became so great that nothing but a sincere desire to see the war finished could have induced me to put up with them.

The British government, justly incensed at the vicious system of government adopted by Don

Pedro's ministers, remonstrated in strong terms against their proceedings, and threatened to withdraw their countenance if a more mild system of government was not adopted. Freire acknowledged the severity of the decree of sequestration, as well as the rigour with which it was executed, and endeavoured to excuse himself on the plea of necessity, remarking at the same time that at Oporto they had no other means of raising money during the siege. Such severity might have been excusable at Oporto, but at Lisbon it could not be justified either in point of justice or policy.

A severe remonstrance was also sent to Sylva Carvalho, the minister of justice and finance, who pleaded the propriety of retaliation, and his hope that confiscation would induce the followers of Don Miguel to abandon his cause, and come to Lisbon to save their properties. He did not take the trouble to reflect that his victims were between two fires; if they absented themselves from Lisbon, their town property was confiscated by Don Pedro; and if they should absent themselves from the provinces, their country property was sure to be confiscated by Don Miguel.

The remonstrances had some effect; better behaviour was promised for the future, and the sale of moveables discontinued. A promise was also made that all prisoners against whom there was not sufficient proof should be discharged. Many were said to have been imprisoned to save them from the fury of the populace; but the Lord help those shut up in a Portuguese prison, nine chances to one they are forgot, and if they have not friends to look after them, they have a very fair prospect of starving.

The general feeling in Lisbon was certainly against the Emperor's ministers, and Don Pedro himself was becoming unpopular. Many excused them on account of the difficulties with which they were surrounded, and it was difficult to persuade others that there was any very great crime in persecuting a Miguelite. Even the most moderate objected to the employment of people who had remained in Lisbon during the usurpation, and Palmella's putting the Count of Porto Santo at the head of the municipality was not generally approved of.

On the 2d of November about six hundred

English and Scotch arrived, chiefly boys. Promises, as usual, made by the Queen's agents, were not kept by the government, and the poor men were the sufferers. Had the agents exceeded their authority, it was the duty of the government to have settled the business with them; but the unfortunate wretches who had been kidnapped ought not to have been ill-treated. Many of them were perfectly unfit for soldiers; some were received as boys on board the Don John; others were sent back to England without any remuneration whatever; and those who went to the depôt were swindled in every direction.

CHAPTER III.

I SHALL now return to Santarem, which the enemy were fortifying, while Saldanha, on the other hand, was strengthening his position, which extended from Val to Azumbujeira. The enemy had their piquets at one end of the Ponte da Asseca, which is a long causeway leading to Santarem: our piquets were at the other. A small river in front ran from Val nearly parallel with the Tagus, and joined it below the bend of the river, opposite Salvaterra ; and up this river vessels brought the supplies for the army. A brig of war was anchored at Villa Franca, the floating battery at the entrance of the creek leading to Villa Nova, and the gun-boats and lighter vessels were pushed up abreast of Salvaterra, which we ought to have occupied and intrenched. The enemy took advantage of our neglect, and passing over a small force at Almeirim, on the 17th marched on Salvaterra, opened a fire on the flotilla next morning, which retired, leaving two barges aground, without making any very great exertion to bring them off.

The possession of this port opened the whole of the south to the incursions of the enemy's cavalry as far as Aldea Gallegos and even Moita ; and had they profited by this advantage as much as they ought to have done, and occupied the island, the water communication with the army would have been entirely cut off. During the occupation of Santarem by the French, the Duke of Wellington never allowed them to get a footing in the south, and his example ought to have been followed. It is true we were much inferior in cavalry, and the south is a cavalry country ; but that ought not to have prevented the occupation of Salvaterra. I repeatedly proposed to Saldanha to attack it, but his views turned more to the north ; and for the present both parties kept looking at each other.

From our position Santarem appeared very strong

and unattackable; and when occupied by the
French with a large army, was certainly accounted
so by the Duke of Wellington; but though not a
military man, I can understand that a position occupied by ten or twelve thousand men is a very different
thing from the same occupied by sixty or seventy.

When our troops first appeared at the Ponte
da Asseca, the old redoubt which raked the
bridge was neither armed nor repaired; and I
think we might have pushed boldly on, and
occupied the ground on the opposite side of the
bridge, between which and Santarem there are
two distinct ranges of hills before you come to the
table-land on which Santarem stands. It would
have required some hard fighting to have gained
it, but still it was to be done; and if we were
able to drive the enemy from before Lisbon without
the assistance of the Peniché division, on their
junction some attempt might have been made to
have driven them into the town, which could then
have been besieged; and abundance of heavy
cannon might have been brought up by water from
Lisbon for that purpose. The fixed battalions,
together with the arsenal battalions, and seamen

from the ships, should have been brought up to support the attack of the regular troops. All this would have been attended with some risk, and it was perhaps judged better to wait till the army was better disciplined, and until reinforcements should arrive from England. At the same time we had no right to suppose the enemy would not take advantage of our inactivity, and penetrate to Setuval, and having possession of the whole of the country, increase their troops, while their friends in England and elsewhere were making exertions to furnish them with money and arms, which, though difficult to land, was still possible, as Portuguese men-of-war were not very well adapted for winter blockades. Don Miguel was, however, ill served. Intrigue was rife, which had driven away Bourmont, and shortly after Macdonald was also obliged to give up the command of the army. Desertion also began to increase to the Queen's colours, and many retired to their homes; in addition to which, sickness made its appearance in their camp, while our troops remained tolerably healthy and were well fed. The Emperor went up frequently to review the army, and Saldanha was indefatigable in forming them, and at each review their improvement in dress and organization was very evident.

On the 26th Leiria declared for the Queen, and and on the 28th the Emperor received at Cartaxo a deputation from that town. On the same day Captain Henry embarked, in two steam-boats, the troops at St. Ubes, composed of Lisbon volunteers, a part of the ninth regiment, and about one hundred and fifty English and Portuguese marines under the command of Lieutenant-colonel Florencio José da Silva. They landed at Fayus, about a league below Alcacer do Sal, which had been occupied for some time by the Miguelites, and after a slight resistance, in which they lost a few men, they abandoned the town, and retired on Evora. Had we been in possession of Salvaterra, this would have been a very proper movement; or, indeed, had we reinforced Baroca d'Alva, where there were a few Portuguese marines, we would have reaped some advantage from this enterprise; but, as usual, we did nothing more, supposing the enemy would be equally inactive, but for once we were mistaken.

General Lemos passed the river at Santarem with about fifteen hundred men, and on the morning of the 2d of November attacked our position, in advance of Alcacer do Sal, which in point of fact was no position at all. Colonel Florencio had his troops drawn up on a plain, with a wood on each flank, which he did not occupy. The English and Portuguese marines were thrown out in front as skirmishers. Our force was inferior to the enemy, particularly in cavalry, which circumstance ought to have confined the colonel to the defence of the town only; but unhappily he advanced. Captain Birt, who commanded the marines, on seeing the approach of the enemy's cavalry, formed his men into a rallying square, and twice repulsed them with great loss. He then formed in line to receive a column of infantry who were advancing; and hearing a firing in his rear, he turned round, and observed the Lisbon volunteers and ninth infantry fire off their muskets and take to their heels as fast as they could run, without having ever seen an enemy. He immediately commenced his retreat, covering the fugitives as well as he could;

Appendix, No. IV.

but the colonel, instead of occupying a convent on his right, and endeavouring to rally his men, made for the marshes by the river side, where every thing got into greater confusion. The cavalry closed, and cut them down in all directions. Captain Birt managed to conduct his men in tolerable order to the river, leaving only three men behind, when, for want of boats, they got into confusion, threw away their arms and ammunition, and took to the water.

In this affair the loss of marines was two officers taken prisoners, and between thirty and forty non-commissioned officers and privates killed and taken. The loss of the Lisbon volunteers and ninth regiment could not have been less than eight hundred men in killed, wounded, and missing. The greater part of those taken were delivered up by General Lemos to the guerillas and put to death; and he had the hardihood to announce this transaction in his public despatch. Report of this disaster found its way to Lisbon a day or two before the official account, and a Belgian regiment having arrived on the 30th of October, which was being clothed on board the sheer hulk, with great difficulty, and after vacillating half the day, I persuaded the minister to allow me to embark two hundred of them in a steam-boat, and carry them to Setuval, where I arrived at daylight of the 4th of November. The town was in great confusion; the principal people were embarked, and not a soul was left to defend it. The Belgians were put into the castle, and the Donna Maria's broadside brought to flank it. This timely succour saved the town. What General Lemos was about after the affair of Alcacer do Sal God knows; he had only to make his appearance, and he would have been received with open arms by the inhabitants, the greater part of whom were staunch Miguelites. As I could hear nothing of him at Setuval, I concluded he would march on Sinnes, and surprise the garrison in that town, for which place I started, and finding it not defensible, I withdrew the garrison, (consisting of two hundred marines,) and the principal inhabitants, and brought them to Setuval. On the same day the rest of the Belgian regiment, who I requested might be sent, arrived, as also the cavalry, who, after the affair of Alcacer do Sal, had retired on

Almada; and this important post was again placed in security. General Lemos, finding I was beborehand with him, was content with surprising Baroca d'Alva, and I apprehend the detachment there had never been acquainted with the affair of Alcacer.

After restoring order, I returned to Lisbon, and pressed the minister to pay the Belgian troops at Setuval the bounty that had been promised them on landing. This, however, was as usual delayed, which happened more or less with every foreign soldier who arrived. Abundance of promises were made in England, but were so ill kept by both parties in England and at Lisbon, that the men got discontented on their landing, and many were sent back without having ever joined their regiments.

The Algarves were still suffering from the depredations of the guerillas, and I was much pressed by the governor of Lagos to come to his assistance. I had frequently sent him provisions from the naval arsenal, and I now decided on collecting all the marines I could muster, and endeavour at once to free that unfortunate kingdom from the miseries of war. This was approved of by the minister, who gave me full power to command the forces there; and my friend Colonel Loreros, one of the best officers in the Portuguese service, but who was not employed, accompanied me, as also the young Count Ficalho. The weather was still fine, and I was in hopes it would continue so for a few days; but on our arrival at Setuval, the cavalry I had expected to embark with me had been ordered in the neighbourhood of Aldea Gallego or Moita, were surprised, and cut off. This detained us a day, and we were obliged to proceed with about twenty cavalry and fifty mounted guerillas, and between four or five hundred marines, including those who had escaped from Alcacer and were now re-equipped. Before starting I took upon myself to order an advance to the Belgians from the customhouse coffers, they were still unpaid, and were nearly in a state of mutiny. This delay was occasioned not from any intention of breaking faith, but simply from the indolence with which every thing was carried on in the war department; and this indolence extended to every branch of the establishment. In more than one instance, I had sent provisions to the Algarves when starving, and which arrived there before even an order had been issued for their supply; and once from the neglect of the authorities in the naval arsenal the whole flotilla in the south were reduced to the last extremity, and on inquiry at the inspector's office their demands had been thrown on one side and entirely forgot. Such was the manner in which war was carried on in Portugal on both sides, and with the exception of the minister of finance, who was most zealous in procuring funds, the ministry deserve not a particle of credit for bringing the war to a successful termination; and although I have no doubt they will feel much offended at reading this narrative, it is proper the Portuguese nation should know that it was to the Emperor and his officers in the field that the whole merit of their deliverance is due, and not to the imbecilles who amused themselves from morning to night issuing out a parcel of foolish decrees.

I arrived off Lagos about the middle of November. The weather had been threatening for a day or two, and it now became so boisterous, that it was difficult to approach the coast. The vessel was very crowded with men and horses, who were drenched with wet; nevertheless the old governor of Lagos, who saw our approach with pleasure, managed to send off boats sufficient to carry between one and two hundred marines on shore. We then proceeded to Faro, but found it impossible to pass the bar. The weather was getting worse, and to mend the matter, the captain of the steam-boat reported that he had only one day's fuel and water on board. This was not a pleasant situation to be in, and we were obliged to return to Setuval. The other steam-boat persevered and succeeded in landing the guerilla cavalry at Faro. I was much annoyed at this, as I hoped to have been able to set things to rights in the Algarves, and still more annoyed when on our return to Lisbon I found the captain of the steam-boat, who did not like the weather, had framed the excuse of having only one day's fuel and water on board to induce us to return to Setuval.

The weather was now too unsettled to undertake

any more excursions of this description, and I was obliged to content myself with the reinforcements I had thrown in, and leave the Portuguese marines to reinforce the garrison, and bring the English ones back to the Don John, where they might be ready for any future enterprize.

During my absence in the Algarves the Emperor had been with the army, and decided on sending a detachment to destroy the mills at Pernes, from whence the enemy received the greater part of their flour. On the 10th November the fourth and fifth columns stationed at Azumbujeira were directed on Pernes by the road of Tremes, another column marched from Rio Maior by Alcanede, the whole under the command of Brigadier Joao Nepomucenos de Macado. The enemy, consisting of the fourteenth, a battalion of the fifth infantry, and one of royalist volunteers, had time to form, and were attacked in two columns, one consisting of the twelfth caçadores and ninth of the line, the other by the three English regiments, supported by several pieces of artillery. They were immediately driven from their positions, leaving in our possession twenty-eight prisoners. The loss on both sides was trifling; the mills were destroyed and the detachment returned, and occupied the positions of Sicurio and Mucarria near the main body of the army.

When the columns marched on Pernes, Marshal Saldanha advanced to the Ponte da Asseca, which he occupied with the first column; the second and third were in reserve at the Ponte de Celeiro. This demonstration prevented any interference with the expedition to Pernes.

The marshal was much dissatisfied with General Nepomuceno for not having proceeded to Thomar agreeable to his orders, and in consequence relieved him from his command. It appears to me the risk was too great, which was probably the general's reason, but Saldanha thought otherwise, and he was an officer who would have his orders obeyed, taking the responsibility on himself, Nepomuceno was nevertheless esteemed a good officer, and was very generally respected by the army.

After this affair and that of Alcacer do Sal, both parties seemed satisfied with what they had done, and were inclined to repose. Don Miguel hunted, and Don Pedro became unpopular through the acts of his ministers. The tobacco contract had been given to the Count Farola, who shared it with another party, himself pocketing a large sum. This was wrong; it ought to have been put up to public auction. He had certainly advanced large sums of money when Don Pedro was in distress at Oporto, and at considerable risk; and it was right he should be rewarded, but people were of opinion that his remuneration was too high, and even hinted that a douceur had been applied in the proper quarter.

The old contractor offered a much higher sum, which so enraged the ministers that they persuaded the Emperor to issue out a very severe decree, calling upon Joao Paulo Cordeiro and Company to pay up within ten days a large sum due to the government, on pain of having the tobacco machinery, &c. seized. It was quite notorious how great had been the exertions of this

Appendix, No. V.

company against the liberal cause; nevertheless the decree was considered by right-thinking men as most unjust, because it was impossible for the old contractor to receive remittances from the country occupied by the Miguelites. The commission appointed declined to carry the decree into execution, and Lord William Russell laboured in vain with Don Pedro to induce him to modify it.

<small>Appendix, No. VI.</small> This called forth a strong letter from the Count de Taipa to the Emperor, which, however, had no effect.

After this decree came another, repealing a former one, which placed certain foreign coins considerably higher than their intrinsic value. This in itself was not reprehensible, had not the bank been previously made aware of it, and issued their foreign coin the day before at the higher value, thereby defrauding the public of a considerable sum of money. This caused general indignation against the government.

The mercantile distress at this time was also great, particularly amongst the English merchants, who could receive no remittances from the prisoners: the exchange was at 52, and had every appearance of getting worse.

On the 23d of November, a council of state was held, and a new tax proposed. The Duke of Palmella took a general view of the state of the country, which was objected to by Don Pedro, and caused an angry discussion. Both Palmella and Guerrero read papers censuring the whole system pursued by the government, and which they deposited on the council table. These papers Trigosa offered to sign, which, however, Palmella declined, as he had no intention of making a formal charge against the government; he only wished to discharge his duty, and relieve himself from the accusation of being a tacit approver of their acts. The ministers announced their intention of replying to what they considered an attack on them by three councillors of state. The tax they proposed was refused unless an exposé of the state of the finances was laid before them, which was not done.

About this time Spain offered to mediate

between the contending parties in Portugal in conjunction with England, and authorised Lord William Russell to make the offer. A confidential agent was also sent to Don Miguel's court to notify that Lord William Russell had been requested on the part of Spain to propose her good offices. This was approved by Don Pedro's government, who also gave their confidence to Lord William, and explained to him that peace on any terms would be a blessing to Portugal provided Don Miguel left the country. Colonel Hare was sent to Saldanha's head-quarters to put himself in communication with the Baron Ramefort, the Spanish agent, and three days were given to Don Miguel to accept or refuse the mediation.

It is, however, singular that the Baron was not instructed by Zea Bermudez to insist on the departure of Miguel as a sine-qua-non, though he had signified to Mr. Villars that instructions to that effect would be given him, and indeed he even proposed to Hare that Miguel's marriage with the Queen should take place.

The Count San Lorenzo did not entirely reject the mediation, but would not accept it till made acquainted with the basis on which they were to treat. Colonel Hare, who was the bearer of Lord William's reply to San Lorenzo, was not permitted to enter Santarem, but delivered his letter to General Macdonnell, and after waiting five hours for a reply, was sent back without it, under the pretext that Saldanha's piquets had fired during the time he was waiting. This was purely accidental, and need not have been noticed, particularly as Hare made no complaint of having himself been fired at by the Miguelites.

Three days more had been granted to accept or decline the mediation, which Miguel refused on the basis offered, but was willing to make any other concession consistent with his dignity. The Baron Ramefort in consequence quitted Santarem.

<small>Lorenzo's Despatch.</small>

This proposal of mediation was followed up by Lord William Russell obtaining permission, with great difficulty, for the Marquis of Olhao (who had been at the head of the municipality when Miguel was declared king) to leave his hiding-place in Lisbon, and proceed to Santarem to use his influence over Don Miguel to induce him to abdicate. He there pointed out to Miguel the great sacrifices that had been made by his party, and that now all hope was gone, it was time he should in his turn make sacrifices to them. Miguel, however, was obdurate, and would listen to no proposal that had for its basis the loss of the crown of Protugal, to which he considered himself fully entitled.

The rejection of the mediation caused a good deal of discontent at Santarem amongst those who saw no prospect of ultimate success, and who were sufficiently moderate to see that the continuance of the civil war would be the ruin of their country, but the ultra royalists were determined to support their king to the last extremity, relying probably on the chapter of accidents, as well as on the hope of Pedro's ministers committing acts that would render him unpopular with his party; and for this they did not wait long. Count de Taipa had written a second letter to the Emperor, which was seized, and an attempt made to arrest him in the street: this he resisted, and sought refuge in the house of Count Ficalho,

Appendix, No. VII.

a high-spirited young nobleman, and one of the Emperor's aid-de-camps. He threatened to put to death the first person who dared break in on the sanctity of his house, and sent to the peers to inform them of what had taken place; the peerage who supported the Queen's cause consisted of only nine, and yet Pedro's ministers were foolish enough to affront them. I will not call it either courage or boldness, for they possessed neither the one nor the other; it was nothing but downright folly, and had the peers gone in a body to the Emperor and insisted on his dismissing his ministers and sending them out of the country as men totally incapable of conducting the affairs of the nation, they would have acted right, and the Emperor must have complied, because they would have been supported both by the army and navy; but they were more moderate; they drew out a protest, and sent a deputation, consisting of the three youngest, viz. the Marquises of Loulé and Fronteira and Count Ficalho, to the palace, to deliver it to the Emperor. They acted with great spirit and told him that they had fought for their own privileges as well as for the Queen; and if

Appendix, No. VIII.

redress was not given, they would sheath their swads and retire from the contest. The Emperor pleaded ignorance of the case, but said he would consult his ministers and reparation should be made.

<small>Appendix, No. IX.</small> This reparation consisted in a reply to the peers being inserted in the Chronicle; at this they were justly offended, again assembled, and drew out a second protest, which was delivered by the same peers. The Emperor declined receiving it at <small>Appendix, No. X.</small> present, as he was on the point of setting out for the army, but promised an answer on his return.

Taipa in the meantime took refuge on board the Asia, which was decidedly wrong; had he been arrested, the affair would have been brought to a crisis. From the Asia, he went to the Duke of Terceira's, and no further notice was taken of him.

Pedro probably became alarmed, and wished to consult Saldanha; he was accompanied only by his Brazilian aid-de-camps. On his arrival at head-quarters, he was coolly received by the troops, and Saldanha told him plainly, had he been a peer, he also would have signed the protest. The Emperor was in very low spirits, saw the folly committed by his ministers, was afraid of a collision between the aristocracy and democracy, and requested Saldanha to become prime-minister and form an administration. This the marshal declined, but advised him to conciliate the peers and form a new ministry, leaving out Aguiar and Sylva Carvalho, and bringing in Palmella, Guerrero, and Liberata. Why Saldanha wished to preserve Freire and Majorchi I am at a loss to know; they were both most incapable, which he afterwards found out, while Carvalho was certainly the only minister of finance who had the talent of procuring money: he had, however, a personal antipathy to that minister, which was to be regretted. The Emperor was undecided; he saw no prospect of obtaining money except through Carvalho, and though I believe he led Saldanha to think he would follow his advice, he only did it in part; he kept his ministers and endeavoured to conciliate the peers.

On his return from the army he received the Duke of Terceira with great kindness, and the minister of interior was instructed to write to him; Appendix, No. XI.

this, however, did not satisfy the peers, and indeed nothing but a change of administration could make up for the insult they had received.

The Emperor thought nothing could be done without Carvalho in the way of finance, and he would not separate himself from Freire; the rest were ciphers. As for my old gentleman Majorchi, he was quite immoveable, totally incapable of deciding upon any one question, except what his chief clerk brought before him; and any thing that I wished carried into effect was sure to be neglected, particularly as regarded the English, or indeed any point I wished attended to for the good of the service. On the other, if any complaint was made against an English officer, it was sure to be brought before me in the most indecent terms. The Chart forbid corporal punishment in both army and navy; but still it was found necessary to continue it in both services, and in the navy it was inflicted agreeably to the customs of the British service, sanctioned by the twelth article of Sartorius's contract; and men were not allowed to be beat with sticks, as practised in the Portuguese navy.

It happened that a Portuguese seaman had deserted from the Eliza, and Captain Charles Napier inflicted a dozen lashes on him. The man, by some means or other not very creditable to the party, had it communicated to the minister, and exaggerated to an extraordinary degree. This was too good an opportunity to be lost; and without the least enquiry on the subject, I received a letter from the minister, to which I replied in rather severe terms, and took both letters to the Emperor, and told him I had no choice left but either to disobey the minister's orders, or run the risk of seeing a mutiny through the fleet, which the very act of the minister having written to me on the subject was enough to occasion. I also observed that he was totally unfit for his place, and also told the Emperor frankly, that I had hitherto made a rule not to interfere in any manner with politics, but things had now come to such a push that I considered it my duty to speak my opinion plainly, and that if he did not like it, I should not trouble him again. I then referred to the affair of Count de Taipa, who I did not pretend to say was either right or wrong;

Appendix, No. XII.

but it had created a great sensation, and in fact there was a spirit of discontent in Lisbon; and if he did not take care, there would be a reaction. The Emperor seemed surprised, but at the same time incredulous. I remarked I had done my duty, and that it was the last time I should speak to him on the subject. I wrote, however, a letter, more clearly stating what my sentiments were, but which by the advice of some friends was withheld; but as that letter contains my feelings at the moment, I annex it to this history without any alteration.

<small>Appendix, No. XIII.</small>

After this conversation I absented myself almost entirely from the palace, and simply attended to the duties of my own office, feeling quite convinced that my opinions were neither wanted nor desired.

During the time these scenes were acting in Lisbon and Santarem, Oporto was exposed to considerable danger.

Sir Thomas Stubbs had been left with a very small effective garrison; he was not only desired to send more troops to Lisbon, but was called upon to act himself on the offensive. He had not more than three thousand effective men, but he had from ten to eleven thousand on paper, all fed and paid. The general embarked nine hundred men composed of volunteers and movables in the Superb steamer, who by great good-luck at that season of the year were landed safe at Nazareth. On the 31st of October he made a reconnoissance to Grijo, and towards dark was suddenly attacked by the enemy, who endeavoured to cut him off from the city, and very nearly succeeded. This affair cost him twenty men in killed and wounded.

On the 5th of November Oporto was reconnoitred on the side of St. Mameda by two thousand infantry, two squadrons of cavalry, and fifty lancers; and on the 26th Sir Thomas Stubbs made a reconnoisance with two columns, one on the Cosmo road, the other on Valongo; and after driving in the enemy's piquets returned to Oporto. All this did not please the minister-at-war; he had his map before him of the forces at Oporto, and looked to their numbers and not to their efficiency; and he determined to get rid of Stubbs, who was a very old lieutenant-general, and much esteemed at Oporto; but this was not to be done in an open manner. Letters came to Oporto addressed to old Torres, now the Baron de Pico, as governor, but without any hint to Stubbs; and the Baron shortly after arrived, without any order to assume the command. Stubbs very properly refused to give it up, and both generals were in the habit of receiving letters addressed to them as commander-in-chief.

On the 1st of December the Miguelites again reconnoitred Oporto, and were attacked by two columns. The eleventh infantry, under Colonel Pacheco, advanced on the main road, and the volunteers moved across the open fields covered by the guns on the lines. They were charged by a few lancers and fled; poor Pacheco was obliged to retreat, and in the retreat was killed. He had served the whole war, was an excellent officer, and sincerely regretted by the whole army.

Shortly after this, Sir Thomas Stubbs was formally relieved and created Baron of Villa Nova de Gaya. The only reason I could ever find out for thus treating so old an officer as Sir Thomas Stubbs, and one so highly respected, was his having had too much sense to obey the minister-at-war's orders and risk Oporto. Attempts had been made to induce the Duke of Terceira to go there, which was to be an independent command, and called the army of the north; but he very frankly told the minister he would not go without an effective force; and when I spoke to him on the subject, he gave the same answer, and told me not to believe one word about the paper force the minister shewed me.

On the 1st of December a vessel arrived from the Cape de Verd Islands with the intelligence of their having declared for the Queen. Before the arrival of the transports sent there, several of the political prisoners arrived from thence. The revolution was brought about without bloodshed. Madeira, however, still held out, and the governor seemed determined to be faithful to his employer as long as there was the smallest prospect of saving his cause.

CHAPTER IV.

THE new year was ushered in by the news of the surprise of Marvao on the morning of the 12th of December, by a constitutional force that had been formed at St. Vicente in Spanish Estremadura, about the middle of November, without any knowledge of the government in Lisbon, by a patriotic Portuguese, José Joaquim d'Abreu by name, and other respectable Portuguese. This corps was called the patriotic legion of Alemtejo, and composed of Portuguese of all descriptions, who had emigrated, or quitted the standard of the usurper. Marvao had been for some time the rendezvous of the adherents of Don Carlos, being advantageously situated to carry on their correspondence with Spain; and here they had collected a considerable quantity of arms and ammunition. Though not a regular fortification, it was sufficiently strong, and attracted the attention of this patriotic column.

Its distance from Vicente was about ten leagues, and it is rather singular that the Spanish emigrants had chosen Marvao from whence to disturb the government of the young Queen of Spain, and the Portuguese San Vicente to disturb the government of Don Miguel.

The small force that surprised Marvao was divided into two columns, one commanded by Captain Mattheus José Rouxo de Fonseca, the other by the patriot José Joaquim d'Abreu, accompanied by other constitutional Portuguese; and after overcoming considerable difficulties and obstacles, succeeded in ascending the steep mountain on which the citadel was placed, and at day-light of the morning of the 12th of December surprised it without losing a man. A council of war was called, and Brigadier Pinto Alvares Pereira, who was released from prison, appointed governor of the province, Major José Victorino du Silveira, governor of the place.

Marvao was not regularly fortified, yet sufficiently strong to be defended against any attack except a regular siege; it was not well provisioned, but successful attacks were made on

Portalegre and Castello de Vide, and a considerable quantity of stores brought in. On the 27th the forces which had been collected round Marvao under the command of Landerset, one of the aid-de-camps of Don Miguel, were withdrawn without any ostensible reason, and the governor seized that opportunity of detaching a small force against Castello de Vide, which they surprised, and took fifty prisoners. The governor and many armed peasantry made their escape. On the 28th Pereira again marched on Castello de Vide, but the enemy having collected a force of fifty cavalry and two companies of the militia of Evora, on the road of Esuesa, he was obliged to regain Marvao by a mountain path.

The enemy returned to Portalegre, leaving Castello de Vide without a garrison; and on the 30th a convoy of provisions proceeding from that place to Portalegre, was captured and conducted into Marvao. In a short time the garrison greatly increased; many deserters came from the enemy, and also from Spain, together with a few but good officers, and several respectable families from Portalegre and Castello de Vide took refuge there.

Within the walls all were united, and as the place was well found in ammunition and now tolerably provisioned, the governor determined not only to defend it to the last extremity, but hoped to keep the enemy on the alert in the adjacent country. This was a most important acquisition to the cause of the Queen: situated in the enemy's rear, it served as a rallying point for all her partizans in that part of Portugal, who from want of a place of refuge had been prevented from rising in her favour.

At this time we had a large flotilla in the Tagus, and the command of the river as high as Salvaterra; and I frequently urged the propriety of carrying on operations in the south to straighten the provisioning of Santarem, and also to cover the flotilla in a nearer approach to that town with a view to future operations; but my ideas did not at all coincide with those of the marshal, who perhaps thought want of cavalry made military operations precarious in that quarter, and contemplated other movements which were now carried into execution with comparative success, but without having any definitive effect in driving the enemy from Santarem.

On the 12th of January, the Duke of Terceira took command of the army and fixed his head-quarters at Cartaxo; Saldanha set out the same day for Rio Maior, to which place he had detached a force the evening before; to form a junction with the troops already stationed there and at Alcobaca, the whole consisting of between four and five thousand men. On the 13th the cavalry occupied Os Carvalhos, and the infantry Os Molianos and the adjacent villages. Lieutenant-colonel Vasconcellos, with the first regiment of the Queen's light infantry, marched the same day for Cos, and next day reached Batalho. A heavy rain which lasted forty-eight hours without interruption, had inundated the whole country; but notwithstanding those difficulties, the columns were eager to march on to Leria and attack that city before the enemy had time to escape. The difficulties of a night march were, however, so great that the marshal decided on waiting till the following day.

Lieutenant-colonel Vasconcellos was directed to march by the royal road with the third column, fifty cavalry of the tenth, and all the artillery; the second column under the command of Colonel Xavier, reinforced with the first regiment of the Queen's light infantry, and fifty horse, were appointed to attack by the road of Batalho. Saldanha put himself at the head of the cavalry commanded by General Bacon. The first column under the orders of General Schwalbach were to pass by Liz and the bridge of Cavaleiro, and from thence to Vidigal, to get into the road of Coimbra leading to Leiria. The second column was directed to attack when they heard the firing of the first, and the third, when the second began. On the morning of the 15th, when Colonel Xavier approached the city, the enemy were drawn up beyond their entrenchments to receive him; two companies of the fifth caçadores advanced and drove them back, and the moment they knew that Schwalbach had passed the bridge of Cavaleiro, they prepared to abandon the position of Castello, which, by means of a parapet mounting several heavy guns, was connected with the place of Bispo.

From the village of Poisos, they were seen moving on the road of Coimbra. General Bacon, with two squadrons of the 10th and one squadron of lancers, advanced at a trot, and the moment he charged they were totally routed, scarcely having time to fire more than thirty or forty shots which caused some loss. The cavalry followed them a league, killed and took many prisoners. The staff-officers accompanied the cavalry, and found much delight in dyeing their swords in Miguelite blood. Such is civil war. Colonel Vasconcelles and Xavier, learning from the inhabitants that the city was evacuated, immediately entered and sent the cavalry of both columns in pursuit of the enemy, Vasconcellos occupied the castle and sent a force on the road to Figueira. Xavier and Schwalbach advanced with their columns, but too late, the cavalry having done all the work.

This affair cost the Miguelites fifteen hundred men in killed, wounded, and prisoners; our loss was not above twenty killed, and wounded. Saldanha was well received by the inhabitants, who were chiefly in favour of the Queen, and very properly commenced fortifications, to prevent the chances of war again throwing it into the hands of the enemy.

Lieutenant-colonel Vasconcellos was left governor of the town with a garrison of fifteen hundred men; and on the 24th Saldanha arrived at Aldea da Cruz and Ourem, and before daylight of the 25th marched on Torres Novas. The ground was favourable for a surprise and a squadron of cavalry drove in the enemy's piquets without discovering the marshal's force. A little distance from the town two hundred and twenty of the Chaves cavalry and two hundred royalist volunteers of Torres Novas and Santarem were posted; the cavalry were halted till Schwalbach's column came up, and then marched on two branches into which the road divided, the enemy retiring at the same time. The quarter-master-general accompanied one squadron to the right, commanded by Lieutenant-colonel Simao da Costa Pessoa, and Bacon headed the other, which advanced by the left. Both squadrons entered the town about the same time, the infantry having already marched out, leaving forty or fifty horses in the Rosio, the rest in column on the road; they were immediately charged, and pursued for two leagues. Twice they attempted to form and were overturned, with considerable loss in killed and seventy-eight prisoners.

This advantage was gained without the loss of a man or horse on our side, with the exception of Captain Jose de Vasconcellos, who was a few minutes in the enemy's power and received a slight contusion. The Chaves cavalry had always been considered the right arm of Don Miguel's army, and in no one instance had any of those men come over to the Queen; and this little affair was considered of great importance, as they were expected to fight well, but they could not stand the impetuosity of Bacon, who was always at the head of his men, and in more than one instance with one or two officers rode into the middle of the enemy's cavalry. On the 26th a patrol was sent to Golegäo and Pernes, who brought in a quantity of flour, cattle, mules, and several of the Chaves cavalry, who were found wounded.

During the time these movements were going on, the enemy appeared to be asleep at Santarem. Instead of taking advantage of the absence of Saldanha at Leiria with the best troops of the army, and throwing their whole force on the Duke of Terceira, whom they had a chance of driving from his position, they remained quiet till the arrival of Saldanha's forces at Torres Novas and Pernes. They then appeared to have planned an enterprize, which, if undertaken and vigorously executed at the proper time, might have been attended with dangerous consequences to the Queen's cause.

Before daylight of the 30th they passed over a corps of infantry and cavalry at Vallada, and threatened the communication of the Duke of Terceira with Lisbon; at the same time they showed a force in front of the Ponte d'Asseca. Brigadier Nepomuceno was detached against the first corps, and on the appearance of his cavalry they hastily retired and had time to reimbark under cover of the guns on the oppo-

site bank of the Tagus. At the Ponte d'Asseca
their attack was confined to the firing a few shot,
and showing a few troops. At three o'clock a
severe cannonade was heard in the direction of
Pernes, which the Duke thought was Saldanha
attacking the enemy—at four Captain Jervis, Saldanha's aid-de-camp, arrived at Terceira's quarters
and informed him that on the 28th the Marshal
having received intelligence that the enemy was
marching a large force on Pernes, he had detached
the first Queen's light infantry and a battalion of the
tenth to reinforce Colonel Romao, who occupied that
position, and returned himself to Torres Novas. On
the evening of the 29th the enemy reconnoitred
Pernes in force, and by their disposition evidently
showed their intention of attacking the following
day: their force was supposed to amount to four
thousand five hundred men. At midnight Saldanha
moved his whole force from Torres Novas, and
arrived at Pernes before daylight. At 8 o'clock,
seeing the enemy ready, the marshal put his troops
in motion on the road of Santarem.

The generals Canavaro and Bressaget, who
commanded the Miguelite forces, having ordered

an attack at 10 o'clock in the morning, were not a little surprised to find their piquets cut off by the Queen's cavalry. The enemy were now under arms, and the first, seventeenth, and twentieth infantry being in squares, were surrounded by the tenth cavalry.

Colonel Pimentel, with a squadron of lancers under command of Captain Wakefield, having cut off a few of the enemy's piquets on the left, were attacked by double their number of cavalry, and for some moments the conflict was severe. The enemy were, however, obliged to give way, afraid of being intercepted by a part of the tenth cavalry, who were making for the road by which they must retire. The first company of the second battalion of caçadores were led by Captain Guerriro to some high ground near where the enemy were in square ; their fire caused some unsteadiness in the seventeenth regiment, and Colonel Pessoa, with the tenth cavalry and a detachment of the eleventh, profiting by the occasion, charged and broke them ; at the same time the lancers fell upon the other square, and were equally successful. This finished the battle, and the enemy retired to Santarem, leaving in our possession one of the colours of the first regiment, and both of the seventeenth, seven hundred and ninety prisoners, including twenty one officers, and fifteen horses of the Chaves cavalry, and many dead on the field : our loss was three soldiers and eight horses killed, four officers, thirteen soldiers, and two horses wounded.

It does appear strange, on reading the despatches of the two marshals, that no communication appears to have taken place between them till after Saldanha's action, and too late for the Duke of Terceira to act. Saldanha appears to have known on the 28th of their moving a large force on Pernes; he knew also of it having been reconnoitred on the 29th, and he himself moved at midnight. All this ought to have been communicated to the Duke, which would have opened his eyes to the feints made by the enemy at Vallada and in his front; and he ought to have seized that occasion of attacking the enemy at the Ponte d'Asseca, when a great part of their force were acting on Saldanha, and were on the south of the Tagus. Had that been done, and Saldanha followed up his victory, Santarem would have been taken, and the war ended. Whether this want of concert proceeded from jealousy or other causes, I am not prepared to say; but it proves at all events the folly of employing two men of equal rank with independent commands so near each other. The Emperor, it is true, commanded the army, but the Emperor was not there to direct the movements of the two corps, and in his absence, if he thought it necessary to employ the Duke of Terceira, to him ought to have been given the command of both armies, being senior officer.

The Duke may be blamed, and I think he in some measure deserves censure, after having driven the Miguelites across the Tagus, and seeing the small force they showed at Ponte d'Asseca, for not attacking the moment he heard the firing, as he ought to have judged that their false attack upon him was only to cover their real attack on Saldanha.

The Emperor, on hearing of these movements, joined the army on the 31st. His health had been indifferent, and he was obliged to keep his bed a day at Cartaxo from an attack in the chest and spitting blood. On the 1st of February Saldanha arrived, and his division occupied the same position they did before going to Leria. He now took upon himself the command of the army. Terceira returned to Lisbon, and Sir Thomas Stubbs took command of his division. Saldanha expressed himself to me much dissatisfied at being ordered back to Cartaxo; his wish was to have gone on to Coimbra, and from thence to Oporto. Whether it was the marshal or the minister of war, or both, who planned the expedition to Leiria, I have never been informed; but taking it in a military sense, it appears to have been a bad movement, and had the enemy profited by the absence of Saldanha, it might have been attended with fatal consequences to the Queen's cause. It is true we gained more territory and destroyed about fifteen hundred of the enemy, but we left a like number at Leiria; and when Saldanha re-occupied his positions, the two armies in point of numbers were pretty nearly on the same footing.

Had he remained at Torres Novas and Gallegao, his operations would have more closely shut the enemy up at Santarem, and I should have been enabled to have established a flotilla on the upper part of the river; but he was not strong enough to do so, or even prevent a reinforcement from arriving from the north, who joined the army at Santarem about this time. The project of marching on Oporto could not have succeeded; he must either have kept a strong garrison in Coimbra, or exposed the town to be again occupied by the Miguelites; besides it is not certain that he could have obtained possession of Coimbra: he had the Mondego to pass, which had been swollen by the heavy rains, and at that season it was impossible to calculate on effecting a landing at Figueiras, and affording a naval cooperation; and even had he succeeded in getting possession of Coimbra, from thence to Oporto was a long march, and several rivers, particularly the Vouga, to cross, all of which would or ought to have been disputed by an active enemy. But suppose he had overcome all those difficulties, and formed a junction with the garrison of Oporto, the enemy would have retired on Braga, and if hard pressed crossed the Lima, having Vianna, Caminho and

Valenca in their rear, a strong country to defend themselves, and the richest province in Portugal to maintain them.

Considering all these circumstances, I have no hesitation in pronouncing the expedition to Leiria as altogether dangerous, and the object obtained not at all to be compared with the risk that was incurred. We have seen that the enemy could cross over at Vallada, and as the river or canal leading to Cartaxo was always full of boats, a bridge might have been made of them, and they would have got into the rear of the army and pushed on to Lisbon without difficulty; or a still safer and more enterprizing road was open to them by collecting the whole of the boats in the river, either at Santarem or in the creek of Benevento. They might there have embarked the greater part of their army, leaving a garrison in the town of Santarem, and taking advantage of the first fresh and fair wind, run down the Tagus, and landed in Black-Horse-square, (taking care to occupy the roads leading from Lisbon,) seized the Queen, sent for the patriarch, and married her forthwith to Don Miguel, making the Emperor and Empress witnesses, declared a general amnesty, fired lots of salutes during the day, illuminated Lisbon for three nights, and either kept the constitution or thrown it overboard, as was most suitable to their disposition and the will of the people. Had Don Miguel or those about him possessed courage enough to have executed such a plan, he would have deserved both crown and Queen, and obtained a reputation that would have insured him forgiveness for all his former sins. This is no after-thought; it was my opinion at the time, and I often gave it as a reason for occupying the south of the Tagus.

I again pressed this measure on Saldanha, which he proposed to the Emperor; and it was finally decided that a force of three thousand men, with a proportion of cavalry and artillery, should be crossed over under the command of the Duke of Terceira, as soon as they could be prepared. The Emperor got better, and on the 2nd of February returned to Lisbon, and preparations were made to reinforce the flotilla with a sufficient number of boats to pass over the force required.

CHAPTER V.

On the 14th of February, Lord Howard de Walden arrived at Lisbon as minister in lieu of Lord William Russell, who was appointed to the mission at Wirtemburg. Lord Howard was a disciple of Mr. Canning's, and had been a good deal employed in the Foreign Office. His last appointment was at the court of Sweden. It was naturally to be expected on the arrival of a new minister from England, some attempt would be made by him to bring things to a close. Lord Howard began by pressing a general amnesty, and to allow any Miguelites who desired to leave the country, to embark in a British ship of war. This was approved by the Duke of Terceira and Freire, but objected to by the Emperor; he, however, consented to General Macdonell, who had now resigned and been replaced first by Povoas, and finally by Lomes, to embark on pledging his honour not to serve again in the Peninsula, and not to remain in the Tagus or hold communication with any of the Miguelites in Lisbon. This he refused. When the amnesty was proposed, Freire consented to it, but on condition if the government became unpopular in consequence, England would support them with six thousand men. The property of all those who accepted it would then be restored.

There was little use stipulating for such terms, because the English government would not accede to it, nor could even the moderate Miguelites themselves ostensibly accept it without running the risk of having the whole of their country property destroyed. The feeling for Don Miguel was gone, but they were all too much compromised, and the priests kept up the disposition for absolutism; in fact they were constantly proclaiming religion as the rule of their conduct, while they outraged all its precepts. Pedro's ministers talked as much of liberty, and all their acts were despotic ; both parties hated each other cordially, and whoever became master would be sure to tyrannise over the other. Spain at the same time shewed a disposition to send troops into Portugal to drive out Carlos, and had actually twice crossed the frontier for that purpose ; and it was apprehended she might not be satisfied with that measure and crushing Miguel, but would probably wish to interfere with Pedro's government, while the Portuguese democratic party in return would appeal to the republicans in Spain to assist them, and anarchy and confusion would in consequence spread from one end of the Peninsula to the other.

Since Saldanha's recal from Leria, he became still more dissatisfied with the ministers ; he always disliked Carvalho, and now Freire became odious to him. He requested permission to come to Lisbon under the pretence of settling his affairs, but in reality to endeavour to bring about a change of ministry, in which all proper thinking men agreed with him ; and I believe even the Emperor himself, but he saw no prospect of replacing Carvalho, who always managed to procure funds ;

indeed, he was the only minister good for any thing amongst them, and the Emperor justly dreaded, if he was displaced, the army would be unpaid and the cause endangered. Saldanha was refused leave, and indeed the Emperor wrote to him and begged he would not quit the army at this critical period. These disagreements retarded, and the movements of the enemy put a stop to the expedition to the south.

When Don Miguel became acquainted with the dissentions in Lisbon caused by the folly of the ministers affronting the peers, and the disagreements between Saldanha and the government, he issued out a general amnesty, forgiving all political offences. How much he must have been led astray by those about him to suppose for one moment that it could have the least effect on the supporters of the Queen, who, though disgusted with Don Pedro's ministers, never once thought of turning their views to Miguel. This proclamation he followed up by detaching a force on the left bank of the Tagus in front of Lisbon. The force consisted of two thousand infantry, two squadrons of cavalry, and four pieces of artillery; they quitted Vendas Novas on the 5th of February, and marched on Aldea Gallego, which they occupied together with the village of Alcuhete and Moita. This demonstration had no other effect than proving the incapacity of the minister at war, who with an army at least equal in number to the Miguelites, and much better disciplined, permitted them to beard Lisbon without any other molestation than a brig of war, which I despatched to Aldea Gallego, occasionally firing at them with little effect. The Miguelite minister, equally as incapable as his brother officer Freire, after allowing the troops to take a view of Lisbon, instead of marching them on Setuval, supported by Louis de Bourmont from Alcacer do Sal, ordered Lemos back to Santarem, and Bourmont to Alcacer, having plundered the country of all the provisions they could lay their hands on.

A considerable body of troops had been withdrawn from the lines to Cartaxo shortly after Saldanha's return from Leiria, preparatory to the projected expedition, of which the Miguelites were aware; and Count D'Almer having arrived at Santarem with a division from the north, General Lemos determined on attacking the marshal, and making a bold effort to drive him back to Lisbon. At six o'clock of the morning on the 18th of February a fire was opened from four pieces of artillery, and an obus on the picquets in front of the bridge of Cellerio; the artillery was supported by a force of one thousand infantry and two small squadrons of cavalry. An hour after this a fire from eight guns and an obus was opened from the redoubt at the foot of the Ponte d'Asseca, where was assembled a division of from two thousand to two thousand five hundred men and a strong squadron of cavalry; at the same time four strong columns of infantry and five hundred horse passed the bridge of Calharis, and marched in the direction of Villa Nova de Outeiro and the small village of Santa Maria, making a long circuit round our extreme left. At the first fire of the Miguelites the picquets were reinforced, and preparations made for battle.

From the moment the movements of the enemy were observed, it was evident their main attack would take place on the left; and the first, third, and sixth regiments marched by Atalaia, and the battalions, second and twelfth, by the left to Casal do Paul, on the right of Almoster, holding themselves in readiness to fall with all their force on the enemy as they approached, and at once overturn them. Two pieces of artillery were placed at Outeiro D'Almedelim, which commanded the bridge of Celleiro; and leaving a sufficient quantity of artillery to sweep the Ponte d'Asseca in the event of the enemy attempting to force it, the remainder of the guns and all the Congreve rockets were directed on Casal do Paul. At eleven o'clock the enemy's columns were seen marching on the table-land opposite Almoster. Schwalbach commanded the column which defended this district, and exchanged a few shot with the enemy as they advanced.

The Miguelite cavalry and seventh corps of infantry having shewn their intention of passing to the left of Almoster, the first, third, and sixth of the line, with the second and twelfth caçadores, advanced by the hills on our side, accompanied by a brigade of artillery. Bacon with the eleventh cavalry, the Queen's lancers, and a detachment of the tenth, followed in a parallel line the movements of the Miguelite cavalry, with orders to charge the moment the nature of the ground permitted an attack.

At noon great demonstrations of joy were observed in the Miguelite army, and loud vivas given for Don Miguel; it was afterwards ascertained that this was occasioned by the Miguelite general reading the order of the day, which promised a great victory and a victorious march on the capital. They were to be at Villa Franca on the 19th, and Lisbon on the 22d, and all this might have been accomplished had they chosen the proper way of going about it.

Appendix,
No. XIV.

These shouts were heard with derision by the Queen's troops, and they tranquilly waited the orders of their officers to again conduct them to victory.

Here, then, we have the Queen's army and Don Miguel's fairly out of their respective lines, both equally devoted to the cause they served, numbers nearly equal, and all ready for fight; one party trying to get to Lisbon, and the other to Santarem, and yet neither one or the other accomplished their object. I don't understand these shore-fights; they last a long while, a great deal of noise on both sides, and when both parties are tired, they finish without any result; but to return to my subject.

At three o'clock, the enemy's columns having crowned the heights above the bridge of Santa Maria between Villa Nova and Alforgemel, to the left of Almoster, they opened a lively fire from their tirailleurs, throwing at the same time many balls from eight pieces of artillery and an obus; the Queen's troops, however, stood firm. The marshal knew by his spies that every means had been used by the Miguelite generals to encourage their men; they had been assured that a new squadron would shortly arrive before Lisbon; and that the moment the Queen's troops were attacked they would retire on the capital. Lemos had chosen the best soldiers he had at Santarem, had united the force from the Alemtejo, and Rebocho had arrived with reinforcements from Oporto and Coimbra, and he appeared determined to signalise his having taken command of the army, by a daring attack and great victory. Saldanha was equally anxious to bring the approaching battle to something decisive, and allowed the enemy to approach his position without interruption, intending to cut them off if possible from the Ponte de Santa Maria.

At half-past four o'clock, the enemy, about three thousand five hundred strong, formed their columns and deployed one regiment, throwing out an immense number of light troops in the plain below. Colonel Quieroz, with the second and twelfth caçadores, formed in line, and advanced on the enemy's flank, directing on the bridge two companies to cut them off. At the same time General Brito, placing himself at the head of the sixth infantry in line, and the third in column, attacked their front; the first regiment remained in reserve, formed in line half musket-shot from the enemy, exposed to a heavy fire, which the Miguelites continued with great activity, till being charged by the Queen's troops, they turned and fled with the greatest precipitation to the bridge. The carnage there was dreadful, and the reflection that Portuguese were butchering Portuguese was horrible. The enemy made little resistance, but did not surrender and were slaughtered without mercy. Saldanha in his official letter observed that, except at the breach of St. Sebastian, he had never before seen such a scene, and very seldom so heavy a fire, up to the moment the enemy fled; it must have, however, been very ill directed, as the loss of the Queen's troops was trifling.

In a few moments the heights of Villa Nova, which the enemy had occupied with their artillery, were crowned. Nevertheless Lemos, confiding in his cavalry, ordered them to charge the Queen's troops. Bacon, who was on the left, seeing their danger, came galloping to their assistance with eighty horse, charged with his usual impetuosity, and overthrew them with great loss, leaving only seven horses on the field. It was now nearly dark; Saldanha halted, and the enemy retired on Santarem.*

During the attack on Saldanha's left, the enemy were prepared at all points in the event of success

---

* It was reported that one of the Queen's officers, seeing the cavalry approach, called out "turn by three's," which they mistook for one of their own officers and obeyed.

to push on boldly. At the time the Miguelites attacked the left, a strong column was posted in the plain in front of Almoster, disposed in two divisions, to attack by that bridge and Quinta de Moira; they were repulsed at both points, by three companies of the ninth infantry, and two of the British grenadiers, who bravely drove them to the heights of Valla.

To the left of the convent at this place, the Queen's light infantry regiment kept up a lively fire of musketry and artillery, and the Quinta de Moira was defended by three companies of the tenth caçadores, who behaved with great courage. At the bridge of Cellerio the troops stationed there, supported by those who were posted at the Ponte d'Asseca at the beginning of the day, consisting of two regiments of infantry and two squadrons of cavalry, put themselves in motion in the direction of Almedelim; they were attacked and driven back with much loss by the second column, commanded by José Pedro Celestino Soares, reinforced first by the fourth infantry, and ultimately by a company of the fifth caçadores and one of the fifteenth of the line. During the rest of the day the enemy kept up a sharp fire from the tirailleurs on the positions we occupied near the bridge and mountain, defended by the sixth national battalion, two companies of the fifteenth, and the bridge by fifty of the fifteenth and a company of the fourth of the line.

On the right of the bridge the enemy kept up a sharp fire from their tirailleurs, supported by a fire in ambuscade in the olive grounds of Lezirao.

At noon the enemy's force in the neighbourhood of the Ponte d'Asseca occupying the heights to the right, detached four hundred tirailleurs in front, who opened a fire on General Brito da Franca, commanding the column that defended that position, and as they seemed desirous to attempt a passage by Valla, to give support to their sharp-shooters, it was necessary to extend, as light infantry, almost the whole of the thirteenth of the line, and a company of Scotch fusileers, stationed on that point, and they were afterwards supported by the fifth national battalion. In fact the dispositions of the enemy were excellent, and they neglected no manœuvre to distract our troops, employing the whole force they had in Santarem. Their forces in the south menaced Azambuja, approaching the margin of the river with two pieces of artillery and a hundred infantry; but on being fired at by the picquets and gun-boats they retired on Salvaterra.

During the whole of this affair the artillery kept up an excellent fire at the various points they were stationed, and behaved with great courage and activity.

The small number of cavalry engaged, consisting of only half a squadron of the eleventh, half a squadron of the Queen's lancers, and a few soldiers of the tenth, though opposed by triple their number on the heights of Villa Nova, drove the enemy with considerable loss; the rest of the cavalry were to the right and not engaged.

The marshal observed in his despatch that in his long military career he had never seen more courage displayed or more sang-froid than in this battle; all behaved well and deserved praise. The enemy must also have conducted themselves not only with bravery, but also with considerable talent, for although defeated, they only left two hundred and thirty prisoners in our hands, the greater part of whom were wounded. Our loss was three hundred and five killed and wounded, and three hundred and seventy-two missing.

The battle ended without any advantage to the cause on either side, except proving to Don Miguel's forces that they were not competent to drive the Queen's troops from their positions, far less to arrive at Lisbon, as had been promised to them by their general. It also put a stop to the projected expedition to the south, which was no more thought of, and both armies took up their former positions, and reposed from their labours. It was reported, and at one time believed, that a Spanish regiment in the service of Don Carlos was engaged in this action, but, on every enquiry being made, it appeared incorrect; there were a few Spaniards present, but nothing in the shape of a regular force.

CHAPTER VI.

On the 28th of February, Lord Howard proposed to Freire, that in the event of an opportunity offering for mediation, the terms should be left to England, France, and Sweden, as he was satisfied the opposite party had no confidence either in Don Pedro or his government. This observation was received with great indignation by Freire. With respect to the Emperor, he was wrong, for he was decidedly a man of his word. As to Freire I know from experience no reliance could be placed in him, and the Miguelites knew him well, as did every officer, native and foreign, in the whole army. I cannot speak so positively of the other ministers, but it is certain they had given no reason by their actions to suppose the Miguelites could put any confidence in them. The French minister consented to arbitrate in conjunction with Lord Howard, who submitted a project of a convention.

Appendix, No. XV.

On the 8th, Lord Howard was presented at court, and made a speech to the Queen. I am not much acquainted with diplomatic etiquette, but it appeared to me, as the Queen was a minor and Pedro regent, that he ought to have addressed the Emperor and not the Queen; and I am inclined to think Don Pedro felt it. He was not well disposed to Lord Howard, having an idea that he was instructed to get rid of both him and his ministers, and oppose the Queen's marriage; this interview did not at all tend to do away these suspicions.

On the 11th of March a communication was made from Santarem, that General Lemos, Count San Lorenzo, and General Munich were disposed to treat on the basis that England should guarantee the treaty, and that Palmella should be minister. A hint was also given that £20,000 or £30,000 could be advantageously employed. This communication must have come from some unauthorized person, for in no one instance, even to the last, was there the smallest disposition on the part of any of Miguel's friends to betray him; and about the same time this communication was made, General Lemos had proposed to treat on the basis of Miguel's marrying the Queen, which was of course rejected.

On the 19th of March a despatch was received from Mr. Villars, notifying that Spain would send troops into Portugal if required, that Mr. Sarmentos's arrival at Madrid was agreeable to the government, and the recognition of the Queen of Portugal was only delayed, least the pope should refuse to acknowledge the Queen of Spain. This Lord Howard communicated to Don Pedro, who was very much elated, till he told him that they should not pass the frontier till proper terms were offered to Don Miguel. This was decidedly wrong. Proper terms had been offered on condition he would quit Portugal, and the Emperor very properly refused to treat on any other basis. He, however, had no objection to Lord Howard making proposals, which he did in writing to Freire. This minister, I think, properly declined giving an answer till he had received Sarmentos's despatch, and equally improperly proposed a military convention should be entered into with Spain before she passed the frontier. This was losing time. Spanish intervention ought to have been accepted without any terms, as Great Britain was at hand to see she did not play foul.

On the 21st a decree was issued, depriving Don Miguel of his rank and titles of Infant, and declaring the Infantado national property. At this Lord Howard took fire, as he conceived it would render useless any further proposals he should make to Don Miguel's government, and he at once accused the ministers of wishing to prolong the war. This accusation, I think, was just, as they neither shewed by their actions or military plans that they had any desire to finish it. They were much more taken up with what they called reforms, and issuing out decrees, than in military matters, being pretty well convinced that the war once concluded, their power ceased. The depriving Miguel of his titles and property was however correct, and ought to have been done long before instead of confiscating that of his followers; he was the head offender, the punishment should have begun with him, and been followed up by the confiscation of one or two of his principal advisers, leaving a loop-hole for the inferior culprits to escape by.

In answer to Lord Howard's project of conven- Appendix, No. XVI.
tion, Freire proposed a counter project, which Lord Howard disapproved of. He, however, took his project to Cartaxo, Palmella and Terceira being of opinion he might, in concert with Saldanha, make some alterations without departing from the spirit of the amnesty, and the government would be obliged to accede to it. The alterations Lord Howard contemplated were leaving out the offensive expressions against Miguel, calling him usurper, and excepting him from the amnesty, making the article concerning civil and ecclesiastical appointments more explicit, doing something for the military, and qualifying the engagement of Don Miguel not to return to Portugal without permission of government. The latter stipulation was quite absurd, because, whether he was banished for

a time or for perpetuity, the Cortes would, on meeting, have the power of altering as they pleased.

On Lord Howard's arrival at Cartaxo, he wrote confidentially to the Count San Lorenzo, who declined any other than a public correspondence. Lord Howard in consequence sent his proposals officially.

Mr. Grant was the bearer of them; he was well received by General Lemos, who proposed to meet Lord Howard, which was accepted.

They met on the Ponte d'Asseca, halfway between the outposts. Saldanha and Lemos also met, and shook hands; the former entreated him to put full confidence in Lord Howard. Admiral Parker and Captains Richards and Fanshaw were of the party; and after exchanging compliments, they withdrew, leaving the minister and Lemos to settle the affairs of the nation between them.

After a good deal of discussion the Miguelite General gave him to understand that if the basis of Don Miguel's removal from Portugal was insisted on, he could hold out no hope of reconciliation; and that he would not desert his king, and the same feeling pervaded all his party. He also alluded to their improved resources, and the expectation of a squadron, and a more moderate ministry being appointed by Don Miguel. Lord Howard at once stopped him by observing that any change was now too late. The Duke of Wellington was no longer prime minister of England, Charles Xth no longer king of France, or Ferdinand of Spain; and even if Miguel was successful, these powers were determined not to acknowledge him; he also observed that a squadron was out of the question, and even if they had one, they had no ports. Admiral Napier had surprised Caminho, and taken Vianna, and as they would not be received in Spain, their cause was desperate. Spanish troops were about to enter Portugal, and such terms would never again be offered. This was the first intelligence he had received of the operations in the north. He was much startled, nevertheless he said he was prepared for the worst, and never would desert his king. Lord Howard remarked there was nothing dishonourable in submitting to the chances of war; they had already done all they could for Don Miguel, and he ought to think of them. Both Napoleon and Pedro had abdicated when necessary, and Miguel ought to do the same. He then delivered a letter to San Lorenzo, with the modified proposals, and returned to Lisbon. A few days after he received an answer from San Lorenzo, rejecting the terms.

Certainly Lord Howard had done his best, and was right in doing so, but his failure was a triumph to Pedro, who was not sorry they were rejected. His great desire was to see the Miguelites lay down their arms without conditions, and trust to his generosity. This would be gratifying to his vanity, and give him an opportunity of shewing he was merciful as well as just, and the sequel will show he was right.

CHAPTER VII.

It is now time to take a view of the military operations in the south and north, the latter of which led to the successful termination of the contest.

In the Algarves things remained pretty nearly in the same state. The guerillas surrounded Lagos and Faro, and harassed them with repeated attacks, but without success. They were little thought of at Lisbon, and were often reduced to the greatest distress for provisions. The governor of Faro shewed little activity, and contented himself with acting on the defensive.

I have already shewn that after the Duke of Terceira quitted the south, and marched on Lisbon, guerilla parties spread themselves all over the country, Mertola, Castro Marim, and Tavira;

and indeed all the other towns had fallen into their hands, with the exception of Faro and Lagos. The French regiment had not conducted themselves well, and were in consequence very unpopular with the inhabitants; and this may in some measure account for the guerillas increasing to the extent they did. Had that regiment been kept in constant motion, supported by moveable battalions, which ought immediately to have been formed, the line of the Guadiana would not have been lost; that was the origin of the mischief which afterwards befel that unfortunate kingdom.

Lagos had been twice saved by the marines, but no active operations had been undertaken to any extent; and when I went there, the weather was too bad to land more than two hundred men. The Emperor at last decided on sending the Baron da Sa to the south; he had been kept lounging about the palace for many months in idleness though he was a brave and active officer, but it did not suit the government to employ him. Colonel Loreiros, for the same reason, remained at Lisbon; he was on the Duke of Terceira's staff, and was only employed with him ; he was too honest a man to be a favourite with the ministry.

On the 19th of February the Baron de Sa left Lisbon: he had pressed me very hard to lend him a few marines in addition to those already in the Algarves; but I had so much reduced my own disposable force in succouring that kingdom, that it was quite impossible to accede to his wishes without cramping my own operations, and he was equally unsuccessful with the Emperor and the minister-at-war. The baron, nevertheless, obeyed his orders, and he soon shewed what could be accomplished by an ardent mind. He arrived at Lagos on the 20th, embarked a part of the garrison, and on the 21st took the military command of the kingdom at Faro.

The baron was determined the grass should not grow under his feet, and on the 22d he sallied out with a small column, and attacked the enemy at St. Bartholomew de Pexäo, one league from Faro, drove them from their position, killing between forty and fifty, and making a few prisoners. His loss was five killed and ten wounded;

amongst the former was Pedro Antonio Lobo, a cornet of cavalry, a brave and distinguished officer. The enemy retired and were followed to the heights of Boa Vista, a strong position, and where they had a permanent camp; but seeing the determination of the baron, they abandoned their station, which was occupied for the night by the Queen's troops, who were regaled with the provisions the enemy had provided for themselves. On the 23d he marched on Aldea de Moncarapacho, where the enemy left three field-pieces, an obus, some provisions and horses; he pushed on boldly and entered Tavira, with the cavalry at a gallop, and made some prisoners. This was the head-quarters of the Miguelite General Bandeira. In this town they were well received and found a considerable quantity of powder, military stores, a cahique of war, and a gun-boat, with six thousand rations. Here he published a proclamation. On the 24th he marched on Castro Marim, dispersing a small force at Villa Real, and on the same day a flotilla entered the Guadiana. On the 25th he halted and placed a garrison in

<small>Appendix, No. XVII.</small>

Castro Marim, a military post of great importance, which, assisted by the flotilla, commanded the navigation of the Guadiana. This place had been before protected by an eighteen-gun brig and a flotilla, and ought never to have been abandoned. On the 26th the baron marched, and entered the mountains, following the footsteps of the enemy through roads almost impassable; and in the evening encamped at Altamora. On the 27th he reached Martinlongo, and though only four leagues distant, such was the badness of the roads that they were twelve hours on the march. Having learnt that General Bandeira had quitted the road of Almodovar, on which he was marching, and arrived at Aldea de Cachopo, situated between Martimlongo and Sao Braz, the baron marched on the 28th on that village. Bandeira, hearing of his approach, retreated into the Alemtejo.

At daylight on the 1st of March the baron was again in motion for Sao Braz, and at ten o'clock he observed a force of from eight to nine hundred men, commanded by Camacho, posted on the heights of the Serra d'Alportel; and as he advanced, they threw out a numerous body of light troops, who commenced firing at a great distance. They were immediately attacked by a company of the first battalion of the Queen's light infantry, followed by a column, while the volunteers of Olhao advanced on the enemy's right. In ten minutes the action was over, the enemy flying in disorder to the highest mountains. They lost between twenty and thirty men, and twenty prisoners, chiefly peasants, who were sent to their homes. This had a good effect on the people. Two hours after the defeat of the first guerilla party, the guerillas of Ramochino were met in the Serra do Farrobo, who also fled at the first fire. On the 2d of March he marched on Loulé after the guerillas of Lagos, commanded by Remechido, a man of singular ferocity. They were posted on the heights, and appeared determined to defend the town, but were attacked and dispersed amongst the mountains, leaving twenty dead on the field. The baron had two men killed and six wounded.

After this skirmish he returned to Faro. The

activity of Baron de Sa shews what ought to have been done ; and I have no doubt, had he been left in the Algarves after the advance of the duke, they never would have been disturbed, and much life and property would have been saved.

During the absence of this expedition Faro had been attacked on the 23d and 27th, and the enemy were as usual repulsed. The military governor, Lieutenant Colonel Luna, deserved great praise for the activity with which the works for the defence of the town were constructed. The Baron de Faro, the former governor of the Algarves, had continued in the government at the request of de Sa during his absence, and conducted the defence of the place much to his satisfaction.

A Belgian battalion had arrived at Lisbon, certainly the best organized foreign troops that had as yet arrived in Portugal. One half of the regiment had been very improperly landed at Oporto on the 3d of February, and the other half proceeded to the Tagus, and it was not before the 16th they were united at Lisbon. They were in the first instance ordered to Santarem, but their destination was afterwards changed for Faro, where they arrived on the 4th of March. This was a good reinforcement for De Sa, and after allowing them a few days of rest, he put them in march for Sao Bras, where the enemy had again appeared in force. They were strongly posted on the heights, and as the baron approached, a company of the Belgian battalion, under the command of Colonel Le Charlier, marched on their right, another company, with the volunteers of Beja and Faro, commanded by Lieutenant-colonel Goes, on the left. De Sa, heading the other six companies formed in column, supported by the cavalry, attacked in front.

The enemy opened a heavy fire and maintained their position until the bayonets approached; they then fled from mountain to mountain with such rapidity that there was no coming up with them; indeed nothing short of a hound could compete with an Algarve guerilla. The enemy lost a good many men in this attack; our loss was two killed and seven wounded. Next day they again collected in force in a strong position near St. Bras, and drew up in line, were again attacked and again fled, but were soon lost sight of by the infantry. The cavalry, however, killed upwards of seventy and took fifteen prisoners, much baggage, and a few horses.

On the 12th a company was detached to Tavira, who drove out the guerillas, who had again taken up their quarters in that town. On the 13th the division bivouacked on the Sierra de Penafines, and on the 14th at Alte. Here two men were shot for having endeavoured to excite a revolt amongst the troops. This severe example checked any further disposition to insubordination. After the execution the troops were marched on Ribeira de Merinho, where they halted for the night.

At daylight of the 15th the baron marched on Bartholomew de Messines. This was the rendezvous of Remechido, and the head quarters of the guerillas; they had arrived two hours before, and in their retreat two men were captured, who gave information that the whole of the Algarve guerillas had received orders to rendezvous at the gorge of Val Fortes. Thither the baron proceeded in hopes of surprising them; few only were captured, the rendezvous having been changed in consequence of the baron's movements. On the 16th the divisions marched on Almedovar, a town on the frontier of the province of the Alemtejo. The weather had set in bad, and the troops were much harassed; nevertheless he continued his march in the night, and defiled through the intricate pass of Val de Matta. Here were stationed a small party of guerillas on the mountains that hung over the defile. After firing a few shot, they retired, and the troops halted at Respingadour.

On the 17th they were again in march, and after passing through the mountains of the Algarves arrived at half-past two at Almedovar.

Thus in eight days were two or three thousand guerillas and royalist volunteers beaten and dispersed by about one thousand men, including forty lancers, and the Algarves pretty nearly cleared of the most ferocious band of robbers and murderers that ever disgraced a war. Remechido and his followers, in their depredations, were not over nice who they attacked; it mattered little to them whether they were Miguelites or Pedroites; his object was plunder. Miguel's cause was a secondary consideration, but a good excuse for every species of atrocity.

CHAPTER VIII.

The news of these reverses on the Algarves decided Don Miguel to send reinforcements to the south, and they were entrusted to Brigadier Louis de Bourmont, one of the most active officers Miguel had. Saldanha was aware of their intentions, and had urgently requested Freire to reinforce De Sa; but as usual that minister was much too incapable to look upon things *en grande* and concert measures (which the advantage of steam-boats made easy) to frustrate the foresight of the enemy.

I had long urged the Emperor and minister-at-war to permit me to withdraw the marines who formed part of the garrison of Setuval, in order that I might be ready, on the first appearance of fine weather, to seize the sea-ports still in possession of the Miguelites, and keep the war alive; and I now became more pressing, as all prospect of any future operation being carried on south of the Tagus was at an end. I at last gained a reluctant consent—I say reluctant, for at this time I really believe neither the Emperor or ministers had the least wish to put an end to the war; they were more occupied with hasty reforms and issuing out decrees than planning campaigns; and although the minister-at-war in his Relatorio would have the world believe that what I am now about to describe was brought about by the most beautiful combinations, I have no hesitation in saying that the whole was chance, and indeed against the minister's wish; and that the Emperor was quite right when he said the Baron de Sa and myself were making war on our own accounts, and that he had nothing to do with us.

The minister-at-war says that the Emperor, to cover his intentions in the north, appeared to be occupied with the south, and that the Baron de Sa was sent to the Algarves as governor on the

19th of February with orders to act on the offensive; and that a column of fifteen hundred men was formed at Setuval. Now the Baron de Sa went to the Algarves a few days after the battle of Almoster, and was ordered there at the time preparations were making to occupy the south bank of the Tagus, and which expedition was given up after the attack on Saldanha; but the Baron de Sa did not take with him a single soldier, and it was his own singular activity that enabled him to act as he did. The fifteen hundred men were placed in St. Ubes purely for its defence, and had been gradually increased since the affair of Alcacer do Sal; and with the exception of making a sally out under Colonel Calce de Pina, who was wounded, did no good whatever; and I will show in its proper place, while the Baron de Sa and myself were surprising and conquering on the north and south, Setuval was surprised and nearly taken by the Miguelites.

I sailed for that port on the 16th of March with about one hundred and twenty English marines, and thirty or forty seamen, in the City of Edinburgh steamer, with the intention of embarking the Portuguese marines there, and attacking Figueiras. This much the Emperor and minister-at-war knew, and directions were given to the governor of Leiria to assist my operations. It was given out and generally believed I was going to the south to assist the Baron de Sa. On the 17th I arrived at Setuval, and the weather not appearing settled, I asked permission by secret telegraph to surprise Alcacer do Sal. The garrison there was weak; it might easily have been done, and it was an important position. The answer I received was, " That it is his " imperial Majesty's orders that the admiral " returns immediately to Lisbon in the City of " Edinburgh." I waited till nearly dusk and replied, " My return will have a bad effect—I " shall proceed to my destination." All this may appear very wrong, and no doubt was, but I have before said, this war was unlike all others. So much intriguing and vacillation constantly at work, it was necessary for officers to take much on themselves, or give it up altogether. I therefore decided on not returning to Lisbon till I had struck a blow somewhere.

I left the Baron de Sa, after clearing the Algarves, at Almodovar, preparing to advance into the Alemtejo on the 17th, the very day I was at Setuval, and had prepared to advance on Alcacer. It is very evident, had I been allowed to proceed, reinforcements would not have been sent to the south, and the disaster the baron met with would have been avoided. I was not aware where he was, but I knew he would not be idle, and it was the duty of the minister to have established secret communications with the Algarves, which in civil war is always easy. We shall now see Freire's combinations, of which he boasts in his Relatorio.

On the 19th Colonel Lecharlier was detached to Mertola with half of De Sa's division, having orders to surprise that post, which was garrisoned by a considerable band of guerillas and a battalion of royalist volunteers. The baron with the other half covered the Algarves, least the guerillas should attempt another irruption. The distance from Almodovar to Mertola was seven long leagues, which the troops marched in one day; but the enemy having notice of their approach, had decamped at noon, taking the route of

Beja. On the 21st De Sa joined, and on the 22d the whole marched on that town, and arrived on the 23d. It was also abandoned, and Count Louis de Bourmont had thrown himself into Serpa on the opposite side of the Guadiana.

Beja was a constitutional city, and although they had already suffered severely for having espoused the cause of the Queen after the landing of the Duke of Terceira in the Algarves, their feeling for freedom was in no way cooled, and the troops were received by both sexes with the greatest enthusiasm. Here then was the Baron de Sa and his small division in the heart and capital of the Alemtejo, totally unsupported. It was a bold undertaking, and deserved a better finish than it met with. On the 24th he was in march for Serpa, and crossed the Guadiana on three points without opposition. One of the enemy's videttes fell into his hands, and from him he learned that Bourmont had evacuated Serpa, leaving a garrison in the fort, with orders to defend it to the last extremity, to give time for the arrival of expected reinforcements.

On the approach to Serpa the advanced guard were met by a part of the garrison outside the town; they were instantly attacked and driven into the citadel. Two companies, under the command of Captains Bergé and Poutrain, were ordered to advance without firing, and endeavour to force the gates. The walls were nearly forty feet high, and well lined with troops, who opened a heavy fire as they advanced. They, however, persevered, covered by the rest of the division, but found it quite impossible to force the gates. Both parties abused each other, and the vivas for Donna Maria and Don Miguel, shouted by either party, were heard amongst the noise and confusion occasioned by the heavy dischage of musketry. Stones were thrown down from every part of the ramparts on the assailants, and many men were knocked down by them, as well as killed by musketry. All efforts to force the gates were unavailing, and the gallant troops were ordered to withdraw. One officer was killed, seven wounded, and a considerable number of men. At half past eleven the division retired, recrossed the Guadiana at one in the morning, and arrived next day at Beja at two o'clock. The advanced guard, who were ignorant of the retreat, did not arrive till seven in the evening, and though they passed close to the fortress of Serpa, they were undisturbed by the garrison.

On the evening of the 25th a Miguelite courier was intercepted carrying despatches to General Bourmont, announcing the approach of two columns to Beja, one from Alcacer do Sal, and the other from Evora.

The capture of the courier gave De Sa time to make arrangements for retreat, and at one in the morning of the 26th he was in full march for Mertola, leaving Beja again to the tender mercies of the Miguelites. He arrived there on the 27th, and at daylight of the 31st he retired on the Algarves. The guerillas, having collected a large force, were marching on Loulé, in a parallel line with the baron on his right flank, and separated from him by high mountains about a league distant. On the 2d the division arrived at Loulé, and on the 4th Colonel Lecharlier was obliged to march out and disperse the guerillas, who had made demonstrations to attack him.

The day before the baron quitted Beja

Louis de Bourmont attacked a small body of the Queen's troops in the valley of Barrancos, and forced them to retire into Spain, where they were well received. He then marched to Serpa, expecting to surprise and overwhelm De Sa, who, it has been seen, had timely notice, and retired on Mertola.

The garrison of Setuval, taking advantage of the absence from Alcacer of the greater part of the troops, marched on that town, which they occupied without loss, the enemy retiring on Evora. This obliged Bourmont to return from the south, and having formed a junction with General Cabrera, who commanded a moveable column, and was making towards the Algarves, both retraced their steps to Alcacer, which was now abandoned by the Queen's troops, who retired on Setuval.

The indefatigable De Sa had gone to Faro on the 4th, to celebrate the Queen's birthday, and to put in motion a battalion of the 4th and thirty lancers sent to his assistance, returned on the 6th, and hearing of Bourmont's and Cabrera's return to Alcacer, marched on the 11th to Silves, and from thence to the heights of St.

Bartholomé de Messines, the only road by which the Miguelites could advance into the Algarves.

The baron's first irruption into the Alemtejo, and subsequent march on Serpa, had obliged the enemy to detach a force into that province ; before that force the baron was obliged to retreat, after receiving rather a severe check at Serpa. The return of the enemy to Alcacer do Sal, and the reinforcement he received, enabled him again to advance, and Don Miguel's government now determined to make a last effort to crush him, little thinking of what I was preparing for them in the north. A division of three thousand men, with six pieces of artillery, and between two and three hundred cavalry, was detached from Santarem under the orders of General Cabrera, who boasted that in eight days the Queen's troops should be driven from the Algarves. I shall leave him on his march and relate my own operations in the north.

On the evening of the 15th of March I sailed from Setuval, and anchored under Cape Mondego the following night; I found there the Eliza and Portuense corvettes ; the Isabel Maria, who had been ordered there from Lisbon, had not yet arrived.

At daylight we weighed, and after reconnoitring Figueiras, I decided on landing the marines at Buarcos, a little to the north, under cover of the ships, and if possible driving the enemy into Figueiras, and attacking it by land and sea at the same time. The weather was fine, but on approaching the beach I found the surf so high that it was quite impossible to attempt it, and the bar was equally impassable. I then reconnoitred to the northward of Cape Mondego, intending to land there, and march over the high land, but not a creek or corner fit to land one boat was to be found, much less to disembark five hundred men; indeed, during the whole time the Eliza had been off Figueiras, at no time could the beach have been attempted. The whole coast of Portugal, from the Minho to the Tagus, at all seasons of the year, is rendered extremely difficult of approach on account of the constant swell setting in, and I have never yet been able to make out how the Duke of Wellington succeeded in landing his army in Mondego Bay.

The Lord of the Isles steamer now joined me from Caminha, and as Mr. Gidney gave a better account of the coast to the northward, I decided on attempting a landing there, and immediately started, desiring the Eliza to follow. Next morning we were joined by the Villa Flor and George IVth steamers, and in the course of the day by the Eliza.

The Minho divides Spain from Portugal; in the centre of the river, on an island, stands a strong castle belonging to the Portuguese; this was garrisoned by the Miguelite troops. There are two passages; that on the north belongs to Spain, on the south to Portugal; both passages are safe, when the water is smooth, the Spanish passage the widest. On a close reconnoitre of the bar it appeared practicable, and I landed at the small town of Guarda in Gallicia, to obtain information, reconnoitred Caminha, which is situated five or six miles up the river, and endeavoured to hire boats sufficient to carry over my men. I was well received by an old captain, the Spanish commandant, and by the Portuguese consul, a Spaniard. The commandant conducted me to the top of a high mountain, where we had an excellent survey of the river and town. The scenery was beautiful; the valley of the Minho, the richest in Portugal, and the river running through that valley, extremely picturesque; but I did not come to look at the beauties of the country, therefore will not attempt to describe them; I came to look at the defences of Caminha, and the best way of approaching them, and will give the result of my observations. The fort in the middle of the river was very strong and very high, and a heavy surf rendered an attack there impossible; it was also doubtful whether the bar was passable, and almost certain that we should be discovered in passing, and the town in consequence be prepared for our reception.

Caminha itself was walled round, and ditched on the land sides, but only mounted a few guns. The sea-wall was not ditched, and on the quay where the vessels unload several storehouses were built against the wall. These storehouses I intended should serve for my scaling-ladders, if I could once get up to the town. From Guarda a road leads through a valley on the left of the mountain to a Spanish mercantile establishment just opposite Caminha. Through this valley Marshal Soult drew boats and endeavoured to pass the Minho, but failed; and through this same valley I was very anxious to march my troops and cross over; but Spain was a neutral territory, and my friend the commandant would not hear of it. The judge was a clever young man and a constitutionalist, and so was Don Manuel Espagnol, the Portuguese consul, and both were anxious for my success. They persuaded the commandant to station his men along the banks of the river and prevent any communication with Portugal, and assisted me in in hiring boats to transport the men across the bar.

All this settled, I returned on board, and towards dark we stood into Guarda with the boats and steamers. I had still some doubts of the bar, and I went myself to examine its practicability, and found it so bad that no boat could pass with safety. On my return on board, the judge and consul were both disappointed at the difficulty of the bar, and most anxious to facilitate my operations, but afraid to commit themselves in countenancing our landing; however, after a good deal of persuasion, and threatening to abandon the enterprize altogether, which would have been very much against the interest of the mercantile establishment on the river, which I soon perceived belonged to them, the judge consented that we should land after midnight, when the villagers were in bed, and undertook to manage the affair with the commandant. No time was to be lost; boats were sent off, and by one o'clock we were all drawn up on the beach, and soon after marched through the valley, and arrived about two opposite Caminha, distant two miles across the river. All seemed quiet; no guard boats appeared, and no communication had been allowed during the day. I expected to have found boats sufficient to carry the whole across, but only two passage boats were to be seen, and they were to be pushed across by long poles, and as the ebb tide was strong they necessarily would drift down nearly at the entrance of the river. The boats could only contain about half our force; they were composed of the English marines under Captain Birt, the seamen under

Captain Liot and Mr. Robinson, and a division of Portuguese marines under Major Carvalho. I was not aware of the manner of effecting the passage, nor till after they pushed off did I exactly understand how far they must drift down. I, however, took the precaution of leaving the operation entirely to the discretion of the commanding officer, either to take up a position until I could bring the remainder of the men across, or push on according to circumstances. From the length of the passage and the impossibility of the boats returning before the tide turned, the commanding officer at once saw that no time was to be lost, and having an excellent guide, he pushed on for the town.

About a mile in advance of the town their picquets were surprised asleep; the gates were shut. No sentries were on the ramparts, but they were too high to get over. The guide, no way disconcerted, led them down a lane to the water-side, keeping close to the walls, and thus they marched the whole length of the town in perfect silence, and gained the quay. A sally-port was open, through which they passed;

one party seized the guard, another the barracks, and a third made for the governor's house, who had just time to poke his head out of a window, and cry out "to arms," when he was shot by one of the marines. A priest, at another window, shared the same fate. The soldiers in the barracks made no resistance, and in a few minutes the town was secured, and all was quiet. An officer and a small party had been detached on board the Scorpion cutter under command of Lieutenant Whitaker, of the navy, who had broke the blockade, and very politely requested him to come on deck. As he awoke out of his sleep, he exclaimed "Good God! is it possible! If I had had sufficient warning you should not have had the Scorpion—I should have set fire to her."

During this time I was under great anxiety for the success of the enterprize, and had almost repented of having undertaken it; but my fears were soon relieved by seeing a movement amongst the fishing boats, which were sent over for the rest of the division. Caminha is a strong walled town, but had been much neglected; the garrison consisted of seventy men, who might have defended it for some time had they kept their eyes open. The people were almost all constitutionalists, but afraid of declaring themselves, on account of the smallness of our numbers. A summons was sent to the fort, in the middle of the river, which was immediately given up and garrisoned, and the Minho, in consequence, shut against any supplies from without.

_{Appendix, No. XIII.}

The George IVth steamer was despatched off Figueiras for the marines of the Portuense and Isabel Maria; and the Don Pedro arriving at the same time from England, our garrison was reinforced by nearly two hundred men. Despatches were sent to the general at Oporto, requesting him to put himself in movement, and I turned my attention to securing the town, and preparing for further military operations. The same day I surprised Caminha, the Baron de Sa, it has been seen, entered Beja. Had all this been planned as the minister-at-war would have the nation believe, nothing could have been more beautiful, and planned it might and ought to have been the moment the enemy weakened their force in the north to strengthen Santarem; but, so far from that, we were both accused of making war on our own account; and when Lord Howard congratulated the Emperor on my success he was much annoyed, and said he had nothing to do with it.

The position of Caminha with a sufficient force was excellent for clearing the province of the Minho, but with a small one I was placed between three fires; the fortified town of Valenca was on my left, about four leagues distant, Vianna on the right about the same, and Ponte de Lima, leading to Braga, in front. If I marched on Ponte de Lima, both flanks were exposed, and a certainty of being attacked in front; should the Baron de Pico not act on the offensive. Valenca was too strong to reduce without a siege; but if pressed, I could cross over to Spain and the Spanish general was disposed to support me, and had asked permission so to do; I managed to persuade him that it was probable Don Carlos would endeavour to throw himself into Valenca, and in fact apartments had been prepared there for a great personage. There was also danger of going to Vianna, which was garrisoned by five hundred men with a strong citadel; and if attacked on the left flank, I might find a difficulty in embarking, still it was necessary to do something. The governor of Valenca had detached one hundred men to watch our movements, and the governor of Vianna was posted at Fifo, two leagues off, with the greater part of his garrison.

In the midst of these perplexities the enemy themselves solved the question. On the morning of the 27th twenty men and an officer of the Vianna militia joined my standard. I beat to arms and marched on Fifo, leaving a garrison of one hundred men in Caminha, with orders to patrole on the Valenca road and organize a force in the town. Here, then, I started mounted on my charger, a wicked pony that had belonged to the governor, my staff on mules and donkeys, or whatever they could find, opening my first campaign at the head of five hundred Portuguese and English marines and sailors, as well pleased as the Duke of Wellington at the head of his army. The Don Pedro and George the Fourth steamer followed along shore, with orders to anchor as close as possible to where we expected the enemy would stand. The sailors carrying little weight, were extended on each flank as we passed through a wood, and an advanced guard two hundred yards in front. In this order we marched on Fifo, a village sufficiently strong for defence had it been necessary to pass through it, but as it lay some distance from the sea I determined on taking the beach, and there fighting our enemy should they be inclined to stand, which I thought preferable to mountain warfare. On arriving within a mile of the position where the deserters pointed out the enemy were stationed, a soldier was despatched to parley with their centinels and invite them over. The only answer he received was a shot, and we marched on. They consisted of two or three hundred men of the Barca militia. They preferred the mountains to the beach; and as we were amphibious animals and did not like to be far from the water, each party pleased himself. We pushed on, and the enemy decamped over the hills very civilly, leaving our flank unmolested. We had only now to encounter the Vianna militia and the remainder of the Barca stationed at the former town, the villagers having assured us that our other opponents had made the best of their way into the interior and probably to their homes.

After marching another league, I received a despatch from the colonel of the Vianna militia, requesting me to halt for the night, and he would make an arrangement with the Barca militia, and come over to the Queen. In war delays are dangerous; this might have been a ruse to give time for the other party to rejoin, or he might expect reinforcements; so I preferred marching on, and desired the colonel to meet me outside the town, which he did with the greater part of his regiment, consisting of three hundred men well equipped. The Barca militia declined the honor of the interview and marched out at the other gate. The hymn was now played, and our new comrades led the way into the town; the constitution was proclaimed in the great square, the troops then marched off to their different quarters and strict orders given that the barrack-yards should be shut, and not a soul allowed in the town.

Vianna is a very nice clean place, at the entrance of the Lima, having a strong citadel for its defence. The harbour, like all those on the coast of Portugal, has a bar, only accessible in fine weather. The inhabitants of this town were reported to be strong Miguelites, as well as all the province; but they took no part in the war whatever, or showed any disposition to defend their town, which might have been done successfully against my small force; in fact they wanted peace, commerce, and good government. It is also just to observe that there was very little appearance of joy, and no enthusiasm for the Queen evinced by the inhabitants. We were received with much civility by the English consul, who informed me that the Baron de Pico had marched from Oporto and driven the enemy to Guimaraens. This welcome news left us at liberty to continue our operations without risk of surprise.

The following day I organized the government, and issued a proclamation, ordering the inhabitants to return to their habitations, and gave strict orders to the authorities to allow no person to be persecuted for their political opinions. The rank of the officers of the Vianna militia was confirmed, and half a moidore given to each soldier who came over to the Queen. Towards the

Appendix, No. XIX.

evening I received the submission of Espinosa and Villa de Conde.

At daylight of the 29th I marched on Ponte de Lima, to prevent the enemy, should they be so disposed, from crossing the river and occupying the rich province of the Minha, making Valenca the basis of their operations; and considering the strength and richness of this country, with a strong fortress, that was the line they ought to have adopted.

The march through this province was most delightful; nothing could exceed the richness and beauty of the two valleys of the Minho and Lima, bounded on either side by high mountains. The valleys are well cultivated, the inhabitants peaceable and industrious, taking so little interest in the war, that although we marched within a mile of a village where there was a large cattle fair, not a soul came to see us pass. I rode up to the village, and desired them to give vivas for Donna Maria, which was willingly complied with, and I have no doubt they would as willingly have given them for Don Miguel. This province did not appear to have suffered from the war, and considering the length of time so large an army had been before Oporto, it might have been expected the country would have been entirely drained of cattle. As I approached Ponte de Lima, I received a deputation, informing me the Queen was proclaimed, that the Miguelites had retired from Braga, which had also declared for the Queen, and the country was clear as far as Amarante, to where the enemy had retired. The preventing the Miguelites from occupying this rich province was a great point gained, but be it remembered there was no combination to effect this; it was all chance; the ignorance of both ministers of war was upon a par; but fortune declared in favour of the Queen. At four o'clock we marched into Ponte de Lima, and were received with much enthusiasm. The men were quartered in the houses of the inhabitants, who treated them in the kindest manner, and shewed great enthusiasm for the Queen. This was a constitutional town.

I now determined to march on Valenca, and sent orders to Captain Bertrand of the Don Pedro, who was at Vianna, to return to Caminha, and make preparations to send me guns and mortars for a siege. The Spanish general at Tuy had offered his assistance, and I wrote to him to join me on the morning of the 1st of April, before Valenca, and likewise to Major Carvalho to march from Caminha with his garrison for the same destination.

Before leaving Ponte de Lima on the 30th, a detachment of the Vianna militia brought in three cartloads of copper money, which had been removed from the government coffers, and having organized the authorities, and appointed officers to form a local force for the protection of the town against any guerillas that might appear, I marched on Valenca with about seven hundred men. After a march of five leagues over bad roads and a mountainous country, we bivouacked for the night in a small wood, lighted fires, caught and killed a bullock, and managed to rough it out tolerably well on a beefsteak and a bottle of wine, without bread. I collected the seamen and marines in a clump, and encouraged them in relating their adventures and the reasons that brought them to Portugal. Some of their stories were amusing in the extreme; we had, as might be supposed, all sorts of characters, good and bad. There were broken-down shoemakers, tailors, drapers, man-milliners, poachers, disappointed lovers, several resurrection men; and it was even said there was a Burker or two in the society. Most had entered voluntarily, but several had been kidnapped when drunk, and shipped off without their consent. Nevertheless they were generally very well behaved, and few instances of plundering or maltreating the inhabitants had occurred, and in all cases they were most severely punished.

At daylight we were again on march, and at ten the fortress of Valenca appeared about two leagues distant in the plain below. The mountains here opened into a wide space, which afforded us an opportunity of making our force appear considerably larger than it really was. The troops marched into this space, which overlooked the plain, and the ground allowed them to file off to the right and left without being seen, and return over the hills into the space I have described. Here we halted to refresh the people, and as the country through which we were to pass was well wooded, we naturally expected the enemy would take advantage of their local knowledge, and harass our march to the town. Our skirmishers were thrown out on either flank, and we advanced cautiously, but without molestation, through the wood, and about two o'clock arrived within range of shot of the fortress. The Portuguese marines were quartered in a village on the left, the English marines in the centre, and the Vianna militia on the right; the advanced posts pushed close up to the walls.

Valenca is a strong fortress, accessible on the western side only, where is placed a very strong outwork, totally independent of the fortress, though connected with it by a bridge. The fortress is a little distance from the Minho, over which it hangs; the walls are high, and the ground on which it stands, except on the western side, is almost perpendicular, and surrounded by a covered way for musketry under the guns, with which it was well bristled.

A flag of truce was sent by a young Portuguese emigré with a summons, but he was ill received, and rather pleased to get back safe, the garrison vociferating vivas for Don Miguel, and a letter I sent in by a peasant remained without a reply.

Appendix, No. XX.

In the evening the enemy made a reconnoissance, but were driven back; we lost seven men killed and wounded. We were supplied with abundance of fresh beef and wine, but bread was scarce, the ovens being insufficient to bake for the troops: part of the money taken at Ponte de Lima was served out to the men, which soon produced a good and abundant market. Orders were sent to Captain Bertrand to hurry up the guns and mortars, and next morning I was joined by the detachment from Caminha and two hundred and eighty Spaniards, which the governor of the district put at my disposal.

The Vianna militia were detached to watch the eastern gate, the Spaniards the southern; the Portuguese marines were quartered in a small farm, protected by the brow of the hill from the fortification, and their picquets pushed up to the glacis, under cover of a wall and hedge; the English marines and sailors at head-quarters between the Spaniards and Portuguese, to support either in the event of being attacked. Strict orders were given to each party to defend their position to the last extremity, except the Vianna militia, who were to fall back on the road, being too distant to be succoured. I now reconnoitred the fortress on all points, and decided on attacking the outwork, which appeared to me the only place against which I could bring up the guns with safety, and with a probability of success. The walls were much too high to attempt an escalade even had we been provided with ladders.

I received a visit in the afternoon from Lord William Russell and Colonel Hare, who had put into Vigo on their way to England, and I prevailed on them to accompany me in having a near look at the town; they were not a little surprised to find our men pushed so close up; they had little opinion of marines and sailors being very useful on shore, and after a pretty good reconnoitre, which they made from a covered road which led to the glacis, and looked round a corner to an angle of a bastion, where was placed a gun pointing direct to the opening, they were of opinion I could not succeed. I thought otherwise: fifty guns was a powerful argument to make use of, and to besiege it I made up my mind. In the afternoon the Spaniards reconnoitred the gate on the side they were stationed nearly up to the glacis, and had an officer and several men wounded. An attempt was made to dislodge the Portuguese from under the wall, but without success.

The governor now released the state prisoners; this proved he could not be very well supplied with provisions; many of the unfortunate wretches had been confined in the dungeons for five years, and were in a miserable situation.

About midnight our piquets were alarmed by the appearance of men advancing upon them from the town, and were well nigh commencing a fight with the Portuguese marines, who fancied the whole garrison were marching out against them, got into a panic and bolted in spite of their officers. Fortunately they were discovered, and ordered back to their posts. This was no great encouragement to begin with, and still less, when next morning an order came from the captain-general of Gallicia for the Spaniards to return to Tuy. This was never explained; their departure made a considerable gap between the Vianna militia and the English seamen and marines; nevertheless I was determined to go on. The part of the marine brigade, who had behaved so ill in the night, were paraded, and given to understand a similar behaviour would be punished with shooting every tenth man. This day several men of the Vianna militia (a detachment of whom were in the town) lowered themselves from the walls and joined us. They appeared to think the town would be defended, and great exertions were making to mount guns in various parts of the fortress.

In the afternoon I received a communication from an officer in garrison who requested I would not attack that night. At daylight of the 3d two heavy guns arrived, and six more with two mortars were on their way up the river. I crossed over to Spain and waited on the governor of Tuy; from thence we could distinctly see the separation between the outwork and the town, and the strength of the place towards the river. On my return I found an officer with a flag of truce, offering to surrender the town. *Appendix XXI.*

I wrote a few lines in reply, and desired the officer to say I should march to the glacis in ten *Appendix, XXII.*

minutes and there receive the governor. To this he objected, as it would be necessary to enter into a regular capitulation. I replied I had nothing further to say, and immediately put the troops in motion, and marched up to the walls. There seemed to be some hesitation on the part of the governor, and our position was rather critical, as we were exposed to the fire of the place in the event of his having changed his mind. An aid-de-camp was despatched to say I was waiting, and to request his immediate attendance, which he complied with. Several objections were made to this haste; he was anxious to wait a few days and draw up a regular capitulation. I gave him his choice, either to allow me to march in or he might return; and I should re-occupy my former position. After a shrug or two of the shoulder and a wry face he consented. In we marched, and in half an hour were as comfortable as if we had been in quarters a fortnight.

Valenca is a town of great strength, capable of mounting several hundred guns; seventy were mounted when I took possession of it, and more were in progress; the garrison was fully equal for its defence against my small force, and had they been well managed they might have given me a considerable deal of employment; there was, however, no energy amongst them, and they appeared stupified at the successes we had met with, and were much alarmed at the idea of being stormed by seamen and marines.

Next morning the garrison were ordered under arms, and had the choice of serving the Queen or returning to their homes. They preferred the latter, deposed their arms and marched quietly off. The officers did the same; they consisted of between four and five hundred men of the regiment of Bastos, and part of the Vianna militia, who joined their corps, now named the Vianna volunteers. Thus, in ten days was the whole of the province secured, the siege of Oporto raised, and the enemy entirely cut off from the richest provinces of Portugal.

I may here mention a circumstance to show what little attention was paid by the minister of marine to those who were exerting themselves for the Queen. I had sent the inspector of the arsenal to Brest, to fit out the Portuguese ships that had been taken away by the French, and had appointed his adjutant, a very active man, to act in his absence. Before I quitted Lisbon it had been rumoured that he would be removed, which I communicated to the minister, and exacted a promise that he should remain; but I had hardly got well out of the Tagus before he was superseded. This I learnt at Valenca, which called forth as severe a letter as I could pen. This letter and my success had its effect, and the same gazette that announced the appointment of a new inspector, also announced his dismissal. This shews one specimen of the intrigues that were set on foot against me even before the war was over, and principally caused by wishing it finished while the ministers wished it continued.

Appendix, XXIII.

After having organized the government at Valenca, and sent the Vianna volunteers to Barca, least the militia of that place, who had disappeared from Vianna, should be troublesome, I left, and embarked on board the Don Pedro, and proceeded to Oporto in the City of Edinburgh steamer. The Don Pedro and Eliza were sent to reinforce the blockade off Figueras and Aveiro, and to get all the information they could before my arrival. I found some difficulty in persuading the governor of Oporto to send a battalion of fixos to relieve my men at Valenca, so unaccustomed were the old gentlemen placed in these situations to take responsibility on themselves, and I was obliged to threaten to withdraw my men and leave the place to itself. This had its effect, and the same evening the City of Edinburgh returned to Caminho with a battalion to garrison Valenca.

Oporto was fast recovering from the effects of the siege, and under the direction of Mr. Miranda, the prefect, public works were advancing. Colonel Sorrel took me over the lines constructed by Don Pedro, and as far as I am a judge I should say they were not defensible in any one point, and nothing can speak more favourably of the goodness of the Queen's troops than the constant and successful defence of those lines against so superior an enemy, and in the last attack, commanded by an officer of Marshal Bourmont's reputation. I met with the greatest attention from the inhabitants of Oporto, and in the evening on my appearing at the opera, the whole of the audience stood up, and on some allusion being made to the capture of the fleet and our successes in the north, it was received by vivas, and the waving of handkerchiefs by the fair sex. The same attention was shewn me on leaving the theatre.

CHAPTER IX.

HAVING described my own operations in the north, I shall now relate what took place at Oporto after the news of the surprise of Caminho. The uncertainty of landing on any part of the coast of Portugal was so great that I did not communicate my project to the governor of Oporto. I was also afraid that, in the event of delay, what I wished to keep secret might leak out, and the enemy in consequence get wind of it. I, however, immediately on getting possession of Caminha, sent the City of Edinburgh to Oporto and Lisbon, and at eight o'clock at night of the 25th the Baron do Pico do Celeiro, better known by the name of old Torres, (who so gallantly defended the Serra convent,) marched out of Oporto in three columns, taking the road of Santa Thyrso. Next morning the enemy were attacked in their position of Santa Christina, and driven to Guimaraens. At daylight of the 27th they retired by the road of Lexa. Raymondo José Pinheiro remained in the Carvalho D'Este with some militia and guerillas, whom he was recruiting at that point, and in order to prevent him disturbing my operations in the north, the Baron do Pico detached a force of fourteen hundred men to occupy Braga, and on the 30th his force marched on Raymondo, who was obliged to retire on Salamonde. The rest of the enemy's forces from St. Thyrso and Baltar were now united with a division from the south at Penafiel, and to drive them from thence, the column which had been sent to Braga was ordered back to Guimaraens. One division was directed on Barragus, and Torres made a movement on the right, which obliged the enemy to retire by the road of Lixa. On the 2d of April they occupied a strong position near that place, which they defended for two hours and a half, and finally retired on Amarante, at which place they passed the Tamego, the Queen's troops occupying a position close to that town. The force of the enemy was nearly three thousand men, including two hundred lancers. Their retreat was well conducted; about a hundred killed and wounded were left on the field of battle: our loss was trifling, principally in cavalry.

Our unlooked-for successes in the north now convinced the ministers that their officers in command were not inclined to protract the war if they were, the Duke of Terceira was hurried off with reinforcements to Oporto, where he arrived on the 3d of April, the day that Torres had driven the enemy across the Tamego and the day I entered Valenca; and all the thanks the old general got for marching out of Oporto when he heard I had landed in the north was a reprimand for not having waited for the arrival of the duke of Terceira, which if he had done, I should certainly have neither taken Vianna or Valenca, and in all probability would have been attacked by a very superior force, and probably annihilated, and instead of the enemy being driven across the Tamego, the Douro, the Mondego, and finally to Santarem, by the Duke of Terceira, he would have had to have fought them in the richest and strongest provinces of Portugal, with three fortresses in their rear, which would have occupied him the whole summer, and completely answered the wishes of the minister in protracting the war.

Appendix, XXIV.
On the arrival of the duke, he issued a proclamation to the inhabitants of the north. On the 5th he despatched the twelfth caçadores to Baltar, and on the 6th he took command of the army at Amarante, which was in position close to that place, having a battalion in the town, and the foot of the bridge fortified, with posts of observation on different parts of the river, at present fordable, and the second moveable battalion of Oporto at Canaveyes, with two pieces of artillery to defend the bridge at that place, and observe the enemy's force on the opposite bank, and to keep in check the guerillas which were stationed at Melres, and between the two rivers. A detachment was also placed at Penafiel to maintain order, and give security to the peaceable inhabitants. And

the moveable battalion of the Minho was stationed in the vicinity, and part of another that had been organized at Guimaraens observed the bridge of Carvez.

It may here be as well to observe the rapidity with which these battalions were formed in every town the Queen's troops got possession of. All the young men were armed and accoutred; and though not clothed, it is quite astonishing in how short a time they assumed a military appearance. The life was new to them, and as they were both fed and paid, for a short time it was by no means disagreeable.

As the Baron do Pico de Celeiro had marched from Oporto when he heard of my successes in the north, he had not sufficient time to prepare for a campaign to any distance from Oporto. It now became necessary for the Duke of Terceira, who saw the enemy were cut off from the north, to put himself in a fit state to follow them up to Santarem, on which place it was most probable they would retreat. He therefore ordered the necessary baggage from Oporto, and began to mount the cavalry with the horses he brought from Lisbon; and be it known here that at the time the minister-at-war was sending horses from Lisbon to form a cavalry corps at Oporto, the prefect there was actually preparing to send horses to Lisbon, having more than he knew what to do with, and no men to mount them; so much for the military combinations of the war minister.

During the time these preparations were going on, the duke put his troops into cantonments in Amarante and the quintas along the banks of the Tamego. He relieved the battalion of the Minho at Braga by the volunteers of Lexa, and established a more prompt communication with the detachment stationed at Cavez by placing the first moveable battalion of Oporto at Freirero. They also protected the inhabitants, who were overjoyed at being able to proclaim the Queen. This disposition of his forces along the banks of the Tamego deceived the enemy as to any intention of an immediate attack, and gave the duke an opportunity of observing what might be their intentions.

I shall leave the troops here for the present,

and relate the operations in other parts of Portugal.

After the City of Edinburgh returned to Oporto with the seamen and marines, I had some thoughts of crossing the Douro, and marching on Aveiro, as the most certain means of getting possession of that place, and subsequently of Figueiras; but the smallness of my force, and the uncertainty of that of the enemy, obliged me reluctantly to give up that plan. On my arrival off Figueiras the surf was so bad that landing was impracticable, and after remaining a day or two, I returned to Lisbon. Affairs at Santarem were in the same situation, and the only occurrence that had taken place in the neighbourhood was the attack the enemy had made on Setuval, which was very nearly surprised. On the evening of the 19th of April Captain Ruxton learnt from one of his boats'-crew that the enemy were advancing on Setuval, by the road of Aguas de Moira; the information came from some countrymen who had arrived at Setuval. This intelligence he communicated to the governor, who, however, did not believe it; he said his picquets had just come in from that neighbourhood, and there was no appearance of an enemy. Nevertheless, at half-past twelve the following day the enemy's cavalry galloped into a redoubt that commanded the anchorage. Captain Ruxton was at that time in the English consul's house, and having ascertained the fact, went immediately to the barracks, where he found a company of the 21st infantry under arms. The officer in command acted with great promptitude, and marched to the redoubt, which was immediately abandoned by the cavalry. He had, however, not much time to lose, and had hardly got in when the head of a column appeared on the brow of the hill about two hundred yards off. A very sharp fire commenced from both parties, and several desperate attempts were made to get possession, but without success. By this time the garrison was under arms; a severe fire was kept up on various parts of the defence for a considerable time, but no attack was made elsewhere. The enemy then retired to the heights of Carvalheiro, where they remained some time, and then returned unmolested to Agoa de Moira, and finally to Alcacer do Sal. I hardly know who was most to blame in this affair—the Queen's governor for allowing Miguel's cavalry to surprise the redoubt, or the officer who planned the enterprise, and did not sufficiently support the cavalry who got into it. Setuval was a most important point, and had it been lost it would have been no easy matter to have regained it; and lost it ought to have been half a dozen times over, had the enemy shewed either talent or energy. They had thirty-four men killed in their attempts on the redoubt; their wounded were carried off. Our loss was very trifling.

The attack on Setuval appears to have been intended to draw our attention from the Algarves, as it took place at the same time that Cabrera was marching on that kingdom; and happily for the cause of the Queen it failed. The capture of that place would have been a good set-off for the successes in the north, and probably occasioned the recal of the Duke of Terceira from thence.

Saldanha had expressed great anxiety for the Baron de Sa, and indignation at the ministry for not supporting him notwithstanding his urgent representations; indeed, I have reason to think that several of Saldanha's despatches to Freire relative to the Baron and other military matters had been withheld from the Emperor, and that the marshal had in consequence resigned, consenting to remain only at the urgent request of Don Pedro, and nothing but apprehension of injuring the Queen's cause, and the Emperor's promise that the ministers should not remain in office after the termination of the contest, prevented him from insisting on their immediate dismissal.

On the 9th of April the Emperor went to Cartaxo, but returned immediately both in bad health and bad spirits, in fact he had enough to make him so; he had Saldanha pressing him on one hand to dismiss the ministers, and the ministers pressing to be allowed to keep their posts. His position was painful; he knew he was becoming unpopular through the follies that had been committed; he was convinced no other minister

IN PORTUGAL. 171

could supply money so well as Carvalho, and the sequel has proved he was right. The Spanish government having also suspended the entrance into Portugal of their troops, in consequence of Carlos' retirement to Vizieu, did not tend to raise his spirits. Lord Howard also disapproved of Spanish interference without a military convention and the consent of the English government. All this was wrong. Spanish interference ought to have been courted instead of checked, and it will be shortly seen that the Duke of Terceira accepted their assistance without troubling his head either with application to Pedro's ministers or to the English ambassador, and they were actually carrying on a military operation in Portugal during the time Mr. Sarmento, the Portuguese minister at Madrid, was treating the question.

Before I give an account of the operations of the Duke of Terceira in the north, and my own campaign, I shall return to the Algarves, where I left the Baron de Sa, on the 16th of April, in position on the heights of Bartholomew de Messines, and a strong division of the Miguelites marching to crush him, instead of going to the north to oppose Terceira. This division, under the command of General Cabrera, having united the Miguelite troops in the Alemtejo, bivouacked on the 23d at St. Marcos da Serra, and on the 24th marched on St. Bartholomew; the enemy's force was upwards of 3000 men, that of De Sa not more than 1500, nevertheless he determined to risk an action. A little before noon the enemy advancing, covered by a cloud of guerillas under the command of Remechido, were received by a company of Belgians and repulsed. This attack was followed up by a battalion of chasseurs, with cavalry and a piece of artillery, and the Belgians in their turn were obliged to fall back on the main body, supported by one small gun. Here there was a severe struggle, and the Miguelite tirailleurs were finally driven back on their reserve, who had not as yet moved, but now began to deploy; a squadron of cavalry attempted to turn their left, but were met by a superior force, and repulsed; the enemy now advanced in force, and the attack was severe.

About three o'clock the Baron de Sa, seeing his left was hard-pressed, reinforced them with a part of the Belgians from the centre ; the Miguelite general observing this advanced a strong column on the weak point, and obliged Colonel Lecharlier to return to his former position in time to check the light troops, who covered the enemy's advance. A strong column composed of infantry and cavalry likewise attacked on the right; this was met by part of the fourth regiment, who opened a heavy fire, and obliged them to halt, but were too weak to drive them from the position they had taken; the left was now beat, and the centre could hardly hold their own.

At five o'clock a small detachment, stationed in the ravine, between the high ground on the left and that on the centre, moved to the right, leaving the defile unoccupied ; the enemy instantly penetrated into the ravine, and separated the left from the centre, which they forced, and the whole were obliged to retire to a range of mountains in the rear of the field of battle; the retreat was well managed, but the loss of the Queen's troops was severe. The Miguelites were, however, so roughly handled that the second position was not attacked, and the Baron was enabled to make good his retreat on Silves, where he arrived at midnight. After giving his men a few hours repose he continued his retreat on Villa Nova, but was obliged to leave the badly wounded men behind. He was much harassed by the guerillas, and lost some of the baggage; the same night the active Baron embarked part of his troops, and sailed for Faro; the rest followed on the 26th and 27th, and the whole arrived on the 1st of May.

The enemy, instead of profiting by their victory, and marching immediately on Faro, which would have been an easy conquest, before the arrival of De Sa, reposed themselves very comfortably at St. Bartholomew and Loulé from the 24th of April to the 3d of May, when they appeared before Faro, which they attacked on the 4th, and were repulsed with ease.

On the 7th the garrison and inhabitants of Olhao, without having seen an enemy, took fright and abandoned the town. Fortunately De Sa had time to send a fresh garrison before the enemy had notice of this affair, and saved the place. At six o'clock in the morning of the 9th a Miguelite division appeared and attacked

Olhao, but were repulsed, and on the 13th the whole of the Miguelite forces retired on Loulé.

While the enemy were before Faro and Olhao the garrisons of Villa Nova and Lagos made several sorties and shot and captured a considerable number of guerillas, and, indeed, before this they had been extremely active in clearing the adjacent country of their troublesome neighbours.

It is now time to return to the operations of the Duke of Terceira, whom I left in cantonments at Amarante and the neighbourhood. The enemy had great confidence in the position they occupied, and in the difficulties of the fords, which were only guarded by a small force; their encampment was at a considerable distance, and they appeared to direct their whole attention to the bridge, the passage of which was obstructed in every possible way. The Duke determined to surprise them. One column was directed to the right by the ford of St. Paul, another to the left by a ford half a league above the bridge of Amarante, and as the artillery could not follow the columns they were posted to the right and left of the bridge to bombard the enemy's force in Amarantinho during the attack, and protect the passage of a third column, which was to force the bridge should an opportunity offer.

Such were the Duke's dispositions on the 10th of April, but during the night, having explored the ford to the left, he found it too deep to attempt a passage with success: he, therefore, changed his plan and strengthened the right and centre columns with the troops from the left, and at daylight on the 11th Colonel Queiroz passed the Tamega with a column at the ford of St. Paul, surprised the enemy's advanced posts, and occupied the adjacent heights, cutting them off from the road of Mezão Frio. When this column was sufficiently advanced, General Nepomuceno opened his artillery, and with great gallantry forced the bridge; this and the advance of Queiroz decided the enemy to retire, but not being able to unite their whole force, the cavalry and artillery retreated by the road of Mezão Frio, and the infantry by that of Marao. The Duke now collected his columns, and after giving his troops a little rest, he pushed on by the road of Mezão Frio in hopes of gaining the passage of Regoa at the same time the enemy arrived by Marao. His attack having compromised the enemy's force in front of Canavezes, the first battalion fixos of Oporto was ordered to march on that place by the left bank of the Tamega, and combining with the second moveable battalion already there, dispersed the enemy. The first battalion was ordered to collect the prisoners, and march the next day to Regoa.

The Duke in the mean time pushed on with the cavalry, artillery, and the brigade of Colonel Queiroz, and arrived at Mezão Frio after sunset; he there learnt that the enemy's cavalry were in a state of disorder, and profiting by the terror that the Queen's troops had instilled into them, he left the artillery and the brigade of General Nepomuceno in Mezão Frio for the night, with orders to march at daylight on Regoa, and followed them up with the cavalry and Queiroz's brigade. The enemy's horse, alarmed at being separated from the infantry, and not being able to communicate with their general, had made the best of their way, without halting, to Villa Real.

Two plans now presented themselves to the Duke, one to follow the enemy with a small force, and pass the Douro with another, thereby interrupting their communications with Santarem, or follow them in force, securing both banks of the Douro in Regoa, and thus securing an easy passage into Beira. The second plan appeared to him the best, because the enemy, followed by a small force in a province which abounded in positions, could make a good retreat. He also feared that, knowing they were cut off from the passage of the Douro, they might disperse into guerillas, and spread over the country. As he was about to leave Regoa, intelligence arrived that the state prisoners at Lamego, in conjunction with the inhabitants, had proclaimed the Queen; the first moveable battalion of Oporto was immediately sent there, and the second occupied Regoa; the Duke himself continued his march on Villa Real: the badness of the roads obliged him to halt at Val de Nogueira, and on the 13th at daylight he entered Villa Real, the enemy having retired on Murca the moment he appeared on the opposite heights, without having made one effort to defend the position, which was strong, and they retired on Villa Flor. This march indicated their intention of crossing the Douro at Pocinho. The Duke taking advantage of the enemy's panic, followed them up with his usual activity, and sent his artillery back to Regoa lest it should retard his movements, the roads being bad. The second moveable battalion of Oporto occupied Villa Real, leaving a detachment at Regoa to protect the artillery. The battalion of the Minho and the skeleton of a battalion of volunteers of Beira who were in Oporto, were ordered to Lamego, and the cavalry organizing at Oporto were ordered on Mezão Frio; but Terceira did not calculate that the ministers had sent him horses without riders. Having made dispositions to be ready to unite at Lamego, and watch the movements of any of the enemy's troops in Beira, he continued his march on Villa Flor, where he halted for the night. On the 16th the enemy commenced the passage of the Douro at two in the morning. Brigadier Nepomuceno was ordered from the bridge of Villa Real to march by a cross road on Pocinho, while the Duke with Queiroz's brigade and the cavalry marched on Montcorvo. On arriving there he found the enemy had already passed the river; Queiroz's brigade was halted and the Duke proceeded with the cavalry to join Nepomuceno, who had arrived at the margin of the river. As the enemy were reposing themselves on the opposite bank, the Queen's volunteers and some companies of the eighth opened the fire across the river, and notwithstanding its width and the impossibility of passing, the panic of the Miguelites was so great that they immediately retired without destroying the passage-boat, which however they afterwards partially did with two pieces of artillery from behind the walls. The Duke, finding it impossible to continue his movement that day, left a strong piquet in Pocinho, united his forces in Montcorvo, and opened a communication with General Avilez, who had arrived at Braganza.*

On the night of the 16th the enemy abandoned the banks of the Douro and retired on Trancoso; on the 17th the passage-boat was got hold off and

---

* General Avilez had been long a prisoner in Braganza, and had made his escape to Alcanicas, in Spain, where he had collected a small force consisting of Portuguese emigrants.

repaired, and at daylight of the 18th the Duke passed the river and halted for the night at Freixo de Numão, intending to unite his troops with those in Lamego, procure what he required, and carry his operations into the province of Beira. Not one enemy's regular soldier was left in the Tras-os-Montes, but to ensure the tranquillity of the province he left brigadier Pizarro with the moveable battalion Transmentano, at Torre de Montcorvo, and the second moveable battalion of Oporto in Villa Real, with orders to communicate with general Avilez, and send all the force he could dispose of after securing the safety of the province under his charge.

At daylight of the 19th Terceira received intelligence that the enemy had abandoned Almeida, and that the state prisoners had broken open the prisons and proclaimed the Queen. On the same day he occupied St. João de Pesqueira; there he learnt that the enemy had united a guerilla force, attacked Lamego, and driven the first battalion of Oporto back to Regoa, where they were joined by the Minho battalion from Amarante. Several companies of this corps now passed the river in boats, attacked the army, put them to flight, and regained the town a few hours after they had left it.

On the 20th the Duke occupied Moimenta da Beira, and on the 22d Lamego, where he halted to refresh his men after their continued marches, reorganise his troops, procure information of the force of the enemy in Beira, and endeavour to discover their projects of defence in that province. It will be seen by what I have related, that the Duke of Terceira had lost none of his activity, and the enemy seemed to be entirely paralysed by his movements. From the 23d of March, the day I surprised Carminha, nothing but success attended the Queen's army; neither towns, rivers, bridges, nor positions were defended. In less than a month the two richest provinces of Portugal were entirely cleared of the Miguelites, and without their making any great effort to defend them. These provinces were considered to be favourable to Don Miguel, but they do not appear to have taken any part in the war.

In the Minho not one guerilla appeared, and I passed from Valença to Caminha without an escort a few days after its surrender, and met with nothing but civility. In Tras-os-Montes the Duke of Terceira met with no opposition from the people; in fact they were tired of the war, and only required permission to cultivate their valleys in peace and quietness. The great error committed by the Miguelites was weakening their force in the rich provinces, and sending them to the poor ones in the south, and the only wise thing the minister of war did in the whole campaign was sending the Duke of Terceira to Oporto, and the Baron de Sa to the Algarves.

At Lamego the Duke received a letter from the Spanish General Rodil, then in Guarda, offering to enter into communication with him, and operate in favour of the Queen's cause. In the Duke's instructions there was nothing to lead him to suppose there was any probability of foreign co-operation; but he immediately saw the advantages of Rodil's unsolicited assistance, especially as he was about to commence operations with a force much smaller than was requisite, and much less than he had demanded, particularly in cavalry, which were still organising at Oporto, in addition to which he had been obliged to leave two battalions in the Tras-os-Montes to prevent the possibility of reaction. Under these circumstances the Duke very properly took the responsibility on himself, and sent his first aide-de-camp, Major Mouzinho de Albuquerque, to compliment Rodil, and to thank him for the provisions and money with which he had succoured Almeida, and to combine with him a plan of operations, which had for its object to observe his left flank, as he marched on Vizieu, and to request General Rodil to occupy Almeida, which would enable the Duke to move to Lamego a moveable battalion formed of state prisoners, and which was almost naked. The Spanish general accepted his proposals with great frankness, and on Mouzinho's return with his answer, the Duke prepared to recommence his operations, which could now be carried on with greater safety and a surer prospect of success.

CHAPTER X.

I had prepared the seamen and marines to make another attempt on Figueiras, and requested Marshal Saldanha to support me with a small force from Leiria on the south bank of the Mondego, but the weather was so unsettled that I was not able to leave the Tagus in the City of Edinburgh before the beginning of May. On arriving off Figueiras, the surf as usual was bad, and at no time since I left it, had it been practicable to land. I was joined by the Don Pedro, Eliza, Isabel Maria, Portuense, and Villa Flor, but could not anchor before the 7th. Preparations were made to land the following morning, and the men-of-war got ready to attack the various batteries at the same time, should the beach be practicable. I now shifted my flag on board the Eliza. During the night two English sailors were picked up; they had drifted over the bar, half drunk, and knew little about its localities. Captain Henry was sent in with a couple of gigs in the night to examine the beach, with strict orders not to risk the boats; but Lieutenant Cullis, who commanded one boat, from over zeal approached too near the shore, was struck by a sea, and with the exception of one man all perished. This man was brought before the authorities, and he gave such a flaming account of our force, that next morning the governor, who had been some time ready for a start, abandoned the town, which was taken possession of by the officer detached from Leiria. Boats also came off from Buarcos, and with great difficulty we succeeded in landing. The Marquis Rezendi accompanied me on this occasion, and it was amusing enough to see a knight of Malta in full uniform, decorated with all his orders and crosses, mounted on a fisherman's back, wading through the surf and afterwards seated on a donkey, making his entrance into Figueiras. We were well received by the inhabitants, who were not sorry to get rid of their military friends: their force was nearly one thousand men. I

Appendix, No. XXV. issued a proclamation to the inhabitants, organised the government, and made preparations to commense my second campaign next day. In the evening I received intelligence that the Duke had that day entered Coimbra, another rare and fortunate occurrence. It was to be expected that our troops stationed at Leiria would have cut off the garrison of Figueiras, as the distance from that place to Pombal was considerably longer than from Leiria; but from some unaccountable mistake the whole garrison of Figueiras made its escape, and joined the Miguelite army. The officer who was opposite to Figueiras ought not to have crossed over; he ought to have immediately communicated to Colonel Vasconcellos the retreat of the garrison, and marched himself along the south bank and endeavoured to have prevented their crossing the river, or if too late for that, he might have harassed their retreat, while Colonel Vasconcellos marched upon Pombal; there they must either have been taken or dispersed. Great praise is due to the Miguelite commander for extricating his garrison from their critical situation, and some blame due either to the officer in front of Figueiras, for not sending the earliest intelligence, or to the commanding officer at Leiria for allowing them to escape. Indeed, I have never seen any good reason for a force of three thousand men and upwards remaining at Leiria, while the Duke of Terceira was driving the enemy before him and across the Mondego. It is true the Leiria division formed part of Marshal Saldanha's army, and the Duke of Terceira had no power over them, and probably did not like to take upon himself to order them to move; but what was the minister-at-war about?—had he authority or not? If he had, he ought to have given directions to them to have moved on the Mondego, and disputed the passage of the river with the Miguelites, or broke the bridge down, while Saldanha kept the army at Santarem in check. If he had not authority to interfere, he ought to have resigned his place; but here again is an instance of want of combination. Terceira commanded an independent army, Saldanha another; the Emperor was commander-in-chief, and Freire minister-at-war; all four, in all probability, giving orders at the same time, or, what is the same thing, acting for themselves.

At Figueiras I received information of what had passed in the north from the time I had brought the Duke's operations up to Lamego. General Cardoso, who commanded the Miguelite army, after being driven across the Douro had united with his army the garrisons of Almeida and Lamego, and retired on Vizieu; he had also been joined by a strong brigade from Souto Redondo to the south of the Douro, and which force the Baron de Pico Soleiro had endeavoured to drive back; but his troops were few, consisting only of provisional battalions ill-disciplined, and a few unorganized cavalry; and he had himself been obliged to retire. From Vizieu the enemy watched Lamego, with a small force in Villa Nova a Coelheria, and another in Castro D'Aire.

On the 30th of April the Duke of Terceira, having refreshed his troops, marched on Castro D'Aire, leaving in Lamego the volunteers of Beira, to organize, and the prisoners from Almeida, who were also being organized and clothed; and it is worthy of remark how easily these battalions were got together, a pretty good proof that the country was not very much inclined to Don Miguel, or he would certainly have formed them into battalions when in possession of the country; but, on the contrary, the army of the Queen kept increasing in about the same proportion Miguel's was reducing; it is true the Queen's troops were all paid and fed, while Don Miguel's lived on rather short commons.

The weather was very tempestuous; nevertheless the Duke crossed the serra and surprised the enemy, who were so terrified that they never attempted to defend their position, which (as the Duke remarked) was the strongest he had ever seen in his whole military career. The troops were so fatigued with this difficult and mountainous march that they halted at Castro D'Aire, and the Duke pursued the enemy with the cavalry on the Vizieu road, the greater part of whom were dispersed, and sought refuge in the mountains and valleys. On the 2d of May he advanced on Vizieu, but the enemy made no attempt to defend the line of the Vouga, and they even retired from Vizieu without firing a shot, retreating by Tondella and Mortagoa. At Vizieu the Duke communicated with General Rodil, who, agreeably to his promise, advanced by the road of Ponte de Murcella, and arrived at Gouvea, having dispersed a band of guerillas under the command of the Capitão Mor Botto. On the 4th Terceira had an interview with Rodil in Mangoalde, and agreed that the Spanish army should march by the road of Ponte de Murcella, and the Portuguese on the road to Coimbra. On the 5th he marched on Tondella, leaving General Azeredo, with the first moveable battalion of Oporto, at Vizieu, to maintain tranquillity in the province. On the 6th he bivouacked in Mortagao, which the enemy abandoned on his approach, directing themselves on Coimbra by the road of Botao, and they were followed up by the cavalry for some time, in order to mask the movement the Duke projected for the following day. On the 7th he marched by the Serra Bussaco on Mealhada, which he occupied without opposition; he there learnt that General Bernardino had retired with all haste from the Vouga, and that the General Gouvea Osorio had ordered him to march on Coimbra the same evening that he evacuated Mortagoa. From Mealhada he opened his communication with Oporto by the road of Sardão, in which route the Baron de Pico Celerio was marching in consequence of orders sent from Vizieu. On the 8th he occupied Coimbra, the enemy having abandoned it the night before, notwithstanding the fortifications they had raised, and a superior force, to the Duke.

The 9th and 10th were spent in Coimbra to rest the troops and organize a government, the people having declared for the Queen; and orders were sent to Colonel Vasconcellos to occupy Redinha or Pombal. Terceira had another interview with Rodil at Senhor de Serra, in which it was agreed that while he marched on Thomar, Rodil should march on the right bank of the Tagus, crossing the Serra de Estrella above Castello Branco, thus menacing Abrantes, and being ready to cross the Tagus if necessary at Villa Velha or Alcantara, and reinforce General Pinto at Marvao,* and when united on the left bank of the

* Marvao had been long under siege by the Miguelites, which they raised on the 23d of March, the day I took Caminho, and the day De Sa marched into Beja.

Tagus, would straiten the enemy if they attempted to remain in Santarem. This plan was proposed by General Rodil, and adopted by the duke, because he wished to profit by the co-operation of the Spaniards, at the same time avoiding, as much as possible, bringing them in immediate contact with the enemy, thus sparing Spanish blood in the Portuguese contest, and giving more honour to the Queen's troops. These arrangements made, orders were sent to the Baron de Pico to send his cavalry on, leaving a garrison in Aveiro, and then return to Oporto, and on the 10th he marched on Condeixo.

There being no further occasion for the squadron on the coast, Captain Henry was sent to the Algarves with the Eliza, the Portuense off Sinnes, and the Don Pedro and Isabella Maria to Lisbon, to complete their provisions and proceed to Madeira; and on the 9th I marched for Figueiras, and halted for the night at Mente Mor; on the 10th I was at Lourical, and on the 11th, the day the duke reached Condeixa, I joined Colonel Vasconcellos at Pombal, where he had arrived the day before from Leiria, with between two and

Appendix, No. XXVI.

three thousand men. Colonel Loureiro arrived from the duke, and it was agreed that we should halt a day at Pombal, and while he marched by the road of Velha on Thomar, we should march by Ourem on Torres Novas, and arrive at the former the same time the duke arrived at Prucha. This delay I thought unnecessary; we knew the enemy had a considerable force at Ourem, and the march from Pombal to that place was very long; however, so it was settled.

At daylight of the 12th we marched from Pombal, through a beautiful and romantic country, and I never saw a finer sight than the troops winding along the mountains; the ground was very strong, and every inch of it ought to have been defended had the enemy shown the least talent or enterprize, but they seemed to be now incapable of any exertion. About five o'clock we entered Aldea de Cruz, a small village in the valley, within gun-shot of Ourem, which is an old Moorish walled town, standing on a high hill, and difficult of access at all parts. As the troops marched in, and were taking up their cantonments, the enemy opened a fire from their field-pieces. The seamen and marines were in the rear, and thought the attack begun, and though nearly knocked up with a march of seven leagues, and not very well shod, I was surprised to see them coming in at double quick least they should be too late. At Aldea de Cruz we were joined by Colonel Shaw's Scotch from Leiria and the moveable battalion of Alcobaca, not clothed, but well accoutred; and it is astonishing, notwithstanding that disadvantage, how military they looked. I believe no men in the world are sooner or easier made soldiers than the Portuguese; they are sober and tractable, and take a pride in their profession. It is true these provisional battalions were only to be kept up during the war, and it might have been considered by them an honour to see a campaign, and share in the glory of establishing the authority of the Queen throughout the kingdom. During the night orders came to Colonel Vasconcellos to join the duke at Cham de Macaas, the enemy having united their forces at Thomar, and been joined by a brigade from Santarem. The duke requested me to remain before Ourem with the seamen and marines, reinforced by the Scotch and the Alcobaca battalion and several detachments, in all about one thousand four hundred men.

It now became necessary to see what could be done with this place; it was strong, and not easy to get at, and difficult to blockade, having three gates. The garrison consisted of about one thousand men, and I was very unwilling they should escape. After reconnoitring well the defences, I ordered Colonel Shaw with the Scotch to occupy a convent within musket-shot of Ourem, which the enemy had neglected to do; and this post he was ordered to defend at all risks. The Alcobaca regiment, two hundred and thirty strong, eighty volunteers of Ponte de Mos, and fifty of the tenth were placed on his right, in front of the Leiria gate; they had orders to retire, if attacked in force, till succoured. The British marines, Portuguese brigade, and the seamen remained in Aldea de Cruz, ready to operate where they might be wanted. These dispositions made, a summons was sent to the governor, who refused to capitulate. In the afternoon I went

Appendix, No. XXVII.

to the convent, against which there was occasionally a fire of musketry, and a picquet was pushed up close to the ramparts, where the ground was very favourable to protect them.

I observed the enemy had left a wall standing, which enclosed the convent garden nearly to the town, and a parapet had been thrown up, with a ditch at which they were still working, though disturbed by our musketry. The peasants were employed at this work, and when they attempted to leave it, were pelted with stones by the garrison. After dark Colonel Shaw and myself got close up to the walls, and recommended them to surrender, and a company was afterwards sent up to draw their fire, to ascertain, if possible, a soft place. During the night all was quiet, and next morning scaling ladders were brought, and the Portuguese and English marines and sailors were put in motion, and took up their ground close to the walls on the opposite side to the Scotch, in a small village, which they were ordered to defend. The enemy perceiving our dispositions for attack, sent a flag of truce to the convent, and I took up my quarters in a cuenta close by. The governor asked for twenty-four hours, which was refused, and the capitulation was immediately signed. The Scotch marched in, and took possession ; the Miguelites laid down their arms, occupied the convent, and next day they were all sent to their homes.

I was much pleased at getting possession of Ourem without bloodshed; it was very strong, and had the enemy made a good defence it would have cost many valuable lives. The seamen and marines had seen a good deal of service, but Shaw's regiment were very young, and the greater part had not been in action, and bringing them up to an assault as the first introduction to a military life would hardly have been fair. They were, however, fine young men, and I have no doubt would have done their duty.

At noon next day every thing was arranged at Ourem; the Alcobaca regiment and the volunteers of Ponte de Mos were left in garrison, the Miguelites dismissed to their homes, and I marched on Thomar. I should have preferred going at once to Torres Novas, but the duke requested me to join him at Thomar, and he might have been

waiting for my reinforcement to attack the enemy.
As things happened it was unfortunate, for had I
arrived at Torres Novas that night, I should have
fallen on the flank of the defeated army, and
worked them on their retreat to Santarem; but
we acted for the best, and nothing is certain in
war. We arrived at Thomar after dark and
found the duke had fought the

BATTLE OF ACEICEIRA.

He had been joined on the morning of the 14th
by Colonel Vasconcellos, and in the evening he
occupied Thomar, the enemy having retired on his
approach.

On the 15th he communicated to Marshal Saldanha all that he knew of the enemy's position
and intentions, which it was difficult to divine, as
the information he received from deserters was
very different; but in the course of the day a
letter was intercepted from General Guedes, who
was encamped in the neighbourhood of Aceiceira.
This letter ordered the artillery that were coming

from Santarem to halt at Gollegão, which led the
duke to suppose it was his intention to retire from
his position. This the duke determined to prevent
if possible, and either bring him to action the
following day if he remained, or follow him should
he retire.

On the morning of the 16th he marched from
Thomar by the road of Atalaya, and soon discovered the enemy on the heights of Aceiceira, about
a league and a half from Thomar. As his advanced guard arrived near Santa Cita, they fell
in with the enemy's outposts, who were driven
back to the main body, formed in position on the
heights and in the valleys of Aceiceira. The
duke lost no time, and put his three brigades
into as many columns. Colonel Queiroz advanced on the right, João Nepomuceno on the
centre, and Colonel Vasconcellos on the left.
The enemy, favoured by strong ground and
by his artillery, made a vigorous resistance
and sustained for a long time the position he
occupied, making repeated charges with his cavalry every favourable opportunity; they were
repulsed by the right and centre columns with

BATTLE OFF CAPE ST. VINCENT between THE PORTUGUESE SQUADRONS, 5th July 1833 commanded by Ad. Nap[i]er do P.N.

Plan of Attack.

Donna Maria's Squadron.

A.	Rainha de Portugal	46	**D.**	Portuense Corvette	16
	Frigate Adm.l's Flag		**E.**	Vill.a Flor Brig	16
B.	Don Pedro formerly	40	**F.**	Faro schooner	6
	Wellington Indiam.n			Guns	176
C.	Donna Maria Frigate	42			

Don Miguel's Squadron.

1.	Don Juan	80	6.	Isabel Maria	34
2.	Rainha	76	7.	Tagus	20
3.	Martim Freitas	46	8.	Principssa Real Corvette	22
4.	Princess Royal	56	9.	Audaz	20
5.	Zebecque		10.	Sybille	26
				Guns	372

great gallantry, closely formed, and by their firmness proved they were not to be broken or prevented from gaining the heights, which were finally carried and the enemy totally defeated, and obliged to fly by the roads of Punhete, Torres, Gollegão, and the adjacent mountains and valleys, followed up by the Queen's troops and cavalry, who by a decided charge put the enemy's squadrons to flight, killed and wounded an immense number of men, took fourteen hundred prisoners, including seventy-four officers; four standards and all their artillery and ammunition, consisting of eight pieces. Such was the result of the battle of Aceiceira, the only decisive action that was fought and followed up all the war. Nepomuceno led the Queen's volunteers and the fifteenth regiment to the attack over the roughest ground, animating them by his courage, and giving them confidence by his able dispositions:

Queiroz conducted his column with great bravery and intelligence, and by his able formation of the twelfth caçadores repulsed the cavalry who charged them. Vasconcellos, who commanded the left, was obliged to make a long circuit with his column under the fire of the enemy's artillery, and met with the most determined resistance, which, however, he overcame with his usual ability. The cavalry under Fonseca deserved also great praise, and by their gallantry contributed greatly to the defeat of the enemy; and no less credit was due to the artillery under Major Passoa: in short every officer and man did their duty, and Colonel Loureiro, the chief of the duke's staff, showed his usual talent, and received a severe wound in the chest; the duke also expressed himself highly satisfied with the conduct of all his staff. The dispositions of the Duke of Terceira seem to have been excellent, and could only be excelled by the vigour with which he followed up his attack and profited by his victory; and I shall ever regret I had not marched on Torres Novas instead of Thomar, where I should have had an opportunity, with my division, of finishing the catastrophe.

On the 17th the duke occupied Gollegão. I occupied Torres Novas, and rode over to compliment him on his brilliant exploit. I was anxious he should cross the Tagus to intercept the enemy, who of course would leave Santarem; but the Emperor having arrived at Cartaxo, and taken command of the army, he thought it more advisable to wait for orders. This was another inconvenience attending the system of carrying on the war, and it is very evident by the duke's despatch he thought it so, for he concludes his report giving an account of his campaign, dated in Lisbon on the 8th of August, by saying—" On the 17th I occupied Gollegão, and put myself in immediate communication with the Emperor, who had put himself at the head of the army at Santarem, and this day the operations of the army of the north, which was under my directions, ceased and commenced to operate under the orders of the illustrious chief."

On the Emperor's arrival at Cartaxo he issued a proclamation calling upon Miguel's army to quit his standard, but it had no effect; they were devoted to their master.

Appendix, No. XXVIII.

CHAPTER XI.

AFTER the defeat of the Miguelites, General Guedes reached Santarem with a feeble disorganized force, and General Bernardino crossed the Tagus, and united fifteen hundred infantry and one hundred cavalry at Chamusca. He was reinforced from Santarem by the Chaves cavalry, but they preferred the winning to the losing side, and went over to the Queen's standard. This obliged Bernardino to retire on Evora, very naturally expecting the Duke of Terceira would pass the Tagus in pursuit of him. The garrison of Abrantes took fright when they heard of the loss of the battle of Aceiceira, abandoned the fortress, and retired on Elvas. These disasters decided Miguel to leave Santarem, and retire on Evora. This operation was carried into execution on the 17th and 18th, and conducted so well and so

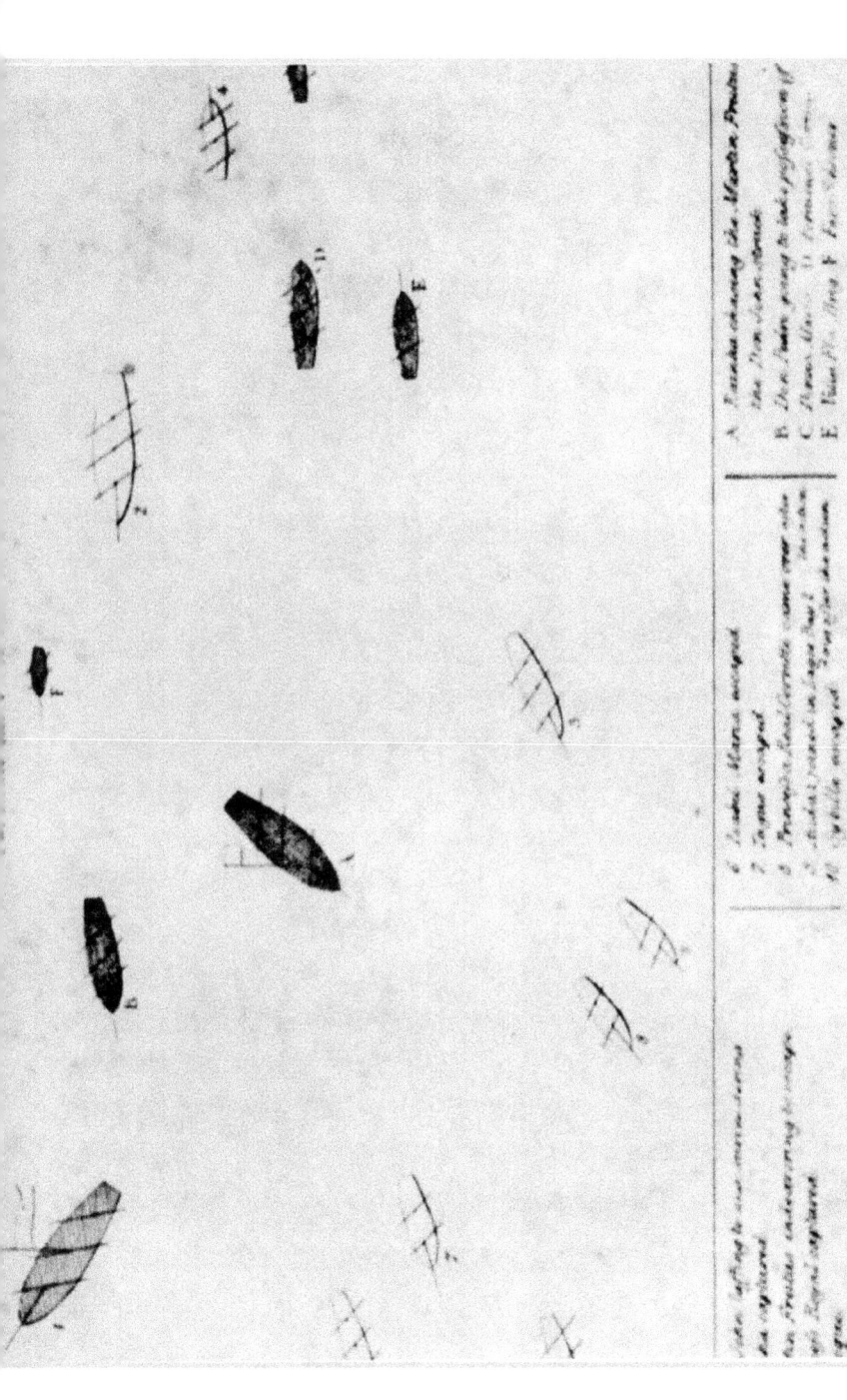

secretly that the whole of the troops and almost all the artillery and baggage were crossed over the Tagus before Saldanha was aware of it. His spies must have served him badly, and this saved Miguel's army; for had Saldanha received proper information, the enemy could never have effected their retreat from thence.

The Emperor now joined the army, and occupied Santarem with a portion of his troops. I joined him there, as did the Duke of Terceira. Both the marshals were anxious to return to Lisbon, particularly the duke. Don Pedro wished each to take command of a division, and pursue the enemy; having independent commands, they saw the impropriety of this, and urged the Emperor to give the command to one or other. He was anxious for the services of both, and unwilling to put Saldanha under Terceira's orders; in fact he wished it to appear that he, as commander-in-chief, directed the operations of the army, and insisted on them retaining their respective commands. It would have been more for his glory had he gone himself, but I apprehend he was beginning to feel the effects of the illness that had hung so long about him, and did not feel himself equal to the task.

Terceira, with much reluctance, put himself at the head of his division, which now consisted of nine thousand men, and crossed the Tagus at Santarem. Saldanha returned to Cartaxo, and crossed with a like number at Salvatierra. The passage of the river occupied two days; both armies then marched, Terceira on Estremoz, and Saldanha on Evora; and I returned to Lisbon with the seamen and marines to make any naval arrangements that might be necessary, should the war be carried into the Algarves or into Spain, both of which operations were still open to Miguel. I also despatched vessels on the southern coast to be on the watch for the usurper should he endeavour to escape, and directions were given in case of his capture to bring him into Cascaes Bay. Don Carlos was in a different situation, and it was with some difficulty that I could obtain from the ministry any directions respecting him, and not before I gave them to understand that unless some specific order was given to me, I should not at all interfere.

Things were now drawing to a close: on the 22d of May General Lemos wrote to Terceira and Saldanha to propose a suspension of arms, and on the 23d he proposed an interview. Terceira received the second communication on his march, and declined a reply till he arrived at Estremoz. Saldanha consented to halt when he received Lemos's letter, and finally agreed to a suspension of arms for forty-eight hours.

Appendix, No. XXIX.

Don Miguel had united at Evora, notwithstanding all his disasters in battle and by desertion, about ten thousand men, and the division in the Algarves, consisting of three thousand, were ordered to join him. General Louis de Bourmont had arrived with fifteen hundred men from Alcacer do Sal. It was now necessary to take a decision—to remain in the plains of Evora and fight a battle was useless; to retreat on Elvas impossible without first beating Terceira. General Bourmont proposed to unite eight thousand of the best troops, and attack one of the divisions of the Queen's army. This was a bold measure, and worthy of the active officer who proposed it; but Miguel had neither men nor officers fit for such a daring measure; they were worn out and fatigued with war, and thought they had already done enough for their master, and in a council of war they did not hesitate to say so.

To retire into the Algarves would have prolonged the war. Faro and the minor seaports might have been taken, and supplies received from Spain across the Guadiana if Miguel had money to purchase them; the generality of the people in the Algarves were favourable to his cause, and the country abounded in strongholds.

It is said that Don Carlos proposed to march into Spain, and that appears to me the plan that ought to have been adopted. It would have been a bold and romantic measure. It would also have had the appearance of generosity in Miguel, having lost his own kingdom, to endeavour to recover the kingdom of Spain for his uncle. Whether such an enterprise would have met with the support of Miguel's officers is doubtful. A French writer observes that with the exception of Colonel Corvo de Camoes, the superior offices were unwilling to die in the plains of Evora, and wished to finish the war; the soldiers, on the other hand, were eager to fight and shed their last blood in Miguel's cause. What, then, should he have done? Why, he ought to have thanked the officers for their services, and dismissed them, giving the command of his army to D'Almer or Bourmont, promoted the officers who chose to remain, and filled their places up from the ranks. With such a devoted army, having every thing to gain and nothing to lose, they would have marched on Madrid, rallied the Carlists, and it is more than probable Carlos would have now been king of Spain, and Miguel might have recovered his crown from thence. Don Pedro was in a much worse position at Oporto, without money, food, or ammunition; but he was obstinate and determined to the last, and finally succeeded. Miguel did not possess these qualities, and deservedly lost his throne.

On the 26th of May a capitulation was entered into, by which Don Pedro forgave his enemies and restored their property, subject, however, to the approval of the Cortes. Miguel lost his rank as Infant, and had a pension conferred on him during good behaviour. The troops laid down their arms and were sent home, and the officers preserved their legitimate rank.

<small>Appendix, No. XXX.</small>

Thus finished the civil war in Portugal, a war undertaken by a handful of men against a large and well disciplined army,—a war undertaken by the ex-emperor of the Brazils to establish his daughter on the throne of Portugal, which had been usurped by her affianced husband and uncle, —a war conducted by imbecile and intriguing ministers, who hardly ever did one act that was not favourable to Miguel,—and a war brought to a successful termination by a chain of events that never could have been calculated upon, and which I shall take a summary of, when I have disposed of Don's Miguel and Carlos.

On taking leave of his troops Miguel in his proclamation attributed his fall to the Quadruple Alliance. Now that alliance had nothing to do with it; it never ought to have been signed, and never ought to have been ratified; in point of fact it was not ratified, there having been some diplomatic irregularity; and had I been at Lisbon when the treaty arrived, I should have used my best efforts with Don Pedro to have prevented its ratification. When the Emperor was in distress, neither France nor England would give him assistance. What, then, was the use of

Appendix, No. XXXI.

a treaty when we had the ball at our feet and were driving it before us? On the contrary, it was owing to that unfortunate treaty that the war is now raging in the Peninsula; it gave the ministers of France and England a right to interfere in the final arrangements, and to their interference is now owing the unnatural strife in Spain, and the possible return of Miguel to Portugal. What instructions the French and English ministers had I know not; but when the treaty arrived, their interference became pressing. Freire was urged to offer terms to Miguel, which he declined until the ratification arrived from England.

That their conduct was guided by motives of humanity I have not the least doubt; it had been currently reported, and I believe it was true, that many of the Queen's officers declared, if an opportunity offered, that they would put both Miguel and Carlos to death; and the English, French, and Swedish ministers pressed Freire to give positive orders to prevent such a shameful act, which he declined as unnecessary. Here Freire was again wrong; he ought to have complied with their wishes, and taken every precaution to prevent such a catastrophe, with the express understanding that the fate of Carlos and Miguel should be left to the entire management of the Queen's government.

This was not done, and instead of Don Miguel being received on board a Portuguese ship of war, stationed off Sinnes for that purpose, an English frigate was sent there to embark him, which was accomplished with some difficulty and danger by Captains Lockyer and Macdougal amidst the hootings of the populace, who showed a strong disposition to put him to death.

This frigate was sent by the consent of the Portuguese ministers, but without making any communication to me; and had there been a Portuguese frigate off Sinnes instead of a corvette, and the officer done his duty, having no orders to permit Miguel's embarkation in an English man-of-war, there must have been something very unpleasant between the two ships.

Captain Lockyer, after embarking Miguel, came to Cascaes Bay in company with the Nimrod, when Admiral Parker made all the necessary arrangements to carry him to Genoa, the town he had chosen for his future residence; and from which place, on the 20th of June he issued a manifesto recalling the submission he had made at Evora.

Don Carlos's friends managed his affairs well, and persuaded the English minister and admiral to take entirely upon themselves the arrangements for his embarkation.

After the death of Ferdinand, Carlos had been hovering about on the frontiers of Spain with a few followers, but he had met with no encouragement to enter that kingdom. When the campaign opened in the Tras-os-Montes and Minho, Carlos quitted Braganza, and retired on Lamego; from thence he repaired to Vizieu, and subsequently to Guarda. With fifty followers he presented himself at Rodil's outposts, in hopes his presence would induce the Spanish army to declare for him; in this, however, he was mistaken, and was obliged to make a hasty retreat to Almeida; thither he was followed by Rodil, and had some difficulty in escaping to Guarda, and finally was obliged to retire to Chamousca. After the defeat of Miguel's army, the defection of the Chaves cavalry, and the evacuation of Santarem, Don Carlos retired on Evora, and sent the Baron de los Valles, a French agent in his service, and one who appeared devoted to his cause, with a letter to Admiral Parker to request he would receive him on board an English ship of war in the Tagus. The baron seems to have managed his mission with all the tact of an accomplished diplomatist; he pretended that Don Carlos wished to go to Italy, and begged he might be conveyed there; this was refused, but he was given to understand he might go any where else. Carlos feigned to be much chagrined at this, and unwillingly consented to go to England, the very place the baron wished to convey him, and on the 1st of June he embarked with his family at Aldea Gallegos in Admiral Parker's barge, his suite following in the boats of the squadron, and was received on board the Donegal under a royal salute, without any restrictions whatever. The treaty was signed by the Duke of Terceira, the Count of Saldanha, and Mr. Grant, the secretary of Legation. Whether they had authority or not from the Queen's government to sign such a treaty I know not, or whether Lord Howard had instructions from his government to do it I am not aware; but it certainly was the most injudi-

Appendix, No. XXXII.

cious and unnecessary act of generosity ever committed by diplomacy, and it will be difficult to persuade posterity that it was not done for the express purpose of embroiling Spain. I do not myself entertain such an idea for a moment, but I repeat, it will be difficult to persuade posterity that it was a diplomatic blunder. By the quadruple treaty Don Pedro was obliged to use all his efforts to drive Don Carlos out of Portugal, and Spain was obliged to employ a military force to drive Don Miguel out; but the Portuguese government, though they would not even allow Don Miguel the title of Infant, and obliged him to sign an engagement never to return to the Peninsula, or disturb the tranquillity of the kingdom of Spain or Portugal, quietly submitted (notwithstanding the demand of General Rodil to deliver up Carlos) to his embarkation without any condition whatever, merely because the English minister thought proper to promise to receive him. He never could have arrived at Aldea Gallegos without permission of the Portuguese government, and instead of embarking him on board a British ship of war, he ought to have been embarked on board the Portuguese flag-ship, there to remain until the four powers had decided on his fate.

After remaining two days in the Tagus, the Donnegal sailed for Portsmouth, where she arrived on the 12th of June. The British government proposed to Don Carlos to renounce his claim to the throne of Spain, which he very wisely refused to do, was landed at Portsmouth, where he remained a fortnight, went to the neighbourhood of London, and in a fortnight more was in the midst of his followers in Navarre:—so much for diplomacy.

The generosity of Don Pedro in giving a full amnesty to the Miguelites was ill received at Lisbon, and the public feeling manifested itself strongly at the opera, where a very disagreeable scene took place. Miguel certainly did not deserve such lenient treatment; his misrule and that of his minister had ruined some of the most respectable families in Portugal, and many had been immured in dungeons for years; and I cannot help thinking a little wholesome castigation would neither have hurt Miguel nor his principal satellites. There are several very nice islands in the western ocean, where he ought to have gone through a probation for a few years. Trusting to his engagement not to disturb Portugal was absurd; he had before, when uncoerced, made solemn promises, all of which he broke; and it cannot be supposed his conscience would suffer much in breaking those he was obliged to make. Don Carlos was in a different position; he had been heir to the throne of Spain in virtue of the Salic law, which was imported into that country by the Bourbons; but still it was the law of the land, and overturning that law promises to keep Spain in civil war for years to come. That the King and Cortes had as much right to change the law of succession in Spain as King, Lords, and Commons have to do it in England, there cannot be a doubt; but still Don Carlos is at liberty to maintain his rights if he can; and for the sake of Western Europe I sincerely hope he will fail; but it is impossible not to admire his perseverance. He threw himself into a corner of Spain to fight for a throne, against an established government, with a large native army, supported by a French and English legion, and assisted by

France and England, feebly assisted it is true; nay, worse than feebly—pusillanimously assisted; and I hope, for the character and honour of this country, that there are reasons, and good reasons too, that prevent England from at once sending an imposing force to expel Don Carlos from the Peninsula. Either let them do that fearlessly and openly, or leave the ring open to the contending parties to settle the succession themselves.

Don Pedro, with a handful of men, was left to his own resources; his cause was the cause of freedom, and hundreds of swords leapt from their scabbards to assist him, and he conquered. Carlos's is the cause of absolutism, and if Spain prefers Carlos and despotism to the Queen and liberty, let her have them ; if, on the other hand, she prefers free institutions, she ought to fight for them, and they will have more stability when conquered than they possibly can have if thrust down her throat by foreign bayonets.

When I sailed with the expedition to the Algarves I made no secret of my opinions, and I I told both the Duke of Palmella and Terceira, and indeed every body, that if I found the people of Portugal were averse to the Queen's cause, I would not be one to force her upon them. I hold the same opinion still, and contend that if Spain prefer Carlos to the Queen, she ought to have him; if, on the other hand, the Queen is preferred, now that we have interfered, it is cruel to her party, and still more cruel to Carlos's followers, to allow them to butcher each other, when we have the power of at once settling the question If Russia is disposed to quarrel with us for interference, the first shot Lord John Hay fired furnished her with as good a reason as if we had landed ten thousand men in the north of Spain; if the expense of the arms, accoutrements, &c. that we have already furnished the Queen's government, and for which we shall never be paid, is taken into consideration, the same money would have gone a great length in paying any troops we sent, and whom we could oblige them to pay before they left the country.

CHAPTER XII.

It may now be as well to take a view of the causes that led to Miguel's downfall.

His first error was in not at once putting down the regency of Terceira; an attempt was made, it is true, which failed, but can it be supposed for a moment, had the resources of Portugal been employed with energy, that insignificant island could have held out a week? His refusal to grant an amnesty, notwithstanding the frequent warnings he had from the Tory administration, was also another cause of his fall. The change of ministry in England, and the French revolution, aroused the energies of the Dukes of Palmella and Terceira; and too much praise cannot be bestowed on them and their gallant followers for their successful attacks on the Western Islands. I was present at these operations, and made acquaintance with the gallant bands that occupied Terceira. I first knew them in adversity, and admired their patience and cheerfulness under all their misfortunes and deprivations, and their moderation after victory.

The arrival of the Emperor from the Brazils took place at this time, and after the capture of the islands, Palmella repaired to London, and concerted means with Don Pedro for future operations. Don Miguel's government quietly allowed them to collect their forces in the Western Islands, without making one effort to interrupt them on their passage, or destroy them when there. They were allowed to cross from St. Michael's to the coast of Portugal without meeting a Portuguese cruizer. General Cordoza permitted them to land without firing a shot, and Santa Martha abandoned Oporto without an effort. After collecting their forces round Oporto, and having known by experience that their troops were not equal to force Pedro's lines, or take the Serra convent by assault, they amused themselves for nearly a twelvemonth in drawing lines of circumvallation round Oporto and the neighbourhood, and collecting an immense number of guns and mortars, foolishly supposing that their firing on the town would force the inhabitants to rise and oblige Pedro to surrender; and to crown this, when Gaspar Texeira took command of the army, he issued a proclamation, calling upon his troops, in the event of taking Oporto, to destroy the whole of the inhabitants. This proclamation gained Pedro every man, woman, and child in the city, whether favourable or hostile to the cause; they felt Oporto was a devoted town, and, if captured, destruction would fall upon their heads, without respecting age, sex, or principles. Had they collected their guns, and established batteries against the Serra convent and the Foz, and issued moderate proclamations, advising the inhabitants to keep quiet in their houses, they would have pounded the batteries to pieces, cut off the communication with the sea, and made friends instead of enemies of the inhabitants of Oporto.

When the expedition sailed for the Algarves,

and appeared off the rock of Lisbon, the Miguelite fleet ought to have put to sea, and made every effort to obstruct the landing; our ships were then crowded with troops, and an action would have been fought under great disadvantage; and if they did not choose to risk an action, instead of following me to the south they ought to have proceeded off Oporto, drove away the numerous merchant vessels, and attacked the Foz in conjunction with the army, and it must have fallen. Even after these errors were committed, had a sufficient force been crossed over to the south, and met the Duke of Terceira after he left Setuval, he would have been placed between two fires, and obliged to gain the high ground by Cape Espichel, to defend himself, till I appeared off; and after the capture of Lisbon, had Miguel's army rallied and marched on the capital, they would have regained it before I had a breeze to bring the squadron to the town.

After Bourmont's failure at Oporto, he ought to have remained before it, and brought all his guns to bear on the Serra and the Foz; he ought not to have calculated that the Queen's minister at war would have slept for three weeks before he began to fortify Lisbon, and when repulsed there he ought immediately to have sent a sufficient force to the south, and occupied Setuval, which town Mollellos never ought to have left, unless he had intended to have retaken the capital.

The failure before Lisbon was followed by the resignation of General Bourmont, caused by the intrigues of Miguel's ministers, who, like Pedro's, fancied they were monstrous clever fellows, and knew the art of war better than the marshals. General Macdonell next took the command of the army, and like his predecessor, was intrigued against, and resigned; he was followed by Povoas and then Lemos, who allowed Saldanha to make a flank movement on Pernes, and afterwards on Leiria and Thomar, and patrole even to Gallegao. Troops were then recalled from the rich and strong provinces in the north of Portugal, and after Saldanha had had time to concentrate his forces, he was attacked at Almoster, the Miguelites beaten back to Santarem; and to complete their follies a strong division was sent into the

Algarves, about the same time we were augmenting our force in the north. The troops before Oporto, instead of retreating to Braga, and detaching a force to save Vianna and Valenca, and drive me across the Minho, (where from the richness of the country and the strength of the ground they could have maintained themselves for ever,) retreated on Amarante, and from thence south, leaving the whole of the north in our possession, with the means of reinforcing the Duke of Terceira's army on his march to Santarem; finally, they did not dispute one inch of ground with the duke as he advanced, and left a garrison of twelve hundred men in Ourem, when they could have been better employed at Acceceira.

Such were, in my opinion, the faults committed by Miguel's government, and I shall now relate all the blunders committed by Pedro's.

Instead of purchasing two bad frigates, and hiring transports to carry the army, they ought either to have hired or purchased ten East Indiamen, embarked their troops, and run them into the Tagus. Such a bold measure would have paralysed Miguel's army, and gained the capital;

which would have finished the war, provided the ministers knew how to rule the country after they got it.

I shall pass over all the faults that were committed in raising men, in breaking faith with them, and disgusting the foreign troops, and shall bring them at once to Oporto. There, it has been shewn, they landed without opposition, but instead of crossing the Douro, and pushing boldly on, they remained in Oporto till Miguel's army recovered their panic, and got the better of their unwillingness to fight against a royal personage.

There was not one wise act done at Oporto afterwards. They intrigued against Terceira, and got him to resign. They lost the wine at Villa Nova. Instead of nursing their troops, they threw away their lives in useless sorties; they disgusted Sartorius, and nearly lost their squadron; they intrigued against Solignac, and wanted him to march out of Oporto, which they were afraid to do when they first landed. They treated all the foreign officers and men ill, and drove the best of them away; and had they been left to themselves, they would have either surrendered Oporto, or escaped from it. Fortunately the Emperor was a strong-minded man, and was determined to defend it to the last extremity; that saved Oporto. Sylva Carvalho, the minister of finance, was a bold financier, and procured money:—he deserves credit.

When the expedition arrived from England, the Emperor was spirited up against Palmella, Mendizabel, and myself; and he was hardly civil to us; nay, more, I believe nothing but fear kept his ministers from either sending Palmella away or to prison. Ten days' precious time was lost by their intrigues and indecision after we arrived, and when the Emperor had decided to go himself with five thousand men, I positively believe he was dissuaded from it under pretence that he ought not to risk his imperial person; but in reality they were afraid to go in the flag-ship with me, and still more to stay in Oporto with Solignac; and when they sent me off troops, they forgot to send water.

When they were shut up in Oporto, I am not aware of one wise statesman-like decree they issued, or one that had the least tendency to conciliate the opposite party; and when they arrived in Lisbon, there was hardly one political act they did, that Don Miguel would not himself have counselled them to do in order to make Don Pedro unpopular. I have no hesitation in asserting that had they staid in Oporto one month, and left Palmella, Terceira, and myself in Lisbon, the war would have been finished.

I assert this from experience; for when I landed at Caminha with between five and six hundred men, only in ten days I gained the whole of the province of the Minho (which is decidedly Miguelite) by kindness and conciliation; and because the troops stationed there had confidence in the promises I made to them, and the people were satisfied that no persecutions for political opinion would be permitted.

With regard to military measures or plans they never had any; Lisbon was left defenceless for three weeks, and they never believed that Bourmont would appear before it. They did not accept the assistance that was offered to them by Admiral Parker under the plea of protecting British property, which would have had a great moral effect on the Miguelites; and when Bourmont approached, they applied for it but were refused. The Duke of Terceira, after having performed the greatest service, was never consulted, and was merely left in command of his division. Setuval, the best port in Portugal after Lisbon, was left I believe two months without any defence. The Algarves were frequently left without provisions. They endeavoured to prevent me from going to the north; they disgusted Saldanha; in fact the only wise act they ever did was sending the Duke of Terceira to Oporto, and then they sent him horses without men to mount them. They disgusted all the foreign troops, and broke faith with them by wholesale, and then were surprised at their being disorderly.

They certainly clothed their own troops well and paid them regularly, and Saldanha organized them; but after the war was over and Saldanha and Terceira unemployed, Freire ruined them. As for the navy, I never could get my old minister of marine to do one single act for its advantage; he was as immoveable as a rock, and nearly as little animated.

After the capture of Figueras I sent a small squadron to blockade Madeira, and on Miguel's army laying down their arms, the governor gave up the island to Captain Bertram, who commanded the ships-of-war. He took upon himself the government *ad interim*, and by his judicious management very soon brought things into a state of peace and quietness.

The inspector of the arsenal had been sent to Brest to fit out the ships the French squadron had taken from Lisbon. France had a demand on Portugal for three or four hundred thousand francs, and Mr. Freire, in his character of foreign minister, negociated the matter so badly that she refused to give the ships up; and for that paltry sum they were left at Brest to run to decay. This minister had the art of disgusting every person he had to treat with, whether native or foreigner. I had prepared the Duchess of Braganza to bring them over, landing me first at Portsmouth, having obtained permission from the Emperor to return to England for a few weeks; and on the 10th of June, the day twelvemonth I hoisted my flag, I sailed from Lisbon, and, after a pleasant passage of fourteen days, landed at Portsmouth, where I was received in the most gratifying manner by the inhabitants. After ascertaining that there was no prospect of the ships at Brest being restored, the Duchess of Braganza went into dock and received some slight repairs. I passed a few weeks with my family, and repaired to Lisbon in the packet, to wind up the affairs of the officers and men, who were all anxious to return to England; which met the wishes of the Portuguese Government, who manifested the most indecent haste to get rid of those men who had served them so well and so faithfully. The officers, by contract, had their choice of remaining in the Portuguese service or leaving it; commissioned officers in the navy receiving four years' full pay, and all others two: but as the Government showed no wish to preserve them, and even positively refused to keep any employed, they all sent in their resignation; and after much trouble and unnecessary delays in paying the men, which delays cost the Government at least £50,000, the whole were sent to England, paid to the time their accounts were made up, and a positive assurance that the six weeks' arrears would be paid on their arrival in England, which, however, has not been done to this day, notwithstanding my repeated applications.

On my return to Lisbon I found the Emperor in very bad health; his troubles, anxieties, and fatigues for the last two years had been too much even for his robust frame, and he was now evidently declining. He had taken up his residence at Queluz, where he hoped quiet might restore his health. During my absence he had visited Oporto with the Empress and the Queen, and the sea-voyage and the excitement attending such a visit had certainly not been at all conducive to his health. The approaching meeting of the Cortes, before whom he was preparing to lay an account of what he had done for the restoration of the Queen and Charter, and also to resign the Regency, kept him in a constant state of excitement.

On the 15th of August the Emperor met both Houses of Parliament in the Chamber of Deputies, and after having given a long account of what he had done, he resigned the Regency and retired. His

Appendix, No. XXXIII.

medical adviser, a Brazilian, the only one he employed, recommended him to try the baths of Caldes, which he did for a few days, and returned decidedly worse.

Both Chambers having decided that the Emperor should preserve the Regency and the command of the army during the minority of the Queen, they assembled on the 29th, at the palace of the Ajuda, where the Emperor took the oaths prescribed by the Charter. He now suffered so much from a difficulty of breathing, that it was with evident pain and inconvenience that he got through the ceremony, and after remaining a short time at the Ajuda, during which he got rapidly worse, he retired to Queluz.

At this time the Chamber of Peers consisted of only sixteen members, for all those who supported Miguel were excluded. Palmella was appointed President for life. Very few of the peers were favourable to the ministry; but, with the exception of the Marquises of Loulé and Frontera, Counts de Taipa and Villa Real, they all voted on the ministerial side. On the 1st of September the

Emperor created twenty-four new peers, the greater part of whom supported the ministry.

Don Pedro became so much worse that on the 17th he sent a message to the Cortes, expressing his wish to resign the Regency; and after a short delay and a little intriguing, the Queen was declared of age, and assumed the reins of government. Taking every thing into consideration, and her approaching marriage, perhaps it was the wisest thing they could have done; but the death of her husband threw every thing into confusion, and left her a young inexperienced woman, without either chart or compass to direct her, hence the constant changes that have since occurred.

Her first act was to confer on Don Pedro the Grand Cross of the Tower and Sword for his services, which he had not assumed when Regent, and a few days after, the Duke of Palmella was desired to form an administration. Whether this was done with or without the approbation of the Emperor, is very doubtful; I am inclined to believe he was far from satisfied at seeing

Palmella entrusted with the re-construction of the ministry, and he, on the other hand, found it no easy matter. Saldanha, who had placed himself at the head of the opposition and declined the peerage, positively refused to serve with Carvalho and Freire; and the Duke was obliged to consign himself again into the hands of the men who had before put him out of the ministry. Mendizabel was anxious to preserve Carvalho, and he would not serve without Freire, and with them Palmella, (by the aid of Mendizabel, who took part in every transaction, even in recommending to the Emperor's medical men how he ought to be treated,) patched up an administration which it was very evident could not last. He became President of the Council without a portfolio; Carvalho Minister of Finance; Freire, who had proved himself unfit for Minister at War, and had ruined the army, took the Marine to ruin that also; Villa Real, Foreign Affairs; Bishop of Coimbra, the Interior Ferraz of Justice; and Terceira, Minister at War. When the ministry was formed I waited on Freire and put into his hands a plan by which the navy should be governed, and in the Appendix, No. XXXIV.

event of its not being adopted, I signified my intention of resigning. I also sent it to the Duke of Palmella, by whom it was submitted to the ministry and rejected. My resignation followed, and I applied myself to the winding up of the accounts of all the officers and men, which was soon effected. Bills were made out in Mendizabel's name and mine, at three, six, nine, and twelve months for the payment of the prize money, and the officers received their gratuity agreeable to their claims.

The minister approved of a list I presented to him for the settlement of the claims of the widows and orphans. This list assigned to the heirs of officers killed in battle or drowned the gratuity which they should have received had they lived. This was also extended to the mothers, wives, and children of those who died in the service. The list was approved by Mr. Augustinho Freire, and I was the bearer of it to England, yet unknown to me this honest minister wrote a letter to the Portuguese minister in London, desiring him to inquire what were the British regulations, and if he found those regulations entitled them to a larger sum than the allowance fixed by me and agreed to by him, they were to have it; but if a less sum they were to have the British regulation. Although representations have been made by me on this subject to every minister of marine, one of which will be found in the Appendix, no attention whatever has been paid to their claims, and at the moment I am writing, many widows and orphans are still starving.

Appendix, No. XXXV.

The complaint of the Emperor, which was originally inflammation of the lungs, had settled into a decided consumption, added to which dropsy had made its appearance; and notwithstanding the violent and torturing remedies that were applied the disease baffled all the skill of his medical attendants, and on the 24th of September, 1834, he breathed his last in the arms of his amiable consort, who had never left him a moment. He was perfectly sensible of his approaching end, and bore his sufferings with Christian fortitude. Shortly before he died he sent for a private of the 5th Caçadores (his own regiment), and by him sent his last farewell to the troops.

His loss to Portugal was great, the services he

had performed were of a nature that entitled him to the gratitude of the whole nation, and had he lived Portugal would have been saved from the misrule that has brought her on the brink of ruin.

It is difficult to describe the character of princes, and none but those who are intimately connected with them have an opportunity of knowing their real sentiments.

Don Pedro was above the middle stature, of a strong robust habit. He had a fine forehead and fierce eye, a sallow complexion, and marked with the small pox, his face was by no means prepossessing. He had the appearance of a savage-looking man, but that was not his character. On the contrary he had no cruelty in his disposition. He prided himself on being a liberal prince, and a friend to free institutions, nevertheless he, like most princes, and indeed like most men, was very fond of having his own way.

He was proud of military renown, and fancied himself a great general. But when Saldanha was at the head of his staff, and had acquired his confidence, he left the command of the army almost entirely to him.

Don Pedro's name will go down to posterity as having freed the land of his birth from despotism, and restored the throne of his daughter, and without having any thing personal in view except the desire of gaining glory.

He was suspected of aiming at the crown of Portugal. But I believe his thoughts were more turned to the possibility of his being called to the throne of Spain, in the event of any thing happening to the young Queen.

He was the most active man I ever saw, rose early, and looked into every thing himself, and knowing the procrastinating character of the Portuguese, he was right; had it not been for his activity the expedition would never have sailed from the Western Islands. He was a man of courage, but not of dash, or he would not have been persuaded to remain at Oporto instead of advancing the moment he landed, or given up his intention of embarking in the squadron with five thousand men.

When his mind was made up, he was firm and determined, and even obstinate; nothing but the last extremity would have induced him to have given up the contest. He was more easily elated by success than cast down by adversity; he was frank and I believe sincere, and hated both intriguing and lying. He was a bad politician and unwise prince, for if he did not like a person he took no pains to conceal it.

He did not easily forgive his enemies, but he was not cruel to them, nor was he very kind to his friends.

To sum up his character, his good qualities were his own, his bad owing to want of education; and no man was more sensible of that defect than himself.

He was universally regretted by the whole nation. The Miguelites even lost a friend in him, and had he lived I believe Portugal would have been in a very different situation than it now is.

His remains were moved from Queluz by torchlight on the 28th of September, and conveyed to the cathedral of St. Vincent de Foro. He was buried with the honours of a general officer, agreeable to his own request. Saldanha, Terceira, and myself were the chief mourners. The funeral was attended by all the principal people and nobility in Lisbon. The streets through which the cortege passed were lighted and lined with the military and national guards: it was a solemn sight. The inhabitants seemed really afflicted at their loss, and few dry eyes were to be seen amongst the females who were at the windows as the procession passed. The ceremony in the church was imposing, after which the coffin was deposited in the vaults. This done, we returned to the body of the church, and Pacol d'Almeida, the Emperor's Chamberlain, with tears in his eyes and much affected, delivered up the keys of the coffin to the Bishop. A paper was then signed by the chief mourners and other officers and people, certifying the day his remains were deposited amongst those of his ancestors.

On the 15th of October I hauled down my flag, and received the following letter from the Queen.

COUNT CAPE ST. VINCENT,

I, the Queen, send you much health. Taking into consideration the weighty reasons by which you are convinced that you cannot continue to exercise the functions of Major-General of the Navy, to which you had been named by the Royal Letter of the 10th June, eighteen hundred and thirty-three, and the extraordinary circumstances of war having ceased which made it necessary to invest you with the command-in-chief of the squadron which was confided to you by the Royal Letter of the said date,

I now exonerate you from the said command-in-chief, as well as from the office of Major-General; notwithstanding you will preserve the honorary post of Admiral, in consideration of your distinguished valour and the various services for which you have deserved my entire approbation and praise.

I communicate this to you for your information.

Given in the Palace of the Necessidades, the 15th of October, eighteen hundred and thirty-four.

A RAINHA.

To the Count Cape St. Vincent.

The House of Peers, on the motion of the Count de Taipa, honoured me with a vote of thanks for my services: this vote was written on parchment, signed by the Peers, to which was attached a gold seal, and conveyed to me by the Duke of Palmella, the president of the Chamber.

Chamber of Peers.

ILLUSTRIOUS AND EXCELLENT LORD,

I have the honour of conveying to your Excellency the resolution of the Chamber of Peers, who express the most sincere and unanimous thanks of the said Chamber to your Excellency for the weighty reasons therein mentioned, and at the same time that I believe that this resolution will be very agreeable to your Excellency, I cannot help assuring your Excellency that I have great pleasure and satisfaction in communicating it.

God preserve your Excellency!

DUKE OF PALMELLA,
President of the Chamber of Peers.

Palace of the Cortes,
December 9th, 1834.

To his Excellency
Count Cape St. Vincent.

The Chamber of Peers of the kingdom of Portugal unanimously resolve that a vote of thanks be given to Admiral Napier, Count Cape St. Vincent, for his brilliant and heroic conduct in the naval action of the 5th of July, 1833, in the waters of Cape St. Vincent, and for the services which he afterwards performed by sea and land, which greatly contributed to the establishment of her Most Faithful Majesty and the Constitutional Charter.

The Chamber also resolves, that to the illustrious and always conquering Admiral their thanks be communicated in this form, as a perpetual testimony of their gratitude.

Given in Lisbon on the 1st of December, 1834.
Signed by the Peers.

Don Pedro had, after the action of the 5th of July, conferred on me the Grand Cross of the Tower and Sword; Commodore Wilkinson and Captain Peak were made Commanders, and the other officers Companions, with the gold or silver Cross agreeable to their ranks. A good many silver Crosses were also given to the men who particularly distinguished themselves. After the campaign in the Minho I had been created Count Cape St. Vincent, and when the war was ended the Duke of Terceira was created Duke, Relation, and Saldanha a Marquis.

On the 1st of November I took leave of the Queen and Empress; the latter presented me with a lock of Don Pedro's hair in a gold locket, and on the 4th I embarked for England in the packet, the minister of marine not having either offered me a ship to carry me home, or even complimented me with a salute on leaving the Tagus.

Shortly after my arrival in England I read in the papers that the Chamber of Deputies had also given me a vote of thanks, as also to the officers and men in the action; the same was given to the Duke of Terceira and Saldanha, and the officers of the army and soldiers.

APPENDIX.

APPENDIX.

No. I.

Oct. 5th, 1833.

My dear Sir,

I enclose your Excellency the copy of a letter sent to me by the Director of the Comptability. If I understand that order right I can be of no further use here, because all appointments and promotions emanating from me must cease, as I never can subject myself to give an appointment to an officer who is not in consequence to be paid. I must also observe, that orders coming direct from the minister of marine to a subordinate officer brings me into contempt with the officer to whom they are addressed, and leaves me completely in the dark with respect to what is going on.

Yours, &c.

To the Director of the Countability,

His Imperial Majesty determines that no receipt belonging to any individual of the marine department shall be noted in the Marine Countability but in virtue of decrees, patents or any other legal documents emanating direct from government, and recommends the most scrupulous execution of this order.

Agostinho Joze Freire.

Palace of the Necessidades,
 Sept. 9th, 1833.

October 6th.

My dear Admiral,

I have just received a letter from you at half-past three, which I sincerely confess has afflicted me.

The fact is that the order, of which you sent me a copy, is no more than the execution of a law which I myself have no right to infringe. It is necessary that appointments of a certain importance ought to be sanctioned by a decree of H. I. M. otherwise they cannot be paid; and if I order them to be paid, I will be responsible before the Cortes, in which case I should have, as you well know, a number of enemies to accuse me, without it being in my power to answer. On the contrary, if I follow a rule, I shall be liberated from responsibility, without your losing any of your powers; besides, you know that I refuse to make any promotion. I could order the payment, but to keep the books in order in the countability, it is absolutely necessary to present decrees.

I yet beg leave to observe that the responsibility weighs exclusively on the minister, and consequently his orders must be on the Treasury. H. I. M. in the quality of commander-in-chief, has himself no previous knowledge of what regards money.

Marshal Beresford and Lord Wellington had also no authority on the treasury or arsenal. By this you will see that there is not, on my part, the least idea of contradicting you, and that you will not be less at liberty to make your appointments.

No. II.

My Lord,

As long as I remained on the list of naval officers I abstained from delicacy writing to your Lordship on the affairs of Portugal.

Your Lordship is aware of the occurrences up to the present moment; they have been great, and fortune has had her full share in placing us in Lisbon. I am, however, far from thinking the affairs of Portugal settled. The enemy have a considerable army on foot, certainly in a state of disorganization, but they are commanded by experienced French officers fighting on Portuguese ground for the Duke of Bordeaux, while Don Carlos is assisting Miguel in order to support his own cause in Spain. It is beyond a doubt that many French officers pass through Spain to join this army; they are also supplied with money, and I dare say with men also, and this can be easily done without it coming officially to our knowledge.

The English government have acknowledged the Queen it is true, but I fear that will not put an end to the misfortunes of this country. She must do more, unless she wishes to see Portugal become a field of blood. Already in various places have the Miguelites been committing the most horrid murders. At Beja, and many towns of the Algarves, the most abominable scenes have taken place, and we have not troops to prevent it. We are organizing men, and establishing lines for the defence of Lisbon as fast as possible; but should the enemy break through them, your Lordship can form no idea of what will happen here. I see only two ways of preventing this; the first is, England sending troops to assist her ally; the second is, France and England insisting on the immediate recognition of the Queen by Spain. There is also another means, which I shall most decidedly advise, let the consequence be what it will: should this horrid war last, and be encouraged by Spain, we must fight her with her own weapons. Your Lordship, I dare say, is perfectly aware were I to appear off Cadiz with my squadron, composed of two sail of the line, two hundred and fifty guard-ships, three frigates, three corvettes, and half-a-dozen brigs, in half-an-hour it would be revolutionized, and Spain would have to look to herself. Now I am far from wishing this: we

APPENDIX. 253

have no business with Spain, if she is quiet; if otherwise, she must take the consequence.

This is my own opinion. I have never conversed with the Emperor or ministers on the subject; but nothing but decision will save this country.

I am sorry to see many of the English papers full of getting rid of Don Pedro. It would be the greatest misfortune that could happen. He is the most active man in Portugal. He saved Oporto; and if it had not been for him, I never would have got the lines begun at Lisbon. He has his faults, like other people, but he is far from being a bad man. He is a great favourite with the army and the people, and it would be no easy matter to displace him. I for one would not lend myself to it. I believe him to be perfectly sincere about the young Queen; he was the first to propose to send for her. As to his ministers, I regret exceedingly Palmella is not at the head of the administration; it will come round, I have no doubt, in time, but the less he is spoken of and brought in competition with the Emperor the better. The way to keep him out is to try to force him in.

CAPE ST. VINCENT.

No. III.

Don Pedro's letter to the Queen of Spain not having been delivered, it is considered improper to publish it.

No. IV.

St. Ubes, November 3, 1833.

My Lord,

I beg to inform you that the enemy attacked our position at Alcasa, on the morning of the 2d instant, in three columns, consisting of infantry and cavalry to the number of about 1500, under the command of General Lemos. The English and Portuguese marines under my command were stationed in front of the constitutional troops as skirmishers, and kept the enemy at bay till the cavalry charged them in three squadrons, when we immediately formed into square and twice repulsed them with great loss. We then prepared to charge a column of infantry, who were advancing, but the Portuguese volunteers and ninth infantry, who were stationed in our rear, seeing the determined manner in which we were attacked, betook themselves to rapid flight without firing a short, leaving my men with some of the Portuguese marines to do the best we could, and when finding ourselves overpowered by numbers we commenced our retreat, keeping the enemy at bay and covering the flight of the Portuguese. I tried to persuade the colonel, commanding our troops, who asked my opinion, to retire to a convent, a strong position on our right, at which place we might have made a good stand, but instead of doing this he led to the marshes beside the river; and here the scene was beyond description, the whole country was strewed with arms and accoutrements, which the volunteers threw away in their

APPENDIX. 255

flight, and the enemy's cavalry closing on them hewed them down in all directions. I kept my men together, and made good my retreat to the side of the river with the loss of only three men; but on coming to the river for want of a sufficient number of boats (the Portuguese troops having taken all) the men were obliged to throw away their arms and accoutrements and swim across the river under a heavy fire of musketry from the enemy, who lined the north bank of the river. In this place, I am sorry to say, my loss was great, in consequence, I fear, of some of the officers and men breaking off to the right and attempting to pass the river lower down, they were all cut off. My loss consists of Mr. Ebsworth, taken prisoner; Mr. Fitzpatrick, drowned in crossing the river; four non-commissioned officers and thirty men, killed and taken prisoners. I assure your excellency I cannot speak too highly of the gallant conduct of my officers and men.

The colonel commanding lost all self command and gave himself up to the enemy; and a great number of the volunteers, when they found themselves surrounded, passed over to the enemy, crying " Viva Don Miguel." The loss of the Portuguese in killed, wounded, taken prisoners, and missing, could not be less than eight hundred men.

The remainder of my men and officers are now on board the Donna Maria, where I wait your Excellency's orders.

> I have the honour to be,
> Your Excellency's
> Most obedient humble servant,
> —— Birt, Captain of Marines.

My Dear Sir,

There has been nothing but the greatest mismanagement displayed here, as you will see by the report of Captain Birt, which I send you.

It appears that the Queen's forces took possession of Alcacer de Sal on the 25th of October, the enemy flying from the place.

Colonel Florenza advanced at four in the morning of the second, about three miles, and took up a position; the enemy made a movement on his left, which brought his troops into a plain, with a wood on each side of him. The Portuguese troops were drawn up across this plain with the English marines and Portuguese brigade in front as skirmishers; they advanced three squadron of cavalry at a gallop; Captain Birt threw the marines into a rallying square, and repulsed them with great loss. The cavalry formed again, and were again repulsed with severe loss, retiring in the rear of their infantry; Captain Birt then formed in line, and advanced against a column of infantry, then coming forward to attack him: at this moment the whole of the Portuguese troops turned round, fired a volley in the air, and fairly run away as fast as they could. He was in consequence obliged to retire, and cover their flight to the town; there the volunteers threw away their accoutrements and ammunition. Captain Birt begged Colonel Florenza to rally his regiment at a castle on this side of the town; but his head was so entirely gone that nothing was done, and away they all went, helter-skelter, through the marshes towards the river. The cavalry took a road to the right, and cut them up in all directions; some escaping in boats, some swimming, many drowning, and the others surrendering. Captain Birt pursued his retreat in good order to the river, where he found all the boats gone down with those who had saved themselves. There were boats on the opposite side of the river, which were brought over by some of his men who could swim, those who could not went in the boats on board a yacht, the others swam off: a party of fifty, with several officers, went lower down the river, where they were charged by the cavalry; those who could swim took to the water, the rest were either killed or taken. Lieutenant Fitzpatrick I believe was drowned; Mr. Ebsworth was taken. Our loss is fifty-four marines and four commissioned officers killed, drowned, and taken. As for the rest of the troops God knows where they are. I heard two hundred are at Palmella, and there may be about a hundred here. I have ordered the men from Palmella, and am rallying the rest as fast as I can.

&c. &c. &c.

No. V.

Is the decree against the old contractors of tobacco, which cannot be found, but the nature of it is stated in the work.

No. VI.

Count Taipa's first Remonstrance.

To His Imperial Majesty.

Sire,

In England the peers of the realm address the sovereign in their individual character, even on ordinary affairs, that have any connexion with the public weal. Raised as I have been by your Majesty to the high rank of a peer of the kingdom, I adopt the same means to make your Majesty acquainted with matters of the highest consequence, in which not only the fair fame of your Majesty is concerned, but on which also depend the interests of the nation so gloriously saved by your Majesty's arms from the most atrocious despotism. This fame evil councillors are attempting to blacken, by casting upon your Majesty's name foul aspersions that have no place there, and by changing into sorrow the enthusiasm and gratitude with which the Portuguese nation hailed your Majesty as the restorer of the national liberties. The suspension of the laws, which ought never to take place but in cases of absolute emergency, has been vilely made use of as a cloak to cover rapine and confiscation, as well as numerous arbitrary arrests, confessedly unnecessary.

Occupied as your Majesty is in carrying on the war, and liable to the misfortune, common to all princes, of with difficulty hearing the truth when the liberty of the press does not break through the veil that surrounds them, your Majesty knows little of what is passing. But I will attempt to enlighten your Majesty with respect to all the complaints that the want of political courage, and the habit of submission to despotic power, prevent reaching your Majesty's ears, trusting that your Majesty, when better informed, will make the constitution a reality while your ministers only wish to make it a falsehood. Let not your Majesty imagine that I am actuated by any spirit of party, or any expectations of favour from some new ministry. I here publicly beg of your Majesty that if at any time that should be presented to you a petition of mine for any favour or office during the present or future ministry, your Majesty will put on the back of it " dishonoured."

The tobacco contract is the business that has principally induced me to offer this letter to your Majesty's notice: it is a business which has given scandal to the whole city, and carried consternation into numerous families by the destruction of their property, by the despotic acts of the minister, and by exactions more tyrannical than those of the most atrocious Roman proconsul. The contract has been given clandestinely to an individual for 1,200 contas of reis, for the space of twelve years, while there were here in Lisbon persons who offered 1,400 contas: so that the public revenue suffers a loss of 6,000,000 of crusadas, an arrangement in which I am sorry to say your Majesty's credit is called in question by those who are not so well acquainted as myself with the elevation and greatness of your Majesty's moral virtues.

260 APPENDIX.

Moreover, Sire, the ministry, after having acknowledged the impossibility of the present contractors to pay their monthly obligations in the royal order of the 10th of September last, for the obvious reason of their not being masters of the contract, in consequence of the provinces being occupied by the rebel forces, has suddenly ordered the property of the said contractors to be confiscated, to the amount of 500 contas of reis, the sum which would be due to the government in case that the commerce of Portugal and the islands were free. Such an act of tyranny was never before practised by any government upon its people; nor can that *summa injuria* be palliated by the *summum jus*, because nobody can exact a right if he does not comply with his own obligations.

If the contractors are bound to pay, the government is equally bound to leave them the means of pursuing the branch of trade which they have undertaken free and unembarrassed; but this is impossible, in consequence of the occupation of the country by the rebel troops.

But, Sire, public opinion does not hesitate to say that this confiscation is neither more nor less than an act of private revenge by a cabal, in consequence of the present contractors having outbid by 200 contas, those on whom the contract has been clandestinely (*camararcamente*) bestowed. Of this indeed there can be no doubt, because laying aside the morality of the case, and looking at it only as a question of interest, it is not with such precipitation, and that too, without consulting the council of state, that a measure on which the existence or credit of one of the principal branches of our trade depends, should be adopted.

Therefore, Sire, out of love to my country, for the honour of your Majesty, for the triumph of justice, and above all that it may not go forth to the world, that your Majesty's government is but little different from a government that bears the very stamp of infamy—that of Don Miguel—I pray your Majesty, after convoking your council of state, and obtaining better information, to act with that justice which is so congenial to your Majesty's heart.

I am your Imperial Majesty's
Faithful subject,
CONDE DE TAIPA,
Peer of the Realm.

Lisbon, October 25, 1833.

No. VII.

Taipa's second Letter.

SIRE,

The Constitutional Charter (chap. 8. § 28) says, " Every citizen shall be at liberty to present in writing to the legislature and executive authorities reclamations, complaints, and petitions; and even to expose any infraction of the constitution by demanding at the hands of the competent authorities the practical responsibility of the infractors." Availing myself of this political right, which the Constitutional Charter allows me, I again throw myself at Your Majesty's feet to expose to Your Majesty the false position in which the present ministry has placed the cause of the Queen Donna Maria II. by rendering a part of the nation indisposed towards Your Majesty, and by preventing such foreign governments as are friendly to us from interposing their good offices to restore peace and tranquillity to this unfortunate country.

The Portuguese nation desires nothing so much as tranquillity: distracted with dissensions ever since the year 1820, she is so exhausted and worn out that nothing but desperation still keeps together to the bloody standard of Don Miguel that portion of the people which, having been deceived or compelled, has followed the cause of injustice. Difficulties are increasing from day to day. The recovery of the kingdom is paralysed by the imbecility of ministers and the discredit of government. The ministry has completely lost the opinion of the public. The most helpless ignorance is displayed in their laws. The merest clumsiness in all the provisions of government. The most scandalous profligacy in almost all the appointments of their officers, and in all their other acts. The present ministry does not represent the interests even of a party: it is purely a faction of ignorant charlatans, anarchists, cosmopolites, without name, without property, without services, without talents; who belong to Portugal simply from the circumstance of their being born within its territory: their only object being to engross for themselves all the fat appointments of the state.

Principles they have none, either good or bad; they were unjustly accused of being ultra-liberal. They are anything and everything, the dregs of all parties; the *caput-mortuum* of all factions, from which they have formed a new and unwonted monster.

Thus alone is explained the strange phenomenon that we see them presenting, at once both friends and enemies, ungrateful and disloyal to their friends, and impolitic to their enemies, they gain no hearts, and make all foes.

Not one of these accusations is vague: I will point out and examine analytically the facts.

Vattel, that great writer on the laws of nations, whose authority is almost received as law among the nations of Europe, says, treating on civil wars, " le plus sur moyen," &c. &c. * * * * * *

The men who compose the present ministry have placed us in the case mentioned in the last sentence which I have just quoted in the words of the author.

The Constitutional Charter says, (chap. 8, § 19) " no punishment shall go beyond the person of the delinquent, therefore in no case shall confiscation of goods or public infamy be extended to the criminal's relations in any degree."

In the present case, Sire, although the Charter does not prohibit confiscations, policy imperatively demands the prohibition. The citizens of Oporto, who, on the for ever memorable day of the 29th of September, 1832, went forth almost unarmed, to face death upon the bayonets of the usurpation, had seen Villa Nova pillaged. It was the defence of their Penates that impelled them to this heroism.

By the decree of the 31st August, 1833, the ministry, after a wily preamble, proceeds to plunder the greater part of the proprietors of Portugal, because the regiments of militia which were compelled, under the pain of seeing their houses burned, to go and fight for the usurpation, are composed of the provincial proprietors. They are too numerous to have the name of rebels: but being desperate of every thing which constitutes the happiness of man they may be elevated to the heroism of desperation—not to conquer, for the cause of the usurper cannot succeed, but to make this war of devastation last long enough to annihilate this wretched country. I fear not, Sire, the execution of this decree : I fear only the terror which it inspires—because there is in it nothing more than the diabolical wish of the ministry, having in itself the salutary principle of its impracticability ; and I will yet quote Vattel, who says, " La punition," &c.   *   *   *   *   *   *

Sire, Your Majesty cannot make laws, because the legislative power is by its nature incommunicable: when the ministers of the restoration in France were wishing to make of the French charter the same mockery which Your Majesty's ministers are seeking to make of the charter which Your Majesty has granted, that illustrious peer of France, Count de Landjuinais, whose voice is always heard in the defence of liberty, said, " Le pouvoir," &c. &c. * * * * * *

But I will grant that the supreme law of public safety authorized every thing: that upon it was founded the dictatorial authority which the government has arrogated to itself; yet this authority could not extend furher than circumstances required.

What circumstances have authorized government to create new places, to establish their salaries, increase them, multiply them infinitely, and then add supernumeraries?

They have assumed to themselves the reformation of the administration of justice, and created a much greater number of judges, doubled the length of the processes, confounded the inextricable confusion of legal chicanery! Jurisconsults as little at home in their country's laws which they have set themselves to reform as in those of the civilized nations which they have copied without having understood; they have published in that disgraceful law of the 10th of May last a solemn record of their gross ignorance and miserable talents. Ragged patches picked by these clumsy hands from the French codes, and with fitting skill stitched, without order or connexion, into a barbarous language, filled with ambiguities (amphibologies) and obscurities, and even grammatical errors which would put a lay brother to shame! Such is the law with which our Lycurguses have presumed to reform the courts and the legislature of their country! Let him who ventures to deny any one of these accusations enter the lists, and I will sustain them one by one upon him.

More scandalous still perhaps is another pretended reform, that of the clergy, secular and regular. No church was in need of more reform than the Portuguese, but the mission was not for such apostles ; and never by such means was the Gospel preached. It would be enough to mention here one name to be more than sufficient : it would be enough to name the priest Marcos Soares Vaz Preto, to whom, from the formulary of his curious sentences, the public have given the title of Conselheiro Profanador. The word profane, although it is not incorrect, has the effect of rooting in the opinion of the people that sophism *ad odium*, the war-cry of " Freemasons," with which our enemies have endeavoured to make us execrated through the ignorance of the people. Common sense is horrified at such stupidity. They have profaned the convents, taken their rents, taken to themselves the subsistence of the secular clergy, not provided for the ecclesiastical revenues of the priests. They have done all this and more; but where appears a single provision for the reformation and improvement, intellectual and moral, of the clergy, either regular or secular ? Where have they restored ecclesiastical discipline ? Where have they caused the canons to be respected ? Where are their councils ? Which of the holy fathers have they invoked for so interesting and useful an object ? " Papam habemus Marcum." Padre Marcos is our Pope, the only authority which governs the Lusitanian church. Who has taught him the canons of the Holy Fathers, that he should know them? Who has established him in the opinion of the people, that his authority might be received with moral submission in a case of such high importance? Let them cast a veil over this subject before the enemies of the cause have seen all the embarrassments which surround the profanation of the sanctuary.

As for the laws of the revenue I will merely say, at present, that we have a million of fiscal employés, with more than a million salaries; many millions of debts and loans, and little money in the treasury. The subject of the gross ignorance of the ministry, and their colleagues and agents, would be inexhaustible; but at my leisure, and with more minuteness, and when I possess some documents which I am expecting, I will again, at Your Majesty's feet, resume the consideration of these affairs. Their unskilfulness and complete incapacity for governing is no less helpless and scandalous — at one time in the internal administration of the country, at another in our foreign relations with the powers of Europe. I know not in what it is not displayed, in such a manner as not only causes horror and shame at the sight of such misery and such want of superintending intellect, but also causes serious apprehensions for the cause of the Queen. And if I speak with so much freedom to Your Majesty, it is because I see, as I have already said, the impossibility of the success of the Usurper's cause; because I see Your Majesty at the head of a valiant army; I see the brave Duke of Terceira, who, by the miracle which his boldness worked, liberated the capital; I see also the energetic Count Saldanha, who under the orders of Your Majesty in the lines of Oporto, broke in pieces the triumphant baton of a marshal of France, the conqueror of Algiers; I see those brave academicians and volunteers of Villa da Praia, who were called by nature to civil appointments, not disheartened when they saw them all given to the busy-bodies of the anti-chambers of the ministry, and continuing at the military posts, in the bivouacks to which honour had called them, ready to make fresh sacrifices. The cause of the Usurper is lost: we must save that of the Queen.

Turn we our eyes to the civil government of the liberated territory. The confusion, the dismay, the anarchy of the administration, is even more astounding; the prefects and corregidors, the new tribunals, and the old Juizes da Fora, the ancient law and the law of grace—Sidon and Babylon (sixes and sevens)—all goes *dancing like mad* (macabra) to the fiddling of these gentlemen. They never cease their sequestrations of the rebels' property that they may have no opportunity of changing sides, and they ruin every body to give places to the turncoats of the ministry, without having reformed a single place, or abolished a single sinecure. Each minister gives his own orders, without connexion with the rest, each subaltern in authority does what he pleases: the people cry, but no one takes notice of their cries. It is true that since I began the letter which I have the honor to lay at Your Majesty's feet, they have at last ordered to be suspended the sale of the sequestrated property; of which and of the manner in which they have made it such scandalous and indecent histories will go forth to the world; but if in the issuing of this same order, the government has yielded to opinion, and confessed virtually the excess which it had committed, they have not thus paid even a moiety of the homage which is due to justice which has been offended, to public decency which has been insulted; and to the cause of the Queen and of liberty, which has been outraged and degraded by such abuses. What has become of the enquiry which was to have been made into the mode and legality of the sales already effected! The ministry has placed itself in such a situation, that it is not enough to do no evil; it is necessary for it to give proofs repeated and continual that it does not evil, and will not allow it to be done. In the delicate state of its credit a mere suspicion is its ruin.

Let Your Majesty enquire if the house of Ascenço de Segueira, a child of four years old, has been sequestrated, if José Balbino Barbosa has been to select furniture, at the unfair price of the valuation, in the sequestrated houses, to pay for them by deductions from his government salary; and if much more of the same sort has not been done: it is of this that Lisbon is full.

Turn we now all our attention upon the state of our foreign relations. We are losing the friends we have gained in some cabinets, we are gaining none; and we are increasing the distance between us and that government which it most behoves us to have for an ally, and without which I do not believe our triumph is possible.

Spain, the legitimate inheritance of the Queen Donna Isabel II., seeks to ally herself intimately with Portugal, the legitimate inheritance of the Queen Donna Maria II.—the cause is the same; the war against the government of order, is the war which is in the present day lacerating the western Peninsula of Europe; the party of those who wish without working to consume the produce of another's sweat, is that which forms the Carlist and Miguelite parties. Let there be established in Lisbon a government which may afford guarantees of order, which will be immediately recognized by the government of order of the Cortez of Madrid. It is not for the difference of the forms of government that this salutary union is not already cemented; it is because Your Majesty's government oppose itself as an invincible barrier, by its discredit with the nation and with Europe. Nor is the recognition of England and France any more than a recognition of right which is evident from the fact that as one of the diplomatists accredited near Your Majesty tells any of the secrets of his cabinet to Your Majesty's ministers, because there is no guarantee that by the return of the packet they might not see such secrets published in the revolutionary journals of Europe to suit the private interests of Your Majesty's ministers and their associates. To remedy these evils I humbly bring to the feet of Your Majesty the following petitions:

First, that Your Majesty will grant an amnesty full and general, excepting only the Usurper.

Second, that you will cause to be quashed all sequestrations for political causes.

APPENDIX. 271

Third, that in order to afford guarantees, and that these measures may produce their effects, and to cure the evils which I have pointed out in the body of the letter, Your Majesty will dismiss your ministers, and proclaim others who may be in the national confidence.

Fourth, that in order that Your Majesty may be informed of the opinions of the public, Your Majesty will command to be put in execution the project of law, regarding the liberty of the press, which passed the Chamber of Deputies in the last legislature, and to which nothing was wanting but the examination of the Peers and the Royal sanction, to become the law of the land.

And the blessings of the Portuguese will be heaped upon your Majesty.

(Signed) DA TAIPA.

No. VIII.

PEERS' PROTEST, No. 1.

SIRE,

The undersigned have the honor of representing to Your Imperial Majesty that there was this morning presented to the Count da Taipa, peer of the kingdom, an order for his arrest signed by one of the criminal judges of this city, which was attempted to be executed, involving, as it would appear, a manifest infraction of the constitutional charter, Art. 26, seeing that they could not shew a case of *flagrante delicto* of a capital crime, which is the only case excepted in the said Article, which is as follows: Art. 26. " No Peer or Deputy, during the time of his being a Deputy, can be arrested by any authority, unless by an order of his own Chamber, except in *flagrante delicto* of a capital crime." The undersigned deeming that it is necessary, in order to the maintaining of the immunity of the Chamber of Peers, that they should ask Your Imperial Majesty to deign to command to be declared whether the articles of the Constitutional Charter, which guarantee the inviolability of the Peers, are suspended by the Decree of the 10th July, one thousand eight hundred and thirty-two, in order that such Declaration may serve as a Rule. — Heaven preserve Your Majesty.

(Signed)

Duke of Terceira,
Duke of Palmella,
Marquis of Fronteira,
Marquis of Ponta de Lima,
Marquis of Loulé,
Marquis of Santa Iria,
Count de Lumiares,
Count de Ficalho,
Count de Parati,

} *Peers of the Kingdom.*

Lisbon, 7th Dec. 1833.

No. IX.

Answer to the Peers' 1st Letter respecting Count da Taipa, from José da Silva Carvalho.

(*Translation.*)

The warrant of arrest issued by the criminal magistrate of the upper district against Count Taipa, and acknowledged by him, was given in consequence of information received. If the person informed against has any thing to allege in his favour, or if any of the noble Peers considers his rights encroached upon, he may have recourse to the means permitted by law. Their inviolability laid down in the 25th Article of the Constitutional Charter will be fully preserved to them. As far as regards the decree of the 10th July, 1832, as it makes no distinction of persons, it comprehends all alike, since according to the Art. 145, cap. 12, of the Charter, " The law is equal for all, in protection and punishment."

Palace of Necessidades,
      (Signed)   JOSE DA SILVA CARVALHO.
Dec. 9, 1833.

No. X.

PEERS' PROTEST.—No. 2.

SIRE,

The representation which certain peers of the kingdom

presented to Your Imperial Majesty (dated the 7th inst.) on the occasion of an order for the arrest of the Count da Taipa issued by the *Corregidor de Bairo Alto*, having been published in the Chronicle of the 11 inst. and been called a complaint (requiramento), with the addition of an official answer, signed by the minister charged with the affairs of Justice,—the undersigned peers of the kingdom find themselves in the harsh necessity of protesting before Y. I. M. as well against the essential alteration, which is made in the character of the representation, by calling it a complaint, as against the form of the answer, which was that of an ordinary despatch, and lastly and chiefly as against the erroneous and pernicious doctrine which the said despatch contains.

The undersigned protest against the calling of the representation a complaint, because complaints are petitions to the executive power upon subjects which it is competent to entertain, and for it to decide upon constitutional subjects, which is a violation of the privileges of the organs of the legislative power, whether permanent or elective, cannot be the attribute of a power to which it is not subordinate. It was for this that Your Imperial Majesty, as Regent in the Queen's name, exercises the powers of government to which by the Charter belongs the watching over the maintenance of the independence of the chief political authorities (Tit. 5, chap. i. art. 71), and to which the peers have recourse in their representation, as it was impossible for them to submit the subject to the consideration of the Cortes. And they protest against the answer being given in the form of an ordinary despatch, for the same reasons as those which they make to calling the representation a complaint.

Lastly, they protest against the doctrine contained in the despatch: forasmuch as the decree of the 10th July, 1832, did not and could not give to the executive prerogative more than was in extraordinary cases conceded to the government by § 34 of the 145 art. of the 8 Tit. of the Charter, which permits the suspension, *for a determinate time, of some formalities which guarantee individual liberty*. Now the immunity of the peers and deputies is not a guarantee of individual liberty, but *of the independence of the legislative power*, and to suspend it, is to make it no longer independent, and in fact annihilates altogether the representative form of government. The despatch argues sophistically enough to make it appear that the independence of the legislature is not endangered, while the peers are secured in the expression of their opinions, as settled by the 25 art. 4 Tit. of the 1st cap. This is not sufficient for the independence of the legislative authority; for a government, which wished to oppress its organs, might do it upon any pretext, by asserting that such opinions were not expressed in the exercise of their functions; and for this reason the learned author of the Charter established as the palladium of the constitutional liberties of all Portuguese, the immunity of the members of both Chambers. Art. 26 of the same tit. and chap.

They are not, Sire, the privileges of an individual,— they are not the legal prerogatives annexed to a dignity, still less are they the pretensions of a class, which the undersigned peers defended before Your Majesty in their representation, and again uphold in their present protest. If such were the subject, if the question did not concern the legal liberties of all Portuguese, the peers would have preserved silence, and most willingly have made this sacrifice for the sake of preserving former harmony; but they are the fundamental principles, without which the representative government, for which so much blood has been shed, would become a counterfeit, and it is the strict duty of the peers to uphold and defend them.

The undersigned peers, in the unfortunate absence of an elective chamber which, with your Majesty and the other chamber, would complete the national representation, acknowledge no legal means but that of availing themselves of an address to the chief of the government in whom resides the governing power; and they cannot see what is the legal resource to which the said despatch refers them if they feel aggrieved ; as they cannot admit, for the decision of fundamental questions of public liberty, any other authority but that of the legislature, or in its unavoidable absence, of the government which they addressed. The undersigned peers would not have so eagerly made the representation of the 7th inst. or the present protest, notwithstanding its great importance, if they had had the least suspicion that the publication of it would be injurious to the happy progress of the important national cause; but they have the fullest conviction that the respectful and frank expression of their opinions in favour of the constitutional government and the legal liberty of the Portuguese can never be favourable to the enemies of that liberty, but that they, on the contrary, prosper, and rejoice at the invasions of power with the violations of the guarantees of the liberty they fight against, and with the annihilation of the rule of the Constitutional Charter, for which the sound part of the nation has made so many sacrifices, and is still fighting with the most laudable enthusiasm and admirable perseverance.

The undersigned peers claiming from your Imperial Majesty, as chief of the government, the Charter entire and religiously observed, have the noble confidence that they are expressing the wish of the nation which is making sacrifices and fighting for that Charter.

(Signed)

DUKE OF TERCEIRA,
DUKE OF PALMELLA,
MARQUIS OF FRONTEIRA,
MARQUIS OF PONTA DE LIMA,
MARQUIS OF LOULÉ,
MARQUIS OF SANTA IRIA,
COUNT OF LUMIARES,
COUNT OF PARATI,
COUNT OF FICALHO,
} *Peers of the Kingdom.*

Lisbon, 11*th Dec.* 1833.

No. XI.

Letter to the Duke of Terceira in reply to the Peers' Protest.

MOST ILLUSTRIOUS AND EXCELLENT SIR,

By order of His Imperial Majesty the Duke of Braganza, Regent in name of the Queen, I communicate to your Excellency, in order that you may make it known to your colleagues who signed the Protest, which on the 11th of this month, and by your Excellency's hands, was conveyed to his august presence.

1st. That His Imperial Majesty has read with every attention the protest drawn up and signed, on the 11th inst. by your Excellency and other peers of the kingdom, to the number of nine, four of whom have not yet taken their seats in the chamber.

2dly. That it does not belong to the moderating power, even " during the compulsory absence of the legislative power," to interpret the Constitutional Charter of the monarchy; nevertheless, if circumstances should occur, such as to oblige His Imperial Majesty to give any explanation upon any article or articles of the Charter, His Imperial Majesty, not as author or as granter of it, but as encharged with the noble mission of saving the country of his birth, and with it the throne of his august daughter, would do so by endeavouring to reconcile the independence of the political powers of the state and the interests of the members of the chambers, with the indispensable execution of justice which is due to society.

APPENDIX.

3dly. That the said protest shall be submitted to the Cortes as soon as we have the happiness to see them assembled, in order that they may decide, with it and the order of the Minister of Justice before them, whether the Constitutional Charter has been infringed or not.

4thly. That His Imperial Majesty is much rejoiced to see the noble peers who signed the protest profess sentiments of respect to His Imperial person, and of attachment to the Charter, for which and for the Queen he has shewn such zeal and submitted to so many sacrifices.

God preserve your Excellency!
Palace of Necessidades, 16th Dec. 1833.
(Signed) JOAQUIM ANTONIO D'AGUIAR.

His Excellency the Duke of Terceira.

No. XII.

SIR,

I have to acknowledge the receipt of your Excellency's letter of the 7th of December, informing me that some English officers have committed the scandalous abuse of ordering Portuguese seamen to be flogged, and that a man so barborously punished is at death's door on board the corvette Eliza. I beg to inform your Excellency, before such an infamous accusation is made against an officer, in all well regulated services it is usual to make inquiry into the subject, and not give ear to reports that are made to your Excellency, in all probability for evil purposes. I should like to be informed who was the person that made such a report to your Excellency. I can inform your Excellency better. The man alluded to received one dozen lashes for desertion, and is not sufficiently punished; and as for the authority of inflicting this punishment, I beg to call your Excellency's attention to the 12th article of Sartorius's contract.

Your Excellency will there observe that I neither can discontinue the infliction of a regular punishment nor reprimand the officer.

I must further observe that so long as I am at the head of the Portuguese navy I will never sanction the habit of beating and bruising the men about with sticks, as is the custom, and can allow no punishment to take place, except it is done in a solemn and regular manner by the captain.

I have the honour to be, &c. &c. &c.

CABO ST. VICENTI.

Dec. 9th, 1833.
 To His Excellency
  the Minister of Marine.

No. XIII.

SIRE,

I took the liberty some time back of telling your Majesty frankly my opinion of the state of things. It was my duty as Her Majesty's admiral so to do. I have no private interests to serve,—no wish but for the prosperity of her cause. My character is above intrigue; and what I shall now state to your Majesty I have no wish should be secret.

I do not like the aspect of affairs. Lisbon, Oporto, St. Ubes, Peniche, Faro, and Lagos are in the power of the Queen, and a small territory as far as Santarem. At Oporto the *regular force* is small; I understand under fifteen hundred men. Marshal Saldanha has, I suppose, twelve thousand men before Santarem; at St. Ubes there may be a thousand; Peniche five hundred; in the Algarves, including the brigade, not more than twelve hundred. I speak of regular troops only. Don Miguel has at least seven thousand men in the north of Portugal and round Oporto; at Figueras, Coimbra, Leiria, and the neighbourhood three thousand men; at Santarem, Salvaterra, and the vicinity twelve thousand men. I believe I state the least probable number. In the other parts of Portugal I have no certain information; but I should suppose there cannot be less than three thousand men. Don Miguel is certainly recruiting and successfully; and his losses by desertion are much below his recruiting. His army, we believe, have not been paid; they are not well clothed; but there can be no doubt they are well provisioned. This leads to prove only that Don Miguel's army is attached to him. I like to stare things in the face. From my position as a foreigner I look at things with impartiality. I do not believe all I wish, and I like to look forward.

Santarem, we all know, cannot be attacked without great risk. At Oporto we can do nothing; at Peniche and St. Ubes we are in the same situation; and in the Algarves the guerillas are organizing themselves, and assuming the appearance of a regular force. They are arming in the Guadiana, and we cannot prevent them. They have even introduced vessels into the river in spite of the force I had there; such is our military position; the force is so nearly balanced that neither can act on the defensive.

Don Miguel clothes and feeds his army, and pays them badly, he has in consequence less cause for money —the great sinew of war. Your Majesty has enormous establishments to keep up; a large army, a navy, and all the public departments; the expense is enormous. Hitherto the government have had considerable loans, but every day it will be more difficult to raise money. The cause is decreasing in interest in England, and the funds have considerably fallen. In Lisbon there is little or no credit. In this department we can get no supplies without ready money. Nobody will furnish stores on credit, and we shall shortly be at a stand. The arsenal has not been paid for weeks, and the men are absenting themselves daily. There is much discontent in Lisbon, and every person is inquiring how this war is to finish.

Should Spain and England interfere there is no doubt the war will be brought to a speedy conclusion; but I am by no means sanguine in their immediate interference, and every day our position will get worse. Should they not interfere, Don Miguel will get money from the

Tories in England, the Carlists in France and Spain, and from the Holy Alliance. The struggle for despotism will be fought on Portuguese ground. We have strong reason to believe Captain Elliott is in England to arm a squadron; I will do all I can to prevent it; but if he has money and support there is no difficulty in purchasing in England as many East-Indiamen as he pleases, who will carry sixty guns each; our ships are not in good condition, and it will require great expense to make them so. I will do all I can, but we cannot command success, though we may deserve it.

I have, as clearly as I can, laid my opinion frankly before Your Majesty; you desired me always to do so; and from the first moment I had the honour of seeing Your Majesty, I have made it the rule of my conduct. Your Majesty will naturally wish to know the remedy I propose.

The first is to form a combined and extended administration, to conciliate all parties, and gain the confidence of the public; to conciliate that portion of the Miguellists who are desirous to treat—to encourage them to abandon the cause of Don Miguel—and to give them confidence in the future. At present they have lost their property; their only hope of regaining it is by adhering to the usurper; it is human nature; they are desperate, and will resist to the last.

I have no fault to find personally with Your Majesty's present Ministers; with Mr. Freire I have always been on the best of terms; but it is impossible for him to perform the duties of two Portfolios. In these critical times a

Minister at War has enough to occupy him all the twenty-four hours, and he must be well supported to carry it on as it ought to be; and Your Majesty knows full well the procrastination of the bureaus. The Minister of Finance has the duties of half-a-dozen offices to do, while his labour in the Finance alone must be enormous; that, God knows, can be no sinecure. The Minister of Marine is I believe as honest a man as lives, but he is unaccustomed to office, and things go on proportionally slow. The Minister of the Interior I have had little opportunity of being acquainted with, but he too must have enough of occupation.

I now approach the most difficult part of my subject, but it is my duty to do it candidly and openly. I have heard that Your Majesty is prepossessed against the Duke of Palmella. Believe me it is without cause; I have known him since he was at Terceira, and there never existed a man more devoted to the cause of the Queen. Will Your Majesty look back to his exertions in planning the expedition that put the Western Islands in the hands of the Queen; there I assisted him all I durst, and I knew what he had to contend with. When in London, I came again in contact with him, and his exertions were without end. This brings me to the fitting out the expedition that placed the Queen on the throne of Portugal. Your Majesty cannot be aware on what slender grounds we began. I will tell Your Majesty. The Chevalier Lima wrote to me to say that Oporto was reduced to the last extremity, and that he had received letters from Sartorius to say the fleet was determined to come to England. Not one shilling could be raised to pay them, or for any thing else; the cause was gone. He requested me to come to town. It was proposed that I should take three steamers and twelve hundred Poles that Mendizabel fancied he could procure at Rochfort, and proceed to the Guadiana, pass the river, and march upon Bega. To put this wild scheme in execution, three English houses offered to advance the money, provided I would go. After some hesitation I acquiesced, provided the Marquis Palmella would go also. On his consenting, the £6000 increased to upwards of £20,000, and five steam-boats were fitted out. There was no great merit then in coming out, the merit was offering to risk life and every thing in the cause of the Queen then in despair.

We arrived at Oporto; after much discussion an expedition was fitted out — the Algarves taken — the squadron captured, and Lisbon occupied in the short space of six weeks, after the most brillant march recorded in history. Your Majesty's activity defended Oporto and conquered Bourmont, fortified the lines of Lisbon; the enemy were repulsed, and finally driven to Santarem; there our success ended, and with all the acknowledged talent of General Saldanha, which he has shewn on so many occasions, it does not appear to me any thing further can be done but by conciliating parties. Far be it from me to point out who are the men Your Majesty should add to the Ministry. Unite all parties, put an end to feuds, gain the confidence of the people in Portugal and of all nations out of it. The funds will rise, the resources will increase, the same enthusiasm that Your Majesty experienced on your arrival will return, the Miguelites will be paralyzed, and the Queen's cause gained without further loss of blood.

I have the honour to be, Sire,

With the greatest respect,

Your Majesty's most obedient servant,

CABO ST. VICENTI.

No. XIV.

The order of the day was calling upon Miguel's troops to exert themselves, and promising they should be at Cartaxo the 15th, Villa Franca the 19th, and Lisbon the 22d.

Nos. XV. and XVI.

Being a project and counter project not acted upon, are withheld, as being improper to be published.

No. XVII.

Inhabitants of the Algarves!

Being named by His Imperial Majesty, the Duke of Braganza, regent in the name of the Queen, to the command of the troops in this kingdom, all my energies will be used to establish order and confidence, which can only exist under the government of Her Most Imperial Majesty.

Algarvians, who have been obliged to leave your homes and your employments, to sustain with arms the cause of your oppressors, return to your families, and be certain that no persecution shall be instituted against you, whatever may be the posts you occupied in the militia, royalist volunteers, or guerillas.

Bernardo da Sa de Bandeira.
Head-quarters, Tavira,
Feb. 23, 1834.

No. XVIII.

Inhabitants of Caminho!

I have delivered you from the tyrannical government of the usurper. I call upon you to come forward, and take up arms in the defence of your legitimate queen. Every man capable of bearing arms will enrol himself under her standard or quit the town.

Sir,

I have surprised Caminho; you cannot be succoured. If you surrender, you shall be well received and retain your rank; if you do not I will storm the fort, and put you and your garrison to the sword.

To the Commanding Officer
at the Fontellezza, in the
Entrance of the Minho.

No. XIX.

Inhabitants of Vianna!

You are now free, and under the government of your legitimate Queen and the Constitutional Charter. Live happy together, and forget political animosities. Those who have left the town will return to their homes; no person shall be persecuted for his political opinions.

Cabo St. Vicenti.

Vianna, March 28th.

No. XX.

(Copy.)

Before Valencia, March 31st, 1834.

SIR,

To morrow I shall be joined by Spanish troops. I have a squadron at Caminho; and if you do not surrender to your legitimate Sovereign, I shall bring up one hundred guns and besiege the town, you will in that case be treated as rebels.

In the event of surrendering, you and your garrison will be well received, and permitted to serve the Queen or return to your homes.

You cannot be succoured, because all the province is in possession of the Queen's troops; I therefore advise you to assist in putting an end to this horrible civil war. Your garrison is small and well disposed to the Queen; and if I decide upon assaulting the town you cannot defend it, and your garrison will be put to the sword.

(Signed)   CAPE ST. VINCENT.

To the Governor of Valencia.

No. XXI.

ILLUSTRIOUS AND EXCELLENT SIR,

I request that you do not make an attack on this place before to-morrow night; for at that time it will be delivered up, in spite of the obstinate resistance of the governor.

God keep your Excellency!
FRANCISCO ANTONIO CALDAS,
Major of the Militia of Bastos.

Valencia, April 2d, 1834.

To the Viscount Cabo St. Vicenti.

(Copy.)

Before Valencia, April 2d, 1834.

SIR,

I know you are a friend of the cause of the Queen. I shall be sorry to shed Portuguese blood, but I am determined to take the place. I shall receive fifty guns to-morrow, and then I shall not treat; at present I am ready to treat.

(Signed) CAPE ST. VINCENT.

No. XXII.

(Copy.)

Conditions for the Surrender of Valencia made by the Governor of Valencia.

SIR,

If I accept the conditions of your Excellency, will you guarantee the life and property of the garrison and inhabitants, and allow them either to serve the Queen or return to their homes, under the condition of not taking up arms against the legitimate sovereign the Queen of Portugal, and assuring us that no person shall be persecuted for their political opinions.

(Signed) THE GOVERNOR OF VALENCIA.

(Copy.)

April 3d, 1834.

SIR,

If you surrender the place I guarantee the life and property of the garrison and inhabitants. The troops may either enter the Queen's service or return to their homes. No person shall be persecuted for their political opinions.

(Signed) CAPE ST. VINCENT.

To the Governor of Valencia.

No. XXIII.

Before the Walls of Valencia,
April 3, 1834.

Sir,

I learn, with equal surprise and disgust, that two days after I left Lisbon, to do all in my power to forward the cause of the Queen, your Excellency appointed another Acting Inspector, and superseded Captain Cunha, whom I appointed.

I am sorry to be obliged to tell your Excellency that you have *broken your word to me*, and put me in a false position; and after the letter I had the honour of writing to you, unless you wished to disgust me this never would have been done. Your Excellency cannot be a judge of the proper persons to assist me in regenerating the Portuguese navy. I make appointments from merit; while a parcel of rascally intriguing clerks, who surround your Excellency, impose on your good nature. Who ought to be your adviser, the major-general or an intriguing clerk? Common sense and a desire to serve the Queen ought to point out to your Excellency that I am the fit person to give you advice. After the services I have performed, and am still performing, I expected a different treatment, and I am sorry to observe that it appears to me to be done on purpose.

I remark that any thing that tends to disgust me is done immediately, there is no delay in your Excellency's office; while at the same time any thing I propose for the good of the service reposes quietly in your portfolio for months; this state of matters cannot continue. I will not submit to affronts, and the Government shall either change the system or dismiss me; and I shall return to England to justify the prophecies of my friends, that I have been serving an ungrateful country.

I have heard of the intrigues of Don Miguel's Government, which lost him his throne; but, by my soul, they never could have exceeded the unworthy intrigues of the existing one.

I feel strongly, and I write strongly, and I do not mean this to be a private letter; your Excellency is quite at liberty to shew it to the Emperor, and, if you do not, I will. The moment I have reduced this place, I shall return to Lisbon. I shall do my duty, because a sense of honour makes me; but, unless I have a most ample apology, I shall call on the Government to fulfil their engagements, and I will retire; and, when this crisis arrives, your Excellency will also get rid of all my officers.

I have the honour to be
Your Excellency's obedient servant,
CAPE ST. VINCENT.

I understand the invalids are still at Lisbon in the Hope, an additional expense to the Government.

No. XXIV.

PROCLAMATION.

Charged, by His Imperial Majesty the Duke of Braganza, Regent, in the Queen's name, with the command of the operations of the north of the kingdom, destined to effect the complete pacification of your provinces, I have much satisfaction, as I feel it to be my duty, to invite the inhabitants of these provinces to aid with their utmost energies the accomplishment of the sacred trust for which the country so much yearns.

Enough have our dissensions desolated the country; enough of our blood has been shed in the struggles between us; and enough of discord has kept back, if not paralyzed, our national prosperity.

I invite you, therefore, to join the standard of the Queen, not, indeed, for battle, but for the enjoyment of her legitimate government. Proclaim it, therefore, for by proclaiming you may have that tranquillity of which you have been so long deprived.

Soldiers of the ranks of the opposite army, lay down your arms and return to your hearths, or come and join yourselves to those who never seek, and have never sought, to return offence for offence, and never harboured in their hearts so unworthy a sentiment as revenge. The party for whom you are fighting have lost the brilliant aspect which perhaps might have dazzled you in former times, and victory in the hands of the

Queen has a force in paternal hands which has the firmest security of sweetness and clemency.

DUKE OF TERCEIRA.

Oporto, April 6, 1834.

No. XXV.

May 8.

INHABITANTS OF FIGUERAS!

The Usurper has lost his last sea-port, and you are free; forgive your enemies, and shew yourselves worthy of living under the just and free Government of the Queen, Donna Maria the Second. I shall follow the enemy up with vigour, and I hope you will soon see not only this province but all Portugal free from tyranny and oppression.

CABO ST. VICENTI.

No. XXVI.

May 8, 1834.

MEM.

You will complete the Eliza and Portuense with provisions; you will then take under your orders the Isabel

Maria, return to Lisbon, complete with provisions, and proceed to Madeira, which you will rigorously blockade; you will endeavour to get possession of Porto Santo, where you will be able to water. Any men of war proceeding to Madeira will be allowed to pass, and you will be very careful in maintaining a good understanding with all foreign ships of war. It is possible an attempt may be made to remove the garrison of Madeira to the Algarves, which you will look out for. It is also possible Don Miguel may attempt to get to Madeira; should you intercept him, you will come to Cascaes Bay, and inform me of the circumstance, keeping it perfectly secret. He will be treated with respect and decorum, but not as a royal personage. You will endeavour to communicate all that has happened to the governor, and do all you can to bring him over to the cause of the Queen.

Cabo St. Vicenti.

To Capt. Bertram,
Ier Imperial Majesty's Ship Don Pedro.

No. XXVII.

To the Governor of Ourem.

May 14.

Sir,

I have the honour of sending you the Proclamation of the Duke of Terceira, with which I perfectly agree. I have only to add that a treaty has been signed with England, France, Spain, and Portugal, to expel from the Peninsula Don Carlos and Don Miguel, and the Spanish troops are actually in Portugal. If you love your country, you will immediately proclaim the Queen; in that case, I guarantee that yourself and officers shall preserve their rank, and the men may join what regiments they please, or go to their homes. If you uselessly defend the place and spill Portuguese blood, you will be held personally responsible; there is now no point of honour, because there is not the possibility of being of the least service to the cause of Don Miguel, who is lost for ever. I have with me the same men who took the fleet on the 5th of July; they are ready to receive you as friends, but you will find them devilish unpleasant enemies.

APPENDIX.

Translation of the Governor's Letter.

To His Excellency,

I have the honour to acknowledge the receipt of your Excellency's despatch, and about its contents, it is my duty to acquaint your Excellency that I cannot agree by any means to the propositions that your Excellency has made to me; for as much as that both the commander of the corps and the garrison are resolved to defend that point; and my honour obliges me to defend with the greatest energy, shewing that I am a Portuguese officer.

I return to your Excellency the proclamation.

14th May, 1834.

Head-quarters at Ourem.

Conditions given for the Delivery of the Castle and Town of Ourem.

1st.

That all the officers and men, and in general every individual who are in the service of Dom Miguel in this town of Ourem, shall be received as if they never acted against the cause of Donna Maria the Second, and that both officers and men shall choose their future destiny as most convenient to them.

2nd.

That the officers shall be allowed to keep their horses and baggage, provided it be their individual property.

3rd.

That all who wish to be excused from serving, passports shall be given them that no person may interfere with them; and during the present war they shall not be obliged to take up arms.

4th.

That all the officers shall pledge their honour, never more to take up arms in favour of Don Miguel, and the troops shall make the same declaration.

5th.

That so soon as this is signed, a competent force of Dona Maria the Second's troops shall take charge of the castle and town of Ourem.

Head-quarters at Aldea da Cruz, 15th May, 1834.

(Signed)   JOAO ANT. DA MOITA,
Governor, &c.
(Signed)   CAPE ST. VINCENT.

No. XXVIII.

(Translation.)

PROCLAMATION.

Unhappy Portuguese, who still follow the banners of the Usurper!

How long do you purpose to continue in the way

of crime, despising the path of honour, which I have so often pointed out to you, and calling you into the bosom of the faithful Portuguese; forgetting all that you have done against me when your King; against my daughter, your legitimate Sovereign, by my solemn abdication; and against your country and her liberty? You see that on all sides the victorious phalanxes are closing round you, and have left you only the ground you tread on; you cannot be ignorant that the people of the northern provinces, those who were the most deluded, have now spontaneously and heartily proclaimed the *Queen* and the *Constitutional Charter* of the monarchy; you must know that you are reduced to the last stage of misery; without pay, without clothing, without shoes, and without all the comforts enjoyed by regular armies: What can you hope for? Whilst the question was doubtful, your obstinacy might be regarded as a point of honour or delusion; now, however, when every thing is against you, you ought to be undeceived; that the squadron, which was promised you, never can arrive; that such a promise was only made to continue the tyranny you are under; that the powerful nations do not protect you; finally, that Spain has already acknowledged the government of *the Queen*, and that the Spanish troops have entered Portugal to support legitimacy, your persisting in crime will redouble your crime. Notwithstanding all, Portuguese, do not think that I breathe vengeance, blood, and death against you; do not judge *me* by your chief: I pride myself on being true, humane, and generous, and to know how to forget injuries done to me. A series of victories assures me a final triumph. Portuguese of every class and opinion, there is yet time—come and join the banner of honour and of legitimacy. I assure you that the amnesty, which, *in fact*, still exists, will by me be ratified justly, and thus you may immediately return to your homes to enjoy domestic pleasures in the bosom of your families, without the fear of persecution, sheltered by the laws, and the clemency which I take pleasure in shewing you, in the name of your legitimate Queen *Donna Maria the Second*.

If you be Portuguese—if you love your country— if you wish for the blessings of your fellow-citizens, who now comprise the majority of the nation, afflict them no longer by prolonging the civil war, *which will soon finish against you*. Abandon the Usurper to his fate; do not fear that this proceeding will be looked upon as an act of treason; on the contrary, it will be considered by all as an act of sincere repentance of your crimes, arising from the love you bear, first of all, to your country; from that same love which has so distinguished, in all ages, true Lusitanians. Come, Portuguese of all classes and opinions, there is still time; I repeat to you, come. I will receive you in my arms; I will pardon you in the name of your Queen; and I will forget all your crimes at the sight of your penitence.

Imperial head-quarters at Cartaxo, 17th May, 1834.

D. PEDRO,
Duke of Braganza.

No. XXIX.

To the Most Illustrious and Most Excellent the Duke of Terceira.

I am authorized to propose a suspension of arms, with a view to open negotiations that no more Portuguese blood may be shed; and if your Excellency consents, the two armies must not approach each other more.

I wait a prompt answer from your Excellency.

Accept the protestation of esteem and consideration with which I have the honour to sign myself

Your Excellency's,

&c. &c. &c.

JOSE ANTONIO DE AZEVEDO LEMOS,
Commanding the Army of Operations.

To the Most Illustrious and Most Excellent the Duke of Terceira.

MOST ILLUSTRIOUS AND EXCELLENT SIR,

Yesterday I sent your Excellency a letter by General Guedes, of which the enclosed is a copy; and as my desire is to cease shedding any more Portuguese blood, and not being certain that you have received my letter, I have taken the determination of sending you an officer of my staff, and I hope by him you will do me the honour of replying.

In case your Excellency wishes to have an interview with me I shall be very much flattered, and you may fix the hour and place.

I profit by this occasion to compliment you.

     Jose Antonio de Azevedo Lemos,
      Honorary Lieut.-General commanding
        the Army.

Head-quarters, Evora,
 May 23*d*, 1834.

To the Most Illustrious and Most Excellent Seigneur Lemos.

Most Illustrious and Most Excellent Sir,

In reply to the letter which on the march I received by your Excellency's aid-de-camp, with the copy of that which your Excellency addressed me by General Guedes, and which I have not yet received, I can only say to your Excellency that I march on Estremoz, and from thence I shall answer to any propositions your Excellency may make. My government and myself have done all we could to spare Portuguese blood, and that same desire dictates my present answer.

    I am, your Excellency,
     &c. &c. &c.
    Le Duc de Terceira.

On the march, May 24, 1834.

No. XXX.

CONVENTION OF EVORA.

His Imperial Majesty the Senhor Don Pedro, Duke of Braganza, Regent in the name of the Queen, the Senhora Donna Maria II., moved by the desire of terminating as speedily as possible the effusion of Portuguese blood, and of pacifying the kingdom, grants, in the name of the Queen, to the troops assembled at Evora, and in other parts of the monarchy, as also to all the individuals who shall submit, and give obedience to the Queen, as follows :—

ARTICLE 1.

A general amnesty is granted for all political delinquencies committed since the 21st day of July, 1826. The execution of the decree of the 31st of August, 1833, is suspended in favour of those who are included in this amnesty, until the Cortes shall have deliberated upon their cases. These persons shall re-enter upon their property; but cannot alienate the same till after the decision of the Cortes. The amnesty does not include restitution of ecclesiastical, political, and civil offices; nor of crown property; nor of orders, commanderies, and pensions: neither does it extend to offences against individuals, nor exempt from responsibility to the prejudice of any third party.

ARTICLE 2.

All persons included in this amnesty, whether natives or foreigners, are at liberty to quit Portugal, and to dispose of their property, in so far as it is not subject to the restrictions of the preceding article ; and they shall give their words never to take part, in any manner whatsoever, in the political affairs of these kingdoms.

ARTICLE 3.

The military officers under this amnesty shall preserve their rank legitimately acquired, and the government undertakes to provide them a subsistence proportionate to it.

ARTICLE 4.

The same rule shall hold in ecclesiastical and civil employments, so far as the holders shall deserve them by their services and merits.

ARTICLE 5.

An annual pension of sixty contos of reis (400,000 francs) is secured to Don Miguel, in consideration of his high birth; and he is allowed to dispose of his personal property, under condition that he give up the jewels and other property belonging to the crown, or to private individuals.

ARTICLE 6.

He may embark in a vessel-of-war of one of the

Powers united in alliance by the treaty of London of
the 22d of April of the present year, which vessel shall
be sent to him at any port he shall name; full assurance
being given to him of security for his person and suite,
and of all the respect due to his exalted birth.

ARTICLE 7.

The Senhor Don Miguel obliges himself to quit
Portugal within the space of fifteen days; and engages
never to return to any part of the Peninsula of Spain,
or of the Portuguese dominions, nor in any manner to
disturb the tranquillity of these kingdoms. In case of
his acting contrary to this engagement, he shall lose all
right to the stipulated pension, and be liable to all the
consequences of his conduct.

ARTICLE 8.

The troops in the service of the Senhor Don Miguel
shall lay down their arms in the place to be pointed out
to them.

ARTICLE 9.

All the regiments and corps now in the service of the
usurpation, after surrendering their arms, horses, and
ammunition, shall separate peaceably, and return to
to their respective homes, under pain of forfeiting the
benefits of the present amnesty.

The commander-in-chief of the forces assembled at
Evora, after having accepted the present concession, in

APPENDIX.

the name of all the persons comprehended in it, has agreed to the following articles to ensure its execution.

ARTICLE 1.

He shall immediately despatch orders to the commanders of all the fortresses, and of all the troops in the field, and to all the authorities who still acknowledge the government of the Senhor Don Miguel, to submit without delay to the government of her most Faithful Majesty Senhora Donna Maria II. under the condition of receiving the benefits of the amnesty.

ARTICLE 2.

The dispositions of the preceding article shall extend to all ecclesiastical, civil, and military authorities of the possessions of the monarchy beyond sea.

ARTICLE 3.

The Senhor Don Miguel shall quit the town of Evora during the day of the 30th of this present month of May, to repair to Sines, where his embarkation shall take place (according to his own desire). He shall be accompanied on his journey by the persons of his personal suite, by twenty horsemen formerly serving in in his army, and by two squadrons of the cavalry of the Queen's armies.

The commander of the forces assembled at Evora shall send to the marshal commanding the armies of the Queen a list containing the names of the persons of the Senhor Don Miguel's suite.

ARTICLE 4.

During the day of the 31st of May instant, the troops assembled round Evora shall lay down their arms in the building of the Seminary of that town, and shall form themselves, according to the nature of their services, into troops, which, under the responsibility of their senior officers, shall repair to the localities hereinafter specified: they shall be provided on their march with their daily rations, and on arriving at the place of their destination shall receive orders of route to repair to their respective homes.

The natives of Lower Beira, to Abrantes;
Upper Beira, — Viseu;
Tras-os-Montes, — Villareal;
Entre Douro-e-Minho, Oporto;
Alemtejo, to have their passports immediately;
Algarves, — Faro.

The militia and the volunteers, of what denomination soever, shall immediately receive the orders for their route to their respective homes.

And that this may be definitively agreed, the marshals commanding the armies of the Queen, and the commander of the forces assembled at Evora, Joseph Antonio de Azevedo-Lemos, have signed in duplicate.

Evora-Monte, 26th May, 1834.

> DUKE DE TERCEIRA,
>   Marshal of the Army.
> CONDE DE SALDANHA,
>   Marshal of the Army.
> JOSE-ANTONIO DE AZEVEDO-LEMOS,
>   Lieutenant-General.
> ANTONIO DE ANDRADE-TORREZAO,
>   Acting Chief of the Staff.

No. XXXI.

Proclamation of Don Miguel to his Army.

SOLDIERS!

The valour you have displayed whenever you have been called to combat for my crown, and your fidelity to my person in the midst of the difficult struggle in which we have been engaged, render you worthy of the highest eulogiums, and deserve all my gratitude.

Nevertheless, since the three great Powers of England, France, and Spain, in conjunction with the government of Lisbon, have concluded a treaty, the object of which is to force me to quit this kingdom, the continuation of the war can only lead to the useless effusion of Portuguese blood which is so dear to me.

This consideration alone has induced me to separate myself from you.

The conventions and arrangements which arise out of this resolution are concluded, and will shortly be communicated to you: you will then learn what stipulations have been made for your safety.

It is no want of confidence in you which has induced me to take this step, but a conviction of the impossibility of overcoming the powers opposed to us, and the desire to prevent the evils to which the presence of foreign armies would expose our beloved country. I have reason to hope, from your discipline and your obedience to myself, as well as from the love which you have always testified towards me, that the troops will conduct themselves in the existing crisis as troops worthy to obey their King; therefore it is that I again recommend to you the observance of order and tranquillity, for which I make the commanders and officers of all ranks responsible.

You will remember that it is no act of weakness which I require of you, but merely one of resignation, in yielding to the disproportionate forces which, in pursuance of the treaty above mentioned, are preparing to pour into this country. You will appreciate as they deserve these reasons, which prudence dictates, for the prevention of calamities that would consummate the miseries of our country.

Again I recommend to you order and resignation. Be assured that I shall never forget your valour, your constancy, and your fidelity. Contribute then by your conduct to the welfare of our dear country.

(Signed) MIGUEL.

At the Palace of Evora,
May 27th, 1834.

No. XXXII.

ARTICLE 1.

His Imperial Majesty the Duke of Braganza, in the name of the Queen Donna Maria II., binds himself to exert every means in his power to drive the Infant Don Carlos from the Portuguese dominions.

APPENDIX. 311

ARTICLE 2.

Her Majesty the Queen of Spain, invited and entreated by his Imperial Majesty the Duke of Braganza, and having moreover very just and serious cause of complaint against the Infant Don Miguel, on account of the support which he has lent to the Infant Don Carlos of Spain, engages to send into the Portuguese territory such a number of Spanish troops as may be sufficient and necessary to co-operate with those of his Imperial Majesty in expelling Don Carlos of Spain and Don Miguel from the Portuguese territory; the Queen of Spain also undertaking to maintain at her own charge, and without any expense to the Portuguese government, the said Spanish troops; which troops shall be everywhere received and treated in the same manner as the troops of his Majesty the Duke of Braganza: and her Majesty binds herself to withdraw her troops from the Portuguese territory immediately that the expulsion of the said Infants shall be accomplished, and that the presence of the said troops shall no longer be required by her most Faithful Portuguese Majesty.

ARTICLE 3.

His Majesty the King of Great Britain engages to co-operate by employing a naval force to second the necessary resolutions and operations consequent upon the present treaty.

ARTICLE 4.

In case the co-operation of France *shall be deemed*

necessary by the high contracting parties, his Majesty the King of the French engages to do all that his Majesty *and his very august allies shall unanimously determine upon.*

ARTICLE 5.

The high contracting parties have agreed, that in consequence of the stipulations contained in the preceding articles, a declaration shall be immediately published, acquainting the Portuguese nation with the object of the present treaty; and His Imperial Majesty the Duke of Braganza, animated with a sincere desire of effacing all remembrance of the past, and of rallying the entire nation round the throne of his daughter, declares his intention of publishing a general and complete amnesty in favour of all the subjects of her most Faithful Majesty who shall within a prescribed time return to their allegiance; and the said Regent also declares his intention of securing to the Infant Don Miguel, as soon as he shall have quitted the Portuguese and Spanish dominions, a pension corresponding with his rank and birth.

ARTICLE 6.

Her Majesty the Queen of Spain, in virtue of the present article, declares her intention of securing to the Infant Don Carlos, as soon as he shall leave the Spanish and Portuguese territories, a pension correspondent to his rank and birth.

ARTICLE 7.

The present treaty shall be ratified, and its ratifications shall be exchanged in London within a month, or sooner if possible.

In faith of which, the four above plenipotentiaries have signed and sealed in London, the 23d of April, 1834.

MIRA-FLORES, TALLEYRAND,
PALMERSTON, MORAES-SARMENTO.

ARTICLE 1.

His Majesty the King of the French engages to take, in that part of his dominions which adjoins Spain, the measures best calculated to prevent any kind of succour, whether of men, arms, or ammunitions of war, being sent from the French territory to the insurgents in Spain.

ARTICLE 2.

His Majesty the King of the United Kingdom of Great Britain and Ireland engages to furnish to her Catholic Majesty all the succours in arms and ammunitions of war which her Catholic Majesty may require; and further, to assist with naval forces if necessary.

ARTICLE 3.

His Imperial Majesty the Duke of Braganza, Regent of Portugal in the name of the Queen Donna Maria II.

fully participating in the sentiments of his august allies, and desiring to acknowledge by a just requital the engagements contracted by her Majesty the Queen Regent of Spain in the 2d article of the treaty of the 23d April, 1834, undertakes to lend assistance, if the necessity should arise, to her Catholic Majesty, by all the means which may be in his power, according to the form and manner which shall be afterwards agreed upon with their said Majesties.

ARTICLE 4.

The above articles shall have the same force and effect as if they had been inserted word for word in the treaty of the 23d April, 1834, and shall be taken as forming part of the said treaty; they shall be ratified, and the ratifications shall be exchanged, within the period of forty days, or sooner if it may be.

In faith of which the respective plenipotentiaries have signed them, and have hereunto affixed the seals of their arms.

Done at London,
18*th August*, 1834.

No. XXXIII.

ARTICLE 1.

His Royal Highness the Infant Don Carlos shall quit

APPENDIX.

Evora, with his family and suite, on the 30th instant, to proceed to Aldea Gallega, and there to embark.

ARTICLE 2.

On this journey the marshals answer for the safety of his Royal Highness, his family, and suite, and will furnish him with such an escort as his Royal Highness shall require.

ARTICLE 3.

All Spanish subjects now in Portugal, and compromised in the service of His Royal Highness, shall be received into a provisionary depôt at Santarem, and shall be conducted thither under the escort necessary to their safety.

ARTICLE 4.

The Portuguese government shall provide them, at the depôt, with the means of existence, until they may without danger quit the depôt for some other residence.

The DUKE OF TERCEIRA, Marshal of the Army.
The COUNT OF SALDANHA, Marshal of the Army.
JOHN GRANT, Secretary of the Legation of his Britannic Majesty.

Evora-Monte,
26th May, 1834.

No. XXXIV.

Speech from the Throne, in the Royal Session of the Extraordinary Cortes of the Portuguese Nation in 1834.

> Worthy Peers of the Kingdom, Gentlemen Deputies of the Portuguese Nation,

The day which I have so anxiously and ardently desired has at length arrived, a day of glory and happiness, in which, after having passed through a vast circle of events nearly miraculous, having extinguished the fury of civil war, overcome the monster of tyranny, and restored the throne of the Queen, my beloved daughter, I see assembled around her the representatives of the nation, rich in wisdom, in prudence, firmness, and patriotism, and nobly eager to promote, by the observance of the Charter, and the enlightened developement of its principles, the stability and splendour of the throne, the consolidation of the constitutional system, and the prosperity and happiness of this honoured and generous nation.

On so happy a day, I must not present to your eyes the sad and gloomy picture of six years of public and private misfortunes; but I cannot avoid alluding in general terms to the principal events of that period, because they belong to history, and must guide your deliberations.

You know, and all Europe knows, that as soon as I

APPENDIX. 317

was called to the throne of Portugal on the lamented death of my august father, it was my first, I may say my only thought, to fulfil the important mission which Providence was pleased to confide to me, by laying down a secure foundation for public happiness, and endeavouring to restore the ancient glory and national greatness, by means of institutions suited to the genius and character, manners and wants of the people, and conformable to the progressive state of European civilisation. And desiring at the same time, to conform to the interests of policy, and the relative situation of the several States which obeyed my Government, I spontaneously abdicated the throne of Portugal in favour of the Queen, my beloved daughter, thus giving to Europe a new and secure pledge of the sincerity of my intentions, and to the Portuguese the fullest proof of the ardent desire which animated me to promote their future prosperity.

The constitutional charter which I granted on the 29th April, 1826, and which entirely fulfilled my inefficient views and the measures which accompanied it, were received by the nation not only with applause and gratitude, but with extraordinary enthusiasm.

All the orders of the State were to obey it. All the Princes who then constituted my Imperial and Royal family gave positive and manifest testimonies of their approbation. All foreign nations recognised the legitimacy of my succession and abdication, and of the measures which I had adopted for the benefit of the Portuguese. In short all sensible and sincere persons conceived the flattering and grateful hopes that with this precious gift there would be obtained, besides its principal effects,. the cessation of discord and of the divergency of opinion which had before been excited and artfully promoted.

Meanwhile a rebellious and fanatical faction directed by secret and powerful forces, and perhaps relying on some foreign co-operation deserted the country, declared itself the enemy of liberal institutions and of the happiness of its fellow citizens, and undertook the base task of supporting the empire of abuses and privileges, of destroying the Charter, of restoring the infamous and abominable regimen of absolute power, and even of calling into question my incontestible and acknowledged rights to the Portuguese throne.

This faction was repressed by the noble efforts of the national army, assisted by the energetic and patriotic union of the people. But the declared enemies of liberty and public happiness did not suspend their dark machinations, but actuated by mad rage, armed with fanaticism, imposture, atrocious calumny, and all the base and perfidious means which desperation and rage suggested to them, they saw in the end the failure of the system of ferocity, which for six whole years oppressed the Portuguese, and gave to the world examples such as never were seen in the most calamitous times of this or other monarchies.

It was a Prince of my family (I cannot record this circumstance without the most sensible grief, but I am obliged to say it)—it was a Prince of my august family, an ungrateful and degenerate brother, who encouraged and promoted the efforts of the rebels, in order to seat himself upon a throne erected upon treason, disloyalty, and perjury. The intimate ties by which this Prince bound himself to observe the Constitutional Charter, and to acknowledge and obey the legitimate Sovereign, by his oath, and promises made and repeated at Vienna, Paris, London, and Lisbon—by the solemn acceptance of the hand of the Queen, who was destined to be his consort— by the confidence which I placed in him in appointing him Regent of the kingdom, and my Lieutenant—lastly, by the very acts of the Government which he exercised under that honourable title;—all this, I say, was despised by him with the most scandalous immorality; and, convoking a vain and illegal phantom of the very national representation which he wished to see annihilated, he caused it to decide a question, which, in reality, did not exist—to declare him King, when he already exercised, in fact, the authority and power of Royalty, and he pretended to justify the enormous irregularity of this rash act by the most notorious falsehoods and gross sophisms.

In this manner the work of iniquity was completed, and by these steps the Usurper ascended to the occupation of a throne which had never been stained by such black and scandalous perfidy. Thousands of illustrious victims were then sacrificed to tyranny, either on the scaffold or in the horrors of prison, or in exile to remote climates, without any crime but their loyalty, without any trial but the will of the Government, and of the infamous satellites of its barbarity.

Consternation and dread, sometimes more cruel than

death itself, continually haunted those who still appeared to enjoy some degree of individual liberty.

Meritorious and respectable persons were everywhere persecuted with injuries and insults, reproaches and sarcasms of a mad populace, who, animated by example, and certain of impunity, perhaps of reward, committed all kinds of violence. The asylum of the house of the citizen was every moment violated. Robberies and murders were continually committed with impunity, not only with the acquiescence, but with the approbation of the Government.

In the pulpits—(I shudder to say it) but you know, and every body knows that I say the truth, in the pulpits, in face of the Holy Altars, in the midst of sacred and august mysteries, the ministers of the GOD of peace and charity preached assassination as a service done to religion, and announced to the astonished people a new gospel of persecution, blood and death.

In short, there was no crime that was not committed, no error that was not defended, no virtue that was not insulted, there was no security or protection except for the wicked, who distinguished themselves by their ferocity and sanguinary zeal.

I refrain from continuing this horrible picture. The facts are notorious, and were repeated in all parts of these kingdoms. There are few honourable citizens who have not experienced them, or witnessed and lamented them in their neighbours, relations, and friends.

My heart was deeply wounded and afflicted by the consideration of the deplorable situation of my country and my fellow-citizens and subjects, whose felicity has been, and ever will be the constant object of my most anxious care; and though I assisted as far as was possible those whom honour and loyalty had driven far from their country and scattered in different parts of Europe and America, all this was not sufficient for my personal sentiments nor for the honour of my exalted dignity, nor to the rights and honour of the Queen, my beloved daughter.

Events certainly inspired, but arising from the inflexible purpose which I had formed never to depart from my word, and the sacredness of the oaths with which I had bound myself to my subjects, brought me to Europe after I had abdicated the Imperial throne of Brazil.

Here two spectacles equally great, but of opposite tendencies, presented themselves to my contemplation. I saw, on one hand, a numerous and distinguished portion of illustrious patriots of honourable and loyal Portuguese incessantly labouring with the most generous assiduity to recover from the hands of the usurpation the throne of the Queen, and ready to encounter for that purpose all kinds of obstacles, opposition, and dangers.

I saw, on the other hand, and experienced myself, the great and redoubled efforts which opposed so arduous an enterprise, whether on the part of the numerous sectuaries of despotism, or of the political interests of the Cabinets; or, lastly, of the powerful force of an association, which called itself Conservative, and which was organized and spread over all Europe.

In the midst of all this it was easy for me to perceive

that the eyes of all, and the sole hope of the loyal Portuguese were fixed upon me; and convinced that PROVIDENCE, by extraordinary and unusual ways, called me to the direction of so difficult though glorious an enterprise, I undertook to place myself at the head of the noble and honourable party of loyalty, and not to neglect any means of saving the honour of the nation, the throne of my august daughter, and the liberty to which the oppressed Portuguese were justly entitled.

From that time forward I did not hesitate invariably to follow my resolution, despising with profound indignation the insulting means which were attempted to make me deviate from my purpose. Every thing, however, was wanting, and every thing was created anew. I regret that I cannot mention individually all that was suffered, all that was done, all that was attempted. I regret that I cannot mention the names of all the noble Portuguese who, with indefatigable zeal, and with sincere and efficacious diligence, employed themselves in supporting so important an undertaking. But I must not omit that the pecuniary resources, as indispensable as difficult to be obtained, were procured by a singular contract, in which the success of the enterprise was the only pledge, my signature the only surety. The zeal and the confidence of the party that gave, and that which received, were equally frank and unlimited.

I assumed the Regency of the kingdom in the name of the Queen, because the enterprise required a centre always present, always active, always vigilant. I enrolled myself the first soldier of the brave and valiant national army, and I had the satisfaction to see that the friends of constitutional liberty in other countries, convinced that the constitutional cause in Portugal was common to them, and in every respect conformable to truly just and liberal principles, came to join us, generously resolved to share in our sacrifices and our reverses, or our triumphs.

In the manifesto of the 2d of February, 1832, I published my intentions, my principles, and the plan of my future proceedings, offering to all peace, good will, oblivion of the past, and even pardon, if they needed it, on the sole condition of their acknowledging their duty, being faithful to their oaths, and obeying the legitimate authority of their Queen.

With these intentions and preparations I left the shores of France and went to the Azores, where a part of the loyal nation was concentrated, and the Regency established which governs those provinces with wisdom and patriotism, and improved their administration.

There was organised the little Portuguese army, small indeed in number, but great, strong, and invincible by its valour, by its civic virtues, and by the noble sentiments which animated it, by the justice of the cause it defended, and by the tried skill of its chiefs.

At the head of 7,500 men I landed on the shores of Portugal, on the ever auspicious day, the 8th July, 1832. The terror which the enemy felt opened a way for this handful of loyal Portuguese, and on the 9th, without the loss of a single man, we entered the honourable and loyal city of Oporto, whose inhabitants displayed from that time the most ardent enthusiasm in the cause of the Queen and of the Constitutional Charter, and a series of prodigies of loyalty, valour, constancy, and patriotic resignation, which may some day be repeated, but can never be surpassed. It is not the place in a short speech to recount the events of the war, and often obstinate and close siege which we gloriously supported there for a whole year. It is for history faithfully to transmit them to posterity.

But I must not omit to mention, at least in general terms, the rare examples of civil and military virtue which I observed in the army and inhabitants, the valour with which they worsted 80,000 men, abounding in resources, and every moment reinforced by all the means which fanaticism and despotism could suggest — the almost incredible firmness and constancy with which we braved death in its most frightful forms, without seeing, even in the most anxious moments, any signs of weakness or discouragement. In short, prodigies of the most exalted patriotism, in the midst of the most dangerous crisis — patriotism and love of liberty, and the efforts of civilization combating servitude, barbarism, and tyranny, and continually gaining signal victories over those monsters.

At the end of a year fertile in events, and which will be ever remembered in the annals of Portugal, the national army was reinforced with some new troops.

A detachment of this little army conquered Algarve, and proceeded to deliver the capital of the kingdom, which it entered on the 24th July, 1833, assisted by the energetic and cordial co-operation of its illustrious inhabitants, and in the midst of their ardent acclamations.

The enemy's squadron was gloriously combated and taken off Cape St. Vincent. The signal victory which we obtained in the lines of Oporto, on the 25th of the same month, over the numerous forces of the enemy, enabled me to join the forces in the capital, where I arrived on the 28th.

I immediately found, as if by enchantment, a new army and a fortified city. Lisbon was defended by miracles of valour and the patriotism of the troops and of the heroic inhabitants, whom I always found around me in the most dangerous conflicts.

On the 10th of October I attacked the 16,000 men who besieged the city with 8,300, of whom scarcely 2,500 were experienced soldiers; but valour made up for every thing. The enemy was thrown back upon Santarem, and the arms of loyalty obliged him to remain there till I judged that the time was come to undertake decisive operations in the North of the kingdom.

From that time everything yielded to the valour of the army. In a few days all the provinces were delivered—the rebellious and disloyal bands dispersing themselves. Oppressed and tortured citizens issued from horrible dungeons—the inquiring and humane army soon showed what were its sentiments, and what a great difference there was between legitimacy and usurpation. The people, bathed in tears of joy, raised their hands to Heaven, and loaded their generous deliverers with benedictions.

On the 27th of May this year, the enemy at length laid down their arms. Having been lately beaten in the obstinate battle of Asseiceira, he abandoned the strong positions of Santarem, and retreated to Evora, still accompanied by a great force.

Here the reign of usurpation expired, after two years of frequent combats, sustained and gained against a vast inequality of force, and with a perseverance superior to all praise.

The Government of the Queen was again every where acknowledged, and the oaths of fidelity to her authority and the Charter were renewed. The nation began to enjoy peace and tranquillity. Some conditions dictated by circumstances and approved by humanity were spontaneously and generously granted to the enemy. And as it was never my desire to make war upon the Portuguese, but only on the usurpation and tyranny by which they were oppressed, I granted them, in the name of the Queen, a second amnesty, conformably to my principles and the dictates of my heart. The articles of both will be duly laid before you.

We feel particular satisfaction in being able to announce to you that during the struggle and since its termination the Government of the Queen has been formally recognised by England, France, Spain, Sweden, Belgium, and Denmark. All other nations are at peace with us, and I expect from the justice, the enlightened policy and good faith which directs them, that they will, without difficulty, hasten to re-establish and to confirm the ties which formerly, to the interest of all parties, united them with Portugal.

The Court of Rome will certainly not be the last in taking so just and wholesome a resolution, since we boast of not being the last to respect and venerate in its head the common Father of the Faithful, and the centre of the Catholic unity, to whom we are indissolubly united by the sacred bonds of Faith and Religion.

We have concluded with Spain, England, and France, the treaty of quadruple alliance, signed the 22d April, this year, the articles of which will be laid before you. Its principal object was to give new securities for the happy and prompt termination of the struggle in which we were then still engaged, and thus to co-operate in the tranquillity and general good of all Europe.

To these three nations, as well as to Belgium, we are indebted for no small proofs of kindness and efficacious friendship; the Government of Spain in particular distinguishing itself by ordering the troops of her Catholic Majesty to pass the frontiers of the kingdom, and by this movement to give an advantageous assistance to our operations. The interest which those nations might expect from their proceeding does not relieve the Portuguese from the duties of gratitude, nor me from the pleasing obligation of recommending it in this place.

Many and very important measures have been taken for the better government of the kingdom and the more easy and prompt observance of the Charter. A new force has been given to the exercise of the judicial power, and to the public administration in its different branches. The army and its civil departments have been organised. Free ports have been established at Lisbon and Oporto, and more regulations ordered for the extension, liberty, and security of trade. Such regulatory laws as seem the most necessary have been made, many obstacles have been removed which impeded the course of business, and opposed the prosperity of the people. Lastly, all the families and associations of religions of every denomination and order have been suppressed; those establishments, considered with respect to religion, were totally alienated from the primitive spirit of their institution, and almost exclusively governed by love of the temporal and worldly interests which they professed to despise, and, considered in a political point of view, they were like denationalised bodies, indifferent to the good or bad fortune of their fellow citizens, and zealously serving a despotic or tyrannical Government, if they expected from it favour and consideration. To their influence over individuals and families, which was the more dangerous in proportion as it was secret, Portugal owes in great degree the evils which it has just experienced. There are indeed, in the individual members, honourable but rare exceptions. The Government has taken everything into consideration.

A detailed account of all the measures and regulations of which I have just spoken will be presented to you by the several Ministers. Many of them were conceived or proposed, and discussed in the preceding meetings of the Representatives of the nation, and in the Regency of the Island of Terceira; and it seemed that they should be adopted or continued, as well to convince the people of the great benefits which they might expect from the constitutional regime, as that at the present wished-for moment of the meeting of the Cortes, experience might have already shown, at least in part, what inconveniences or difficulties were encountered in their development and execution.

Among all these measures, the means which have been employed to establish and increase the public credit, merit your most serious attention. Most important transactions, all founded on justice and good faith, have taken place with that view. The result is notorious. The creditors of the State have been paid, both in and out of the kingdom, with the most scrupulous punctuality. The paper currency, which has for so many years secretly undermined the fortune of the public and of the citizens, is going to be extinguished. The Queen's Government has acquired a respectable name on the Exchanges of Europe, and is now equal in this point to the most prosperous and pacific nations.

The singular situation of the kingdom appeared to make it necessary to suspend some of the guarantees established by art. 145 of the Charter. However no excess has taken place on the application of this measure. It is for your zeal and prudence to deliberate on this subject, and consider what may be most useful and just.

While the Government was employed in such assiduous and important labours, almost all our vast and rich transmarine dominions voluntarily declared in favour of the Constitutional Charter and the authority of the Queen. The inhabitants of Madeira followed the same glorious example as soon as a sufficient force could support their efforts, which were restrained. The Government begins to make its beneficent influence felt in all these dominions.

After having showed you in a short but faithful sketch the principal events of a period which for so many reasons will form an era in the history of Portugal, and having shewn you what has been done to restore the nation, and to raise it from the deplorable state of depression to which it had been reduced by the errors and crimes of the usurpation, I must recommend to you, which I do with the most entire and unlimited confidence in your zeal, the two principal objects which now call for in preference the attention of the Cortes: viz. 1st. Whether the Regency ought or ought not to be continued during the remainder of the Queen's minority. 2dly. To take the proper steps that her Majesty may marry some foreign Prince. Your consummate wisdom and prudence will deliberate and decide upon both points with the discretion which may be expected from the union of so much knowledge, and a happy association of the most estimable virtues.

It is also necessary to fix the amount of the force by sea and land, comformably to art. 15., sect. 10. of the Constitutional Charter, having respect to the circumstances and internal state of the country, and not losing sight of the peculiar situation in which the neighbouring and allied nation may be placed where a Prince pretending to the throne is come again to revive the almost extinguished flames of civil war.

Besides these objects, many others claim your attention. The laws regulating the liberty of the Press, the responsibility of the Ministers and public officers, the inviolability of the residence of the citizen, the law which is to regulate the use and the employment of the property of the citizen for the benefit of the public, and the indemnity which is previously to be given him first, according to act 145, sect. 21, of the Charter, the organization of public instruction and study in all their branches, the pious and charitable establishments, the laws for the protection and promotion of manufactures, commerce, and arts, and of agriculture, which is the queen of them all; the measures for improving the situation and administration of our transmarine dominions, from which so many inestimable advantages hitherto overlooked or despired, may be derived; every thing, in short, which the Charter prescribes or recommends. All that public necessity requires, and all that may contribute to the prosperity of this honourable nation, and to restore its ancient glory and greatness, must deserve the zeal and labour of the Cortes, and will, doubtless, be the constant object of their thoughts and attention.

Gentlemen Deputies of the Portuguese Nation,

The Minister of Finance will present to you the present state of the public funds, and the estimate of the resources necessary to meet the ordinary and extraordinary expenses of the State. It will be for you to examine this subject, and to enable the Government to fulfil its obligations.

Worthy Peers of the Kingdom,

Gentlemen Deputies of the Portuguese Nation,

I most cordially rejoice with you and the whole nation

at seeing our country restored, the Constitutional Charter enforced, and the august throne of the Queen established, and to see you united around it, ready to employ your talents aad your zeal to promote its splendour, and to raise the Portuguese to that station which belongs to them in the number of civilised nations.

For myself, I reserve only the glory of having placed myself at the head of so brave and honoured a people, and of the national army, and of having co-operated with them to maintain the rights of a daughter whom I love and esteem so highly, and those of a nation which has rendered itself so illustrious in the world by its heroism in war, and by its virtues in peace.

The Extraordinary Session is opened.

Palace das Necessidades, Aug. 5.

No. XXXV.

Lisbon, July 26th, 1834.

My dear Sir,

When people are to work together I think it is always best that they should thoroughly understand each other; it hinders many disagreements afterwards, therefore I think it better to put on paper the substance of what I spoke to you about this morning.

Fourteen months' experience has clearly shewn me that, constituted as the offices of minister of marine and major-general now are, a good understanding cannot long subsist between them, were they at the beginning the best friends in the world. The offices are, in a certain degree, independent of each other; one may be giving one order, at the same time that another is contradicting it, and both be in ignorance of what the other is doing; this begets jealousy, and opens a wide field for the intrigues of clerks, which, I am sorry to observe, I have suffered much from, and have only been patient because I was bound in duty to remain till a final settlement had been made with my officers and men, who so nobly supported me on the 5th July; that settlement is now nearly completed, and the formation of a new ministry is the proper time for me to state my opinions clearly and distinctly.

It appears to me that the two bureaus of minister and major-general should be consolidated into one, with a number of clerks sufficient to do the duty, and no more. The whole of the correspondence, except between the ministers, should be addressed to the major-general direct; this correspondence should be examined by him, and what was competent for him to decide should be done immediately; any changes of importance, or any thing that required the decision of the minister, should be laid before the minister of marine by the major-general in person; there should be no correspondence between them; every thing should be done *viva voce;* he should be the naval councillor of the minister; neither the inspector of the arsenal, rope-walk, countability, hospital, or any other department belonging to the marine, should have the power of corresponding direct with the minister; this is the spirit of the major-general's present instructions, which has, however, been widely departed from, and he has long since ceased to be the minister's adviser. Whatever he proposed has been referred to a clerk to give his opinion, and hence I have had repeated affronts heaped upon me, and the service has suffered. Experience has shewn very evidently that the system of education, and indeed the whole detail of the Portuguese navy is bad; it requires regenerating, and that can only be done by adopting the British system, which is proved to be good, and no man of honour can conscientiously consent to receive a salary, when he is intimately convinced that he is doing no good to the country he serves, nor will he risk his reputation in executing any commission he may be sent on, unless the materials he has to work with are good, and if he is not permitted to make them good, he has no business to remain and receive his pay.

His Excellency
Agostinho José Freire,
Minister of Marine, &c. &c. &c.

APPENDIX.

No. XXXVI.

Purbrook, July, 1835.

Sir,

Before I left Lisbon I submitted to your Excellency lists of officers and men who had been killed in the Queen's service, and your Excellency agreed with me, both in conversation and writing, which I have now before me, that the heirs of the officers and men who fell in battle were to receive the same gratuity as the survivors who had been discharged from the Queen's service, and that the mothers, widows, and children only of those who died in the service were to be allowed the gratuity. On this assurance I wrote to the parties concerned. I find, however, that your Excellency made me the bearer of a different communication to the Queen's minister in London, which communication states that inquiry was to be made into the custom in the British navy, and if the sum allowed in this country was more than stated by me, they were to have the amount awarded on the lists, but if it was less, they were to have the British allowance. Such a system is not a proof of gratitude to the officers and seamen who were so instrumental in saving the cause of the Queen, and is moreover a breach of faith to me. The pension to be allowed is stated both in the contract and the minister's instructions to be agreeable to the British regulations, but up to this time nothing has been heard, and I receive daily complaints from the widows and orphans. I have, therefore, to request, nay,

APPENDIX.

I demand that your Excellency fulfils your promise to me, and which promise is in your Excellency's own handwriting. I have also written to your Excellency on other subjects, and to which I have to request your Excellency will be good enough to reply.

> I have the honour to be,
> Your Excellency's obedient humble servant,
> CHARLES NAPIER,
> *Count Cape St. Vincent.*

His Excellency
 Senor Augustinho José Freire,
  Minister of Marine.

ERRATA.

Page 8, last line, *for* though at once alarming *read* though at one time alarming.
— 44, line 7, *for* port *read* post.
— 46, — 18, *for* Macdonald *read* Macdonnell.
— 57, — 6 *for* Farola *read* Faroba.
— 59, — 1, *for* prisoners *read* provinces.
— 83, — 9, *for* were attacked *read* was attacked.
— 83, — 10, *for* double their numbers *read* double his numbers
— 91, — 3, *for* Lomes, to embark *read* Lemos, embarking.
— 91, — 14 & 15, *for* accede to it *read* accede to them.
— 91, — 16, *for* accept it *read* accept them
— 135, — 17, *for* reconnoitred *read* reconnoitre.
— 135, — 19, *for* endeavoured *read* endeavour.

MARCHANT, PRINTER, INGRAM-COURT, FENCHURCH-STREET.

www.ingramcontent.com/pod-product-compliance
Lightning Source LLC
Chambersburg PA
CBHW070752300426
44111CB00014B/2382